The Politics of Latino Faith

The Politics of Latino Faith

Religion, Identity, and
Urban Community

Catherine E. Wilson

NEW YORK UNIVERSITY PRESS

New York and London

NEW YORK UNIVERSITY PRESS
New York and London
www.nyupress.org

Library of Congress Cataloging-in-Publication Data
Wilson, Catherine E.
The politics of Latino faith : religion, identity, and urban community /
Catherine E. Wilson.
p.   cm.
Includes bibliographical references and index.
ISBN-13: 978-0-8147-9413-5 (cl : alk. paper)
ISBN-10: 0-8147-9413-0 (cl : alk. paper)
ISBN-13: 978-0-8147-9414-2 (pbk. : alk. paper)
ISBN-10: 0-8147-9414-9 (pbk. : alk. paper)
1. Church work with Hispanic Americans. 2. Hispanic Americans—
Religion.   I. Title.
BV4468.2.H57W55 2008
361.7'508968073—dc22   2007052101

Manufactured in the United States of America

10 9 8 7 6 5 4 3 2 1

Contents

Acknowledgments

This book is the result of a long and scenic life journey. Latino culture and the Spanish language first piqued my interest while I was a grade-school student at Ancillae Assumpta Academy (AAA) in Wyncote, Pennsylvania. Sitting in third-grade Spanish class, I can still recall the gentle commands of Sister María Antonia—an immigrant from Cuba—to the students: "*siéntense, chicos*" (sit down, children) and "*cállense, por favor*" (please be quiet). It was not unusual to have a Cuban American as a teacher at AAA, as the order of religious sisters (the Handmaids of the Sacred Heart) was founded in Spain in the late nineteenth century and had established convents throughout Latin America. I continued my studies in Spanish at Gwynedd Mercy Academy High School in Gwynedd Valley, Pennsylvania, where I received the Spanish Medal on graduation day.

Upon entering Villanova University, I developed a genuine liking for Latin American literature and poetry, after taking classes with Estrella Ogden and Carlos Trujillo—an internationally recognized Chilean poet—and spending a summer semester in Concepción, Chile. This liking was broadened after stumbling across a text on the shelves of Villanova's Falvey Library—*Latin American Political Thought and Ideology*, by Miguel Jorrin and John D. Martz—which served later to shape my senior thesis on the foundations of the Christian Democratic movement in Chile. I am indebted to the many formative discussions outside the classroom at Villanova with professors Colleen Sheehan and Lowell Gustafson, during which I came to realize how ideas—political, religious, and otherwise—certainly have consequences.

While at Georgetown University, I met Roberto Esquenazi-Mayo the first day of classes at the opening reception for the Center for Latin American Studies, the master's program with which I was affiliated. After a brief conversation, he convinced me to enroll in his class on the "*ensayo latino-americano*," dedicated to examining Latin American political thought. This was one of the best decisions I ever made, as Esquenazi-Mayo later served as a mentor during my years at Georgetown and throughout my professional life. My decision to enter the doctoral program in political science at the University of Pennsylvania was based on my desire to continue researching the role ideas have played in shaping social movements, political parties, revolutions, and constitutional orders in Latin America. A few years into the program, however, I extended my academic interest from the politics of Latin America to Latino religion and politics in the United States. John DiIulio, a recent transplant from Princeton University, served as my adviser at Penn. I could not have asked for a better adviser, especially given his extensive research on the role faith-based institutions play in revitalizing America's inner cities.

Choosing this present study as my research topic, I wove together all the areas of scholarly research that have influenced me deeply throughout my years of schooling: Spanish language, Latin American and Latino religious culture, politics, and public policy. I am especially thankful to those Latino faith-based organizations (FBOs)—Latino Pastoral Action Center (LPAC), Nueva Esperanza (Nueva), and The Resurrection Project (TRP) —that served as case studies for this work. The willingness of Latino FBO leadership and staff to give generously of their time—spending hours and even weeks of time explaining the ins and outs of their respective organizations—was greatly appreciated. I am particularly grateful for the leadership of Reverend Raymond Rivera, executive director of LPAC, Reverend Luis Cortés, Jr., executive director of Nueva, and Raúl Raymundo, executive director of TRP, who opened the doors of their organizations to me. Without their assistance and keen interest in my research area, this work would not have been possible. I also extend a special thanks to all those external actors—government officials, nonprofit leaders, community activists, and corporate officers—who agreed to be interviewed for this study. Their insights and attention to detail have greatly contributed to a more nuanced presentation of this work.

My deep appreciation goes to my research advisers at Penn—DiIulio, Jack Nagel, and Henry Teune—who encouraged me to engage in this under-researched area of study. This project owes much to DiIulio, who not only served as an outstanding mentor, but also provided me with a research fellowship at the Program for Research on Religion and Urban Civil Society (PRRUCS) at Penn, where I met other doctoral candidates— from the fields of political science, social work, and city planning—conducting research on the impact of religion in the inner city. I wrote my manuscript alongside one of my PRRUCS colleagues and cubicle mates,

Nisha Botchwey, and my first round of manuscript edits alongside David Hodge, a trusted colleague. I am grateful for Rebecca Kowal's valuable insights, Lia Howard's profound capacity to listen, and Hara Wright-Smith's ability to see the big picture. An additional round of thanks goes to the PRRUCS extended family: Cindy Brodbeck, Chuck Brutsche, Chaz Howard, Sheria Sellers-Crawley, Marc Siegel, and Joe Tierney. Writing this work without the presence and support of my PRRUCS colleagues—now very good friends—would have been an impossible feat.

I would like to thank the Bradley Foundation for the generous grant I received to conduct my research in 2001–2002. Many thanks are also due to Alex Simmons, a former Villanova student now attending Haverford College, who served as an excellent research assistant for this study, gathering critical data at a moment's notice. I received incisive comments from the best editor anyone could ever have, my father, John Franklin Wilson III, Esq., who could leave his job any day and work for a publishing company. Furthermore, I am grateful to the Villanova Center for Liberal Education (VCLE) and to the Department of Political Science at Villanova —under the respective leadership of Jack Doody and Craig Wheeland —for providing an encouraging environment in which to edit my book. As a faculty member in the Visions of Freedom Learning Community in the VCLE since 2005, I appreciate the collegial spirit shared with Doody, Sheehan, Andrew Bove, and Joseph Prud'homme. Special thanks are reserved for NYU Press and my editor Ilene Kalish, for providing excellent comments on my manuscript and guiding my editing process in the right direction.

Finally, I would like to name a few others who share in the success of this book. I am grateful to Kate Barker, Melissa Benner, Heather Cameron, Father Anthony Costa, Kristin Hodgson, Caroline Horstmann, Father James V. Schall, S.J., Jenny Schlegel, and Christine and Reed Wilmerding for their emotional, intellectual, and spiritual support. Furthermore, I am thankful to my wonderful brothers and sisters and their families: Judy Wilson, Jim Wilson, Anne, Tim, Kiley, Katie, and Kiera Mahoney, and John Vasthi, and Logan Wilson. Finally, I am eternally grateful to the enduring love and support of my parents, Anne and John Wilson, who have never ceased believing in me.

It is my hope that this book has captured the life and work of LPAC, Nueva, and TRP so that readers may have a glimpse into the diverse ways these Latino FBOs are building and rebuilding America's inner cities. It is to these organizations this book pays special tribute.

Introduction

In "On the Look-Out," the opening chapter of Charles Dickens' novel *Our Mutual Friend* (1865), the reader is presented with two individuals in a small boat riding down the Thames River in the thick of night with nothing more than a "rusty boat hook and coil of rope." The narrator tells us they are "doing something that they often did, and were seeking what they often sought." The reader learns later that the two individuals work on the river as independent operators, routinely dredging up human bodies that have fallen to the bottom. It is on the river that these workers eke out a living in the severe, urban London environment. After lifting the bodies to shore, their duty is to turn over any of these new "findings" to police so that they can be properly identified. A criminal case often ensues. Meanwhile, the workers return to the cold setting of the river, distinctively bounded by the stone of London Bridge and the metal of Southwark Bridge.[1]

According to literary critics, *Our Mutual Friend* accounts for Dickens' most pressing social critique of urban life in late-nineteenth-century London. With the backdrop of the city as "central brooding image," modern urban society is viewed as "an institution without content."[2] While Dickens strongly criticizes the existing state of urban society for its lack of content, he does make suggestions for the "possible emergence of a new and better society," one based on the concern of "mutuality."[3] This same concern for mutuality drives central urban actors—congregations, government agencies, community-based organizations, and faith-based organizations—to be "on the lookout," lifting up not bodies, but urban dwellers who fall to the bottom of America's inner cities. Poor and often marginalized, these dwellers eke out their living amid the stone of congested city streets and the metal of urban skyscrapers.

Latino religious institutions place a great emphasis on the value of mutuality—or the genuine flourishing of community life—in the inner city. Guided by the Christian narrative, they consider themselves called to "live

peaceably with all" (Rom. 12:18) and to "love one another with mutual af-
fection" (Rom. 12:10). In lifting up the human persons that fall to the bottom of urban society, these religious actors strive to put in practice this
narrative by privileging those who are weak, marginalized, and powerless.
As Christian believers dedicated to the plight of urban dwellers, they take
their biblical tradition seriously, paying specific attention to the words of
Jeremiah: "Seek the welfare of the city where I have sent you into exile,
and pray to the Lord on its behalf, for in its welfare you will find your
welfare" (Jer. 29:7). Latino religious institutions consider themselves commissioned to promote the city's welfare not only through the "healing"
of the city's wounds, but also through the advancement of its "prosperity
and security" (Jer. 33:6).

Over the past 20 years, Latino religious institutions—congregations
and faith-based organizations alike—have played a significant role in the
urban revitalization of America's toughest inner cities. These institutions
have made a long-term commitment to the crises many of their neighborhoods have been facing for decades.[4] In addition to providing havens for
immigrant populations and engaging in community economic development, religious institutions influence the daily life and politics of Latinos.
Although Latino congregations have been long-standing indigenous faith
communities in U.S. urban areas, Latino faith-based organizations are
newly emergent urban actors in public life, wielding a considerable degree
of social, spiritual, and cultural legitimacy not only with their own community "constituents," but also with key local, state, and national political
players.

Distinctions must be made as to congregations, faith-based organizations (FBOs), and community-based organizations (CBOs). For the
purposes of this study, congregations will be defined as religious sites—
churches, synagogues, and mosques—whose primary objective is to provide a spiritual place of worship for community members. Although some
congregations provide social services to their community members, this is
not necessarily the case for all congregations. Congregations "are considered tax-exempt entities by virtue of being religious organizations and the
assumption that they are charitable organizations." There are more than
350,000 congregations in the United States today. Thus, they account for
the "most common and widespread institution in our society."[5]

FBOs are far fewer in number than their congregational counterparts.
Unlike congregations, no approximate figure exists for the number of
FBOs in the United States. In contrast to congregations, FBOs are orga-

nizations whose very purpose is to provide some type of social service for the community they serve. These organizations are "required to register with the Internal Revenue Service and get a formal certificate of incorporation."[6] While having a religious foundation, FBOs also are required by law to avoid the intermingling of proselytizing with social-service provision. Ultimately, having a religious foundation distinguishes the FBO from its secular counterpart—the CBO—because the two kinds of organizations tend to perform the same type of community work.

This book, *The Politics of Latino Faith*, is the first systematic treatment of Latino FBOs in the United States. The main objective of this study is to introduce the concept of religious identity politics,[7] defined here as the content and context of religious values, beliefs, and culture that drive social and political action in community life. Religious identity politics manifests itself in how Latino FBO leadership interprets the Christian narrative. Such an interpretation in turn influences the kinds of social and political activities in which these institutions become involved on behalf of their own "constituents." Latino FBOs are emerging and "potential sources of political influence,"[8] and I shall demonstrate in this study that it is impossible to understand these institutions socially and politically without first understanding them in terms of their theological drives and commitments.[9]

The Latino FBOs under study are: the Latino Pastoral Action Center (LPAC), a para-church organization located in the Highbridge section of the South Bronx in New York, led by a Pentecostal minister, Reverend Raymond Rivera; Nueva Esperanza (Nueva),[10] an interdenominational Protestant organization located in the Hunting Park section of North Philadelphia, led by an evangelical pastor, Reverend Luis Cortés, Jr.; and, The Resurrection Project (TRP), a Roman Catholic, lay-driven organization led by Raúl Raymundo, with a membership base of twelve Catholic parishes representing the neighborhoods of Pilsen and Little Village—and an auxiliary membership of two churches consolidated into one parish from Back of the Yards—in Chicago. These Latino FBOs in no way represent the entire Latino community-serving ministry sector, but they are the three largest and most reputable Latino FBOs in the United States, with operating budgets in excess of $2.5 million as of mid-2007.

Despite the fact that all three Latino FBOs manifest a religious identity politics, they do not engage in the same types of Christian ministry. The varieties of Christian ministry exhibited by these Latino FBOs are based on the public theology[11] each organization advances. (This is documented in more detail in chapter three.) While Christian denomination serves to influence these public theologies, ultimately the articulation of each public theology is a function of how FBO leadership interprets the Christian narrative in the urban context. As the later case studies will attest, LPAC manifests a ministry of *personal outreach*, Nueva advances a ministry of *institutional development*, and TRP embraces a ministry of *community empowerment*.

These varieties of Christian ministry have real implications in social and political life.[12] LPAC manifests a ministry of *personal outreach* through its provision of personally oriented services, such as gang outreach and psychological counseling in the largely Puerto Rican and Dominican neighborhood of the South Bronx. Moreover, this ministry of personal outreach is exhibited by the political involvement of LPAC's leader, Rivera, who personally has endorsed political candidates in New York City and at the national level. In contrast, Nueva advances a ministry of *institutional development* in the largely Puerto Rican corridor of North Philadelphia through its macro-level, business approach to ministry. Of the three Latino FBO leaders under study, Cortés of Nueva is the leader who engages most with state, national, and international political actors. Neither endorsing nor financially contributing to political candidates, Cortés has acted as lead host of the National Hispanic Prayer Breakfast since 2002, bringing together central political figures from both Democratic and Republican political ranks. TRP, meanwhile, displays a ministry of *community empowerment* through the organization's attention to building a healthy community for the largely Mexican neighborhood of Chicago that it serves. Raymundo, TRP executive director and lay leader, advocates the need for both the "bricks and mortar" side to community development—the building of housing units—and community development's more human side, the celebration of Mexican culture and religious tradition.

The Significance of Latino Religion

It is only natural to study the role Latino FBOs play in urban life. According to a 2007 study jointly conducted by the Pew Forum on Religion and Public Life and the Pew Hispanic Center, approximately 68 percent of Latinos surveyed consider religion "very important" in their lives. In addition, 66 percent of Latinos surveyed deem religion to be very important or somewhat important in their political thinking. Unlike Dickens' image of urban society as an institution without content, Latinos would regard urban religious congregations and FBOs as institutions *with* content. Nearly 90 percent of Latinos surveyed self-identify as "Christian."[13] Thus, Luis Pedraja's assertion that the Christian congregation is the "central location" for the Latino community should not be passed over lightly. In providing Latinos with a "community of faith," the Christian congregation helps safeguard Latino cultural traditions and religious customs.[14] Along with congregations, FBOs help the Latino community to mediate its religious sensibilities and, in so doing, prepare this community for social and political involvement in the urban context.

With an estimated 42.7 million Latinos living in the United States as of 2005, this ethnic group constitutes the nation's largest minority, representing 14 percent of the total population.[15] These numbers are bound to increase, as estimates predict that Latinos will account for 25 percent of the total U.S. population in 2050. Given this "demographic revolution," the spread of Latino values, beliefs, and culture will continue to permeate U.S. society.[16] In religious terms, Latinos are poised to make a significant impact on American society in three ways: (1) the growth of the "renewalist" movement—an umbrella term given to charismatic Protestants and Catholics who worship in an expressive manner, (2) the phenomenon of the "ethnic church"—a faith community characterized by the desire of Latinos to worship together in their native Spanish language, and, (3) the impact of Latino religion on politics[17] to the degree that Latinos "see religion as a moral compass to guide their own political thinking."[18]

The political significance of Latino religion cannot be overstated, as evidenced in the last six National Hispanic Prayer Breakfasts, spearheaded by Esperanza USA, Nueva's national subsidiary. On June 15, 2007, nationally recognized political figures from both sides of the aisle spoke to a crowd of approximately seven hundred at the J. W. Marriott Hotel in Washington, D.C. The official roster of speakers included President George W. Bush, former Governor Howard Dean, chairman of the Democratic National Committee, Senator Ted Kennedy (D-MA), Senator Mel Martínez (R-FL), and Senator Hillary Clinton (D-NY). The director of an evangelical nonprofit (and non-Latino) seated at my table remarked that "no other group" but Latino people of faith "could command such a powerful lineup as this one." After a raucous welcome, President Bush approached the dais to comment on how the "nation is more vibrant and more hopeful" due to the "armies of compassion" unleashed by Latino congregations and FBOs. Bush characterized these armies as faith-based movements that care for "one heart, one soul, and one conscience at a time." These armies advance, he said, "*el sueño americano para todos*" (the American dream for everyone). Building on Bush's address, Kennedy discussed what lies at the foundation of being an American. Referring to the Senate bill on comprehensive immigration reform, Kennedy stated that America is "not just defined by its geography, it's defined by its values." Meanwhile, Cortés ended the three-hour-long breakfast by reiterating the core religious values cherished by Latino Christian believers—"values to do for the powerless and not the powerful."[19]

Politicians who advocate a new approach—or a "third way"—to American politics have been speaking the "language of values." It is a "common set of values" that binds Americans together, maintains Senator Barack Obama (D-IL) in his latest book, *The Audacity of Hope*. This set of values is what "people use to map their world. It is what can inspire them to take action," he states.[20] Whether secular or steeped in religious belief, values are "cultural resources," claims Ann Swidler, as they provide a template for a particular strategy of action.[21] In practice, the Christian virtues of faith, hope, and love serve as templates for the varied kinds of ministry advanced by the Latino FBOs under study. By definition, these groups are defined as "faith-based" and "charitable organizations" that care for "the least of these" (Matt. 25:45). However, these organizations can also be regarded as *institutions of hope* in those inner-city neighborhoods they serve. Plagued with adverse socioeconomic conditions, inner cities are places of constant struggle. Rooted in the biblical tradition, these institutions of hope "do the extraordinary"[22] by enabling urban residents to believe in the possibility of change through Christian faith in action.

The religious values, beliefs, and culture that comprise religious identity politics in the Latino community cannot be captured simply by quantitative research. In fact, this study will challenge faith-factor research —usually consisting of quantitatively and survey-driven studies—which has dominated studies on religion and public life. By documenting the ubiquity of religious communities in low-income neighborhoods and by measuring the social outcomes of religious involvement, faith-factor research[23] has done much to further a greater appreciation by the social sciences concerning the extent and efficacy of faith.[24] Nevertheless, this research tends to do two things: (1) overemphasize the commonalities that exist among distinct religious groups and (2) code distinctions as "very distinct," displayed in the dichotomous variables "churched" and "unchurched." In contrast to survey and quantitative studies that comprise faith-factor research, I will present a third stream of research on religion —the *political ethnography*.[25] Through my research, I show how religious identity politics informs the degree and kind of social and political activities in which these Latino FBOs involve themselves for the betterment of their urban constituents.

These different kinds of religious identity politics can be viewed best through *lo cotidiano*, or the "everyday life," of LPAC, Nueva, and TRP. Like the work of Bartkowski and Regis in *Charitable Choices* (2003), this study will consider Latino religious commitment as a "lived" experience, brought to life by the narratives of Latino FBO leadership and staff, clergy, public officials, nonprofit leaders, and community activists as well as the range of FBO community initiatives.[26] As carriers of strong religious sensibilities, Latinos are a community that takes its faith seriously. However, the term "faith"—even "Christian faith"—does not mean the same thing to everyone in that community. The Christian ministries of LPAC, Nueva, and TRP display the degree to which faith motivates and inspires people to social and political action in varied ways. A Christian believer may point to a well-cited biblical passage to explain the variety of Latino faith-based activity:

> We are one body in Christ, and individually we are members one of another. We have gifts that differ according to the grace given to us: prophecy, in proportion to faith; ministry, in ministering; the teacher, in teaching; the exhorter, in exhortation; the giver, in generosity; the leader, in diligence; the compassionate, in cheerfulness. (Rom. 12:6–8)

Because the faith in "faith-based" is multifaceted, an ethnographic approach proves valuable in uncovering the variety and complexity of Latino faith-based involvement in America's inner cities. Furthermore, such an approach is worthwhile in considering the nuanced understandings of faith that influence the religious identity politics for each organization.[27]

There has been limited research by social scientists on the nature of the "faith" in faith-based. Even more recent works have treated faith (or religion) as a means to something else, such as political mobilization, social-service delivery, and social capital.[28] Social capital theory is limited when describing the religious motivations of faith-based actors, state Bartkowski and Regis. Specifically, the theory "lacks a language for analyzing moral motivations for social action," thereby running the risk of reducing such action to a "self-interested entrepreneurial endeavor."[29] Instead of conceiving of religion simply as a form of "social capital," this study will consider religion on cultural grounds. As a "cultural resource," religion is a "public phenomenon—a collection of symbol sets to which many different actors have access," says Rhys Williams.[30] To Christian believers, however, religion is a guide for action and, more importantly, a source of personal, communal, and public truth. Because a cultural account of religion involves understanding the lived experience of faith—from the viewpoint of the believer—it is only fitting that research on LPAC, Nueva, and TRP was conducted from a qualitative and ethnographic approach. When relevant, the book will include scriptural passages in both English and Spanish (from the New Revised Standard Version and Nueva Versión Internacional Bibles, respectively) to drive home the influence of the Christian narrative on FBO leadership and staff. In the end, this study will not concern itself as much with the levels of social capital produced by these Latino FBOs as with coming to grips with the religious culture of each organization. It will consider how the interpretation of the Christian narrative by FBO leadership shapes the religious identity politics of LPAC, Nueva, and TRP.

Personal Background

My first witness of the social, political, and cultural salience of the role of faith among those of Latin American heritage was during my trip to Concepción, Chile, where I was enrolled as a student at the Universidad de Concepción during the 1994 summer session, taking classes in Latin American history and Chilean poetry. At the heart of the plaza in Concepción, and indeed at every other plaza I visited in Chile, was a large Catholic church situated across from the municipal building, signifying the importance of both the institutional church and the church as place of devotional gathering. Walking the streets of Concepción, I always seemed to bump into American Mormon missionaries, who tended to stand at the local post office inviting Chileans and other foreigners to participate in their church services. Off in the distance, a megaphone would blast the *Evangelio* (Gospel) from an open-air Pentecostal service—the first I had seen of this kind—while I was visiting my host family's relatives in the poor coal-mining town of Lota.

I returned to Chile in 1995 and, one year later, to Argentina as a Latin America consultant for a global financial services company. During the summer of 1996, between my first and second years as a master's student in Latin American Studies at Georgetown University, I personally constructed and conducted surveys about the newly privatized pension plan in Argentina. I spent weeks asking random passersby—in the heart of Buenos Aires on Avenida Florida and in the provinces of Mendoza and San Juan—about their thoughts on the new pension system. I returned yet again to Latin America in 1997, this time as a full-fledged employee for the same financial services company in a marketing capacity. Stationed in Buenos Aires, I was reminded by the influence of faith I witnessed in every city I visited in Argentina of my initial experience in Chile, and I wondered how faith as such made an impact on a Latin American "culture" so steeped in family, community, and tradition.

Although my Latin American experience is distinct from the Latino context of the inner city, my visits to the Southern Cone still enabled me to gain a "feel" for Latino culture. Through improving my fluency in Spanish and my experience in living in a closely knit Latin American community, I was able to appreciate more fully the values, beliefs, and culture that serve to shape Latino identity in the United States. Debates continue over the existence of a Latino "identity." While *Rethinking Latino(a) Religion and Identity* (2006) provides a series of essays concerning the relationship between Latino religion and identity,[31] other commercial studies have considered the economic implications of Latino identity. The Latino Cultural Identity Project unveiled by the Association of Hispanic Advertising Agencies (AHAA) in 2006 exhibits how the marketing sector—broadly speaking—views the relationship between Latino cultural identity and commerce. Acknowledging that "Latino identity is as complex and perhaps, as fragmented as the general market," the project identifies a set of "interrelated values" that constitute such identity. In this project, AHAA likens Latino cultural identity to a heart with four chambers, consisting of (1) interpersonal orientation, (2) time and space perception, (3) spirituality, and (4) gender perception. With respect to the third "chamber," i.e., spirituality, the project affirms how religion and spirituality "influence nearly every aspect of U.S. Latino life, and they affect how Latinos see the world."[32]

Debates continue over whether it is more appropriate to use the term "Hispanic" versus "Latino."[33] The terms "Latino" and "Hispanic" tend to be used interchangeably by scholars, community leaders, and business professionals. However, according to Arlene Dávila, while the term "Hispanic" evokes Spanish conquest and colonization, "Latino" tends to be a more "politically correct term."[34] For the purpose of this study, I will use the term "Latino" when referring to anyone who is either a U.S. citizen of Hispanic heritage or an immigrant from Mexico, Central America, South America, or the Spanish Caribbean,[35] although FBO leadership and staff —like the aforementioned business professionals, scholars, and community leaders—tend to use both "Hispanic" and "Latino" (as well as "Mexican," in the case of TRP) when referring to "their community."

Fieldwork Methodology

For this study, I conducted approximately ten months of fieldwork in 2001–2002 at three Latino FBOs in Chicago, New York, and Philadelphia, for a month at a time. Like political scientist Richard F. Fenno's research on members of Congress in their home constituencies,[36] I engaged in ethnographic research to study LPAC, Nueva, and TRP in their "natural settings." I examined these organizations from the perspective of leadership and staff "engaged in real-life activities"[37] as well as from the point of view of external actors with whom the organizations have collaborated. As part of this fieldwork, I interviewed leadership, staff, and board members of these Latino FBOs. I also interviewed external actors to the organizations—corporate, foundation, community, and government leaders—who either partnered with one of the FBOs in question or had knowledge of its activities in the community. In addition, the Latino FBOs under study extended to me an open invitation to attend any and all events hosted by their respective organizations. As a participant-observer, I attended staff and board meetings, block club meetings, homeownership workshops, community policing meetings, job readiness workshops, gang prevention conferences, and local church services and celebrations.

While mindful of advice from anthropological circles to avoid "going native"[38] with such ethnographic research, I have endeavored to balance such warnings with my own concerns about "going foreign." In contrast to "going native," I would argue that "going foreign" imposes a whole set of theoretical devices, derived from graduate training, on the popular expressions of faith and politics. Therefore, throughout this study, instead of speaking for my research groups, like Chicana novelist Sandra Cisnernos, I aim to "allow what comes in from the neighborhood"[39] and let people speak *for themselves* and *on their own terms.* While the "people" in question—particularly Latino FBO leadership and staff—are arguably community leaders in their own right, many of them were raised in the inner city and/or continue to live in the very neighborhoods where LPAC, Nueva, and TRP are located. Because much of the leadership and staff of these organizations have experienced personally the harsh reality of urban life, their voices should be heard—especially when they speak on behalf of their Latino community constituents.

I created four separate questionnaires, one for FBO founding members and members of the board of directors, a second for FBO leadership and staff, a third for government and community leaders, and a fourth for foundation and corporate leaders. (See appendix for a sample of one such questionnaire.) Questions addressed organizational establishment, organizational objectives, community and political involvement, strategic partnerships, faith identity, and community impact of each FBO. I conducted approximately 125 open-ended interviews, mostly in English with a few in Spanish, for an average length of one hour.[40] To engage in a more open dialogue, I opted to record interviews in pen as opposed to tape-recording them. While the overwhelming majority of interviews were conducted face-to-face, a small number of telephone interviews (6 of the 125) were conducted of the same average length for those who were unable to participate in a face-to-face interview. In February 2007, I held follow-up interviews (via telephone and face-to-face) with Rivera of LPAC, Raymundo of TRP, and Reverend Danny Cortés, brother of Luis Cortés and senior vice president of Nueva, in an effort to incorporate up-to-date information on organizational initiatives—past, present, and future—in the study.

Despite being a political ethnography, this study is not a "thick description." Instead of using lengthy quotes from interviewees to describe specific initiatives, events, and accomplishments at each organization, this ethnography is laced throughout with quotes. Because the purpose of this book is to analyze the kinds of religious identity politics that inform LPAC, Nueva, and TRP, the quotes selected are brief and to the point. Written in narrative form, the book draws its analysis from interviews and participant observation as well as from a variety of secondary sources, such as local city newspaper and magazine articles (both in Spanish and English),[41] earlier scholarly works written about these Latino FBOs, and general works on cultural anthropology, political science, city planning, and Latino studies, broadly speaking.

Outline of the Book

Before turning to the individual case studies of LPAC, Nueva, and TRP, this book begins with three chapters that help lay the foundation for this political ethnography of Latino FBOs. In chapter one, I develop the concept of *religious identity politics* by drawing on scholarship from the fields of political science, sociology, theology, urban studies, literature, and anthropology. Rooted in the lived experience of the Christian believer, this form of identity politics regards religion as a distinct form of culture—one grounded in the Christian narrative. Chapter two provides a structural look at these Latino FBOs, by examining the *context* of the values, beliefs, and culture that constitute the religious identity politics for each organization. In addition to providing an overview of the organizational history and urban setting of LPAC, Nueva, and TRP, this chapter will briefly document the long line of involvement by religious institutions and Latino CBOs—urban predecessors of the Latino FBOs in question—in the U.S. public square. Chapter three explores the *content* of the values, beliefs, and culture that constitute religious identity politics, through an examination of how human agency—i.e., Latino FBO leadership—influences the organizational life of LPAC, Nueva, and TRP. As *new liberationists*, these leaders promote three distinct versions of Christian ministry through the nonprofit structure of the Latino FBO.

Although the kinds of religious identity politics advanced by LPAC, Nueva, and TRP are categorized as three different versions of Christian ministry, these versions are not inflexible categories. More than anything, such versions are framing devices that serve to highlight how the advancement of a particular public theology at each organization has real social and political consequences. It is possible, therefore, to note some overlapping tendencies among the three ministries. For instance, it is clear that "community empowerment" is a driving force not only at TRP, but also at LPAC and Nueva to the extent that all three Latino FBOs believe strongly in the empowerment of their urban Latino constituents. Furthermore, although all three organizations can be said to engage in a type of "personal outreach," LPAC is most fully dedicated to this ministry. The same can be said with respect to Nueva and its ministry of institutional development.

In addition to three theoretical chapters, this book includes three case-study chapters, one on each Latino FBO. Chapter four outlines how LPAC manifests a ministry of *personal outreach* through attention paid to the specific context of the South Bronx and to its personally oriented services, such as gang outreach, martial arts, and psychological counseling. Chapter five focuses on how Nueva advances a ministry of *institutional development* through the organization's concern with building Latino-owned and -operated institutions in the low-income Philadelphia neighborhood of Hunting Park and on a national scale. Chapter six displays TRP as furthering a ministry of *community empowerment* through a consideration of the organization's attention to faith-based community in the densely concentrated Mexican neighborhoods of Pilsen, Little Village, and Back of the Yards in Chicago.

As discussed in chapter seven, the case studies of LPAC, Nueva, and TRP presented in this work serve to invite the disciplines of the social sciences (and other related fields such as religious studies, sociology, and public administration) to engage in a dialogue about what exactly constitutes a religious identity politics. By emphasizing the need to demystify language around popular expressions of religiosity, this political ethnography seeks to create a place for the discipline of political science in qualitative research on religion—usually conducted by sociologists and cultural anthropologists. Additionally, such a study endeavors to reserve a place for religious identity politics in the conceptual vocabulary of political science. Lastly, such a work strives to display how the Latino FBOs in question "seek the welfare of the city." Each kind of identity politics furthered by LPAC, Nueva, and TRP both reflects the Christian message of "God's activity on behalf of the oppressed"[42] and responds to the severe conditions posed by inner-city life for Latino residents. Through their respective ministries, these FBOs exhibit the varied ways they go about healing the wounds of the city as well as promoting its prosperity and security.

1

The Development of a Religious Identity Politics

[There is a difference between] a scientific knowledge and an experiential knowledge of a community. Faith-based organizations live in the community and serve with passion [because] they recognize . . . that any change comes from the power of God.
                                                    —Bishop Roderick Cesar[1]

The development of a religious identity politics constitutes a new approach in the field of political science. Religious identity politics is treated here as a broadly defined term and refers to the *content and context of religious values, beliefs, and culture that drive social and political action in community life.* Such a politics comprises personal, communal, and public levels. On the personal level, the believer engages in activities related to personal devotion—i.e., prayer, fasting, Bible study, and worship. On the communal level, the believer enlarges his or her personal sphere through an institutional attachment to a religious congregation. As for the public level, the believer's institutional attachment does not stop at his or her place of worship, but also extends to his or her neighborhood, racial and ethnic community, and nation.

Because this study of Latino FBOs is ethnographic in nature, religious identity politics will be treated from the perspective of the Christian believer as opposed to the social-science researcher. In so doing, this chapter seeks to uncover how the "experiential knowledge" of the believer—to which the above quote refers—is at the heart of religious identity politics. Anthropologists have suggested that this kind of knowledge can be viewed in four distinct ways: as "open to critical reflection; mostly contextualized; . . . a repository of timeless realities, or [as] a conditional stage of understanding."[2] The religious experiences of the Christian believer, while personal and private, have social and political consequences, as manifested through the pastoral leadership and varied ministries of LPAC, Nueva, and TRP. These experiences, however, do more than simply shape social and political involvement. While the content of religious values, beliefs, and culture help one to "make sense of [religious] experience,"[3] the believer's experiences also serve to bring to life these values, beliefs, and culture.

For many political scientists, religion is a means to something else in American public life, i.e., political mobilization, social capital, and social-service delivery. In *Voice and Equality* (1995), Sidney Verba et al. contend that religion is a domain highly relevant to American politics, as religious institutions are often the sites for "deliberate attempts to mobilize the ranks to political action."[4] Moreover, in *Bowling Alone* (2000), Robert D. Putnam contends that religious institutions are the "single most important repository of social capital in America."[5] Other scholars view religion as being a commodity in the marketplace and argue that sheer competition for members is exhibited among religious denominations.[6] Lastly, some researchers deem religion a social construction. In his famous study of a black Pentecostal church, Melvin D. Williams characterizes religion as "one available means by which man can create his social reality."[7]

The development of a religious identity politics resists any categorization of religion as a political, economic, or social variable. In many cases, the Christian believer views religion and politics not separately, but as continuous entities. In *The Interpretation of Cultures* (1973), Clifford Geertz contends that the political and religious contexts may not only appropriate the same symbols, but also commingle political meanings with their religious counterparts.[8] While religious identity politics is indebted to the intellectual discipline of cultural anthropology for its conceptual development, it also finds its heritage in the subfield of political science known as political culture. The full development of this type of identity politics reaches beyond these fields, incorporating conceptual tools from theology, philosophy, sociology, literature, urban studies, and public policy.

This study contributes to the field of political science in that it considers religion not merely for its instrumental worth (i.e., as a means to political mobilization, social capital, or social-service delivery), but for its intrinsic value. In contrast to viewing religion as another form of social capital, this study explores how religious values and beliefs constitute what anthropologists call "public culture." Written from the perspective of the believer, this study takes religious values and beliefs seriously and acknowledges that religion in general—and the Christian religion in particular—is subject to different social and political expressions, i.e., "religious identity politics," due to the way in which Latino FBO leadership interprets the Christian narrative in their respective urban contexts.

There are five main sections contained within this chapter to help illustrate the development of religious identity politics. These sections emphasize the important role urban faith plays in the Latino community. Whereas the first two sections provide a theoretical discussion of the study of religious identity politics, the last three sections offer a practical account of the link among Latino religious culture, urban community development, and social and political involvement. The first section begins with a brief summary of how the subfield of political culture lays important groundwork in the development of a religious identity politics. The second section, on the other hand, discusses the way in which cultural anthropology understands religion as an aspect of public culture, by exhibiting six impacts that religion has on public culture. This section will draw heavily from Clifford Geertz's research with respect to culture—and religious culture more specifically—due to the indebtedness the field of anthropology has to the Geertzian view of making "the cultural object . . . [the] center stage" in ethnographic accounts.[9] While the third section illustrates the intimate connection between religious institutions—churches and FBOs alike—and urban community development, the fourth section explicates the content of Latino religious culture and how such culture informs social and political involvement. The fifth section maintains that there are varying expressions of religious identity politics by displaying three versions of Latino Christian ministry, as attributed to LPAC, Nueva, and TRP. Lastly, the chapter concludes with a short summary of the themes treated above.

The Value of Political Culture

The central purpose of including a brief summary of the legacy of political culture is to show how such a subfield in political science shapes the language of religious identity politics. As previously stated, religious identity politics is defined above as *the content and context of religious values, beliefs, and culture that drive social and political action in community life*. Much of this definition is indebted to the concept of political culture, which is conceived of as "political orientations" by co-authors and political scientists Gabriel Almond and Sidney Verba in their seminal work *The Civic Culture: Political Attitudes and Democracy in Five Nations* (1963). Generally speaking, political culture is described as "attitudes towards the political system and its various parts and attitudes toward the role of self in the system." Beyond these general terms, Almond and Verba note that different "types" of political culture exist based on the level of one's personal orientation to the political system.[10]

A study of the varying expressions of Latino Christian ministry—picked up at the end of this chapter—functions in a similar manner as an analysis of diverse types of political culture. Such expressions embody a distinct approach to religious identity politics, or better yet, a particular theological orientation to the larger social and political order. These ministerial expressions slightly extend the argument presented in *Civic Culture* that political culture amounts to personal "knowledge of system . . . feelings towards it, and . . . judgment of it."[11] Religious identity politics revolves not only around personal orientations (or in theological terms, acts of personal devotion), but also around communal and public orientations, exhibited in the institutional attachment the believer has to congregational life and the larger community.

The subfield of political culture emerged in the mid-1950s but did not rise to full stature until the publication of *Civic Culture* in the early 1960s. In this publication, Almond and Verba carried out extensive fieldwork and survey research in five so-called "democratic republics"—the United States, the United Kingdom, Mexico, West Germany, and Italy—to measure levels of interpersonal trust and "commitment to democratic institutions." The co-authors regarded trust and commitment as essential ingredients to "effective political participation" and "for the functioning of the democratic rules of the game."[12] Although this cross-national study was considered cutting edge for its use of methodological techniques drawn from behavioral psychology, public opinion research, and cultural anthropology,[13] many scholars critiqued its treatment of culture as "an instrumental device for allying citizens and system."[14]

Shortly after the publication of *Civic Culture*, Verba and Lucian Pye, another representative of the political culture school, co-edited a work entitled *Political Culture and Political Development* (1965). In this work, Verba broadened the concept of political culture, characterizing the term as "the system of empirical beliefs, expressive symbols, and values" that describes the context of political action.[15] The development of religious identity politics is even more indebted to Verba for this later understanding of political culture. As an early proponent of political culture, Verba relied on anthropology to generate increased knowledge concerning the "beliefs," "symbols," and "values" that constitute the notion of culture. Even with such reliance, Verba understood culture not for its own intrinsic value, but merely for its instrumental worth, or "as an attribute of a political system."[16]

As the study of political culture experienced its peaks and valleys during the 1970s, that study reemerged with a new face in Almond and Verba's edited volume, *The Civic Culture Revisited* (1980). In addition to having a range of authors comment on current trends in political culture in the United States, the United Kingdom, Mexico, Germany, and Italy, Almond and Verba included various critiques of their original concept of political culture, as presented in *Civic Culture*. Carole Pateman's essay, contained in the edited volume, maintains that Almond and Verba's earlier work on political culture generated numerous assumptions. For example, she notes that in speaking of the type of political culture of a particular nation, Almond and Verba implied not only that "a model of the civic culture" existed, but that such a model "was relevant across the whole community."[17] Indeed, Verba himself criticized that model as "bold," "incautious," and even "foolhardy." He argued that the scope of the work was far too broad, and that the work lacked a "rich contextual knowledge" of the nations under study.[18] Almond contended that while the concept of political culture presented in the earlier work stressed the "value orientations toward political objects and processes," missing was an emphasis placed on "attitudes towards public policy."[19] Even with these critiques, Verba commended the original *Civic Culture* for "add[ing] to progress and to culmination in the study of comparative politics."[20]

Current literature on political culture—as seen in the works of Robert Putnam and Samuel P. Huntington—builds on the legacy of *Civic Culture* by viewing personal orientations as highly instrumental to the functioning of a stable democratic culture.[21] In *Working with Culture* (2002), Anne M. Khademian focuses on how culture acts as a "commitment" in the field of public management. Defining the "common understandings held by people working together in an organization or program" as the "commitments" of a culture, she argues that commitments provide a "context" for how "people approach their work" and a "guide for action and reaction."[22] Other recent studies have extended Almond and Verba's treatment of political culture by researching two new areas: (1) the "process" by which political culture is "institutionalized" and (2) how such culture is "produced" and "consumed." In these recent studies, political culture "encompasses a wider range of spheres of social life and of states of mind."[23] Additionally, nontraditional renderings of political culture have employed a "more flexible cultural approach," one attentive to identity politics and symbolic analysis.[24]

These renderings have carved out "general principles of a cultural approach to politics"[25] that pays close attention to the theoretical devices found in the field of anthropology. The development of a religious identity politics amounts to a cultural approach to politics. Such an approach acknowledges culture, and more specifically, religious culture, *for its own sake*, both in content and context. Like Khademian, understanding culture as a "commitment" helps one to view religious commitments as a "reference point, sometimes consciously applied, sometimes unconsciously."[26] The next section discusses the meaning that leading anthropological scholars assign to the words "culture" and "public culture." Culture is more than a characteristic of the political system or an attribute of the social order. Religion, as a specific kind of culture, must be described *on its own terms*, as it constitutes a distinct worldview with its own set of theological commitments and outcomes. As a form of culture, religion "does not unilaterally determine organizational outcomes, but it does provide powerful structuring tendencies shaping those outcomes."[27]

Religion and Public Culture

As the primary subject matter of anthropology, culture is understood as public because it "consists of whatever it is one has to know or [to] believe in order to operate in a manner acceptable to its members."[28] For Ward Goodenough, public culture is a "system of rules" that gives rise to a domain of "public values." Such values embody a code of ethics by informing both personal and communal action. Public values lay down the foundations for rights and responsibilities within a particular community.[29] These values proscribe an acceptable range of activities in which community members can engage, both out of self-interest and for the betterment of the community as a whole.

According to Geertz, while most everyone knows that the field of anthropology concerns culture, "no one is quite sure what culture is." Culture is both a "multiply defined" concept and an "essentially contested" one.[30] Because anthropology embraces the multiplicity of ways in which people exist and survive, the employment of an imprecise definition for culture makes sense. As a distinct kind of culture, religion is one such contested concept. Religion embodies a "set of values," and these values act as a bridge between one's personal faith and the faith community to which one belongs. These values are public in that they influence one's participation in the larger political order.[31] Religious culture matters, argues Peter Wood, "because it is taken seriously by large numbers of people —and thus orients their lives either toward or away from political engagement and the habits of the heart that can sustain it."[32]

Geertz maintains that the discipline of anthropology has discovered four different types of worldviews: the commonsensical, the scientific, the aesthetic, and the religious. Like the other worldviews, the religious worldview is a "particular way of looking at life, a particular manner of construing the world." And yet, the religious worldview differs considerably from these three other perspectives. First, the religious worldview transcends the commonsensical approach by embracing *supernatural realities*. Second, the religious worldview challenges the "institutionalized skepticism" of the scientific outlook and the premium that skepticism places on detachment and analysis. This worldview not only advances scientific knowledge, but also holds a place for concepts like *commitment* and *encounter*, typically associated with experiential knowledge. Lastly, the religious worldview questions the surface-oriented approach of the aesthetic perspective[33] by advocating a deeper, more *phenomenological account* of reality to explain all that lies beneath such surfaces.

This study proposes that religion impacts public culture in six ways: *sacred symbols, sacred doctrine, dynamic presence, divine purpose, public language,* and *social action.* In the paragraphs that follow, there is a brief treatment of the first three impacts of religion on public culture, namely, sacred symbols, sacred doctrine, and dynamic presence. (These three impacts are discussed further in chapter three, where an account of the theology of the new liberation is presented.) Then there will be a more detailed account of the three additional ways religion impacts public culture, i.e., divine purpose, public language, and social action.

First, religion impacts public culture to the extent that it believes spiritual meaning to be "stored" within sacred symbols. Symbols are the "primary means" by which individuals assign meaning to the world and to human existence. In that most people are unaware of how symbols filter these meanings, symbols have a "taken-for-granted quality." Symbols serve to create order and provide an explanation for the way things are, i.e., "a way of understanding the world."[34] The sacred symbol of the cross, for instance, serves as a visible reminder of Christ's suffering, redemption, and resurrection for Latino Christians. This understanding of the cross as a sacred symbol "sum[s] up . . . what is known about the way the world is . . . and the way one ought to behave in it."[35] This sacred symbol not only builds religious identity at the personal level, but also at the institutional level, i.e., the level of the congregation, whereby the congregation draws upon "accepted cultural icons . . . within a context of traditional Christian meaning" to communicate shared truths.[36]

Second, religion impacts public culture through the spiritual meaning not only stored within sacred symbols, but also within sacred doctrine. The existence of more than 350,000 congregations in the United States today[37] attests to the fact that sacred doctrine, i.e., theology, varies from denomination to denomination much in the same way a congregational use of sacred symbols may differ. While both Latino Protestant and Catholic traditions display a "vibrant spirituality" and a "thirst for the sacred,"[38] how these two traditions express their sacred doctrine differs. Due to the rich liturgical life of the Catholic Church, Latino Catholics place greater emphasis on participation in the sacraments and expressions of popular religiosity—novenas, celebration of feast days and holy days, and Eucharistic processions. Furthermore, there is a premium placed on the veneration of the Virgin Mary by Latino Catholics. Although such devotion "symbolizes ethnic identity" and is a "constant reminder of home," veneration of the Virgin Mary serves to unite Latino Catholics from all cultures "in their shared experiences of migration, oppression, and hope."[39] Latino Protestants, on the other hand, stress the proclamation of the Word of God, whether it is through reading the Bible, delivering sermons, or giving personal testimonies.[40] The locus of spiritual activity for Latino Protestants is the "local church community." In contrast to their Catholic counterparts, Latino Protestants have a more informal liturgy in which the "preaching of the Bible dominates."[41]

The third impact of religion on public culture, dynamic presence, relates to the teaching role of the Christian church. As a teaching community, the church's "distinctive claim" is that of being called to be the "Body of Christ" in the world. The church is called to be a dynamic presence to all, seeking to be "the place where Christ is to be made present in word, sacrament, and service," with a special welcome extended to the poor and marginalized.[42] In striving to be such a presence in society, Christianity amounts to more than an "intellectual horizon," notes Peter Wood. "It is also a religion with a substantive content, the espousal of which genuinely and frequently disrupts and transforms people's lives."[43] Inasmuch as the Scriptures act "within a particular social, economic, and cultural context," the substantive content of Christianity is always contextually based. This is due to the fact that the central feature of Christianity, i.e., the Incarnation, is itself an "example of God's contextual activity . . . where God enters human history and culture embodied in human flesh."[44]

Fourth, religion impacts public culture because the church is a moral community with a divine "purpose for the created universe."[45] Latino FBO leaders like Rivera, Cortés, and Raymundo understand that their institutions possess a divine purpose. This purpose is not rooted solely in Latino ethnic pride, but "in the recognition of an infinite and eternal God,"[46] who confers divine purpose on those who are willing to listen. This institutional dimension of divine purpose embraces the discovery, maintenance, and furtherance of organizational culture and mission. As members of this moral community, the believer strives, along with his or her church, to discover his or her divine purpose. This divine purpose is nothing other than a new personal identity in Christ and a vocation to fulfill a particular role in the world. St. Paul proclaims: "You have stripped off the old self with its practices and have clothed yourselves with the new self, which is being renewed in knowledge according to the image of its creator" (Col. 3:9–10). As St. Paul's quote displays, this new identity is accompanied by a rejection of the old persona. However, such an identity does not result in one being alienated from society. On the contrary, those who are transformed are called to "liv[e] fully within their world and tak[e] responsibility for it."[47]

Such an emphasis on the believer as "bearer"[48] of religious identity, who then lives out one's divine purpose within the larger faith community, illustrates the personal and communal sides to the development of a religious identity politics. The personal and communal faces of religious identity politics are not so clear-cut to the Christian believer. Although the believer "puts on" a new identity in Christ, such an identity can only be brought to fruition within a faith community. Communal worship connects one's personal identity to such a community "largely by making one's experience consciously social, that is, by producing a realization that even what is private to me is shared by another."[49] In this process, the personal identity of the believer is never absorbed by the faith community

—that is, such personal identity is kept intact as the believer "adds on" a new communal dimension to the self.

The participation of the believer in the larger political order displays further how Christian identity is not only personal and communal, but also markedly public. The Latino FBOs presented in this study—LPAC, Nueva, and TRP—are new entrants to the public square. As such, these FBOs manifest different Christian versions of a religious identity politics. This politics is rooted in a mandate[50] theological in nature and, therefore, distinguishable from the mandates of both the public and private sectors. While the mandate of the public sector focuses on equity and the provision of a public good, the mandate of the private sector emphasizes efficiency, profit maximization, and "individual decision-making."[51] In contrast, a theological mandate challenges these traditional public-private divisions of political life because this mandate lies "at the boundaries of the private and public spheres of activity." Through this theological mandate, "religion moves from the private sphere of individual devotion and household practices into the public arena of collective worship and social activities and back again."[52]

Fifth, the use of public language is an additional impact of religion on public culture. Latino FBOs, as one type of urban institution, are not unique in their public display of a shared mandate rooted in their theological beliefs and values. For part of what makes culture "public" is the degree to which leadership makes the values of each institution "public." Attention to sacred symbols, sacred doctrine, and dynamic presence centers on the content of values, beliefs, and culture for the religious group in question. But public language further "fixes the reference" point of such content by allowing FBO leadership to proclaim publicly the meaning that such shared values, beliefs, and culture have for a particular community.

World-renowned linguist Noam Chomsky maintains that to understand a shared value or belief is to know "its sense in the shared public language."[53] Whether at organizational sessions, community events, or national rallies, Latino FBO leadership continues to make public their theological mandate for involvement in urban community development. Similar to the vision of the church in American public life advanced by Reverend Dr. Martin Luther King, Jr., this FBO leadership declares that their institutions are neither the "master[s]" nor the "servant[s] of the state." Rather, these FBOs are called to serve as the "conscience of the state,"[54] or as its "prophetic interrogator."[55]

Rhys Williams describes the religious language used by such Latino FBO leaders as one that grounds "its public claims in a transcendent authority outside society." Such an authority, as Williams notes, "must be hooked to some sort of supreme or divine source." Due to the denominational nature of Christianity, Williams admits that "access to sacred words" and "liturgical truth" are limited to those congregations of which such language and ritual are an integral part. However, once religious language becomes "public," it can no longer remain "sectarian." He writes, when "religious language crosses social boundaries, its interpretations, meanings, and impact are open to variation and contestation." Because religious language has these "universalizing" tendencies, it can be made "democratically available" to the general public.[56]

In addition to forming "bridging social capital" across varied social relationships in American public life, religious language also produces "bonding social capital" within a particular social group.[57] Emphasis on the use of the Spanish religious language is essential to the preservation of Latino culture, as the native vernacular fashions a "bedrock for member unity and institutional commitment."[58] In addition to sacred symbols and doctrine, the Spanish language is one of the "main transmitters of religious meaning systems"[59] available to urban immigrant congregations. Use of the Spanish language serves to maintain the existence of a cultural link between the newly arrived and the American-born Latino. Moreover, such use provides immigrants with a "comfort zone" as they continue to adjust to a new social, economic, and political setting with its own challenges.[60]

Sixth and last, social action constitutes the final impact of religion on public culture. Ann Swidler asserts that culture "equips" one for social action by "shaping" one's "internal capacities" and the effect those capacities have on particular circumstances.[61] The same could be said of how religious identity politics "equips" one for engagement in social ministry, which Heidi Rolland Unruh and Ronald J. Sider describe as the interplay between "socioeconomic transaction" and "spiritual venture," or "faith in action." Religious beliefs and values, they argue, not only shape "how people define their involvement" in social action, but also "the priority [people] assign to various social concerns" in general.[62]

At the institutional level, these religious values and beliefs—constitutive of religious identity politics—provide "strategies of action" by "shaping the patterns into which action is routinely organized" in the public culture. As the case studies of LPAC, Nueva, and TRP demonstrate, religious identity politics both enables and "constrains [social] action"[63] of Latino FBO leadership. It enables social action in the manner by which this leadership's interpretation of the Christian narrative serves to combat socioeconomic ills specific to their neighborhood. On the other hand, religious identity politics constrains social action by FBO leadership's reliance upon tried-and-true patterns of religious behavior within the Christian denominational framework of the FBO in question.

The previous discussion of the six impacts of religion on public culture—namely, sacred symbols, sacred doctrine, dynamic presence, divine purpose, public language, and social action—emphasizes the fact that religion consists of a set of values and beliefs that influence public life. In the following sections of this chapter, the role of urban faith in the Latino community will be presented from a number of different angles—the geographic context of the inner city, the social context of the urban religious institution, and the theological context of Latino FBO leadership. Viewed together, these separate but related contexts paint a portrait of Latino urban life as one in which key urban actors—congregations and FBOs—strive to build genuine community amid the many challenges that beset urban dwellers on a daily basis.

Faith and the Inner City

Religious institutions have played an integral role in urban community development and are considered key actors in community building in the inner city.[64] Because urban restructuring "emptied the inner cities of almost all viable neighborhood institutions save the church,"[65] religious institutions have been left with the task of building community as an outgrowth of their theological mandate. Along with the family and community, Ernesto Cortés, southwest regional director of the Industrial Areas Foundation (IAF), characterizes religious institutions as among America's "major institutions"[66] in the field of urban community building in the United States. As the Christian values and beliefs that ground these religious institutions dictate, such institutions are called not to compete with the public or private sectors but to serve responsibly the urban context in which they find themselves.

The term "community building" is a recent approach to community development in the literature of city planning and accounts for a redefinition of community development as a holistic enterprise. Community building emphasizes not only the economic needs of inner-city neighborhoods, but also their social and psychological needs. This holistic approach endeavors not only "to create opportunities, but also [to] raise the expectations of the people, forge bonds of community and trust, improve social justice and equity, and establish a sense of accountability and ownership within the community."[67]

By expanding the role that diverse social networks play in community life, community building seeks to advance the widening and deepening of community development initiatives at the local level. One example is the "indigenous participatory initiatives"—advanced by LPAC, Nueva, and TRP—that have come into existence over the last twenty to thirty years in response to government devolution.[68] These initiatives point to a kind of internal community development where the "internal capacity of the community" is considered first.[69] Religious institutions—congregations and FBOs—are particularly attuned to this type of internal community development due to the emphasis they place on the empowerment of the urban Latino context. These institutions are called to exist within the harsh environment of inner-city life that so many urban dwellers face. But such a calling does not stop there. In providing tailored solutions to personal and communal problems, such institutions strive also to ignite the hope and aspirations of the neighborhoods they serve.

Religious institutions, as central urban actors, serve to remind neighborhood residents of their common goal of advancing and flourishing genuine community life. In so doing, these institutions maintain their focus on areas considered by many to be "morally and socially inconsequential."[70] As previously stated, community building is a holistic term. Urban religious institutions regard the community building process as a simultaneous empowerment of the community and the human person. While providing for the tangible goods for the community at large, community building also entails an acknowledgment of the mystery and intangible goals of the human person.[71]

Patricia A. Wilson contends that community development always begins with "the individual, interior person" in mind. She maintains that such development must start with the "interior person" "by touching the heart [and] changing values and beliefs. . . . This does not imply 'working on' the individual but working with the individual, calling on the person's higher values."[72] Christians here are reminded of the passage in Ezekiel in which God tells His people, "I will give you a new heart and place a new spirit within you" (Ezek. 36:26). With this new heart and spirit, God promises to rebuild the desolate cities. Those "ruined" cities will be "inhabited and fortified" (Ezek. 36:35).

Anthropologists have long understood community development as both an exterior and interior phenomenon. Development "must come from within," Goodenough writes, as "the agent of change is only a catalyst." Goodenough maintains that the cultivation of development from within the community is critical, as that particular community will be responsible for sustaining any such changes made without external assistance. These changes, if they are to be lasting, must become constitutive of the community's social identity or its way of life. The biggest challenge, therefore, for development agents is not to stimulate such physical changes on behalf of those living in the community, but to awaken within the community "a desire for change" that precedes any external prompting.[73]

Latino FBOs, as one type of urban religious institution, engage in community development from the holistic perspective of community building. Like city planners and anthropologists, Latino FBOs understand the community development process as a three-pronged effort to advance: an "inner transformation" of the human person, an "outer connectedness" to public and private actors and vital community resources, and a rebuilding of perishing neighborhood institutions. The Christian faith, in which these Latino FBOs are steeped, reminds one to look beyond oneself to the public good. Faith disciplines a human person, and in serving as a "primary control," it provides one with the "principle restraints and incentives" necessary for community life.[74]

The inner city embodies a dense network of social, political, and cultural relationships. Urban ethnographies, like those of Elijah Anderson, serve to exhibit the cultural meaning of those who inhabit a particular urban space. In *A Place on the Corner* (1976), Anderson conducts his research in urban taverns, viewed as "special hangouts" or "social clubs" to those who frequent them.[75] Meanwhile, in *Code of the Street* (1999), Anderson studies street life and its many "codes" in his case study of Philadelphia. Both studies point to the reality of the urban neighborhood and how interpersonal relationships are a central part of public culture in the inner city. Moreover, these studies illustrate how the structuring of urban space displays a distinct kind of experiential knowledge of one's community life that is shared with other urban dwellers. Whether believers or not, urban residents rely on "shared activities, experiences, and values, common loyalties and perspectives, and human networks"[76] to make everyday urban life meaningful. Just as some dwellers seek out urban taverns as meeting places for fellowship, other urban residents rely on the dense networks of faith in their effort to build community in the inner city.

Although much progress has been made in anthropologizing the city, urban ethnographers continue to underestimate the comprehensive nature of religion in the lives of urban dwellers. The tendency of scholars is either to reduce religion to merely one of many "roles" dwellers play[77] or wholly to neglect religion and the unique perspective it brings to bear on urban life.[78] As in urban ethnographic accounts, the field of urban history presents relatively few studies that document the way in which religion is a vital part of the urban landscape. Without even analyzing whether the religious perspective is important, many American urban historians have tended toward an implicit acceptance of the secularization theory.

According to Kathleen Neils Conzen, what typically is left unexplored in the field of urban history are a threefold series of research questions: (1) Why has religion had power in the inner city? (2) What has the religious impulse meant to the lives of urban dwellers? and (3) What does urbanization mean for religion?[79] What is often left in its place is described by James Morone in his recent work *Hellfire Nation* (2003)—a privatized view of faith communities in urban life as simply a work of "redeeming us" and "reforming them."[80]

In the 1960s, scholars like Harvey Cox contended that urbanization marked the age of secularization. For Cox, all public marks of traditional religion had faded away in the city, leaving only the private realm of faith in its stead. In contrast to the "juvenile dependence" of the sacred city, the secular city exhibited "maturation and responsibility." The advent of the secular city taught urban dwellers to "speak of God in a secular fashion." Thus, all theology was to be interpreted with a specific social or political goal in mind.[81] Such an interpretation advanced an instrumental approach to religion—categorizing religion as a social, political, or economic variable—in contrast to understanding religion on its own terms, as possessing intrinsic value to the believer. Thirty years later, Cox revised his stance on the link between urbanization and secularism in his work on Pentecostalism, *Fire from Heaven* (1995). In contrast to his earlier research, in this work Cox argues that secularity, as opposed to spirituality, is "headed for extinction." Religion, he writes, "seems to have gained a new lease on life" in the city.[82]

More than any other institutional feature, ethnic immigration has defined the U.S. inner city for more than a hundred years. Cities "constitute ideal laboratories for examining new immigrant congregations as well as their religious components," argues David A. Badillo.[83] Whereas sociologists of religion in the 1960s claimed that ethnic loyalties were much stronger than their religious counterparts among second and third generation immigrants,[84] Badillo writes that "churches continue in their role of identity transmission across generations" in the inner city. Even in the second generation, Latino immigrants maintain strong transnational contacts with their "homeland parishes" in Latin America. Further, Latino churches play a central role in the "preservation of community" and Latino religious culture at the neighborhood level, even to the extent of advancing a "pan-ethnicity" based on a common language among diverse Latino subgroups.[85] Institutional attachment to ethnic congregations has permitted the reproduction of native culture for Latinos. This reproduction has been achieved through physical aspects, such as church architecture or special dress for religious festivals, or through devotional activities, as in the Catholic celebration of Mexican patron saints like Our Lady of Guadalupe. Whether on the personal or institutional level, these religious expressions allow immigrants to pass down age-old religious customs to future generations.[86]

As the next section illustrates, the Latino community has displayed a marked resilience to retaining its loyalties to Christian culture and tradition. The community's attachment to the Christian faith provides a strong indicator of how Latinos have developed a religious identity politics in the urban context. A religious identity politics may serve to bridge intercultural divides among Latino subgroups so prevalent in the inner city by reminding the Latino community at large of the common, unifying threads of Christian culture that bind the group together. As Segundo S. Pantoja writes, "religion forges and maintains community and ethnic identity" for Latinos by "bringing various nationalities together to negotiate common grounds for preserving their culture and solving common problems."[87]

Latino Religious Culture

Over the past several years, social scientists Michael A. Jones-Correa and David I. Leal have maintained that "the central role of the church among Latinos is particularly striking."[88] Many recent texts on Latino thought and politics have addressed the centrality of identity, culture, and citizenship in the lives of Latinos but have neglected to articulate a special kind of culture, i.e., Latino religious culture. If culture plays a central role in the definitions of identity politics and citizenship, then Latino religious culture should be included as well. Latino religious culture is one possible source from which the Latino community derives its public values about social and political involvement in the inner city.[89]

Religion is an "identity marker,"[90] as the development of a religious identity politics suggests. The perpetuation of Latino religious traditions both serves to preserve ethnic identity and acts as a catalyst for community building for those of Latin American descent, not only within the United States but also on a transnational level. The impact of urban Latino congregations is far-reaching. In addition to providing "new spiritual homes"[91] for Latinos in the United States, many congregations have deployed missionaries to establish new churches in Latin America. These new churches offer support to their populations, whether it be in the form of material resources or nonmaterial resources like prayer and worship.

In striving to preserve its religious culture, the Latino community displays a preference for a policy of cultural pluralism in the United States, as opposed to a policy of ethnic assimilation.[92] For Latino Christian believers, the *narrative role* of religion is at the heart of cultural pluralism, informing personal devotion and the "human need for story,"[93] as well as an institutional attachment to one's congregation, community, and nation. In allowing the biblical narrative to serve as a central backdrop for other narratives, urban Latino believers display their desire to keep religious culture alive as they wrestle with the severity of everyday life as residents of the inner city. Christian worship makes this biblical narrative present in the context of the urban Latino congregation. Such worship serves as a "community of memory," recalling the "story of the relationship of the community with God" in liberating the chosen people from Egypt and in redeeming humankind by Jesus Christ.[94]

Nowhere is Latino religious culture displayed with such richness as it is in Latino literature. In fact, a dominant theme of Latino literature is the "vital role" religion plays for the Latino community.[95] Over the years, Latin American literature was made famous for its literary device known as "magical realism." This device, displayed in the works of Colombian novelist Gabriel García Márquez and Chilean novelist Isabel Allende, requires the reader to suspend disbelief by accepting an otherworldly realm of supernatural phenomenon. Unlike magical realism, Latino literature has constructed a literary device known as "the new reality"[96] or "fantastic realism." Puerto Rican novelist Rosario Ferré describes this device as a tool to exhibit "a reality that is very palpable in our environment," an environment in which "there are no great differences between fantasy and reality."[97] Fantastic realism does not view supernatural occurrences as belonging to an otherworldly realm detached from *lo cotidiano* (everyday life). As the ordinary practice of Christian devotion displays, Latino religious culture is as much of an "interior reality" to the believer as it is an "exterior reality" in the Latino community. This religious culture acknowledges the link between inner religious experience and the conveyance of "shared cultural values"[98] for Latinos in the United States.

A sense of fantastic realism is present throughout the novel *Under the Feet of Jesus* (1995) by Chicana author Helena María Viramontes. Written in the "social-realist" vein of John Steinbeck's *Grapes of Wrath* and Upton Sinclair's *The Jungle*, Viramontes' *Under the Feet of Jesus* portrays the life of migrant fruit workers in California through the eyes of thirteen-year-old Estrella.[99] The novel is a tale of survival for Estrella and her family. It is also an archetypal story of struggle for Latinos for both "inner space" and "physical space" in a new land.[100] Characteristic of fantastic realism, Viramontes features Latinos as having an "ordinary, everyday" religious culture. For instance, the "lacy diamond pattern" of the tire tread reminds Estrella instantly of the "scarf doily" her mother Petra spread under the statue of *Jesucristo* (Jesus Christ). Additionally, there is the "lopsided poster of the holy Virgin, Our Lady of Guadalupe," positioned between the posters of Elvis Presley and Marilyn Monroe, that graces Petra's kitchen wall behind the vegetable tubs. Further, one notes the use of the *aspiration*, or short prayer, "Sweet Jesus" by the main characters in various parts of the novel. The narrator's use of the aspiration, "Sweet Jesus, how she wished it would rain and they wouldn't have to go to the fields today,"[101] drives home how religious culture permeates the life and livelihood of Latinos like Estrella in the United States.

All the foregoing examples demonstrate the everyday nature of Latino personal devotion. In a larger sense, Estrella's and Petra's instances of such devotion are a symbolic rendering of the meaning the Latino community assigns to the Christian narrative. Like other narratives, the Christian narrative "provide[s] a rich source of information about how people make sense of their lives, put together information, think of themselves, and interpret their world."[102] Additionally, this narrative provides a theological approach to community life, privileging solidarity over solitude and "collective intimacy"[103] over autonomy.

As Jean Bethke Elshtain asserts, the role of Christian religious institutions is to serve "as interpreters of the culture to the culture." From the

Christian perspective, community life is "mediated" through union with Jesus Christ and communion with others as lived expressions of fraternal love. It is a "concrete embodied community" whose very theology suggests the mark of inclusiveness, particularly for those who are marginalized in mind, body, or spirit. Most of all, the Christian community is a haven of hope, constituted by a body of believers who seek the kingdom of heaven as their final goal and also endeavor to fulfill their temporal mission of "transform[ing] a wounded culture."[104]

Like neighborhoods, districts, precincts, and communities, the religious institution is one such "social context" in the inner city. A social context refers to the environment in which people "interact with one another." For urban residents, religious institutions are rallying forces that encourage the advancement of shared values and beliefs. In addition, such key institutions account for a "special culture," distinct from the culture of other secular institutions in the urban environment. Not only are such institutions "genuine communities" that transmit public values, but also they are "political contexts"[105] in that they influence the political behavior of their members. Through sermons, church publications, pastoral messages, and adult education classes,[106] religious institutions exhibit the different theological varieties of Christian religious culture. Indeed, these theological varieties are significant because they translate into different kinds of social and political action for the Latino community.

Three Versions of Latino Christian Ministry

Just as there is not "one" universal narrative for all peoples, there is not "one" Christian narrative, as the religious traditions of the Latino FBOs under study attest. Despite their shared belief in the Christian faith, these organizations present distinct theological accounts of Christian community life. These accounts endeavor to provide a response to the temporal conditions of human existence in the inner city—real-lived experiences of despair, marginality, inequality, and even hope. As a religious community leader in the Bronx commented, while focusing on the kingdom of heaven, Latino FBOs never forget "the hell the[ir] congregation lives on earth."[107] Latino FBOs provide their people with an accessible public language, steeped in Christian belief, which speaks both to the community's marginality as well as to its ideals of hope. This public language also rallies the community around the demands of justice proclaimed in the Old

Testament, as well as around the "liberating power" of the gospel. Through a shared identity in Christ, urban Latino dwellers seek to find their place in an unjust world as human persons with inherent dignity.[108]

Public language also plays a central role in differentiating the prophetic role of those working in the Latino community-serving ministry sector. TRP, Nueva, and LPAC form part of this ministry sector in the United States. Each organization is either led by or staffed with leaders from the Christian ministerial profession and is affiliated with an institutional church or grouping of churches. While belonging to this sector, "ministry" means something fundamentally different to each Latino FBO. These differences are based on the unique way in which FBO leadership interprets the Christian narrative. As the twentieth-century Spanish philosopher José Ortega y Gassett stated, one word with the same meaning can mean different things, depending on the "living situation" in which the word is used.[109] So it is with the term "ministry," which cannot be understood apart from the particular version of the Christian narrative that gives it life.

With respect to the three Latino FBOs under study, the term "ministry" displays a range of meanings, shaped both by the particular context in which each organization finds itself and by the indigenous pastoral leadership driving the organization. Like most other words, "ministry" is "inseparable from the person who says it, from the person to whom it is said, and from the situation in which this takes place."[110] For instance, LPAC executive director and Pentecostal minister Reverend Raymond Rivera views ministry as *personal outreach*. The principle of liberation, the first of LPAC's "four principles" of holistic ministry undergirding the organization, reflects this personal approach to ministry. According to Rivera, liberation does not emerge merely from a communal deliverance from societal vices, but more from a deeper personal liberation through knowledge of Jesus Christ. It is precisely this kind of liberation that begins with the human person and ultimately leads to healing, community, and transformation—the other three principles of LPAC's holistic ministry.

Seeing itself as a "wounded healer," LPAC strives to help community members confront the depersonalization they experience on a daily level. Through the opportunity to gather at LPAC's in-house Sanctuary, community members are invited to participate in Sunday worship. In contrast, the younger generation gathers for religious services on Fridays at LPAC's Holy Hood. Complete with graffiti on the walls, this "hip-hop" church offers a relational ministry to the youth of the South Bronx, providing them with an alternative style of worship. Moreover, LPAC aids urban dwellers by providing social services as individually oriented as free psychological counseling, gang intervention and prevention programs, and weekly Aikido classes for the community. In September 2002, LPAC received a one-year grant of $4 million from the Federal Emergency Management Association (FEMA) to provide free and confidential post-9/11 counseling. With a ready staff of 80 counselors—indigenous to the community and from eight hub churches throughout New York City—LPAC was under contract to serve nearly 60,000 people by September 1, 2003.

At LPAC, Aikido is taught in its pure form but is given a Christian bent. Instructors frequently read Scripture passages throughout sessions to prompt students to embrace the "liberating power" of the gospel. Meaning the "essence of life," this Japanese martial art form calls the human person to overcome fear by practicing discipline on both the physical and mental fronts. Like LPAC's first principle of holistic ministry, the ultimate goal of Aikido, according to LPAC Aikido sensei and handyman Victor Rodríguez, is liberation of the human person. Aikido students are urged to "learn about what makes [them] weak, so [they] can become strong."[111] The organization's interest in providing Aikido classes is closely linked to the physicality present in Pentecostal spirituality—speaking in tongues, laying on of hands, and other works of the Holy Spirit. As a Pentecostal minister, Rivera has realized that it is often easier to reach at-risk youth —those who usually attend these classes—first at the physical level before approaching them on the spiritual level.

Nueva takes a different approach to ministry. The organization views ministry as *institutional development*, as its primary focus is to build community assets through real estate, educational, and employment initiatives. This institutional understanding of ministry emphasizes the important role of building structures in the inner city. Nueva's macro-level approach to ministry lies at the opposite end of LPAC's personal, or micro-level, approach, to ministry. Nueva's mission is to advance "the establishment of Hispanic-owned and -operated institutions that lead to the familial, economic, and spiritual development of our communities."[112] The organization begins with an emphasis on institution building to drive authentic community development. Many "compare Nueva to a small business," claims Arthur Haywood, senior vice president of the organization. As both a "competitor" and "collaborator," Nueva's chief interest is to "bring new resources to the table" to incrementally create more opportunities for local residents who have no resources.[113] Some community leaders find that Nueva's institutional approach to ministry has a downside because Nueva has become "more influential with politicians than with the Latino community" and because Nueva knows how to play the "inside politics" game with national and state politicians extremely well.[114]

Reverend Luis Cortés, ordained Baptist minister and executive director of Nueva, has captured a great portion of the national political spotlight in recent years. In addition to serving as lead host of the National Hispanic Prayer Breakfast in Washington, D.C., since 2002, Cortés has been the central Latino religious adviser to President Bush's Office of Faith-Based and Community Initiatives. In 2002, Nueva was one of the community organizations and universities nationwide selected to receive a $2.4 million Compassion Capital Fund grant from the Department of Health and Human Services to build an "emerging Latino social-services infrastructure" in Philadelphia, New York City, Los Angeles, Seattle, Tucson, Boston, and Miami. As its institutional approach to ministry suggests, with this new infusion of capital, Nueva has created Esperanza USA—the organization's national subsidiary—to provide leadership training, capacity building, and technical assistance to smaller Latino nonprofits throughout the nation so that they can compete eventually for their own federal grants.[115]

TRP lies roughly between LPAC and Nueva in the range of ministerial meanings. Representing a largely Mexican community in the Chicago neighborhoods of Pilsen and Little Village, TRP views Christian ministry chiefly as *community empowerment*, understanding the many societal prejudices and challenges Mexican Americans and newly arrived Mexican immigrants face as a community of color. While advancing new housing developments in Chicago, TRP leadership contends that community development means more than the tangible assets of bricks and mortar. According to executive director Raúl Raymundo, TRP's ministry centers on finding a way "to act on faith and values in a community setting." For that reason, intangible assets like the celebration of language, culture, and the "spirit of the community" are just as central to community development.[116] This understanding of ministry as community empowerment is captured well in the organization's motto of "building relationships, creating a healthy community."[117]

It is the twelve member Catholic parishes (and one auxiliary member parish) of TRP that act as the driving forces of community development. TRP founder and board member Father Charles Dahm, O.P., understands fully that for the predominantly Mexican community the organization serves, "there is identity and pride with being connected to the church."[118]

Therefore, participation in religious feasts, novenas, street masses, and re-enactments of the *Via Crucis* (a Mexican rendition of Jesus Christ's Way of the Cross) on Good Friday serve to foster a cultural appreciation of Mexican heritage and encourage the community to preserve such heritage. In August 2002, musician Carlos Santana filmed a video for a new song in front of the mural of Our Lady of Guadalupe in the TRP plaza in Pilsen, a popular site for TRP summer street masses.

As TRP seeks to transform its plaza into a Mexican *zócalo,* or town square, Santana's visit reflects the organization's interest in community empowerment through the development of the tangible and intangible assets of community life. Alvaro Obregon, community organizer at TRP, states that the creation of a *zócalo* is an attempt to make Pilsen "the premier place for Mexican culture in the Midwest."[119] TRP has actively engaged in renovating the buildings that surround the plaza. In one such building, Bank of America has agreed to place one of its branches for increased community access to this financial institution. In developing the plaza, TRP aims to increase commercial business activity along bustling Eighteenth Street in Pilsen by welcoming neighborhood vendors to sell their wares in the shared public space. At the same time, the organization endeavors to empower Mexican heritage by inviting local artists, dance troupes, and craftsmen to present their cultural works to the public.[120]

As the theological understandings of community life held by the Latino FBOs under study exhibit, Latino religious culture, like other kinds of culture, informs the public values that its community holds. But there is more to this culture. As the religious imagery in *Under the Feet of Jesus* manifests, Latino religious culture embodies the language, symbols, and narratives without which a community cannot live on a daily level. With the Christian narrative as "something lived and not just held,"[121] this culture suggests that tracing social and political action back to theological commitment becomes an important undertaking. It is only in this tracing back that one can come to understand what constitutes a *religious identity politics* for a particular Latino FBO in question.

Conclusion

The aim of this chapter has been to present a new approach in political science. The development of a religious identity politics constitutes such an approach. Religious identity politics is an approach to politics that understands religion *for its own sake* and *on its own terms*. Thus, such a politics rejects any categorization of religion as a political, economic, or social variable. In this work, the study of religious identity politics employs conceptual tools from a variety of disciplines in analyzing, generally speaking, religion's impact on public culture and, specifically, the importance of urban faith for Latinos. Latino religious culture has a particular resilience for the community as displayed in the attachment such a community has to the Christian narrative. The varieties of Latino Christian ministry—briefly documented in the last section of this chapter and more extensively treated in chapters four to six—attest that there are different responses to the Christian narrative. These varieties affirm the definition of religious identity politics as the *content and context of religious values, beliefs, and culture that drive social and political action in community life*.

The religious identity politics of Latino FBOs in the inner city is a "new politics"[122] that does not view religion and politics separately but as continuous entities. This politics, grounded in the Christian narrative, is one that emerges from below and speaks to the challenges and aspirations of Latino community residents. To the believer, Christianity is not merely a pattern of orientation to action, it is a "new orientation towards [all of] existence."[123] Acceptance of the Christian narrative aids the Latino FBO leader to renew one's promises to be a person of faith and use that Christian worldview in the service of genuine social and political change.

Before discussing how the interpretation of the Christian narrative leads to diverse kinds of ministries, it is appropriate to lay some groundwork for the three Latino FBOs under study. The next chapter will provide a brief summary of the organizational history as well as the urban settings of LPAC, Nueva, and TRP. In so doing, the chapter will examine how the structure of these particular neighborhoods has influenced both the establishment of these Latino FBOs and the types of political and social involvement in which these organizations are involved. Moreover, the next chapter will explore how earlier urban religious participation and community-based involvement by Latino CBOs has laid a foundation for present involvement by Latino FBOs in the inner city.

2

Latino Faith-Based Organizations and the Urban Context

[Latino faith-based organizations] tackle systemic problems in the gathering place [of the inner city]. [They are] vehicles for social change.   —Patricia Garza[1]

As mentioned in the previous chapter, Latino FBOs are central actors in urban community building. These organizations employ a holistic approach to community building, integrating community development with their Christian faith. Such an approach involves understanding community building not as the provision of "one point of service"—like affordable housing *or* psychological counseling—but as the recognition that building a community has *both* exterior and interior dimensions. Because LPAC, Nueva, and TRP were established from the "bottom up," they are considered "indigenous participatory initiatives,"[2] with organizational leadership and staff hailing from the urban neighborhoods they serve.

LPAC, Nueva, and TRP clients all face the following common struggles in their respective neighborhoods of the South Bronx, North Philadelphia, and Lower West Side Chicago: lack of affordable housing, crime, gang activity, drug dealing, unemployment, poor educational opportunities, lack of access to health care, and feelings of ethnic inferiority. At the same time, each neighborhood has its own distinctive character as well as its own unique history. This chapter will provide an overview of each urban setting with its particular Latino concentration as well as the organizational history of LPAC, Nueva, and TRP. (In documenting the population and ethnic concentration of each urban setting, this chapter will rely on U.S. Bureau of Census statistics from 2005 for the cities of New York, Philadelphia, and Chicago and from 2000 for the smaller boroughs, districts, and neighborhoods within these cities.) In addition, this chapter will briefly examine the urban involvement of religious institutions in the U.S. public square from the period of abolition to the civil rights movement. Lastly, this chapter will reflect on more recent social and political involvement by Latino community-based organizations (CBOs) in the United States. The main objective of this chapter is to explore the role that geographic, ethnic, and organizational *structure* plays in the life of a Latino FBO. This structural view involves describing the urban setting of these organizations and the history of how each Latino FBO was established. This view takes into account how religious involvement in social and political issues over the centuries and community-based involvement by Latino organizations over the past few decades have set the stage for the entrance of Latino FBOs onto the U.S. public scene.

Latino Pastoral Action Center (LPAC)

Urban Setting

LPAC is situated in the Highbridge section of the South Bronx at 170th and Plaza streets, just a few steps from the 170th Street stop on the No. 4 subway. A neighborhood of roughly 120,000, Highbridge is just north of Yankee Stadium at 161st Street. In the 1830s and 1840s, Irish immigrants escaping the Great Famine settled in this section to work as fruit farmers and construction workers on the George Washington Memorial Bridge.[3] Once largely Irish Catholic and Jewish, the neighborhood boasts a large Puerto Rican, Dominican, and African American population, with 40 percent of households headed by single mothers.[4]

The ride to LPAC's complex is a unique experience. At one of the changes at Lexington Avenue, a Cuban man plays guitar, salsa-style, to the tune of "*America, America, God shed his grace on thee*," then whistles the next verses. Proceeding to 149th and Grand Concourse, a young girl passes by with blaring headphones. She is wearing a black T-shirt with the words "I love nothing" in white lettering. From 149th to 170th, as one gazes out the subway window, it is astonishing the care with which people hang their clothes amid graffiti-covered high-rises and rowhouses. On this ride, one particular graffiti message stands out—"*It's just the beginning*"—as Pentecostal and Evangelical storefront churches stand off in the distance. Since the September 11th attacks, one observes many people wearing New York Police Department (NYPD) and Fire Department of New York (FDNY) hats on the streets and subways of New York City.

In front of the subway stop at 170th Street is a small area of benches lining Jerome Avenue. LPAC is located a few steps from the subway stop, next door to the 16th Council District office of City Councilman Wendell Foster and nearby a battered-looking Equator Lounge. Across the street from LPAC is a host of fast-food places, including Burger King and Popeyes, as well as an "El Cheapo 99 cents Plus Store." Proceeding east on 170th Street is a Dunkin' Donuts, and an Arkansas Fried Chicken Pizza place announces a special for a $1.49 pizza slice. Although it is before lunchtime, the sidewalks of this section of Highbridge are full of African Americans and Latinos eating at the Munch Time Coffee Shop or shopping at the Great Ocean Fish Market, or waiting in line at various auto repair shops on West 170th. In addition to national chain stores like Rite Aid, local businesses such as the Ponce de León Federal Savings Bank dot the neighborhood.

District 16, accounting for both the neighborhoods of Highbridge and Morrisania in the South Bronx, comprises a population of 54 percent Latino, 43 percent African American, 2 percent non-Hispanic white, and 1 percent Asian. One-third of the population of this district is below the age of eighteen. District 16 ranks 51st out of fifty-one districts in New York City in terms of median income. In 2001, the median family income there was $20,112, less than half the $48,200 median income citywide. Neighborhoods in that district are plagued by the highest rates of unemployment in the city, the worst-performing schools, high crime rates, and a shortage of affordable housing.[5] The Highbridge neighborhood sits nestled in the northern section of the South Bronx. With a population of approximately 1.3 million, the Bronx is the second smallest in size of the five New York City boroughs. Within the larger jurisdiction of the Bronx, one finds the Albanian and Italian neighborhoods of Belmont, the Jewish neighborhood of Riverdale, the African American neighborhood of Marble Hill, and the largely Puerto Rican neighborhood of the South Bronx.[6] According to Census 2000 figures, the Bronx boasts the largest concentration of Latinos in New York City, with a population of 644,705 out of a total borough population of 1,332,650, or 48 percent.[7]

In 2005, the number of Latinos living in New York City totaled 2,221,906 out of 7,956,113 residents, approximately 28 percent of the total city population. While Dominicans and South Americans are the largest Latino subgroups in the boroughs of Manhattan and Queens, respectively, in the whole of New York City, Puerto Ricans register the largest numbers.[8] Of the total number of Latinos, Puerto Ricans accounted for approximately 35 percent of the population in New York City and Dominicans and Mexicans registered 24 and 11 percent, respectively.[9]

Puerto Ricans have lived in New York City longer than any other Latino subgroup.[10] Making East Harlem their home, they arrived in New York shortly after the Spanish American War as the city increasingly became both an important port for sugar exported from the Caribbean islands and for agricultural and industrial products exported to the islands. With the granting of U.S. citizenship to Puerto Ricans in 1917, they officially became the largest Latino group in the city. By the 1950s, most Puerto Ricans lived in the Bronx, between 149th Street and 3rd Avenue, where they largely dwell to this day.[11] Between World War II and 1965, Puerto Rican immigration witnessed a dramatic increase in the city, so much so that by 1965, "the Puerto Rican presence in New York City became practically coextensive with the Latino presence."[12]

While Puerto Ricans account for approximately six out of ten Latinos in the Bronx, since the 1990s, ethnic composition has been changing due to the arrival of Dominicans and Mexicans. Dominican influx into this New York City borough brings with it some interesting trends. Dominicans are the first Latino subgroup to come to the neighborhood that is not yearning to return to their native land. In other words, they do not tend to view life in the United States as transitional. Moreover, Dominicans are extremely involved in entrepreneurial pursuits, as their increasing involvement in corner *bodegas* (grocery stores) attests, either established as new businesses or purchased from Puerto Ricans. Because males account for a strong majority of Dominicans and single females largely head their households, Dominican–Puerto Rican liaisons and intermarriages are commonplace.[13]

Organizational History

A large multipurpose building is the official site of the Pentecostal-led organization of LPAC. The building was formerly the site of the New York City Mission Society (NYCMS), the oldest social-service agency in New York City. Along with the building, NYCMS presented LPAC with an endowment and helped the organization with raising additional funds.[14] The sign outside the building reads "Latino Pastoral Action Center Urban Ministry Complex," and to describe it otherwise would be a mistake. It is a sprawling complex. As one walks through the front door, a poster board with pictures from Ground Zero decorates the reception area with closeup photos of Americorps workers taken with President George W. Bush, Senator Hillary Clinton, and former Mayor Rudy Giuliani. Construction-paper flags welcome visitors to LPAC with the message "God Bless America" from the Family Life Academy Charter School Kindergarten (FLACS), housed in the basement of the LPAC complex.

Due to generous support from the NYCMS in the form of grants—including a project grant from the Pew Charitable Trusts—and the gift of a $5 million multipurpose building, Reverend Raymond Rivera was able to establish LPAC in 1992 with the express desire to develop holistic ministries within Latino churches. To help develop these ministries, LPAC focused on promoting leadership development and technical assistance. Recognizing that the "Latino church has a rich tradition of helping people spiritually," Rivera signaled the need for these churches "not to stop helping people spiritually, but to start helping in other ways as well."[15]

Rivera had ample involvement in New York City's public square. In the late 1960s and early 1970s, he was community coordinator of Lutheran Medical Center, organizing outreach programs for clergy and CBOs. During this same time, Rivera co-founded the Sunset Park Redevelopment Corporation, in the Sunset Park community of Brooklyn, whose mission was housing redevelopment. In the mid-1970s to the early 1980s, he served as president and founder of the RAP Foundation in Sunset Park, an organization dedicated to offering after-school programs and employment training to youth. In addition, Rivera simultaneously served as the national executive for the Hispanic Council of the Reform Church in America (Hispanic Council) and as a member of the Board of Trustees of New York Theological Seminary (NYTS). As national executive for the Hispanic Council, Rivera called for the empowerment of churches in both the Latino *barrios* (neighborhoods) of the United States and in Latin America's poor, urban areas. As a member of the Board of Trustees of NYTS, he developed ministry training initiatives for Latino and African American clergy serving in U.S. inner cities.

Along with NYTS President Dr. George W. Webber and other prominent evangelical and Pentecostal clergy in New York City, Rivera in the mid-1970s created Acción Cívica Evangélica (Acción Cívica), a social and civic action movement composed of the city's evangelical and Pentecostal churches as well as approximately forty Latino Protestant denominations. In developing a range of social services for the urban poor, Acción Cívica intended to forge "a new role in affairs of the community and New York City."[16] In October 1976, in response to vandalism and arson in churches on the Lower East Side, Acción Cívica mobilized area congregations to protect the vulnerability of religious buildings. Meeting with the NYPD, Rivera and other Latino clergy stated the need to increase the number of Latino policemen in the Lower East Side of New York City. In addition, they advocated the demolition of vacant buildings in the vicinity of churches. On October 29, 1976, then New York City Mayor Abe Beame reassured Acción Cívica leadership that efforts would be taken to prevent church vandalism in the city.[17]

In 1981, with the support of other Acción Cívica leaders, Rivera officially endorsed the formation of the Unity Party on the editorial page of the *New York Times*. This party, a grass-roots multiracial coalition of working-class people, presented a candidate, Frank Barbaro, to enter New York's mayoral election that year. Surprisingly, Barbaro won 36 percent of the overall vote in the Democratic primary in 1981, but not enough to enter the general elections. Considered an alternative to the "politics of polarization" witnessed under Mayor Ed Koch's administration,[18] the Unity Party, neither Democratic nor Republican, continues to be an independent progressive political party representing all communities of color. Its goal is to create "community-based, popular, political power" that functions "in the interest of the people." The party strives to drive a wedge between the dominant two-party system so as to build a "powerful progressive movement for positive change."[19]

Rivera's pastoral mandate of empowering the Latino, and largely Puerto Rican, community around the institutional strength of its churches echoes the Unity Party's political objective to effect "positive change" around community power. As pastor of Melrose Reform Church, Rivera relied on the strength of the Latino church in addressing social needs in the neighborhood. He quickly came to realize that "the only infrastructure in the Latino community that is authentically Latino is the churches."[20]

As the affiliation of hundreds of churches throughout New York City attests, LPAC is a para-church organization. In Rivera's perspective, it is the churches themselves that serve as the "vehicle for change" within the community. LPAC's goal is to create a "holistic ministry" that addresses both the body and spirit of the Latino urban dweller. Rivera has developed a "practical theology" around Pentecostalism so as to "participate in both worlds," both spiritual and physical, and "lay out expectations" for this community.[21] While using the language of social justice to critique the "unjust structures" that constrain the Latino community in the Bronx, LPAC's ministry always begins with a focus on *personal outreach*. It is within a faith-based organization such as LPAC that one finds a "sense of personhood and meaning."[22]

Nueva Esperanza (Nueva)

Urban Setting

Nueva Esperanza is located in the Hunting Park section of North Philadelphia at the intersection of North Fifth and Bristol streets. The immediate neighborhood of Nueva is marked by a score of abandoned factories, such as the old Wagner Chemical factory, a red-brick complex constituting almost a whole city block on Sixth Street between Wingohocking and Cayuga streets. The offices of Nueva are situated in a rehabilitated factory managed by Hunting Park Properties. Nueva shares space in this complex with Belco Corporation, La Fortaleza, Lancer Textiles, and Temple Community Medical Center, among others. Directly behind Nueva's headquarters lies Nueva Esperanza Academy, also housed in a renovated factory at Fifth Street and Hunting Park Avenue.

Fifth Street is the bustling epicenter of North Philadelphia. In addition to the regular check-cashing outlets and Latino mini markets, one finds a chain of Cousin's Supermarkets on Fifth Street. Run by Arab Americans, Cousin's provides ethnic food for the Puerto Rican community in North Philadelphia. Also located on Fifth Street is Casa del Carmen (a bilingual social-service agency for Latinos), the Catholic Institute for Evangelization, Aspira, and Aspira's Eugenio María de Hostos Charter School. In addition to being an educator and advocate of the Antillean federation in Puerto Rico, de Hostos was a founding member of the *Liga de Patriotas* (League of Patriots), an organization dedicated to pressuring the U.S. government to allow Puerto Ricans to institute a plebiscite to decide their own political rule, shortly after the United States gained control of the island.[23] Proceeding north on Fifth Street from Girard Avenue, "Sam & Haydee's Spanish and American Lunch Bus" sits at Fifth and Allegheny. Sam & Haydee's is a large school bus, painted pink, open 6 A.M. to 4 P.M., with daily lunch specials. Farther north on Fifth, a man sells black and silver rosaries at Rising Sun Avenue. A huge bundle is draped over his arm as he walks up and down the street displaying the religious articles to those cars stopped at red lights.

The largely Puerto Rican section of Hunting Park is marked not only by abandoned factory buildings and trash-strewn streets, but also by a host of auto parts stores. Cruising north on Fifth Street from Ontario, one finds Frank B. Claytons Sons, established in 1895, once a producer of steel fabricators and the famous Flexible Flyer sleds, and clothing manufacturer Ashworth Bros. Inc. Around the corner from Nueva, a vibrant old diner, Café del Marisco, with blue, yellow, red, and white colors, sits next to an auto tag agency, painted bright red over brick with slight yellow stripes. Both Puerto Rican and U.S. flags grace the roof of the agency, while salsa music blares outside from large speakers. No matter what time one drives by the auto tag agency, these Caribbean melodies and rhythms are playing.

North Philadelphia is located north of Vine and Spring Garden streets, between Northwest and Northeast Philadelphia. This section of Philadelphia comprises three smaller districts: East and West Oak Lane/Olney, Upper North Philadelphia, and Lower North Philadelphia. The area of North Philadelphia is home to many hospitals, medical schools, and health clinics. Proceeding north on Broad Street from Roosevelt Boulevard, one sees the Einstein Trauma Center. Proceeding south is a host of medical hospitals and clinics, including Temple University Hospital and Shriners Hospital. Broad Street is marked by the SEPTA Broad Street subway, which runs more than nine miles from the Olney station at 5600 North Broad to the Pattison station at 3600 South Broad. Social-service and government centers line the congested part of Fifth Street known as the "*La Milla de Oro*" (The Golden Mile). The centers include Kensington Welfare Rights Union, the office of State Representative Angel Cruz, District 180 (at Fifth and Somerset), and a storefront medical center at Fifth and Indiana situated in an old diner. Numerous banners line Fifth Street, proclaiming, "*No hay excusa para la violencia doméstica*" (Congreso de Latinos) and "*Servicios, Beneficios, Respeto*" (Health Partners).[24]

Hunting Park, the immediate neighborhood where Nueva is situated, has a population of 21,708. Of the total population in Hunting Park, 57 percent is Latino. Approximately 45 percent of Hunting Park residents register an income below the 100 percent poverty level, in contrast to 22 percent of all Philadelphians. In 2004, the median residential sale price in Hunting Park was $15,250, compared to $60,000 for the rest of Philadelphia.

Residents of Hunting Park have a higher rate of owning housing units (61 percent) than all those living in Philadelphia (59 percent).[25]

In 2005, Latinos numbered 146,856 out of a total population of 1,406,415, representing approximately 10 percent of all those living in Philadelphia. Puerto Ricans continue to be the most dominant Latino subgroup in the city, accounting for 67 percent of all Latinos. The next largest Latino subgroup in Philadelphia, Mexicans, registered 8 percent of the total Latino population.[26] Latinos face many socioeconomic challenges in Philadelphia. Latino households accounted for the largest numbers of Temporary Assistance for Needy Families (TANF) recipients in the city. (TANF is a temporary welfare assistance program—a welfare-to-work program—administered by the U.S. Department of Health and Human Services and allocated to the states). In addition, Latinos registered the only decrease in median household income among all subgroups between the years 1990–1998. In contrast to African American median household income increasing from $17,674 to $23,847 during these years, Latino median household income dropped from $15,255 in 1990 to $12,744 in 1998. Similarly, Latino youth have the highest school drop-out rate—38 percent—among all their peers.[27]

A Latino presence in Philadelphia dates back to the eighteenth century. During the eighteenth and nineteenth centuries, Puerto Rican merchants, cigar makers, laborers, students, and pro-independence exiles and organizers lived and worked in Philadelphia.[28] In the 1920s, large numbers of Puerto Ricans settled in the Spring Garden neighborhood to work in North Philadelphia's thriving industrial sector. By the 1970s, the neighborhood witnessed a wave of gentrification spearheaded by preservation activity, forcing Puerto Rican residents to move east of Broad Street into what is now the American Street portion of Philadelphia's empowerment zone. While able to find affordable housing, the new residents were unable to find jobs. "The language barrier and the exodus of factory jobs ha[d] left many people poor." For instance, hat manufacturer J. B. Stetson Co., once the largest employer in North Philadelphia, providing "medical care, playgrounds, and home mortgages," closed in 1971. However, such closings did not leave the community discouraged. In 1983, the American Street Corridor became a state empowerment zone, thereby allowing the neighborhood to attract businesses to locate to the area through a host of tax incentives.[29]

As stated above, Puerto Ricans account for the majority of the Latino population in Philadelphia (67 percent). In recent years, the city of

Philadelphia has witnessed significant numbers of emerging Dominican, Colombian, Venezuelan, and Mexican populations. This influx has
brought with it not only the diversification of the city's Latino population, but also new problems for the neighborhood. The issue now is how
to build relationships with and among newer immigrant groups, notes
Roger Zepernick, executive director of Center Pedro Claver. While Puerto
Ricans should continue to build intra-community relationships, argues
Zepernick, the Latino community, speaking broadly, must learn how to
build relationships "in a way that supports" this demographic and "is not
competitive."[30]

Organizational History

Nueva was officially incorporated as a nonprofit organization in July
1988, only six years after Reverend Luis Cortés, with six other pastors,
established the Hispanic Clergy of Philadelphia and Vicinity (Hispanic
Clergy), a local religious organization still active to this day. Initially
housed in the Christian Education building of the Primera Iglesia Bautista Hispana at York and Hancock streets in Norris Square, the office was
established to provide a central space where Latino community residents
could gather necessary resources for urban life. With membership today of
more than one hundred pastors representing twenty denominations, from
mainline Protestant to evangelical and Pentecostal, this combined leadership is responsible for nearly 2,500 congregants in North Philadelphia.

Latino pastors have learned that remaining committed to pastoral responsibilities brings with it serious financial obstacles. In 1990, 75 percent
of Latino pastors earned less than $15,000 a year, obligating them to take
on an additional career. Hispanic Clergy widened its efforts in 1989 by
becoming part of the Metropolitan Christian Council, an umbrella group
of Protestant denominations and organizations. Further, the organization
benefited from a generous grant of $160,000 from the Pew Charitable
Trusts in 1988 as well as from World Vision, the global development relief
agency. W.W. Smith Foundation also granted Hispanic Clergy $40,000 to
aid renovation of senior-citizen housing at Second and York streets.[31]

At its inception, Hispanic Clergy engaged in social, political, and economic involvement on behalf of the community. In August 1990, Hispanic
Clergy gathered a crowd of more than fifty people outside City Hall in
Philadelphia to pray and protest the verdict of life sentences in jail for the
five individuals accused in the May 1989 slaying of Sean Daily in the Port

Richmond section of Philadelphia. The slogan for the event was "Proclaiming Peace." The protest centered on what was considered to be an unfair trial for the original ten defendants, nine of whom were Latino. Soon after the life sentences were announced, Cortés founded the Puerto Rican Justice Defense Coalition in 1989 to help advance public justice for Latino youth. "The civil rights of these defendants were violated," remarked an angry Cortés on that August day. Victor Vázquez, representing the Puerto Rican Justice Defense Coalition, added, "there are two separate and unequal systems of justice in this city. There is one for those who are rich and white, and another for those who are poor and black and Puerto Rican."[32]

In 1995, acting on behalf of Hispanic Clergy, Cortés, along with other area religious leaders, fought to oppose the legalization of riverboat gambling in Philadelphia. Arguing on principle that such legalization would bring with it organized crime and economic exploitation of Latinos living in North Philadelphia, Cortés exclaimed, "Atlantic City is not an example that we need in our neighborhood."[33] Finally, drawing national concern, Cortés, representing Hispanic Clergy, spoke alongside civil rights advocates Reverend Al Sharpton and Martin Luther King III at a two-hour rally and prayer service in July 2000 at Morris Brown AME Church in North Philadelphia. That event was an interfaith rally with representation from both Muslims and Christians to protest the Philadelphia police beating of Thomas Jones, carjacking suspect, and to make a broader national statement against police violence in general.[34]

"Strong, vibrant and radical in a Hispanic religious sense," Hispanic Clergy began a "tradition of political, social and economic involvement" in the predominantly Puerto Rican community of North Philadelphia.[35] Theologically formed during the radical times of the 1960s and 1970s, the original group of "activist ministers" affiliated with Hispanic Clergy was in their twenties when they began to engage in community organizing. These ministers were influenced strongly by the Latin American "reflection on praxis" theological model of Protestant missiology, which emphasized the role of critical reflection in the praxis of mission.[36] (A more thorough explication of this model will be presented in chapter three.)

Among the original group of Hispanic Clergy ministers, there were varying degrees of social activism. While some ministers, like the Panamanian Reverend Floyd Naders Gamarra ("Father Butch"), were influenced heavily by the more radical thought of liberation theology, others were more conservative in their theological stance.[37] Ministers affiliated with Hispanic Clergy quickly became new models for Latino neighborhood residents in North Philadelphia. Culturally speaking, these residents had been unaccustomed to this kind of social and political engagement by members of Hispanic Clergy. (To this day, three ministers from the original Hispanic Clergy leadership group sit on Nueva's board: Reverend Raúl Le Duc, Reverend Bonnie Camarda, and Reverend Sergio Martínez.)

Hanging from the wall in Nueva's smaller conference room is a large framed picture from the Greater Philadelphia Billy Graham Crusade in June 1992. Seen in conjunction with the April 1992 crusade by the Argentine evangelist Alberto Mottesi, the Graham Crusade was viewed as a strategic effort to evangelize large numbers of Latinos in the Philadelphia area. Hispanic Clergy assumed general sponsorship for the Mottesi Crusade while also encouraging Latino attendance at the Graham Crusade in June.[38] Being associated with Hispanic Clergy has opened doors for Cortés on various levels, notes Fritz Bittenbender, former secretary of administration for the Pennsylvania state government. Cortés' affiliation as a clergyman "brings instant credibility;"[39] however, he makes it clear that Hispanic Clergy and Nueva are two separate entities.

Nueva has no involvement with mass evangelization events such as those described above. And yet, Nueva's religious identity is a central component of its urban community building. Nueva's mission statement targets the "familial, economic and spiritual development" of the Latino community, or "our communities," as it is written.[40] From Nueva's inception, the vehicle for such community development initiatives always "has been the churches."[41] Organizationally, however, Nueva reflects more of a capitalist corporate structure than a church structure.[42] Nueva can be characterized best as having a "business approach to ministry,"[43] or engaging in a ministry of *institutional development*. For Nueva, creating Latino-owned and -operated institutions "speaks to permanence" in the neighborhood of North Philadelphia due to the "ongoing and lasting impact" these institutions have on the Latino community at large.[44]

The Resurrection Project (TRP)

Urban Setting

TRP's headquarters is in Pilsen, an area of Lower West Side Chicago, conveniently located roughly four miles from Chicago's downtown area called the "Loop." Pilsen is most popular for its bustling town center on Eighteenth Street. At the heart of Pilsen are some three hundred businesses, mostly stores attracting the area's large Mexican population. Interspersed banners line Eighteenth Street with the words *"Tenochtitlán"* and *"La Diechiocho."* Mexican music is heard blaring from the rolled-down windows of cars and pickup trucks. A plethora of *restaurantes, panaderias, librerias,* and *casas de cambio* mark Eighteenth Street. One such restaurant is the brightly colored Nuevo León Restaurant, established in 1962 and located on Eighteenth Street between Laflin and Ashland avenues. One may also see the chain of *taquerias* called "Los Comales." *Chelas,* or the Mexican term for beer, are advertised for sale in just about every *fruteria* and *carniceria* in town. As a stray cat makes its way through a Pilsen alleyway, one notices various businesses along Eighteenth Street, from "Servicios Legales" to "Clinica Pilsen: Foot and Dental."[45]

Pilsen is accessible both by the Chicago Transit Authority (CTA) buses and the "L," the elevated train. In fact, TRP, which sits at Eighteenth and Paulina streets, is a few steps from the Eighteenth Street CTA "L" stop on the blue line. Near the "L" stop, a young married Mexican couple is bundled up in the middle of December selling grilled *elotes* (corn) and fried pork rinds. They constantly bag mounds of rinds and turn the corn every so often so as not to blacken it entirely. The Dollar Store sits catty-corner to TRP on Eighteenth Street, and across the street is the new Goldblatt's Department Store. The "L" stop is adorned with brightly colored murals, some of which depict the Virgin Mary dressed in blue, the laying of Jesus in the tomb, and other native indigenous motifs from Mexico such as a mound of skulls for the "Day of the Dead." From the Eighteenth Street stop, one may view the rooftops of Chicago's trademark bungalow houses. Over the loudspeaker, the announcement rings that "an inbound train headed for the Loop will be arriving shortly."

In 2005, there were 778,234 Latinos living in Chicago, accounting for 29 percent of a total population of 2,701,926. Of those Latinos, a predominant number were Mexican (73 percent) in comparison with their Puerto Rican counterparts (15 percent).[46] The area of Pilsen registered a population of 44,031 in 2000, with Latinos comprising 89 percent and 37 percent non-citizens. In addition to only 26 percent of housing in Pilsen being "owner-occupied," 27 percent of Pilsen's population lives below the poverty line.[47] Back of the Yards and Little Village—which border Pilsen —make up even larger areas of Chicago, with respective populations of

61,950 and 91,071. However, these areas have less of a Latino presence than Pilsen. While 83 percent of Little Village was Latino in 2000, Latino residents accounted for only 36 percent of the population of Back of the Yards.[48]

The neighboring areas of Little Village and Pilsen have the largest population of Mexicans in the Midwest. Pilsen was named after a West Bohemian town, whose etymological root also bore the word Pilsner Urquell, or any other type of "pilsner" beer. Pilsen had the largest Bohemian American population in the United States prior to World War II, and it has since attracted great waves of immigration from varying ethnic groups, gaining its name as a "port of entry." Mexicans began migrating to Chicago in the early twentieth century during a time of "economic, political, and religious upheaval" in their native land. Due to a labor crisis fueled by World War I, the U.S. government admitted 660,000 Mexicans into the country between the years of 1910–1925 to fill the labor gap. These new immigrants worked in low-paying jobs, such as on the expanded railroad network.[49] It was not until the 1950s that Mexican families began dwelling in Pilsen, after a wave of Poles came in the early twentieth century, following the earlier Czech migration even decades earlier.[50] Including all of Chicagoland—a term encompassing the Chicago metropolitan area—there are currently more than one million Mexicans.

There is a common phrase depicting Pilsen, "*tan cerca de Chicago y tan lejos del cielo.*"[51] Living primarily in multiple-family units, Pilsen is densely populated and considered one of the most overcrowded areas of Chicago. This is due to the constant flow of immigrants from Mexico, who live with friends and family members in rather small spaces while they find jobs. "This is how immigrants—all immigrants—start their lives," notes Rosa Valenzuela of the Illinois Coalition for Immigrant and Refugee Protection.[52] Bordered by the University of Illinois at Chicago to the north, the Illinois Medical District to the west, and the industrial corridor to the south,[53] Pilsen is an attractive ground for increased property development due to its proximity to Chicago's downtown. And, as Pilsen has "entered into its gentrification process," this has taken away even its supply of rental housing, argues Dan Alexander, former residential development manager at TRP.[54] Many property developers have increased the rents of residential and commercial space in the neighborhood, thereby causing housing displacement for many of Pilsen's Mexican American poor.

Organizational History

Since its establishment in 1990, TRP's core mission has been "to build a healthy community" in its various areas of involvement, whether it is constructing affordable housing or community organizing. As of 1990, TRP's only financial resources were a $5,000 investment from each of its then six Pilsen member parishes (St. Adalbert, St. Procopius, St. Pius V, Holy Trinity, Providence of God, and St. Vitus), totaling $30,000. Today, its resources have increased exponentially to leveraging more than $140 million in community reinvestment assets.[55] Since 1994, Raúl Raymundo, a native of Pilsen, has been TRP's executive director. As a parishioner of St. Pius V, Raymundo, came to learn "the broadness and richness of Catholicism." He understood that TRP's "immediate concern was to decide how to act on faith and values in a community setting."[56]

TRP originally began as an organization dedicated first and foremost to community organizing and development. Community organizing in Pilsen did not begin with TRP in 1990. In the 1960s, the Pilsen Neighbors Community Council (PNCC) was established to "effect social, economic, and political change around issues of concern to the general population." Troubled by the declining rates in intermediary institutions, such as labor unions, churches, and other voluntary associations, PNCC community organizers encouraged local churches to "open their parish halls" for organizing meetings and to identify community leaders from within the congregation. Through the churches, PNCC aimed to form broad-based relationships with a host of community actors so as to be a voice for the community against the "exploitative designs of corporate and governmental entities." At that time, St. Pius V Church[57] was the core "institutional supporter" for PNCC.[58]

PNCC registered many victories in the community, such as (1) the establishment of a high school, Benito Juárez High School, to serve the Latino population in Pilsen, (2) the founding of a Catholic Youth Center adjacent to Benito Juárez High School, (3) the establishment of a technical training school on the west side of Pilsen, and (4) the formation of a credit union to help residents secure loans to buy and rehabilitate houses.[59] Despite those accomplishments, Father Charles Dahm, O.P., former pastor of St. Pius and TRP founder and board member, maintains that the organization failed to engage in ongoing community leadership development. PNCC leaders were interested in adopting a top-down version of leadership. In controlling all aspects of leadership—including the selection of parish leaders—the organization isolated the very community it sought to help. PNCC leaders lost many lay participants as a result of the organization's inflexibility over leadership style. These leaders regarded participants who were "unable to act with sufficient anger or to dedicate significant time to the organization" as "unsuited" for leadership. When those participants left the organization, PNCC quickly "abandoned them" and found new replacements. According to Dahm, PNCC's "one-dimensional" leadership style sharply contrasted with the purpose of parish life, which is to build "a strong Christian community that lives the values of God's kingdom."[60]

In response to the actions of PNCC, in 1988 a group of local Pilsen pastors hired Mike Loftin as new community organizer for a Pilsen cluster of parishes. Shortly afterward, Loftin established the Catholic Community of Pilsen (CCP), comprising two representatives from each Pilsen parish to work on pressing issues in the community, namely, gangs, neighborhood cleanup, and housing. Loftin desired to form lay leadership in the parishes as a separate organization from the parishes themselves. One year later, the Interfaith Community Organization (ICO) was born in response to this desire. ICO intended to be an ecumenical organization; however, of the three mainline Protestant churches and 20 evangelical churches invited, only one Protestant church joined the organization for a short period of time. In 1994, the ICO merged with the Pilsen Resurrection Development Corporation (PRDC), the Catholic parishes' economic development arm, founded in 1990, and later became known as The Resurrection Project (TRP).[61]

According to Raymundo, TRP operates under a "new paradigm for community development."[62] One might rightly call TRP's promotion of an integrated community development—the merging of physical development with a "pro-family" human development[63]—a ministry of *community empowerment*. Linking the local celebration of Mexican arts and culture to the goals of economic development, TRP has made a definite stake in the community by striving to understand the community's hopes and needs at the neighborhood level. At the heart of the organization's ministry is the desire to build healthy relationships in the neighborhood, and with a host of external actors. TRP's identity as a faith-based organization lends legitimacy to these efforts as the organization strives to maintain its connection to a Mexican community deeply influenced by religious tradition and values.

The objective of the sections above was to account for the roles that geographic, ethnic, and organizational structure play in the three Latino FBOs under study, LPAC, Nueva, and TRP. In describing the urban setting, ethnic concentration, and organizational history of each FBO, one gains a greater understanding of how structural constraints may determine the distinct social and political contribution these organizations make in their respective neighborhoods. The next section provides additional information on the history of urban religious participation in the United States. It will examine the long line of involvement by urban churches and other Christian religious actors in social and political issues from the time of abolition to the civil rights movement. This previous involvement by urban religious actors displays how the emergence of Latino FBOs is not a new phenomenon in the United States, but rather is part of a larger American tradition.

A Brief History of Urban Religious Involvement

For more than a century, religious institutions have assumed a public role in the United States speaking out on varied issues such as slavery, child labor, war, civil rights, abortion, and nuclear disarmament. The first religious congregations on the urban scene to denounce slavery publicly were the Quakers. As early as the late seventeenth century, Quakers proclaimed that "holding slaves violated God's fundamental precepts" of the "universality of God's love, the brotherhood of man, and the sinfulness of physical coercion." Incidentally, this antislavery posture was considered a minority position in the congregation until the mid-1700s, when a great movement regarding abolition began in Quaker meeting houses up and down the East Coast. For Quakers, the eradication of slavery signaled "God's broader plan for human progress," in which freed slaves would be "transformed into upright workers" and masters would "learn sobriety, thrift, and responsibility."[64]

Subsequently, during the Great Revival of the 1820s, many evangelical Protestants were added to these abolitionist ranks. Evangelical leaders, such as Lyman Beecher and Charles G. Finney, preached to their audiences that all had "a personal responsibility to improve society." Congregants were encouraged both to both pursue "holiness and choose a new life of sanctification" and engage in social activism, especially in the "crusade against slavery." A direct response to this call was the establishment of the American Anti-Slavery Society in 1833. Founded in the city of Philadelphia, its objective was the immediate emancipation of slaves. The Society delegates vowed to organize antislavery societies in all U.S. cities and towns, as well as to distribute antislavery newspapers, with the express desire to "convert ministers and editors, men with direct influence over public opinion" to the abolitionist cause. A strong Christian impulse motivated the Society's Declaration in that delegates were roused to conquer "prejudice by the power of love—and the abolition of slavery by the spirit of repentance."[65]

Like the American Anti-Slavery Society, the rise of the Social Gospel Movement (1865–1913) displayed how Christian theology inspired social and political engagement in U.S. cities at the turn of the twentieth century. As a theology of social change, this movement was predominantly Protestant in character, with leadership from urban pastors like Reverend Walter Rauschenbusch, author of *Christianity and the Social Crisis* (1911) and *A Theology for the Social Gospel* (1917). Directly responding to societal challenges posed in the aftermath of the Industrial Revolution, this movement advanced a "revolutionary Christianity" that called for the transformation of the world.[66]

As a result of the capitalist forces driving the Industrial Revolution, Rauschenbusch contended that the human person had been reduced to "a thing to produce more things." Moreover, workers were considered to be "hands and not men." Christianity was summoned to respond to the social ills unleashed by untrammeled capitalism, by espousing a "public morality" that would make society realize the worth and dignity of all humanity—regardless of class or ethnicity. Such a public morality was not simply to "confine itself to theology and the Bible," but was to be incarnational, and thus to encompass a larger domain. Christians were called to be agents of transformation, elevating their motivations and aims in social life. This Christian spirit would "hallow all the natural relations of men and give them a divine significance and value," thus advancing the kingdom of God on earth.[67]

The Salvation Army (the Army) was a leading force in the Social Gospel Movement in urban areas of the United States. Army workers, known as "Salvationists," recognized that the social problems plaguing the inner cities were consequences of economic changes taking place during the Progressive Era (1890–1930). In response to such problems, Salvationists provided relief for the needy, regardless of race, creed, or religion. In addressing the challenges of unemployment and urban decay, the Army offered an "alternative model" to that of the Progressive Era. This model,

firmly rooted in the Social Gospel, had as its mission putting into practice the message contained within the gospel of Jesus Christ as opposed
to accepting the consumerist messages characteristic of the "gospel of
wealth."[68]

Less radical than Rauschenbusch's stance, the Army was more closely
attuned to the theology of: Josiah Strong, author of the muckraking book
Our Country and secretary of the American branch of the Evangelical Alliance; Washington Gladden, founder of the Committee on Capital and
Labor (1892), which later evolved into the Commission on Social Service
(1934);[69] and Lyman Abbott, a lawyer and Congregationalist minister. In
contrast to calling for a "revolutionary Christianity," the Army sought to
maintain the inherent relationship between personal transformation and
social service in the alleviation of suffering for the urban poor. This relationship, in the Army's view, was more fully representative of the Christian spirit.[70]

Like other nineteenth-century Social Gospelers, the Army came to
see urban America as an important mission field. As an action-oriented
religion, the Methodist faith of the Army aimed to "transform the secular world into God's kingdom" through the saturation of symbols affiliated with the movement. The modest dress of Army uniforms witnessed
to "Christian service and commitment" and served a unique function of
emphasizing the wearer's social identity. Moreover, the Army successfully
used the culture of theatre in productions like *Laughing Sinners* and *The
Miracle Woman* to suffuse "urban space with religious imagery." Women
volunteers in World War I, known as "Sallies," took the expression of Army
faith abroad as they baked doughnuts for U.S. soldiers on the front lines
"with heart and hands consecrated to God." In turn, the doughnut came
to symbolize the Christian faith, representing the cherished virtues of love
and sacrifice—the same values for which U.S. soldiers were fighting.[71]

The establishment of the Industrial Areas Foundation (IAF) endeavored to carry out the legacy of social-structural change advanced by urban
religious leaders of the Social Gospel Movement. Founded in the 1930s
by Saul Alinsky, IAF began as a "foundation that organized in the areas
[neighborhoods] surrounding industry."[72] An agnostic Jew and internationally recognized figure in community organizing, Alinsky elaborated
on his model of community organizing in two books: *Reveille for Radicals*
(1969) and *Rules for Radicals* (1971).[73] In *Reveille for Radicals*, Alinsky related that his motives for community organizing derived not from a theological mandate but from a "belief in people." The "radical," or the one

who "genuinely and completely believes in mankind," was central to the organizing effort, as he or she "personally share[d] the pain, the injustices, and the sufferings" of humanity. The chief concern of the radical was the provision of human rights for all, especially "economic welfare and intellectual freedom" for those most disadvantaged.[74]

Alinsky's model of community organizing employed "disruptive tactics" to challenge the co-optation of the poor by local machine bosses. In developing "independent political power" from the bottom up, Alinsky urged urban communities to stay locally rooted in neighborhood concerns. Although tied to support from the Catholic Church, Alinsky "was not particularly interested in the culture and belief systems embedded in the churches he recruited." In response to Chicago Monsignor John J. Egan's desire to include more religious discussion within IAF, Alinsky responded, "You take care of the religion, Jack, we'll do the organizing."[75]

According to Jim Rooney, author of *Organizing the South Bronx* (1995), to this day, IAF leadership strives to incite current and potential members both to understand their "abiding sense of powerlessness and . . . breakdown in spirit" and to make effective positive changes through community organizing. Rooney's research on the IAF affiliate—South Bronx Churches (SBC) in the South Bronx, New York—has held that community organizing at IAF is not fashioned on values but along lines of power. In fact, Rooney describes IAF leaders as being "brazenly explicit about their appetite for power." As a "power-oriented" organization, the IAF relies on partnerships with "mediating institutions" like the family, neighborhood groups, schools, and churches to gain triumphs in urban public-policy debates. As a broad-based movement, the IAF seeks constituents of diverse races, ethnicities, and religions to represent urban life. These constituents do not band together out of common values. Rather, they form alliances out of self-interest. In the IAF view, self-interest is the "motivational engine" of building relationships.[76]

Later works on IAF affiliates, such as Mark R. Warren's *Dry Bones Rattling* (2001) and Richard L. Wood's *Faith in Action* (2002), take a more nuanced look at the organizing principles of IAF. While not denying the role interests play in community organizing, Warren characterizes one IAF affiliate—Communities Organized for Public Service (COPS) in San Antonio, Texas—as promoting a "value-based politics." While religious institutions provide a "moral foundation" for IAF community work, "faith values" are always held "in tension with practical interests," such as the achievement of concrete policy goals.[77] Wood's research on another IAF affiliate—the Pacific Institute for Community Organizing (PICO) in Oakland, California—has maintained that the faith-based model employed by PICO makes a "direct appeal to religious culture as the basis for organizing" through the institutions of neighborhood churches. Through collaboration with these churches (and other community organizations), PICO leadership has moved beyond the pursuit of "organizational and self-interests," claims Wood. Such leadership now seeks ways to advance "common interests."[78]

The kind of community organizing model advanced by these IAF affiliates has its roots in the civil rights movement. During the 1960s and 1970s, community organizations emerged for a number of reasons. First, there was a noted failure of urban renewal policies in the 1960s. Gentrification policies largely were succeeding in many urban locales in the United States. Under the name of "revitalization," these policies tended to sanction the removal of low-income populations from bustling city corridors, replacing them with a "new urban gentry." Second, the civil rights movement and anti-war efforts gained legitimacy and were considered "viable mechanism[s] for empowerment." Third, the same leadership figures involved in civil rights and anti-war efforts also were interested in the development of grass-roots organizations that would speak to the current challenges of urban dwellers. Last, there was an increase in available financial resources from government agencies, churches, and private foundations.[79]

A key resource for black churches during the civil rights era was an indigenous pastoral leadership. Black pastoral leaders were able to rely on already existing relationships of collaboration among churches while forging ties with those "discontented groups" outside the church structure that wanted to unite in collective action.[80] The theological position of indigenous pastoral leaders, such as Reverend Dr. Martin Luther King, Jr., was influenced by the black church tradition and its belief in "the social injustice of racial oppression."[81] This position served to inform King's activities in the community. King believed the black church had a special duty to fight the existence of racial oppression, recognizing that "if the church does not recapture its prophetic zeal, it will become an irrelevant social club without moral or spiritual authority."[82] Viewing his 'beloved community' as an outgrowth of an "active participation"[83] in the kingdom of God, King served to provide the black church with a distinctive religious identity politics that would shape its entrance into the larger political struggle in which it was embroiled.

The impact of the civil rights movement on American society was pro-found. The movement did not simply help eradicate the legal constraints that had formerly limited both the personal and political freedoms of blacks. In a much larger sense, the movement "penetrated far beyond the black community" in that it offered other marginalized groups "organiza-tional and tactical models" to engage in a politics of protest. The move-ment was not limited to blacks, as the establishment of the IAF affiliates demonstrate. The fight for civil rights extended to all oppressed groups, and a central legacy of the movement was that "organized nontraditional politics was a viable method of social change."[84]

This section has provided a brief history of urban religious participa-tion in the United States from abolition to the civil rights movement and also has displayed how Latino FBO involvement is part of a larger Ameri-can tradition of religious institutions playing a public role in urban life. The following section presents the history of Latino CBOs in the United States. Like the previous section, it attempts to explore how LPAC, Nueva, and TRP are indebted to the important social and political roles that La-tino community-based involvement has played over the past decades.

The History of Latino Community-Based Organizations

According to Enrique T. Trueba, "the training ground for political or-ganization in Latino communities was the civil rights movement of the 1960s and 1970s."[85] During that time, the establishment of Latino CBOs fought for the recognition of Latinos as emerging groups in political life. This early involvement by Latino CBOs in "making public the oppressed self"[86] preceded much later community involvement by Latino FBOs. That later involvement by the Latino FBOs under study accounts for the "new forms of solidarity"[87] established in the inner city. Because LPAC, Nueva, and TRP all minister in large part to Mexican, Puerto Rican, and Dominican populations in the United States, a brief history of social and political involvement by these groups will be provided in the paragraphs that follow.

In comparison to Mexicans and Puerto Ricans, social and political in-volvement by Dominicans in the United States has a relatively short his-tory. Organized Dominican involvement surfaced in the United States during the mid-1960s. Earlier, movements such as the Partido Revolucio-nario Dominicano (PRD) were formed to combat the dictatorial regime of Rafael Trujillo in the Dominican Republic (1930–1961). New York City served as this movement's base of operations. In the 1980s, Dominicans in New York witnessed gains in political empowerment as many from the community joined or were elected to local governance bodies. Although Dominicans today account for the fourth largest Latino subgroup in the United States, the community suffers from a "political invisibility." Historically, Dominicans have been left out of reference publications that treat the multiplicity of ethnic groups in the United States.[88]

Like other Latino subgroups such as Puerto Ricans, poverty rates are generally high for Dominicans, especially because they tend to belong to "lower-income brackets." Dominican immigrants tend to have "high rates of employment in declining economic sectors" as well as "below average educational skills." These trends seem to be changing with the second-generation Dominicans, who typically have better access to educational opportunities and higher-income occupations. While New York registers the largest concentration of Dominicans in the United States, there has been a dispersion of the Dominican population into other states over the past decade. This follows a similar pattern of dispersion by earlier Latino subgroups, most notably the Puerto Ricans.[89]

Puerto Rican activism dates back to the mid-1800s, when newly arrived Puerto Ricans in New York City advocated Puerto Rican independence from Spain. After the economic havoc created by World War I, small community movements began to emerge, like the Alianza Puertorriqueña and the Puerto Rican Nationalist Association. With waves of Puerto Rican migration to the United States occurring after World War II, community organizations began to develop to provide for the social, economic, and political needs of the Puerto Rican community, living largely in New York City. During the 1960s and 1970s, organizations such as the Puerto Rican Forum, Aspira, and the Puerto Rican Legal Defense and Education Fund were established in New York, while the more radical Young Lords Party emerged in Chicago and later in New York and Philadelphia, marking "the political awakening of a new generation of young Puerto Ricans."[90]

More than any other Caribbean or Latin American nation, the history of Puerto Rico cannot be understood outside of large diaspora to the United States. While 3.8 million Puerto Ricans resided on the island in 2000, approximately 3.4 million lived in the United States. This has given rise to the reality of "another Puerto Rico" in many communities across the United States, "introducing a new dimension of the construction of identity and to the notion of what it means to be Puerto Rican."[91] Puerto

Rico has a unique relationship of dependency with the United States, nicely summarized in the bumper sticker, "*vive tu vida, no la mia,*" or "live your life, not mine." Since the Spanish American War in 1898, the United States has had a paternalistic relationship with the island of Puerto Rico. In that year, the island officially came under U.S. control. When, in 1917, the island was granted U.S. territory status, Puerto Ricans became American citizens. In 1952, Puerto Rico became a U.S. commonwealth. Although Puerto Ricans are U.S. citizens, residents on the island have no voting representation in the U.S. Congress and cannot vote in presidential elections.

Because all Puerto Ricans are U.S. citizens, it is not appropriate to use the term "Puerto Rican American" to designate them as a group. They are not "hyphenated Americans," argues María E. Pérez y González, because "whether one favors or opposes U.S. involvement in Puerto Rico, to state that one is Puerto Rican is synonymous with saying that one is American." Although they are American citizens, Puerto Ricans still struggle with issues of "self-preservation and [cultural] affirmation." Furthermore, Puerto Rican males struggle with having the lowest labor force participation rate of all ethnic groups in the United States. And, Puerto Ricans, generally speaking, continue to have a socioeconomic status as "among the poorest ethnic groups in the United States."[92]

With respect to Mexican American (or, Chicano) movements, initial political agitation by CBOs began with the outbreak of the Mexican American War (1846–1848), during which time the United States acquired the northern territory of Mexico. Almost a century later, between the 1930s and 1950s, national Chicano organizations, such as the Mexican Congress and the Unity Leagues, developed in California alongside grass-roots, state, and regional Chicano political organizations, such as the Council of Mexican-American Affairs and the Mexican American Political Association. Lacking resources and base community support, David Rodríguez maintains that "none of these organizations had the necessary political power to fundamentally challenge . . . Anglo political hegemony." It was not until the 1960s that a form of Chicano politics called "protest politics" emerged. New organizations headed by charismatic leadership strove to confront unjust social structures. Among others, these organizations were: Alianza Federal de Pueblos Libres, headed by Reies López Tijerina; Crusade for Justice, led by Rodolfo "Corky" Gonzales; La Raza Unida Party, founded by José Angel Gutiérrez; and, United Farm Workers (UFW), established by César Chávez.[93]

Although considered a leader of a secular Latino social movement, César Chávez of UFW demonstrates how indigenous Latino leadership has relied and continues to rely on theological mandates found in Christian teachings to advance its social and political causes. This is nicely documented in Frederick John Dalton's work, *The Moral Vision of César Chávez* (2003). Dalton describes the moral or "prophetic vision" of Chávez as one that gave witness to a life lived for justice, where the underlying motivation for such justice was "an expression of faith in God."[94] Chávez combined his role as a radical labor organizer with his Catholic identity as a Cursillista, or follower of the Cursillo Movement. A pre-Vatican Council II manifestation of popular religiosity, this movement "provided a significant sharpening for Latino Catholic identity"[95] by offering liturgies in Spanish and serving as a base for the development of Latino leadership, particularly for the working class and poor.

As a Mexican American, Chávez endeavored to integrate his Catholic faith with his public opposition to farmworker treatment through "his use of Catholic symbols like the banner of Our Lady of Guadalupe, the *peregrinación* (pilgrimage), his fasting, and his appeal for Catholics to support his cause."[96] The plan drafted by UFW for the Delano grape strike (1965–1966), calling for "pilgrimage, penance, and revolution" is a case in point. "Seeking social justice in farm labor," this plan emphasized the need for the unity of all workers in their struggle against injustice through the protection wrought by the religious symbols of "Our Lady of Guadalupe," the "Sacred Cross," and the "Star of David."[97]

While the previous examples of Mexican CBOs display active engagement in public affairs, most Mexicans, even second-generation ones, tend to distance themselves from the world of politics, because they view such a world as "contentious, divisive, and therefore 'un-Christian.'"[98] Virgilio Elizondo explains that this lack of engagement stems from the oppression Mexicans suffered during the Spanish colonial expansion, resulting in a cultural identity of "inferiority and worthlessness."[99] This situation is exacerbated further in the United States, where Mexicans "consider themselves even more impotent." Many Mexicans face great obstacles that prevent them from engaging in community involvement—poor English skills, long working days, and discrimination. And, undocumented Mexicans have even more to fear, realizing that such involvement could ultimately lead to their deportation.[100]

Anti-immigrant sentiments have served to maintain a Mexican identity apart from the United States. At the same time, however, recent immigrants have developed "an ethnic identity and consciousness that integrates a sense of 'American-ness.'" As the May 1, 2006, marches for "immigrant rights" attest, Mexican immigrants eventually gain awareness of their rights as U.S. residents, whether as legal residents or as undocumented workers. In other words, they simultaneously navigate a dual identity of "immigrants" and "New Americans."[101]

Conclusion

As the definition of religious identity politics suggests, it is both the context and content of religious beliefs, values, and culture that inform social and political action. This chapter explored the *context* of these beliefs, values, and culture by examining the role that geographic, ethnic, and organizational structure can play in the day-to-day operations of a Latino FBO. Moreover, the chapter examined how urban religious participation —from abolition to the present "protest politics" of the IAF—and community-based involvement by Latino CBOs historically have set the stage for the emergence of Latino FBOs like LPAC, Nueva, and TRP in the U.S. public square. In documenting how the *context* of religious beliefs influences such participation, the chapter displays how structural constraints —such as urban setting, ethnic concentration, organizational history, and the history of urban religious participation and Latino CBO involvement in the United States—can determine the political and social contribution made on behalf of Latino FBOs in their respective neighborhoods.

The next chapter will examine the *content* of religious beliefs, values, and culture that inform the direction that each Latino FBO leader takes in his ministry. Instead of examining structure, the next chapter will focus on the role of *agency*, and particularly how FBO leadership interprets the Christian narrative to effect social and political change in their communities. Anthony Giddens' work on the development of the term "agency" should be considered here. Giddens acknowledges that there is, in fact, a "cycle of agency and structure" to the degree that institutions result from human agency at the same time that human agency is in turn shaped by institutions. Whereas agency is understood as the realm of "human action" or "individual efforts," structure involves the "cumulative consequences of those efforts" on social systems.[102]

An investigation into the theological influences of Rivera of LPAC and Cortés of Nueva will bring to light this realm of human agency in the institutional life of Latino FBOs. In place of Raymundo, TRP's executive director, the next chapter will explore the role that select liberation theologians have played in the life and work of Father Charles Dahm, O.P., TRP founder and board member, and Dominican priest. Raymundo credits the faith-based focus of the organization to the influence of the religious orders affiliated with TRP member parishes—the Jesuits, Claretians, and Dominicans—and especially to Dahm's theological articulation of TRP's ministry of community empowerment in the neighborhoods of Pilsen, Little Village, and Back of the Yards, Chicago.[103] Although theological influences may differ among Rivera, Cortés, and Dahm, viewed together, they may be considered to be proponents of a "new liberationism," directing their Latino constituents to unleash a spiritual renewal and democratic revitalization in the urban context.

3

The New Liberationists

Liberation theology was a sweeping critique of the way things were. [Its] solution was to take power and change things. [This was at the heart of the] Medellín generation. There will not be another one.   —Phillip Berryman[1]

Liberation theology has been read, discussed, taken over and transformed by Latinos in the United States.
                                        —Reverend Nelson Rivera[2]

Whereas the previous chapter viewed how the *urban context* of LPAC, Nueva, and TRP has influenced and continues to influence the emergence of these Latino FBOs in American public life, this chapter examines how leadership—Reverend Raymond Rivera of LPAC, Reverend Luis Cortés, Jr., of Nueva, and Father Charles Dahm, O.P., of TRP —understands the *religious content* of each Latino FBO. This chapter will consider the role that human agency—i.e., the realm of "human action" and "individual efforts," as suggested by Giddens—plays in the organizational life of LPAC, Nueva, and TRP. All three leaders under study are not merely religious professionals in a narrow sense, but professionals who "shape the course of political affairs" through their ministerial involvement in the inner city.[3]

This chapter will treat how Rivera and Cortés articulate the religious content of LPAC and Nueva in their respective ministries of personal outreach and institutional development. Dahm's reflection on TRP's religious content will be considered in place of Raúl Raymundo, executive director of TRP. Raymundo is indebted to Dahm's theological articulation of TRP's ministry of community empowerment summarized in the organization's central slogan of "building a healthy community." An understanding of the theological commitments of these leaders is "politically significant"[4] in that their social and political involvement is "rooted . . . in deep-seated theological perspectives and their associated social theologies."[5]

The chief aim of this chapter is to explicate the theological sources of religious identity politics for each organization. This identity politics is not attributable solely to the denominational affiliation of Rivera, Cortés, and Dahm. Rather, this identity politics is shaped by how leadership reads, interprets, and applies the Christian narrative to the urban context. Although Rivera, Cortés, and Dahm advance distinct kinds of religious identity politics through their organizations, their respective ministries of personal outreach, institutional development, and community empowerment share important similarities. These Latino FBO leaders believe in the power of the Christian narrative to drive social and political change for their constituents in the inner city. They are the *new liberationists* who have "read, discussed, taken over, and transformed" Latin American liberation theology, as the quote above suggests.

For new liberationists, as for liberation theologians, theology and politics are continuous entities. Theology informs political decisions, political activities, and political collaborations. In the tradition of liberation theology, Rivera, Cortés, and Dahm do not consider themselves as articulating a new theology. Rather, they demonstrate a "new method of doing theology."[6] This new method is accomplished not simply through academic scholarship, traditional congregational life, and pastoral ministry, but through the para-church and nonprofit structure—the Latino FBO.

New liberationists are "new" for several reasons. First, Rivera, Cortés, and Dahm are new kinds of leaders in that LPAC, Nueva, and TRP are among the first grass-roots Latino FBOs on the U.S. public scene, established approximately fifteen to twenty years ago. Second, the leadership model of these institutions is unique in that these organizations are not denominational churches demanding merely a pastoral background. Instead, the leadership model required of Rivera, Cortés, and Dahm is one of an institutional actor who leads an ecumenical institution known as a para-church organization, or the Latino FBO. While "faith-based," these organizations are ecumenical entities run like community-based organizations, offering holistic services for Christian believers and nonbelievers alike on the local level. Depending on the organization, services include, among others: affordable housing, gang intervention programs, free psychological sessions, educational opportunities, and political advocacy on issues such as comprehensive immigration reform.

Third, Rivera, Cortés, and Dahm do not view personal and communal expressions of religious devotion—i.e., popular religiosity—with disdain, as did some proponents of Latin American liberation theology. In contrast, these leaders believe deeply in the connection between popular religion and liberation. (This theme will be examined more closely in the last two sections of this chapter.) Fourth, new liberationists do not desire revolutionary or "sweeping changes" of the political and economic orders, as in the case of Latin America. Viewing democracy as a "sham" in Latin America, many Latin American liberation theologians advocated "revolutionary socialism" as a path to participatory democratic politics. Rivera, Cortés, and Dahm hold no such attitude toward U.S. political structures. Last, the new liberationists tend, on the whole, to be less critical of capitalism than their Latin American counterparts, many of whom likened it to a "monolithic totality."[7] (To varying degrees, these Latino FBOs consider private corporations a legitimate source of funding for their program areas. Nueva, for instance, receives $350,000 a year from corporate sponsors for the National Hispanic Prayer Breakfast.)[8] Instead of viewing democracy and capitalism in a negative light, these new liberationists view them as "partial and contradictory creatures, amenable to change and recombination."[9]

As in U.S. Latino theology, "a culturally contextualized theology of liberation" is at the heart of the new liberationists' ministerial activity in urban life. Each leader understands the need for a cultural approach to theology to "highlight those features that make Latinos unique" and provide them with a space to assert "collective cultural identity." However, as Benjamín Valentín claims, Latino theology needs to "go beyond" themes of "culture, identity, and . . . difference" through the cultivation of a "public theology" that takes into account how religious culture can "engage with and influence public discourse." Through the advancement of a particular kind of religious identity politics in LPAC, Nueva, and TRP, the new liberationists are, in effect, taking up Valentín's challenge. As a result of their theological commitments and personal histories, Rivera, Cortés, and Dahm have succeeded in crafting public theologies that have "capture[d] the attention of a wide and diverse audience, including many who have ceased to take either religion or theology seriously."[10]

This chapter has four main sections. The first section provides a brief overview of the variations of political activity displayed by LPAC, Nueva, and TRP, illustrating the way in which these organizations are political actors. The second section provides a detailed treatment of the theological influences on Rivera, Cortés, and Dahm. This section discusses the legacy of Latin American liberation theology and explores the relevance that particular strands of such theology have played in the leadership of LPAC, Nueva, and TRP. The third section lays the foundation for a U.S. Latino theology, with special attention paid to the role of the *mestizo* (racially mixed person) and popular religion. Finally, the last section concludes with a brief look at the theology and practice of the new liberation, as displayed through the ministries of the Latino FBOs under study.

Latino Faith-Based Organizations as Political Actors

During my first visit to Chile in 1994, I decided to enter a bank in Santiago to exchange my American dollars for Chilean pesos. Upon approaching the bank teller, I asked in my broken Spanish, "*se cambian los dolores?*" instead of asking "*se cambian los dólares?*" What I did not realize at that moment was that I had asked the Chilean teller if he exchanged "sorrows" instead of "American dollars." Quickly recognizing my mistake, the teller responded, "*sí, y también las tristezas,*" or "we do exchange sorrows, and also sadness."

My Chilean experience above relates well to the phenomenon of Latino FBOs in the inner city. Many tend to view Latino FBOs as merely social-work agencies that exchange "sorrows" and "sadness" in the neighborhood. While it is correct to see these organizations in this light, such a perspective does not portray how they are "encouraged to be political actor[s]" in the community. These organizations supplement the very limitations of Latino political power in public life in three distinct but related ways: (1) through the legitimacy they wield with their community constituency; (2) through the influence they hold with a host of community, corporate, foundation, and government actors; and, (3) through their reputation as successfully leveraging public and private resources to provide for a public good. FBOs are, in fact, "political organizations," notes Michael Leo Owens, by the very fact that "they are engaged in a movement that is providing an alternative model or vision to government" and private enterprise. They are mediating institutions offering both a "range of services" and engaging in a "range of political activities" at a time when

government provision of such services in urban neighborhoods is perceived to have failed.[11]

According to Kraig Beyerlein and Mark Chaves, approximately 40
percent of all congregations are politically active in some fashion. The
types of political activities—in which evangelical/conservative Protestant,
mainline/liberal Protestant, black Protestant, and Catholic congregations
are involved—differ considerably. Each religious subgroup has its own
"distinctive way of engaging in politics."[12] These different ways of engaging in politics are attributable to the religious identity of the respective
congregations. In other words, the content of theology can play a chief
role in determining forms of social and political behavior.

Most religious institutions in the United States espouse similar beliefs
that aid the survival of the democratic political process, namely, freedom,
participation in community life, and public trust in governmental office. But these institutions do more than serve democracy; they "perform
the important task of reminding us that public decisions inescapably involve and reflect values."[13] As Beyerlein and Chaves point out, there is
"religious variation in political participation" among congregations in the
United States, and such variation is qualitative in nature. Although Beyerlein's and Chaves' research displays the strong affinities that lie between
religious tradition and type of political involvement, they admit that such
research does not attempt to uncover the sources of these affinities. It is
the task of future research in the social sciences, they argue, to investigate
the "sources of religious variations in congregational political activity" in
the United States.[14]

Recent scholarship has been conducted on how religious traditions
shape the types of programs in which congregations involve themselves.
In highlighting the "spiritual foundations" of congregations in the United
States, Nancy Tatom Ammerman summarizes four main areas in which
congregations engage in the "spiritual work of building faith": worship-
ping together, nurturing individual spirituality, conversion, and educating
the faithful.[15] Moreover, in *Congregations in America* (2004), Mark Chaves
provides a treatment of the varying kinds of civic engagement among
white conservative and evangelical Protestants, white liberal and moder-
ate Protestants, black Protestants, and Roman Catholics. Further, Gastón
Espinosa elaborates on the distinctions of social-service provision by Latino Protestant and Roman Catholic congregations.[16] Similar research has
been conducted at the level of the faith-based organization. For instance,
Heidi Rolland Unruh's and Ronald J. Sider's *Saving Souls, Serving Society*

(2005) provides a look at the "religious dynamic in faith-based ministries," typologizing FBOs as well as their mission orientations.[17]

In studying the religious variations among congregations and FBOs in the United States, the aforementioned research has moved the fields of religion and politics and sociology of religion in a very positive direction. At the same time, this research is largely descriptive as opposed to analytical. In other words, these works do not examine *in-depth* the theological sources of social and political activity within these religious institutions, i.e., the "values, teachings, and ideas" of the congregations or FBOs themselves. Clearly, there are inherent limitations in using theological explanations for political behavior. Theological explanations are "far from complete" in that certain religious traditions tend to be "elastic," or changing over time. Nevertheless, Kenneth Wald believes that understanding the sources of religious variations is a worthwhile task, even if theological content is "imperfectly captured by denominational affiliation, church attendance, and religion."[18]

Because LPAC, Nueva, and TRP display variations in political activity, it is essential to examine such differences from a political view as well as a theological standpoint. According to Clifford Geertz, an anthropological study of religion must address the values underlying patterns of social and political behavior. Such a study is a "two-stage operation": (1) an analysis of the system of meanings within the symbols that constitute religion and (2) the relation of these systems to larger social-structural and psychological processes. Much of the growing dissatisfaction within the field of anthropology, comments Geertz, is not that it overemphasizes the relationship between religion and these larger processes, but that it downplays an analysis of the system of meanings contained in religion.[19] Only with such an analysis can a greater understanding of religious identity politics —of Latino Christians engaging in politics—be brought to light.

Variations in Political Activity

As organizations relatively independent from the theological directives of an institutional church, LPAC and Nueva are structurally freer than TRP to give their leadership a political and even partisan face. However, Reverend Rivera of LPAC, in contrast to Cortés of Nueva, has not only been politically active in New York City, but also has engaged in partisan politics through the personal endorsement of Fernando Ferrer, the

2001 and 2005 Democratic primary candidate for New York City mayor. Moreover, Rivera has formed ties with other significant political figures in the Democratic Party, namely, Adolfo Carrion, Jr., Bronx borough president, and Congressman José E. Serrano of the 16th District in New York City. And, Rivera has decided to offer his help to Senator Hillary Clinton's 2008 presidential campaign. All these political activities have taken place outside the organizational structure of LPAC. Reflective of LPAC's ministry as personal outreach, these activities point to the reality of Rivera as an "independent operator" in both policy circles and community collaborations. Such political involvement is nothing new for Rivera. After all, he endorsed the creation of the grass-roots, multiethnic Unity Party in the 1980s.

LPAC relies on its management philosophy of "ministry as ministry."[20] In showcasing its HIV and AIDS facility, Liberation Manor, as well as its first faith-based clinic, located in Queens, LPAC displays how the organization is a "wounded healer" to its community, putting into effect the words proclaimed in Isaiah: "by his bruises we are healed" (Isa. 53:5). While working alongside other evangelical and Pentecostal Christians in leadership development and technical assistance, Rivera also has maintained long-standing partnerships with area Buddhists and Quakers to foster community building in the South Bronx—largely atypical behavior of traditional Pentecostal preachers. Over the years, LPAC has neither had a structured leadership nor a strong board of directors. In 2007, the organization began the process of renewing its leadership model to meet the demands of its desires for longevity. In addition to hiring five new program directors, Rivera has named his daughter, Susana Rivera-León, vice president of the organization. Furthermore, he has created an institutional board, thereby building an organizational structure that will survive the charismatic leadership of Rivera himself.[21]

Neither endorsing nor financially contributing to politicians, Cortés views himself not as a separate entity but as a part of Nueva. Concerned with program effectiveness and internal operations, Cortés' institutional approach to ministry is reflected in his attentiveness to business management concepts like "strategic planning" and "core competency." Entrepreneurial and progressive in its own right, Nueva strives to be a staff-led corporation along the lines of a company listed on the Nasdaq. While the Nueva website often contains information on political advocacy at a national level, the organization has no existing organizing arm within the local community. Perhaps Cortés' statement that "when you institutionalize, you de-radicalize"[22] offers an explanation why such an arm does not exist. As a nationally recognized leader, Cortés often engages in high-level political appearances, testifying before the Senate Judiciary Committee in support of comprehensive immigration reform in July 2006.

In May 2007, Nueva hosted the sixth National Hispanic Prayer Breakfast in Washington, D.C. For the last six years, approximately seven hundred people have attended the breakfast, ranging from Hispanic clergy and laypeople to lobbyists, political advocates, and U.S. political leaders. Reverend Danny Cortés (D. Cortés), Luis Cortés' brother and senior vice president of Nueva, argues that, at a local level, the breakfast has "opened up a series of experiences" that has made a profound impact on Latino churches. Politically speaking, the breakfast has helped "raise the voice of the Hispanic faith community" at the national level, encouraging U.S. politicians to "take this constituency seriously." D. Cortés admits that the breakfast has provided Nueva with public access to both political parties. Over the years, speakers at the event have included, among others: President George W. Bush, former U.S. Attorney General Alberto Gonzales, Senator Mel Martínez (R-FL), Senator Hillary Clinton (D-NY), Senator Harry Reid (D-NV), and Senator Ted Kennedy (D-MA).[23]

Although engaged in politics, TRP is extremely careful when entering the public square due to its close affiliation with the Catholic Church. Reflective of its political face, TRP was part of a bipartisan community entourage welcoming President Vicente Fox of Mexico to Chicago during his visit in July 2001. In a later TRP staff meeting, Raymundo, in his typical "bottom-up" style, invited staff to comment on the potential political ramifications of President Fox's event for Mexican immigrants living in the United States. Among the ramifications TRP staff discussed were legalization of undocumented Mexican workers, permission to allow undocumented Mexicans to attend institutions of higher education, and permission for Mexican immigrants to obtain driver licenses. All present at the staff meeting were engaged in conversation about how they would be able to hold their political officials accountable to get such items listed on their policy agendas.[24] More recently, TRP has been actively engaged in the fight for comprehensive immigration reform, helping organize the mega-marches across Chicago in May 2006.

As a Latino FBO leader advancing a ministry of community empowerment, Raymundo is attentive to addressing the concerns of the Mexican community, especially its large and burgeoning undocumented sector. Whether engaging in marches for comprehensive immigration reform, opposing gentrification of the neighborhood, or setting up information booths at Chicago cultural events, TRP seeks to both empower and preserve the Mexican community from an encroaching Anglo way of life centered on individualism. TRP's concern for Mexican community empowerment is displayed in the famous "one-on-one" meeting with potential or existing collaborators. Building relationships through the one-on-one has been a central "practice of relationship building" for organizations like IAF.[25] Relational in nature, through the one-on-one, TRP staff seeks to educate external actors about the challenges, hopes, and accomplishments of the Mexican community in Chicago. As the member parishes affiliated with TRP exhibit, this community empowerment is not complete without its grounding in the Catholic faith. In 2007, TRP established Social Ministry Action and Reflection Teams (SMART) at its member parishes to keep community organizing at the heart of TRP and to drive home further the intimate connection between faith and community empowerment.[26]

The Latino FBOs under study exhibit variations in their respective political activities. These variations are qualitative in nature and manifest, as Beyerlein and Chaves suggest, unique ways of engaging in politics. These variations have been characterized as distinct kinds of ministries: *personal outreach* at LPAC, *institutional development* at Nueva, and *community empowerment* at TRP. The section below will examine the theological commitments of Rivera, Cortés, and Dahm to understand more fully the degree to which such commitments shape the social and political involvement of their organizations.

Theological Influences on Rivera, Cortés, and Dahm

The Latino FBOs under study are not simply political actors; they are "moral communities." Institutional leadership and organizational staff "bring[s] deeply held moral commitments" to these organizations. Such commitments arise from "religiously grounded presumptions" about one's rights and responsibilities as a human being. In bringing these moral and theological commitments to the fore, Latino FBO leaders provide a counterweight to the "instrumentalizing tendencies of power politics."[27] Whereas the basic power source located in the political world is secular, that of religion is "of another quality," or "otherworldly."[28] According to Dr. King, religious power, at its best, is nothing more than "love implementing the demands of justice."[29]

This section will explore the theological commitments for Rivera, Cortés, and Dahm. It will examine both the intellectual and nonintellectual factors that have shaped such commitments, as displayed in the ministries of LPAC, Nueva, and TRP. For James Cone, nonintellectual factors—i.e., a "theologian's personal history"—are highly influential in shaping the content and methodology of theological reflection.[30] Intellectual factors will also be considered to the extent that the central theological commitments of Rivera, Cortés, and Dahm are rooted, albeit in varying ways, in the legacy of Latin American liberation theology. Taken together, these nonintellectual and intellectual factors display how theological commitments and personal theological reflection can translate into the crafting of a public theology at the institutional level—the level of the Latino FBO. It is to this topic that our attention now turns.

The Legacy of Latin American Liberation Theology

Emerging in Latin America in the 1950s, liberation theology sought to "understand the workings of the larger social world,"[31] especially for those who had been marginalized from direct engagement with it. Influenced both by Roman Catholic social teaching and neo-Marxist writings on class struggle, liberation theology challenged rampant materialism by uniting in solidarity with the poor, characterized as "victims of . . . oppression."[32] To liberation theologians, like brothers Leonardo Boff and Clodovis Boff, the poor did not refer simply to the plight of an individual person but to a collectivity known as the "popular classes." According to the Boffs, this categorization of the poor as the popular classes accounted for a wider definition of poverty than the Marxist term "proletariat." The category of proletariat only included those who were the industrial working class, while the term "popular classes" embodied a more expansive sphere—those in whom the face of the "suffering servant, Jesus Christ" was made manifest.[33]

Apart from the use of the term proletariat to designate the poor, Latin American liberationists tended to view certain tenets of Marxism as compatible with Christianity. Protestant theologian José Miguez Bonino noted that for both Marxism and Christianity, the human person was not an "autonomous reality," but one who shared in a "common humanity" marked by collective features of sin and redemption. Moreover, Christianity shared with Marxism a common ethos that rejected untrammeled capitalism.[34] For Gustavo Gutiérrez, key proponent of Latin American liberation theology, Christianity and Marxism both believed in the "revolutionary struggle" and "the need for power for the common people" to construct a new society.[35] Ernesto Cardenal asserted that "revolution . . . is a synonym for love" and that "participation in this revolution [in Nicaragua] has meant faith in Jesus Christ."[36] This compatibility between Christianity and Marxism would prompt the redefinition of Christianity "in light of the call to revolution" and serve to inform the creation of this new society. Such a society would echo the objectives laid out by Christ, "to bring good news to the poor . . . to proclaim release to the captives and recovery of sight to the blind, to let the oppressed go free, [and] to proclaim the year of the Lord's favor" (Luke 4:18–19).

Liberation theology not only embraced the workings of the larger social world but also "highlighted the political significance of all theological work."[37] That liberation theology was a contextual theology was evident as it preached a "theology of salvation incarnated in the historical and political conditions" of the day. Such a theology was considered a "critical reflection on the historical praxis." Thus, Gutiérrez referred to it as the "second act," whereas the "first act" was the "commitment to create a just fraternal society."[38] Liberation theology was also a political theology in that it claimed to restore the "public meaning of Christian faith against the privatization of the faith by the Church."[39] Jürgen Moltmann, German theologian and one of Gutiérrez's mentors, was critical of the "privatization of religion in modern society." He called for a broader understanding of the kingdom of God as "radically relational or public."[40] In Moltmann's view, the kingdom of God did not entail merely personal salvation, but the "realization of the eschatalogical *hope of justice,* the *humanizing* of man, the *socializing* of humanity, *peace* for all creation."[41]

Christian Smith notes that there is not just one single liberation theology; there are multiple liberation theologies.[42] Latin American liberation theologians are a diverse group, with Catholic, mainline Protestant, and evangelical Protestant representation. Even given this rich diversity, Latin American liberation theology can largely be considered an ecumenical movement, as the scholarly, social, and political collaborations evidenced by Catholic and mainline Protestant groups attest. Catholic proponents include, among others, Gustavo Gutiérrez, Leonardo Boff, Jon Sobrino, and Ignacio Ellacuría,[43] while José Miguez Bonino and Rubem Alves represent examples of Protestant liberation theologians. Further, Orlando Costas, leading proponent of the "Misión Integral" movement, represents evangelical Protestant leadership in Latin American liberation theology. Costas is not considered a "prototype" of Latin American liberation theology. Instead, he is regarded as a "unique phenomenon" among liberation theologians. Generally speaking, liberation theology was not considered successful among evangelical Protestants in Latin America.[44]

For both Catholics and mainline Protestants alike, the impulse for a clear articulation of the principles of liberation theology was the result of the confluence of several intellectual currents in Latin America during the 1960s. First, there was the leadership of socially progressive bishops such as Dom Helder Camara in Brazil. Second, there was the significance of the World Council of Churches' Conference on Church and Society held in Geneva, Switzerland (1966), and particularly the call pronounced by Richard Shaull, theologian at Princeton Theological Seminary, for a "theology of revolution" in Latin America.[45] Third, Pope Paul VI's social encyclical *Populorum Progressio* (1967) set the stage for such an articulation by discussing the notion of "integral development" of the human person. Fourth, the Latin American Bishops Conference (CELAM II), held in Medellín, Colombia (1968), furthered such an articulation by discussing the "moral validity" of the politically repressive governments active throughout Latin America. Last, the first publications of liberation theology (1968–1969) began to be circulated worldwide by authors like Gutiérrez and Alves. Taken together, these intellectual currents advocated a "new social commitment to the poor" that previously had not been pronounced with such intellectual rigor.[46]

Evangelical Protestants did not join Catholics and mainline Protestants in this new theological movement at its outset. In fact, many evangelical leaders viewed liberation theology with suspicion for its Marxist emphasis and revolutionary theory "about how and why to change reality."[47] The drafting of the Lausanne Covenant (1974), and especially its section on "Christian Social Responsibility," brought about a renewed commitment from evangelicals to the themes of social responsibility embedded in liberation theology. This document maintained that "social responsibility and evangelism" were constitutive of one's Christian duty. Involvement in social and evangelistic activities, therefore, was a "necessary expression" of "love for our neighbor and our obedience to Jesus Christ." Unlike other writings in liberation theology, the Lausanne Covenant rejected any attempt to "equate salvation with political and economic liberation." In so doing, it retained traditional Christian language of salvation as a personal "deliverance from evil."[48]

For Costas and the evangelical Protestants, liberation theology had a "missiological implication,"[49] that of "mobilizing the faithful for witness."[50] Liberation was not simply a social or political event but embraced the "radical nature of conversion" on the personal level. There was no "new social order," according to Costas, without a "new person." Although Costas contended that the emergence of liberation theology did much to "liberate theology from academic imprisonment," he observed how the movement posed some significant problems for evangelical Protestants. In addition to overemphasizing the primacy of the political sphere, liberation theology advanced a "too optimistic view of human nature." This movement also downplayed the role of the Bible in theology. Liberation theologians tended to view theology as a "reflection on praxis," thus leaving little room for viewing the Bible as anything more than a "reference point." Nevertheless, Costas claimed that Latin American liberation theology presented some important challenges to evangelicals. Among others, these challenges included its protest against the "sterility of academic theology," the pronouncement of the ethical importance of a social commitment to the poor, and the intricate relationship between personal and social transformation.[51]

Scholars have characterized Latin American liberation theology as a "transforming movement," identified by its "Christian motivation, presence, and energy."[52] Such a movement is inspired by St. Paul's proclamation to the Romans, "Be transformed by the renewing of your minds, so that you may discern what is the will of God—what is good and acceptable and perfect" (Rom. 12:2). As the writings of Catholic, mainline Protestant, and evangelical Protestant liberation theologians have exhibited, liberation theology constitutes a public theology that reflects and acts upon the context in which "culture, religion, tradition, social, economic, [and] political systems confront each other."[53]

Although liberation theology had its heyday in the 1960s and 1970s, Gutiérrez argues that the movement "has not lost validity" in present times.[54] Liberation theology may not be the dominant pastoral approach in Latin America today, but religious movements continue to be laced with themes of liberation. As the newer expressions of liberation theology attest, "liberation theology" is not a single category. There are now African American, Asian American, Latino, feminist, and gay liberation theologies thriving in the United States.[55] Additionally, there are the "new liberationists." These new liberationists derive their central theological commitments from the legacy of Latin American liberation theology.

However, they have also been influenced by other theological discussions of liberation contained in black theology, Neo-Thomist philosophy, educational pedagogy, and sociological studies of religion.

The treatment of the theological influences of Rivera, Cortés, and Dahm, discussed below, serve to display how leadership reads, interprets, and applies the Christian narrative to the inner-city neighborhood. On the one hand, all three leaders share the belief that a public theology guides their ministries. On the other hand, the content of each theology is unique. Through their respective ministries of personal outreach, institutional development, and community empowerment, Rivera, Cortés, and Dahm display that just as there are multiple liberation theologies, there are also multiple applications of such theologies.

All three leaders have been shaped by their experiences in Latin America: Rivera worked for the Reform Church in Chiapas, Mexico, during the 1970s; Cortés spent time in Cuernavaca, Mexico, in the 1970s to understand the plight of the Mexican poor; and, during the 1960s, Dahm lived and worked as a Dominican missionary in Bolivia. While Dahm was most influenced by the Catholic strands of Latin American liberation theology, Rivera and Cortés claim to be affected most—theologically speaking—by the writings of Orlando Costas, evangelical Protestant representative of liberation theology. As the following sections attest, Rivera and Cortés provide distinct applications of Costas' Misión Integral movement manifested in their ministries of personal outreach and institutional development.

Rivera: A Theology of Captivity

Rivera's vision for LPAC emanates from his own conversion experience at a storefront Pentecostal church in New York City at the age of fifteen. Five years later, he was ordained a minister. At that time, Pentecostalism was an "otherworldly theology," acknowledges Rivera, in which the theology of hope that emerges is only hope for the second coming, which is a "future world."[56] Rivera's ministerial response to an otherworldly faith such as Pentecostalism was the provision of holistic services to Latinos in the South Bronx, uniting faith with community-building initiatives. Articulated most clearly in his "theology of captivity," Rivera's ministry of personal outreach addresses ways to deliver the Latino community from situations of captivity, especially those forms of captivity affecting the life and work of the individual.

While respecting its theological principles, Rivera distanced himself from the radical political campaign advocated by early pronouncements of liberation theology among Roman Catholic circles in the 1960s. Instead, Costas' theology of 'Misión Integral' "provided a theological and scholastic affirmation" of Rivera's "inclinations."[57] It was argued that under the evangelical Protestantism of the Costas sort, "personal transformation was possible." Therefore, the human person had the ability to be "freed from vices."[58] For Costas, liberation from captivity entailed a two-pronged approach: (1) preaching the gospel and (2) taking into account the cultural, structural, and institutional context of the times. He argued that both of these approaches would serve to aid the link between evangelization and community development. Liberation, therefore, had "missiological implications" in that it involved "mak[ing] disciples of all nations" (Matt. 28:19) as well as "mobilizing the faithful for witness."[59] Preaching this "spirituality for combat," as Costas would call it, demanded a holistic vision "sensitive to the fullness of the world to which God has sent us."[60]

Rivera has extended Costas' vision in the articulation of LPAC's "Four Principles of Holistic Ministry," a central force behind his theology of captivity. These principles—liberation, healing, community, and transformation—serve as a spiritual foundation for all LPAC's program areas. Liberation is the first principle of holistic ministry, summoning the individual to "confront powers" and to "call systems back to submission."[61] However, for Rivera, liberation is also inherently personal, i.e., the liberation from sin that results from having a personal relationship with Jesus Christ. Rivera acknowledges that the concept of personal liberation also may be expressed in the secular language of "pro-activity," which promotes a "life that is controlled by one's values and not one's circumstances."[62]

The second principle of healing points toward the "wounded healer" of the Book of Isaiah, which foreshadows the testimony of Jesus Christ in the New Testament: "Out of his anguish he shall see light; he shall find satisfaction through his knowledge. The righteous one, my servant, shall make many righteous, and he shall bear their iniquities" (Isa. 53:11). The principle of community has two dimensions, reflected in the Greek words "*coinea*" and "*diacoinea*." "*Coinea*" refers to fellowship, interdependence, and the desire for "authentic Christian community." "*Diacoinea*," on the other hand, is a call to mission and entails "service to the larger community." Lastly, the principle of transformation is a "call to perpetual growth," reflected best in the scriptural pronouncement to be continually "transformed by the renewing of your minds" (Rom. 12:2).[63]

One may also find Costas' influence—as it relates to Rivera's theology of captivity—in the more recent development of the "Five Dimensions of Personal Development" at LPAC. These dimensions provide a foundation for LPAC's ministry of personal outreach, challenging each person to live out Jesus' two main commandments: "you shall love the Lord your God with all your heart, and with all your soul, and with all your mind, and with all your strength" and "you shall love your neighbor as yourself" (Mark 12:30–31). According to Rivera, loving God with all one's heart, soul, mind, and strength accounts for the respective spiritual, emotional, mental, and physical dimensions of personal development. Loving one's neighbor as oneself, on the other hand, involves the social dimension of personal development. Rivera understands that one may not grow simultaneously in these dimensions of personal development. He comments, one "can be a spiritual giant and an emotional midget."[64]

In addition to Costas, Rivera acknowledges that other black religious figures have helped to shape his theology of captivity, including Malcolm X, Dick Gregory, Cornel West, and Eldridge Cleaver. In fact, Rivera's clear, theological articulation of the "Four Principles of Holistic Ministry," as well as the "Five Dimensions of Personal Development," is reminiscent of Malcolm X's advice concerning evangelizing: "I had learned early one important thing, and that was to always teach in terms that the people could understand."[65] This advice is further expanded on in *Pedagogy of the Oppressed* (1971), by another of Rivera's mentors, Brazilian educator Paulo Freire. In describing such a pedagogy, Freire states that this teaching method must be dialogical in that is created "*with*, not *for*, the oppressed (whether individuals or peoples) in the incessant struggle to regain their humanity." Freire's understanding of liberation serves to influence Rivera's ministry of personal outreach. Likening liberation to a kind of painful childbirth whereby "the man or woman that emerges is a new person," Freire comments that such a person "is not longer oppressor or oppressed, but human in the process of achieving freedom."[66]

According to Reverend George W. Webber, as a Protestant urban pastor committed to the plight of the marginalized, Rivera is an "agent of liberation."[67] Rivera's objective for LPAC is to promote liberation from captivity in the Latino community. In that the biblical Fall was "cosmic," not only individuals but also systems and structures have been held captive and need liberation. However, Rivera contends that while personal and structural forms of captivity are intertwined, liberation from such captivity always begins at the individual level. Thus, the chief goal of LPAC's ministry of personal outreach is to serve in this situation of captivity, acknowledging, as St. Paul does in his letter to the Romans, that although "all have sinned and fall short of the glory of God" (Rom. 3:23), all people are also in the "process of renewal."[68]

Cortés: Misión Integral at the Institutional Level

A native New Yorker, Cortés attributes his theological formation on the streets of New York City as the vehicle that "moved him towards the church." Cortés himself argues that he "came from a radical position." He was influenced both by Robert McAfee Brown and James Cone while studying for his master of divinity at Union Theological Seminary.[69] After traveling to Cuernavaca, Mexico, to come to grips with the socioeconomic situation of the poor and marginalized, Cortés worked at the Interreligious Foundation for Community Organization (IFCO) under its founding director, Lucius Walker. In addition to fighting against apartheid in Africa and for social justice in Central America, IFCO has played a central role in supporting the fight for self-determination in Puerto Rico.[70] Cortés later settled in Philadelphia to study under and serve as associate to Orlando Costas, professor of theology and co-founder of Eastern Baptist's (now renamed the Palmer Theological Seminary) School of Christian Ministry. In fact, Cortés' brother, Danny, decided to do the same.

At first glance, it would appear that Cortés' radical theological past conflicts with Costas' theology of Misión Integral. However, this is not the case. Through Nueva's ministry of institutional development, Cortés, in effect, has institutionalized Misión Integral. While Hispanic Clergy has extended the work of the local church in its mass evangelization events as well as in its provision of marriage education classes, at Nueva Cortés helped create institutions in the neighborhood that can compete with its peers. For Cortés, "those who do not own [institutions] do not play." Institutions "speak to permanence" by creating "assets that bring positive benefits" to a neighborhood rife with political, economic, and social problems. In light of Brown's and Cone's more radical theology, Cortés has focused Nueva's attention on addressing these structural problems in the neighborhood through the creation of institutional assets that help liberate residents from abject poverty and helplessness. At the same time, Cortés' consideration in viewing these structural problems as "symptomatic" of something spiritual reflects the spiritual overtones of Misión Integral to the degree that there is no new political, social, and economic order without a "new person."[71]

Brown argues that Christian spirituality "includes all of life." Since "all the domains of human existence" are discovered in Christianity, it is a holistic spirituality.[72] Thus, Christian spirituality also includes the realm of liberation. He claims there are three levels of liberation: (1) liberation from oppressive political, social, and economic structures, (2) liberation from fate, and (3) liberation from personal sin.[73] Viewing spirituality as a communal enterprise, Brown argues that conversion is not merely an acknowledgment of individual sin, but involves the "recognition that ours is a sinful situation, containing structural causes of injustice." Because Christianity is "rooted in the immediate human situation"—politically, socially, and economically—it demands a communal response.[74] Cortés' communal response at Nueva has been the advancement of its ministry of institutional development in the inner city of North Philadelphia and more recently—through the vehicle of Esperanza USA—throughout the nation.

Because the nature of Christian spirituality is communal, for Brown human rights should be understood as "social rights," namely, those rights to employment, health care, food, and affordable housing. Cortés has institutionalized this vision of Christian spirituality at Nueva through the provision of educational and development opportunities for Latino community constituents. Cortés would concur with Brown concerning the need for theologians to equip themselves with a new set of tools—those of the social sciences—to better understand the political, social, and economic structures that constitute human society.[75] Viewing theology through the lens of social science becomes an important charge in that theology itself, according to Cone, is first an "investigation of the socio-religious experience" of those affected by such institutional structures. One is reminded here of Gutiérrez's claim that theology is the critical reflection on praxis and, therefore, the "second act." For Cone, there is such a thing as "black truth" or "Latino truth," because it emerges from the context of a particular experience and a particular culture, namely, an oppressed culture. Even amid such cultural diversity, Cone admits that the Bible provides a way for distinct cultures to dialogue across cultural lines in their proclamation of liberation for the oppressed.[76]

Costas himself had direct experience in advancing a ministry of institutional development of sorts. After completing biblical studies at Nyack Missionary College, Costas returned to his homeland of Puerto Rico as he "became convinced that in order to minister to Latino people he needed to work and study in a Latino country." For approximately seven years, Costas taught and performed missionary work in Costa Rica with the Latin American Mission and later with the United Church Board for World Ministries, during which time he became engaged in the relationship between theology and community activism. In 1973, he founded the Centro Evangélico Latinoamericano de Estudios Pastorales (CELEP) which was, in essence, the evangelical equivalent of the Roman Catholic Instituto de Pastoral Latinoamericano (IPLA).[77] At the time Costas completed his doctorate at the Free University of Amsterdam—under the famous Dutch missiologist Johannes Verkuyl in the mid-1970s—he was a globally known speaker and author on Christian mission "from the periphery," representing those "who had not been the main actors of the missionary enterprise—Asians, blacks, Hispanics, and Native Americans.[78]

Costas understood Latino churches, like other racial churches in urban areas, to be "centers of survival" in four main ways. First, these churches serve as centers where congregants find "personal meaning" or empowerment. In this sense, they address a type of psychological survival. Second, they display cultural survival through the use of language as "the essential tool for the expression of the Latino self." Third, Latino churches promote solidarity with others and, in so doing, build social survival. Last, they further spiritual survival by emphasizing the Christian virtue of hope, or "the drive to live on." While responsible for cultivating "the internal life of the individual" within the congregation, the urban church must also advance "a liberative engagement" of the congregation as a whole "with its social context."[79]

Under the leadership of Cortés, Nueva can be viewed as a "center of survival." In contrast to LPAC, Cortés would argue that an emphasis on psychological survival is the work of local churches and Hispanic Clergy. Instead, as a Latino FBO devoted to institutional development, Nueva's focus centers on the melding of spiritual and social survival through the creation of educational and development initiatives in the urban context of North Philadelphia. Costas would contend that this engagement with the urban context has theological roots in the incarnation, i.e., God becoming man through the person of Jesus Christ. This reality of the incarnation has important implications for Christian ministry in setting forth a "biblically holistic approach to Christian mission." Costas speaks both of the "inward journey and activist outward journey"[80] as informing the Misión Integral movement. While Rivera's LPAC has emphasized the "inward journey" of Misión Integral in its ministry of personal outreach, Cortés of Nueva has highlighted the other half—the "activist outward journey." In so doing, Cortés has, in effect, institutionalized the movement in his deliberate attention to "income producing realities" in the inner city of North Philadelphia.[81]

Dahm: *The Communal Praxis of Liberation*

As a missionary sent to Latin America, Dahm spent five years living, teaching, and ministering in Bolivia in the mid- to late-1960s. It was there he became engaged in the praxis of liberation theology and in the formation of *comunidades de base Cristiana* (CEBs), or Christian base communities (CBCs). Dahm states, "In a way, I grew up with Gutiérrez." He argues that small CBCs and worker movements in Brazil predated the explosion of theories of liberation theology on the Latin American scene in the late 1960s. Liberation theology "didn't drop out of the sky," but was a "culmination of a progressive movement and vision" stemming from Vatican Council II, which advanced greater lay involvement in the Catholic Church. Theories of liberation theology, especially in the Latin American context, developed from practical examples where new forms of pastoral ministry were practiced.[82]

After returning to the United States, Dahm pursued a doctorate in political science at the University of Wisconsin, seeking to understand how Christianity and public policy could work together to address areas of oppression. Back in Chicago, he co-founded the Eighth Day Center for Justice and became pastor of St. Pius V Church in Pilsen in 1986, "at a time when the existing efforts in community organization were in need of new inspiration."[83] TRP "grew out of Pilsen and Charles Dahm," argues friend and former Panamanian missionary John Donohue. TRP's emphasis on community empowerment issues—like the provision of affordable housing—"reveals . . . [Dahm's] desire" that TRP become a "prophetic voice in the midst of oppression" in the Mexican neighborhoods of Chicago.[84] The organization's ministry of community empowerment began with the formation of nearly sixty CBCs during the Lenten season of 1990, at which time priests and laypeople reflected on Scripture to act on the prevailing community concerns affecting the neighborhood of Pilsen. This activity is captured well in Dahm's recent book, *Parish Ministry in a Hispanic Community* (2004).

Freire's work, *Pedagogy of the Oppressed* (1970) and his model of *educación popular* (popular education), has been a major influence on Dahm in laying out a communal praxis of liberation to combat various forms of oppression Mexicans face in Chicago. Freire's pedagogical method is people-centered in that it helps people, as opposed to just leaders, to understand oppression from their own perspective and discover ways to address its various manifestations in their daily lives.[85] Freire speaks of the importance for people to be "masters of their thinking" through "critical and liberating dialogue," i.e., reflection on their situations. Reflection, however, must go hand-in-hand with community action. For Freire, there is a "radical interaction" between the two: "If one is sacrificed—even in part—the other immediately suffers." This kind of dialogue does not simply enable the oppressed to "name the world" around them. Critical and liberating dialogue is existentially necessary in that it helps the voiceless "achieve [their] significance as human beings."[86]

The radical interaction between reflection and action—of which Freire speaks—was present in the work of CBCs in Pilsen. Classes were given in both Spanish and English to lay leaders and parishioners, centering on "the prophetic teaching of Jesus, the role of the church in seeking justice, and the importance of building people power for justice." Two classes, Christian commitment to social issues and building relationships of trust, each had six sessions. Then pastor of St. Procopius, Father Don Nevins claims that, through these sessions, the central questions became: "How do we respond to the challenge of Scripture? How do we make the world a better place?"[87] In light of Dahm's firm belief in a communal praxis of liberation, emphasis was placed on forming Christian relationships of "community and solidarity for power to challenge and change unjust conditions." To conclude the training sessions, more than four hundred participants congregated at St. Pius V Church to meet with Chicago city officials from the Department of Housing and the Police Department and other Illinois state departments.[88] For Dahm, CBCs thus functioned as models of "participative democracy" aiming to build "relationships of trust."[89]

According to Daniel Levine, CBCs make their impact through the "appeal of religious messages and structures." Therefore, to understand the work CBCs perform, it is important to take the religious beliefs that undergird them seriously.[90] As Gutiérrez states, the "first act" of changing oppressive structures precedes the "second act" of theological reflection.[91] Whereas Freire does not employ explicit religious language in outlining his pedagogy of the oppressed, Gutiérrez states that it is a Christian duty to place oneself "fully in the world of oppression." "Participat[ing] in the struggles of the poor and oppressed for liberation" should not lead to a privatized faith, but toward a reinterpretation of the gospel in a public sense for those who have been repeatedly excluded from the social and political order.[92] It is a Christian imperative to fight for the oppressed, because Christianity is a "social practice" that is "born on meditating on the Word of God and taking its inspiration in the activity of God coupled with human beings."[93]

Gutiérrez points to the influence that Jacques Maritain, French neo-Thomist philosopher, had on the development of Latin American liberation theology. He writes that "Christian social thought sprang up, and it was backed by [such] Thomistic philosophy." For Gutiérrez, Maritain's insight of a "new Christendom" was an attempt to "open up moderately the Church to values of the modern world and to the ideals of freedom and democracy."[94] In *Integral Humanism* (1936), Maritain discussed this new Christendom in terms of bringing about a "Christian culture." In contrast to the aim of Christian religious order, the objective of Christian culture was "to work on earth for a socio-temporal realization of Gospel truths." Maritain understood well that a Christian culture will never be built if, while affirming the inherent dignity of the human person, one "does not work to transform conditions which oppress him, and to bring it about that he can eat his bread with dignity." This is the reason Maritain emphasized the need for the creation of new political formations. These formations are to be "intrinsically Christian," as they "presuppose . . . a profound spiritual revolution" of the heart both for political leadership and their constituencies. While steeped in Christian roots, such formations are to be "temporal fellowships" as they seek to advance the common good of political community.[95]

To the degree that TRP engages in social and political activity as an outgrowth of its Catholic conviction, the organization is an example of the kind of new political formation of which Maritain speaks. Interestingly, Dahm argues that he was reading Maritain's works as a Dominican missionary in Bolivia. It may be argued then that TRP's ministry of community empowerment is based on a synthesis of the Catholic strand in liberation theology and neo-Thomist philosophy. Moreover, this ministry is founded on a communal praxis of liberation that began with the establishment of CBCs in 1990. Similar in form to the original CBCs, TRP has recently developed an initiative called Social Ministry Action and Reflection Teams (SMART) at each TRP member institution. The purpose of these groups is to recommit the organization to the mission of faith-based community organizing as lived out in its ministry of community empowerment.[96]

The paragraphs above detail both the intellectual (i.e., theological sources) and nonintellectual factors (i.e., one's personal history) that have influenced the public theologies driving LPAC, Nueva, and TRP, as articulated by Rivera, Cortés, and Dahm. Of the three leaders, Rivera has most clearly articulated a customized, public theology for LPAC through his elaboration of a theology of captivity. Rivera has gathered his theological principles in two soon-to-be released books: *Four Principles of Holistic Ministry* and *Doing Ministry in a Situation of Captivity*. As evidenced in their respective ministries, Rivera, Cortés, and Dahm have read, interpreted, and applied the Christian narrative in distinct ways. They all have been influenced by the legacy of Latin American liberation theology. However, just as there are multiple liberation theologies, so too are there multiple applications of these theologies. Rivera and Cortés have demonstrated how one might interpret Costas' Misión Integral movement from either a personal or institutional perspective. On the other hand, Dahm has displayed how Gutiérrez, Freire, and Maritain all contribute to a communal praxis of liberation. The next section will show the degree to which U.S. Latino theology builds on the tenets of Latin American liberation theology. Moreover, that section will show how Latino theology parallels the distinct public theologies articulated above by these Latino FBO leaders.

Foundations of U.S. Latino Theology

Latin American liberation theology has inspired U.S. Latino theology in many ways, specifically with respect to the construction of a theological method that has as its primary objective liberating those who are marginalized. María Pilar Aquino contends that such a "praxis-oriented" methodology is an "intercultural enterprise" that takes into account the cultural context of the Latino community as a whole. This theological method acknowledges the rich variety of traditions, customs, and cultures present in the Latino community. Nevertheless, such a theological method underlines the common reality Latinos share as residents of the United States—as Spanish-speaking peoples who live in adverse social, economic, and political situations. The construction of a theological method does not simply provide an understanding of the cultural context of U.S. Latinos but rather "implies a direction" of liberation. Like the goal of method for Latin American theologians, the aim of method in Latino theology is not "new doctrines, but new relationships and lifestyles."[97]

Notwithstanding similarities between Latin American and Latino theology, Latinos in the United States face a different social, economic, and political context than that experienced in Latin America during the 1970s and 1980s. First, unlike in their native lands, Latinos are ethnic minorities in the United States. Second, U.S. Latino presence is not homogeneous but draws from multiple ethnic, religious, and cultural traditions. Third, Latinos do not live under the shadow of dictatorships and guerrilla groups that plagued Latin America for decades. Instead, they dwell in a less violent, largely democratic order in the United States. Last, although Latinos face adverse circumstances as urban dwellers in the United States, such an existence is unparalleled to the kinds of suffering—starvation, massive unemployment, and serious social and political unrest—faced daily by millions of Latin Americans.

U.S. Latino theology was established in the wake of the civil rights movement, during which time the Latino community was "coming to [its] own politically within the larger society."[98] Central Catholic figures in the field of Latino theology include, among others, Virgilio Elizondo, Roberto Goizueta, and Ada María Isasi-Díaz. Justo González is a key figure in mainline Protestant circles, and Eldin Villafañe and Samuel Solivan represent central forces in Pentecostalism.[99] Issues of "powerlessness and poverty," like those witnessed in Latin America, served much to inform the writings of U.S. Latino theologians. Central to the U.S. Latino context, however, was the "legacy of racism in U.S. society and church," which such theologians placed at the heart of social and political concern.[100] Rivera of LPAC acknowledges the "cycle of despair" in which Latinos are placed, having suffered, "through years of racist conditioning . . . from an ethnic stereotype that predetermines failure and self-hate."[101]

In *The Galilean Journey* (1983), Elizondo treats the experience of Latinos living in the United States. He uses the term *mestizo,* or half-breed, to describe the "marginal status" of the Latino. Elizondo contends that the *mestizo* suffers "cultural marginalization," as he or she is "perceived as a threat to the barriers of separation that consolidate self-identity and security" in U.S. society.[102] Although feared by established groups, the *mestizo* can challenge unjust social, political, and economic institutions by serving as a reminder of the abundant cultural pluralism in life. For Latino Christians, a *mestizo* identity finds its meaning in Jesus Christ, because—like other ethnic minorities—he "personally suffered the pains of marginalization and dehumanizing insults." The "cultural suffering" Christ experienced provides a "new understanding" of the kingdom of God on earth, one that speaks to the challenges and aspirations for those most marginalized in society.[103]

Latino *mujerista* (feminist) scholars provide a more expansive definition for the term *mestizo*. Ada María Isasi-Díaz claims that, in addition to racial minorities, the term includes the "lived experience of Hispanic women" as oppressed peoples. The task of *mujerista* theology is to demonstrate how Latinas integrate the personal, communal, and public spheres of religious experience rather than create a "false dichotomy" among them. Such a task is accomplished through an understanding of the popular religion that informs Latina identity. She notes that the Christian church need not be the "point of reference" for such expressions of popular religion. The kind of Christianity that became a central part of Latino culture is "one that uses the Bible in a very limited way," argues Isasi-Díaz, in merely "emphasizing the traditions and customs of the Spanish church." In contrast, popular religiosity operates much like a "religious subculture," to the degree that Christian religious practices undergo a reinterpretation by the people themselves. In many ways, argues Isasi-Díaz, popular religion constitutes one of the most "creative and original parts" of Latino culture, as it provides "*fuerzas para la lucha*," or "strength for the struggle."[104]

Popular religion is at the heart of the varied manifestations of Latino culture—i.e., its "language, customs, symbols, worldviews, and faith expressions." The multiple forms of personal and communal devotion associated with Latino popular religion find their primary source of "symbolism and imagery" in the Bible. Devotion does not refer merely to individual or communal acts of piety. As displayed in the public theologies of the Latino FBOs under study, popular religion also has a political dimension "imbedded in the hearts of the people from their exposure to the Gospel." Such a dimension has real "liberative potential" in that it privileges values and beliefs that challenge sinful structures and institutions.[105] This understanding of popular religion differs considerably from the writings of Juan Luis Segundo, acclaimed Latin American liberation theologian. Segundo considered such personal and communal acts of devotion as a "highly charged superstitious" display of religion that served to legitimize the existing political order.[106] In the words of Michael Candelaria, Segundo regarded popular religion as "alienating, moribund, and incapable of being disestablishing."[107] Moreover, such an understanding contrasts sharply with earlier institutional pronouncements, like those from the International Week of Catechists held in Bogotá, Colombia (1968). During this conference, popular religion was defined as "conservative," "conformist," and incapable of "commit[ing] itself to the transformation of the prevailing social system."[108]

Latino theologians maintain that popular religion has a personal, communal, and public side as it may be "practiced by individuals, families, or whole communities." Popular religion is a way in which the Latino community "make[s] sense of the world and provide[s] a concrete point of contact with the Divine."[109] The cross on which Jesus Christ died is the Latino community's most important expression of popular religion for both Catholics and Protestants. Participation in this sacred symbol, according to Orlando Espín, empowers the community to embrace the cherished values of "solidarity and compassion"[110] over more self-seeking goals. The words Jesus uttered on the cross, "My God, my God, why have you forsaken me?" (Matt. 27:46), remind the community that, like its members, Jesus had to suffer in this life. Suffering, unlike sadness, has "active and communal dimensions" that help engender "solidarity and hope." Sadness is an individual experience, but one always suffers "with" someone else.[111] As believers prayerfully gaze up at the cross, they are reminded that they are not alone. They unite their own sufferings with those of Christ on behalf of humankind.

U.S. Latino theology begins with the "faith of the people" in mind. Such a theology acknowledges *lo cotidiano* (the everyday) as the central space in which Latinos "live, understand, and give direction"[112] to personal devotion, communal involvement, and public action. In *Jesus Is My Uncle* (1999), Luis Pedraja approaches Latino theology from a particular vantage point—the Latino community's act of naming its children "*Jesús*." Pedraja notes that such naming reveals Christ as the "one who is near to us" and the one who shares in the daily sufferings of the community. Moreover, use of the name "*Jesús*" is characteristic of the community's "sense of solidarity with Jesus." Because "*Jesús*" is the name of many friends, relatives, and neighbors in the Latino community, Pedraja maintains that such an act is not considered a sacrilege but an honor and a "reminder of God's nearness" in a most familiar sense.[113]

In summary, U.S. Latino theology draws extensively from the tradition of Latin American liberation theology. However, in contrast to Latin American liberation theology, Latino theology places greater emphasis on expressions of popular religiosity. Together, Latino Protestants and Catholics highlight the importance of the sacred symbol of the cross and how this symbol teaches the community at large about solidarity in the face of suffering. With respect to the cross, one finds that popular religion not only inspires personal devotion, but also has "liberative potential" and thus assumes a communal and public face as well. Moreover, Latino theology is praxis-oriented in that it takes into account the cultural context of Latinos and points the community in a direction of new relationships and lifestyles, based on an interpretation of the Christian narrative. While Latino theology shares this appreciation of cultural context with its Latin American counterpart, it is clear that the contexts in question—the United States and Latin America—are very distinct. The next section will discuss how Rivera, Cortés, and Dahm apply this theology of the new liberation to the context of the inner city.

A Theology and Practice of the New Liberation

Many Latinos bear a marginalized status in an urban society that challenges "their right to exist with human dignity." Urban neighborhoods are plagued by violence, drugs, gang involvement, decrepit housing, poorly funded schools, and high unemployment. New liberationists believe, however, that even amid this environment, God, in the person of Jesus Christ, is present in a real way. These leaders remind urban believers to experience Christ both as the suffering, crucified Christ "accessible to those whose own suffering requires comforting" and the glorified Christ who "overcomes death and the sins of the world." Whereas the image of the suffering Christ provides a point of reference of daily life for urban Latinos, the image of the glorified Christ spurs believing Latinos to rise above the day-to-day struggle by reminding them of the salvation that awaits them "beyond history." This strong belief in the person of Jesus Christ in no way suggests that new liberationists encourage their respective communities to embrace a kind of "privatized Christianity," out of touch with the social context of urban life.[114] While not discounting the value of personal faith, Rivera, Cortés, and Dahm invite those they serve to acknowledge the transforming link between such faith and social and political involvement for the betterment of the community.

Under the leadership of Rivera, LPAC has chosen to address the personal dimension of Costas' Misión Integral movement, by focusing on the "inward journey" of the Latino urban resident. Rivera has taken a personal approach to politics, endorsing local and national candidates. Moreover, he has set his sights on building a ministry of personal outreach in the neighborhood of Highbridge, addressing ways to lift urban residents out of captivity. In viewing his ministry as a "ministry," Rivera has paid special attention to the development of LPAC's "Four Principles of Holistic Ministry" and "Five Dimensions of Personal Development," as they inform all the programs in which the organization involves itself. Rivera concurs with Malcolm X and Freire that the message of liberation —as articulated in these principles—must be delivered in terms that people understand.

Cortés of Nueva, on the other hand, has chosen to institutionalize Costas' movement, emphasizing instead the "activist outward journey" of the organization. Likening Nueva to a "center of survival," Cortés has applied a business approach to ministry through the creation of Latino-owned and -operated institutions in the inner city of North Philadelphia. In agreement with Brown, Cortés has understood that structural forms of injustice are "sinful situations" that demand a communal response. Additionally, these situations demand the use of a new set of tools borrowed from the social sciences—and in Cortés' case, from the field of business management—to address the underlying causes of these unjust structures. It is through Nueva's ministry of institutional development that Cortés aims to encourage urban residents to embrace ownership in the community, thus lifting them out of the manifold situations of hopelessness in which they find themselves.

TRP's communal praxis of liberation, as articulated by Dahm, provides a third kind of public theology for the Latino FBOs in question. Underlying TRP's ministry of community empowerment is Freire's call for the "radical interaction" between reflection and action in community life. Critical dialogue, which lies at the heart of Freire's *educación popular*, has been a central force behind TRP's "bottom-up" style, from the inception of CBCs to its staff meetings and various one-on-one meetings with leading community actors. Dahm agrees with Leonardo Boff that Christianity is a "social practice." TRP has advanced the social practice of Christianity not only through its involvement in advocacy issues like comprehensive immigration reform, but also in its decision to establish SMART groups at every TRP member institution in Lower West Side Chicago.

Theologically speaking, these Latino FBOs all belong to the same Christian faith tradition, a tradition that emphasizes the incarnation of Jesus Christ, the kingdom of God on earth, and personal salvation at the end of one's earthly journey. But given a closer look, these organizations represent three distinct expressions of the Christian tradition, namely, Pentecostalism, evangelical Protestantism, and Catholicism. According to a 2007 study conducted by the Pew Forum on Religion and Public Life and the Pew Hispanic Center, approximately 68 percent of Latinos living in the United States self-identify as Catholic, and 20 percent consider themselves Protestant. Of those who are Protestant, 70 percent call themselves evangelical or "born-again" Christians.[115] This shift from Catholic to Protestant identity among Latinos, coined the "conversion movement," has far-reaching consequences, especially on the political order. Contrary to Catholicism, the religiosity characteristic of evangelical Christian and Pentecostal denominations tends to be "less institutionally driven"[116] but "more socially and theologically conservative."[117]

Denominational differences alone do not explain these distinct kinds of religious identity politics. As the different versions of ministry and variations in political activity of LPAC, Nueva, and TRP attest, a theology and practice of the new liberation involve how Latino FBO leaders read, interpret, and apply the Christian narrative to their particular urban context. Often such an interpretation of the Christian narrative does not fall along denominational lines, as indicated in the medley of theological influences informing Rivera, Cortés and Dahm. Rather, these new liberationists are, in fact, quite ecumenical in the application of their theological commitments.

Over the years, doctrinal differences between Protestants and Catholics have been a source of division in the Latino community. Due to the urban conditions under which Latinos live, however, believing Christians—both Protestant and Catholic—are joining forces to combat social, political, and economic injustices as demonstrated by the recent book commissioned by Nueva, entitled *Who Is My Neighbor?* Co-authored by Justo González and Virgilio Elizondo, this book provides an ecumenical treatment about how the Latino church can best attend to the adverse social, political, and economic conditions affecting its community. "The net result" of initiatives such as these, argues González, is that Protestants are finding themselves "walking along the same path with Roman Catholics."[118] This path recognizes the validity of "faith" combined with "works" in the urban context, as in the passage, "for just as the body without the spirit is dead, so faith without works is also dead" (James 2: 26).

For Latinos, religious institutions such as churches and FBOs are not merely community organizations but religious sites that allow what Latina novelist Sandra Cisneros calls "insider discourses"—specific to the local Latino community—to be pronounced. Cisneros writes that the faith of "ordinary people," manifested in the "exchange of prayers and religious services for offerings made and thanks given," is constitutive of such a culture.[119] One need only turn to the poetry of Puerto Rican author Judith Ortiz Cofer to elucidate this point. In her poem, "Cada Día," or "Every Day," Cofer displays the ordinary faith of the Latino in an embellishment of the universal Christian prayer, the "Our Father":

> *Padre*, who sits on a cloud,
> danos el pan de cada día,
> Madre, who stands on his left
> and just a little behind,
> ruega por nosotros,
> Hijo Santo, de ojos azules y
> corazon sangrante y grande,
> listen to the pleas
> of the little live things
> crawling on this planet
> given to you for Christmas.
> Please do not toss us
> into a dark corner
> of your vast universe
> and forget us.[120]

Selected poems like "Cada Día" manifest how Latino literature abounds with religious imagery, particularly in depicting the collective struggle of the Latino community.[121] The narrator begs the Father not to "toss *us*" —not simply me—"into a dark corner/of your vast universe/and forget us." For Latinos, "there is no such thing as an isolated individual." Instead, they believe their community is "defined by relationships" among each other and with God. Even one's personal devotion to Christ is mediated by relationships. "Jesus is never just Jesus," admits Goizueta, "he is always also our brother, father, co-sufferer, [and] friend."[122]

Conclusion

The central aim of this chapter was to explore how the *new liberationists* —Rivera of LPAC, Cortés of Nueva, and Dahm of TRP—understand the religious *content* of their organizations. In contrast to chapter two, this chapter considered the realm of human effort, or "human agency," in its examination of how these leaders read, interpret, and apply the Christian narrative to effect social and political change in their urban neighborhoods. Rivera, Cortés, and Dahm are all indebted to the legacy of Latin American liberation theology. However, their theological influences are not confined to a particular Christian denomination or tradition. In fact, these new liberationists have gathered a medley of influences along the way, that, along with their respective faith traditions, have served to impact the public theology driving each organization.

Like Latin American liberation theologians, Rivera, Cortés, and Dahm understand the political significance of all theological work. These new liberationists, however, would not go as far as Jürgen Moltmann in calling for a "political theology." Instead of a political theology, these Latino FBO leaders advance distinct "public" theologies at the helms of their organizations. Rivera, Cortés, and Dahm all claim theology is the "second act," as Latin American liberation theologians have suggested. However, through the careful fashioning of their respective public theologies, these leaders also demonstrate that theology can be simultaneously the "first act." For it is not only the urban context that serves to give the respective ministries of personal outreach, institutional development, and community empowerment shape and direction, but also the theological commitments and personal histories of Rivera, Cortés, and Dahm.

Like Latino theologians, new liberationists concern themselves with the role of race in urban society. They regard *mestizo* identity both as a challenge and as a key factor in societal transformation for Latinos living in the United States. Rivera, Cortés, and Dahm find meaning in the suffering Jesus Christ endured, as it provides them with a new understanding of the kingdom of God on earth. In order to combat issues of marginalization in the inner city, they advance a community building that is ecumenical in nature. While they are dedicated to the plight of the Latino, their respective organizations address unjust social, economic, and political situations shared by urban dwellers of diverse faiths, cultures, and ethnicities. In so doing, LPAC, Nueva, and TRP serve as "vehicle[s] for liberation,"[123] and the leaders of such organizations serve as the "new liberationists."

Having provided a sketch of the new liberationists in this chapter, we now turn to detailed case studies of LPAC, Nueva, and TRP. These case studies will provide the reader with a fuller understanding of the day-to-day management and operations of Latino FBOs. Such an understanding will offer insight into the different kinds of religious identity politics guiding these organizations, as displayed in the three kinds of ministry —LPAC's ministry of personal outreach, Nueva's ministry of institutional development, and TRP's ministry of community empowerment.

4

Latino Pastoral Action Center
A Ministry of Personal Outreach

> The indigenous religious community has benefits not apparent
> unless one "goes below the surface." . . . It is a collective support-
> ive community that affirms and legitimates [urban Latino youth],
> telling [youth] that leadership is within reach.
> —Reverend Raymond Rivera[1]

Commenting on the recent creation of the White House Office
of Faith-Based and Community Initiatives (OFBCI) in 2001, Reverend
Raymond Rivera, Pentecostal minister and executive director of LPAC,
stated that "there is room for indigenous organizations that are closer to
the community" in the social service system. This system "is in need of
renewal, and we can be part of that renewal."[2] Conversant with the urban Latino experience in the United States, LPAC is one such indigenous
religious community. In "affirm[ing] human dignity and personhood,"
Rivera claims that the organization provides a "counter-cultural assimilation tool"[3] for urban Latinos against the traditional "white and mainline-
dominated" culture of the U.S. social-service structure.[4]

As of the beginning of 2007, with total assets of $6.7 million and an
operating budget of $2.5 million, LPAC received 90 percent of its funding
from public sources. This is a significant change from earlier years. When
the organization began in 1992, approximately 97 percent of its funding
was private—all foundation money with the exception of some small city
government grants. Ten years later, LPAC received one-third of its funding from the federal government, specifically the U.S. Department of Justice and Americorps, as well as negligible city government grants for small
community projects.[5] At present, Rivera desires to restart discussions with

officers from the original foundations that were instrumental in establishing LPAC, namely, the Pew Charitable Trusts, the Lilly Endowment, the Rockefeller Foundation, and the Ford Foundation, to advance more effectively its five program areas: (1) fund development, (2) program development and services, (3) community engagement, (4) leadership development, and (5) organizational development.[6]

As a para-church organization in the South Bronx, LPAC has approximately three hundred local clergy in its immediate network and a mailing list of two thousand clergy who take an interest in community issues like police brutality, parenting, and at-risk youth.[7] With the award of a $708,000 federal grant from the Compassion Capital Fund on September 30, 2005, LPAC transformed itself from a "community and city-wide faith-based organization" to one national in scope. That grant allowed LPAC to share its approach to ministry with approximately two hundred churches in the areas of New York and Chicago as part of the organization's National Holistic Ministry Development Project.[8] Rivera's long-term objective is to continue to take LPAC's model of urban ministry to the "national level" by providing personal development training, leadership training, and capacity building to FBOs and CBOs across the United States.[9]

Because the research gathered on LPAC predates the organization's more recent national focus, the paragraphs that follow will explore LPAC's ministry of personal outreach at the neighborhood level of the South Bronx. This chapter aims to examine Rivera's theology of captivity as well as relevant concepts pertaining to religious identity politics in light of five specific themes: (1) gangs and the faith community, (2) engaging the hip-hop culture, (3) the indigenous religious community, (4) the dimensions of personal development, and (5) leadership in the Bronx.

Gangs and the Faith Community

"We are who we are, we come out of a faith context that is unapologetically faith-based," proclaimed Rivera, in his opening prayer at the organization's first annual PRAISE conference for gang prevention on April 3, 2002.[10] PRAISE, which stands for Providing Recreation Arts, Inner Healing, Service, Education for our youth, is the gang prevention unit within LPAC that centers on at-risk youth between the ages of fifteen and twenty-one by providing alternative activities to help reduce street involvement. Ranking among other nationally recognized faith-based programs, such

as Boston's Ten Point Coalition and the Lake County, Illinois, Gang Outreach, PRAISE focuses on gang prevention and intervention in one of
New York's roughest inner-city areas.

The "presence of gangs and drug crews" in the large New York City
borough of the Bronx drove the organization's involvement in this serious area of social concern. LPAC realized it needed a vehicle both to address and attempt to reduce gang involvement in the inner city. Moreover,
the organization wanted to serve as "liaison between law enforcement and
gangs." Adrian Bordoni, former coordinator of PRAISE, admits there are
rather large obstacles to be overcome with law-enforcement officials in
the community. LPAC staff acknowledge the need to "strike a balance to
cooperate with local law enforcement," but ultimately not be co-opted by
them. LPAC also faces considerable challenges in representing the needs
of at-risk youth in the community. Neighborhood youth tend to view
any intimate dealings with the New York Police Department (NYPD) as
"snitching." With an objective to provide outreach to youth at risk in the
community, Bordoni recognizes that LPAC is involved in a long-term
process to forge strong "connections with street kids and young adults."[11]

LPAC's direct involvement in gang prevention began in 1996 through
Rivera's initial contact with José Ramos, a.k.a., "Green Eyes," once head
of the Universal Zulu Nation (Zulu Nation) gang. Ramos met with Rivera and "became connected," leading to Ramos' initial stint as an Americorps worker at LPAC. Other former Zulu Nation members currently
are LPAC staff members.[12] A large part of this connection between Zulu
Nation members and LPAC came as a result of the spiritual beliefs held
by the gang. While standing for "knowledge," "freedom," and "justice," as
its website indicates, Zulu Nation also stands for "facts, faith, and the one-
ness of God." The core of its Fifteen Beliefs include, among others, the belief in one God (No. 1), the belief in the Bible, Koran, and many prophets
of God (No. 2), the belief in the "mental resurrection of the dead" (No.
9), and the belief in universal peace and justice (Nos. 12 and 13).[13] Recognizing the role of prophecy in daily life, Zulu Nation attaches equal importance to passages from the Old Testament as to ones from Krishna,
ancient Norse prophecy, and Shambhala.[14]

According to Bordoni, faith is a "very effective tool even among a very
violent gang culture." He reminds the approximately forty people in attendance at the April 2002 PRAISE conference that it was the neighborhood
youth, not LPAC leadership, who chose the name "PRAISE" for LPAC's
Gang Prevention Unit. These youth wanted to place "praising the Lord" as

the central focus for the organization's outreach activities.[15] As evidenced in the following poem, "even in a gang lifestyle, [there is a] certain respect for God," as noted in both its title as a "Blood Prayer" and its call for peace:[16]

> When I die bury me 5 feet deep not 6
> with 2pitch fork going across my chest
> with a heart tatoo placed on my chest
> and my red rag around my head 2 double
> barrel shotguz going down my legz
> with my 3 burns going down my right
> arm standing for the u.b.n.[17]
> peace blood
> Bloody flesh
>
>   —"Blood Prayer," n./t.g.

Identified by the wearing of the color red, gaining membership in the Bloods requires a "Blood-in," or the spilling of blood from either oneself or another. From April 1 to August 31, 1997, Bloods were responsible for more than 50 percent of the "stabbings and slashings" in New York City prisons, using razors as their weapon of choice. Bloods have an elaborate organizational structure that displays respect for "the commands of the higher rank." Moreover, its code of conduct requires "lifetime allegiance to the group." A failure of loyalty is met with "inner-disciplinary punishment" ranging from the performance of menial tasks to physical assault and death.[18]

Whereas only 9 percent of Bloods were Latino in 1997, one must have a Latino bloodline to be a member of the Almighty Latin King and Queen Nation (ALKQN). The majority of ALKQN members are Puerto Rican. Established in Chicago in the 1940s, ALKQN spread to New York City in the late 1980s, first through the New York State Prison system, then to the streets through the organization of chapters, or "tribes." Animal names like "Tiger Tribe," "Wolf Tribe," and "Lion Tribe" most commonly were used in labeling the various chapters.[19] Like the Blood poem above, an excerpt of an ALKQN prayer below, entitled "74 Prayer," manifests a similar faith dimension of many gang leaders and members. Prayers of this kind are used heavily by leaders to "train and instruct" others within the gang as well as to recruit additional members:

Bless my folk both old and new
Bless ones in the Penetentiary to
Bless shorty mac of King star of light
Who crown King David both day and night
Bless our Queens who we love to please
stack "6" times to the sky then back
    down to our knees. . . .[20]

Due to its reputation as the largest and most violent gang in New York City, ALKQN was subject to a massive Racketeering Influenced Corrupt Organization (RICO) investigation in the mid-1990s by the United States Attorney's Office, NYPD, and the New York branch of the FBI. The investigation resulted in the arrest of numerous ALKQN members on charges from arson to murder. In 1999, the Brooklyn District Attorney's Office, the Bronx District Attorney's Office, the U.S. Attorney's Office, the FBI, and NYPD spearheaded another investigation known as "Operation Crown," resulting in the arrest of more than one hundred members of ALKQN on charges ranging from narcotics possession to murder.[21]

Interestingly, Hector Torres, Latino community activist and former spiritual adviser to ALKQN in New York City, spoke at the PRAISE conference. Donning white athletic socks without sneakers, a New York Yankees black knit cap, and a hooded Falcon jacket, Torres gave all the signs of suffering from dementia as a result of being in a late stage of HIV/AIDS. Drinking periodically from an orange juice carton, Torres commented—in a largely incoherent manner—on the Lord speaking to him: "When everyone abandons you, I will not abandon you." Torres first met Reverend Rivera at a church with more than one thousand members of ALKQN in attendance. While speaking, Rivera made an "altar call" through which he "saw the potential to minister to young people." In this large gathering of gang members, he witnessed a genuine openness to the spiritual dimension.[22] As spiritual adviser to ALKQN, Torres frequently spoke out against institutions that used "fear and intimidation" tactics against racial minorities. He likened the plight of Latinos in New York to the nativity narrative in Christianity, with the Virgin Mary as "an unwed teenage mom with a problem" and Joseph as "an unemployed laborer who can't get any work." Then Mayor Rudy Giuliani was symbolized as King Herod in his desire "to kill every black or Latino who does not know his or her place." The Three Kings referred to the Latinos, "knowing that Giuliani was sabotaging their path to get to [the] child Jesus." Similar to the Kings, the Latinos would "have to find a different way, even if it mean[t] going through the desert and suffering the heat."[23]

Current Trends in Gang Membership

Since 1999, the ethnic and racial composition of gangs in the United States has remained relatively constant with 47 percent Latino, 31 percent African American, 13 percent non-Hispanic white, and 7 percent Asian.[24] The most prominent gangs in New York City include ALKQN, Asociación Ñeta (Ñetas), Bloods, and Crips. In addition, Latin American nationalist gangs operate in the city. Dominican gangs like Matantes and Trinitarios as well as Central American gangs like Mara Salvatrucha 13 (MS-13) are present alongside La Gran Familia and La Gran Raza, which are overwhelmingly Mexican gangs.[25] The phenomenon of gang globalization has grown increasingly more visible in the inner city. Latino gangs such as the MS-13, the M-18, and the Ñetas have created transnational bonds around the drug trade between the Americas.[26]

With roughly four former youth gang members—male and female— present at the PRAISE conference, Norma de Jesús, branch chief for the New York City Office of Probation, Family Division, asked the conference crowd why youth join gangs. Alphonso Sealey, youth leadership trainer of the community organization Families Reaching in Ever New Directions (FRIENDS) and chaperone of the adolescents, answered that it stemmed from "an absence of love." Others in the audience answered similarly, citing a "need for family," a "sense of mentorship," and the understanding that "all seek community." A young adult from the audience named Jay contended that it was boredom that makes a youth "at risk" for gang involvement. The number of recreational opportunities for youth living in the inner city is extremely limited. This vacuum causes adolescents to seek excitement elsewhere, sometimes on the streets.

Reverend Willie Reyes combines his experience as a former member in the largest cocaine gang in Philadelphia with his newfound faith in Christ to dialogue with the gang culture of the South Bronx. Reyes contends that his involvement in gang activity and drug dealing stemmed from his family dysfunction. Gangs are, according to Reyes, nothing more than a "family nucleus."[27] As an Anabaptist pastor and integral part of LPAC's PRAISE team, Reyes claims that in seeking membership in gangs, individuals are actually in search of God. He cites St. Paul's address at the Areopagus to make his case:

> For as I went through the city and looked carefully at the objects of your worship, I found among them an altar with the inscription, "To an unknown god." What therefore you worship as unknown, this I proclaim to you. The God who made the world and everything in it, he who is Lord of heaven and earth, does not live in shrines made by human hands, nor is he served by human hands, as though he needed anything, since he himself gives to all mortals life and breath and all things. From one ancestor he made all nations to inhabit the whole earth, and he allotted the times of their existence and the boundaries of the places where they would live, so that they would search for God and perhaps grope for him and find him—though indeed he is not far from each one of us. (Acts 17:23–27)

According to Reyes, in this passage St. Paul is arguing that even though the Athenians do not profess knowledge of God, their actions manifest their deep desire to find him. The end of the passage reads, all "grope for him and find him" as he is "not far from each one of us."

St. Paul's observation of the Athenians parallels Reyes' contention that gang members are also seeking God, albeit in very perverse and even violent ways. In addition to being a heroin addict for nearly eighteen years, Reyes spent eleven years in and out of penitentiaries. After his cocaine gang was disbanded, Reyes, then twenty-nine years old, returned home to hide out in North Philadelphia while bounty hunters were on his trail. An elderly man invited him in to share a meal, after which he asked Reyes to allow the man "to pray with [Reyes] and to ask Jesus Christ into [his] heart." Reyes responded in tears, exclaiming, "I'm sorry." Reyes attributes his first spiritual experience of God to this encounter.

Two weeks later, Reyes was sent to Graterford Prison with severe symptoms of heroin withdrawal. Because Graterford is a state prison, Reyes was unable to receive methadone treatments, routinely administered to heroin addicts. Catching a glimpse of himself—a grayish-colored, sickly body and weighing a measly ninety-three pounds—in a prison mirror, Reyes entered his cell and prayed to God: "If you're for real, you have to touch me. Because if you are, I'll die and I don't know where I am going." This experience shaped his later entrance into Ashland Theological

Seminary in Ohio, where he received a master of divinity, clinical psychology and homiletics, and thereafter his four years as Anabaptist pastor in the Amish town of Sullivan, Ohio.[28]

Implementing the Principles of Holistic Ministry

While the mission of PRAISE is to foster proactive community involvement around the issue of at-risk youth, its methodology is the "Four Principles of Holistic Ministry," as elaborated by Rivera: liberation, healing, community, and transformation. Liberation refers to calling "systems back to submission." In the case of urban youth, it emphasizes deliverance from unhealthy street acquaintances. Healing, both spiritual and emotional, "challenges people to be wounded healers" through the infusion of divine grace and personal healing. The model of "wounded healer" is Jesus Christ, who "was wounded for our transgressions [and] crushed for our iniquities," but, "upon him was the punishment that made us whole, and by his bruises we are healed" (Isa. 53:5). The principle of community urges youth to "become one" through fellowship, or "*coinea*" in the Greek sense. Moreover, it reassures youth that they are "called to mission," challenging them "to serve the larger community" in the Greek sense of "*diacoinea*."[29] And, transformation calls for the dual process of "ongoing renewal" at both the personal and communal levels. It points to "the culmination of spiritual, emotional, and physical enrichment."[30]

LPAC's Four Principles are a main force behind Rivera's theology of captivity. Rivera recognizes that his organization serves in an environment of captivity, especially when considering at-risk youth in the Bronx. These youth are, in effect, "held captive" by their involvement in gangs and drug-dealing activities, often seeing no hope for the future. The response of the PRAISE team to these situations of captivity is a ministry of personal outreach, challenging Latino youth on an individual basis to turn away from the streets and seek a better and more fulfilling life. In so doing, the team emphasizes the attainability of such concepts as "comfort, love, salvation, and peace"[31] for gang members through engagement in meditation, healing, the martial arts, and—as one will later see in the next section—the visual and performing arts.

In its response to an environment plagued with distrust and violence, LPAC provides a particular kind of "faith in action" to the gang culture of the South Bronx. This faith-based social action has not escaped recognition by leading actors in the public sector, at both the city and national levels. The creation of PRAISE was a direct result of LPAC's receipt of a $1 million grant from the U.S. Department of Justice to develop a gang prevention and intervention program specifically tailored to the South Bronx. DOJ designated the office of Congressman José E. Serrano (D-NY) of the 16th Congressional District in the Bronx as the official funnel for this grant money. In a show of support for LPAC's activities in gang prevention, Luis Pérez—representing Serrano's office—was present at the April 2002 conference.

Additionally, LPAC collaborates with many local agencies in the area of youth-at-risk, such as the New York City Department of Probation. Speaking at the PRAISE conference, Norma de Jesús, branch chief of the Juvenile Intensive Supervision Program of the Probation Department, applauded LPAC's efforts in gang prevention and intervention. Responsible for four hundred youth city-wide, de Jesús works alongside other law-enforcement agencies and a host of CBOs and religious organizations in the area of at-risk youth. Claiming that "no one can do it by themselves," she emphasized the importance of these community partnerships in "develop[ing] positive alternatives" for youth to meet their social, psychological, and physical needs.[32]

The PRAISE conference was the launching pad for LPAC's establishment of a gang prevention and intervention unit. Just recently, LPAC leadership has eliminated the acronym "PRAISE," placing the unit under the domain of the Greater Heights program, headed by Rivera's son, Stephen Rivera.[33] According to Bordoni, the Christian identity of the unit will continue to provide LPAC with the necessary tools to offer a holistic antidote to problems endemic to the gang culture of the South Bronx.[34] This identity is rooted deeply in a ministry of personal outreach, helping deliver Latino youth from situations of captivity, especially those that hold the individual in spiritual or physical bondage. Due to the great struggle urban youth face in freeing themselves from such captivity, Rivera would agree with his mentor Orlando Costas that LPAC's ministry is nothing more than "spirituality for combat."[35]

Engaging the Hip-Hop Culture

As the PRAISE conference wound down, a cultural performance ended the activities for the day. A lean-looking hip-hop dancer named "Bam Bam" emerged on the auditorium stage amid a backdrop of select Bible verses. In Bam Bam's words, he does "positive hip-hop"—from a distinctly Christian perspective. Wearing a silver lamé hat and vest and black pants, he glided across the stage with incredible agility to a pulsating music beat. This performance, used in high schools in the Bronx area and other New York City boroughs, attempts to showcase the redeemable features of the Bronx-born hip-hop music craze. As a follow-up to the performance, a team of LPAC professionals provides workshops in local high schools on various topics like peer pressure, gang prevention, gang awareness, and crisis intervention.[36] The team also offers meetings for parents' associations with Christian motivational speakers and musicians. The chief aim of these meetings is the discussion of alternatives to violent lifestyles through the cultivation of the virtues,[37] such as those touted by proponents of "character education." Virtues such as courage, honesty, generosity, and fortitude are summarized best by adherence to the Golden Rule, i.e., "do unto others as you would have them do unto you"—a "universal and timeless" truth shared by "rich religious and historical traditions."[38]

Hip-hop developed in the Bronx as a form of street dancing in the 1970s. This musical style "emerged as a cultural space shared by Puerto Ricans and blacks," pointing to their "intermingling placement in the . . . political and economic geography" of the inner city.[39] Generally speaking, hip-hop comprises four elements: the disc jockey (DJ), the emcee, graffiti writing, and break dancing. "The birth of hip-hop is credited to the DJ," and particularly to three DJs: Kool Herc, Afrika Bambaataa, and Grandmaster Flash. Instead of turntables, DJs began using mixers, allowing them to combine two records together "to keep the beat going." Increasing importance given to the emcee accompanied the surge of activity in DJ mixing. The mission of the emcee, or the rapper, was to "rock the crowd" by helping maintain the crowd's high enthusiasm for the music. Using a call-response technique, taken from the tradition of African music and the Jamaican art form of *toasting*, rappers tend to rely on good lyrics, "rhymed over the DJs' beat without faltering." Graffiti art entered the hip-hop craze as musical artists began "tagging" their names throughout the city for publicity. Finally, there was breakdancing, or the b-boying tradition, which traces its origins to the African martial arts form *capoeira* or *capoeta*, used by rebellious slaves in Brazil.[40] Waning in performance during the early 1990s, breakdancing has enjoyed a recent revival, as the motions of Bam Bam attest, adding a distinct flavor to the hip-hop tradition.[41]

Hip-hop includes "the thinking, the dress, the language—the whole thing." Partly due to the opposition the musical craze was facing, hip-hop "became more sophisticated as the years went on." Hip-hop is the reflection of a marginalized, inner-city, and multiracial culture. Artists like KRS-One cite hip-hop's alleviating and predictive characteristics in a culture facing violence and distrust. He writes that "not only does hip-hop relieve human suffering, but knowing it or having the sight and awareness that hip-hop has, gives you the ability to predict what's going to happen in the inner cities before it happens."[42]

LPAC Cultural Coordinator Danny Padilla uses "hip-hop culture" as an umbrella term to summarize the totality of cultural offerings provided by the organization, namely, dancing, singing, rapping, DJing, acting, miming, modeling, writing, and graffiti art. As executive director, Rivera is deeply interested in the hip-hop culture and the "continued connection" such a culture creates "between blacks and Hispanics" in the Bronx. Every night from 6–8 P.M., area youth between the ages of sixteen and twenty-one are invited to participate in any of the aforementioned cultural offerings. Total numbers of youth participating in LPAC's cultural offerings number three hundred to four hundred.[43]

LPAC engages the hip-hop culture of the South Bronx in two fundamental ways through its ministry of personal outreach. First, youth are exposed to positive, faith-filled role models at the organization. According to Padilla, these youth take notice that "moral living and moral values [are present] in the building. They see a difference. This comes out of faith, of living right and speaking right." In witnessing this, youth are "seeing the kingdom at hand." Even given LPAC's faith-based environment, conversion is never a precondition to engage in the cultural arts. Of course, as Padilla argues, his hidden agenda is ultimately to "bring [youth] to Christ." However, he acknowledges that "God didn't call me to save people, but to serve people. I am his hands and feet. I keep it my business to keep it separated. I leave the rest to him."[44]

Second, LPAC also seeks to make a difference for neighborhood youth through the business of referrals. Many of its youth participants in the cultural program hail from the same high schools where PRAISE has offered cultural performances and workshops on gang awareness. Talk of LPAC's unique cultural offerings draws many youth to participate in the organization's various activities. Padilla notes that public schools largely have cut music programs out of their budget, especially in urban areas, due to lack of funding. This is problematic for neighborhood youth, especially since "the Bronx has its own flavor, culture, and rhythms." Thus, the varied cultural offerings provided at LPAC serve as an outlet for youth whom "the system has ignored."[45]

While interviewing Padilla in the rehearsal room behind the stage, I could hear a schoolchild practicing for the next day's concert to the song "Lift Every Voice and Sing" by James W. Johnson (1871–1938): "Lift ev'ry voice and sing, till earth and heaven ring, Ring with the harmonies of liberties. . . . Let us march on till victory is won." Providing various kinds of cultural activities in which neighborhood youth can participate, LPAC allows youth to understand their urban situation through artistic expression, with the end goal of achieving their human potential. Realizing the strong pull of gangs and other societal pressures in the streets, LPAC serves as a "nurturing community" interested in the transformation of lives at the individual level.[46] Through its cultural offerings, the organization aims, much like the song cited above, to lift up every voice of Bronx youth.

LPAC as a Dynamic Presence

After the terrorist attacks of September 11, 2001, LPAC responded in late October with a musical celebration and rally entitled, "Beyond Revenge," dedicated to "our fallen heroes." Attendants listened to mesmerizing musical performances from Christian artists Corey Red & Precise and Godz Finest, as well as to a moving speech from William "Blinky" Rodríguez, former world champion kickboxer, member of the *Black Belt Magazine* Hall of Fame, and gang intervention specialist. A native of Los Angeles' San Fernando Valley, Rodríguez's sixteen-year-old son was killed during a gang-related drive-by shooting in early 1990. In response to his son's death, Rodríguez formed the Valley Unity Peace Treaty, of which he serves as executive director. With representation from the Valley's seventy-five gangs and more than 10,000 gang members, Rodríguez holds weekly meetings to discuss ways to "maintain the truce and improve the quality of life." He admits that, "for a lot of these gang members, there's not a lot of other things to do. We are trying to give them a vehicle to transfer out, but you can't expect this to change overnight."[47]

Through cultural events like the Beyond Revenge rally, LPAC endeavors to provide neighborhood youth both with a vehicle for artistic expression and an alternative to life on the streets. Culture is "embedded in Hispanic heritage," claims Padilla. "We are such a cultural and musical people." Youth participating in LPAC cultural activities have a favorite phrase, notes Padilla: "Just be real." In offering youth an array of activities reflecting the hip-hop culture, LPAC strives, in turn, "to be real with them." Padilla views the cultural arts, then, as "educational tools" not only for the youth, but also for the larger community. His goal is to help the youth use "what they have to the max." Whether through dance, rap, or theater production, LPAC "brings in [the] community." Because many urban dwellers in the South Bronx do not have the means to see a Broadway play, Padilla remarks that LPAC strives to "bring the arts to them."[48]

As discussed in chapter one, culture implies a set of commitments shared by a particular community. Religion, as a special kind of culture, involves particular kinds of commitments or values, which serve as a link between one's personal faith and the faith community to which one belongs. Religious values, however, are also public in that they influence one's participation in the larger public order. In describing LPAC's cultural offerings as "educational tools," Padilla describes the way in which the religious identity politics of the organization impacts the hip-hop culture through dynamic presence, which, as previously stated, is one of the six impacts of religion on public culture. This impact relates to the teaching role of the Christian church. Reyes nicely summarizes how LPAC acts as a "dynamic presence" to the hip-hop culture of the South Bronx. He states:

> Latino Pastoral Action Center is a vital institution because we get to be mentors and someone to talk to. Through events, we can guide and give [youth] the type of stability and understanding that there is another lifestyle and [that there] is hope. . . . There is a sense of unity because our purpose, objective, and goal are still: Love fulfills the needs that communicate the Gospel towards salvation.[49]

In serving as "mentors and someone to talk to," LPAC manifests its teaching role to the urban youth of the South Bronx. It is important to recognize that such a teaching role is always contextually based. As Padilla remarks, the "flavor, culture, and rhythms" of the South Bronx is the context out of which LPAC personally ministers to youth. Taking a lesson from Malcolm X, in engaging the hip-hop culture, LPAC is aware of the importance to "always teach in terms that the people [can] understand."[50]

Other Community-Based Programs for Youth

In addition to those cultural offerings listed above, LPAC's Greater Heights Ministry (Greater Heights) engages the hip-hop culture by providing a late-night alternative to the streets for young adults. Greater Heights meets Mondays through Thursdays in the LPAC complex and offers college and career tutoring, General Educational Development (GED) preparation, English as a Second Language (ESL) classes, and opportunities for spiritual development through the youth hip-hop chapel, "Holy Hood," and Sunday Sanctuary services. While groups entitled "My Brother's Keeper" and "Sister's Circle" provide weekly support for male and female urban youth, another program, "Serve Our Youth," helps youth become more civically engaged. Greater Heights also provides youth and young adults with a range of recreational activities like weightlifting, volleyball, Aikido, dance, and basketball. Whereas more than four hundred youth visit LPAC each night, approximately one hundred twenty youth between the ages of nine and eighteen participate in LPAC's basketball program, traveling to different states to play in games.

Greater Heights is very explicit about the kind of behavior expected from its youth. Outside the gymnasium is posted a sign by the ministry prohibiting all of the following: "the use of foul language or obscene hand gestures, fighting (verbal or physical), . . . weapons, gang relation (flagging, hand gestures, or gang content), graffiti, . . . gambling, racism, sexism, contraband (illegal substances), improper attire." It then proceeds to state, "and finally we will not tolerate any sexual activity. This includes the exchanging of numbers, sitting on each others lap, etc. Anyone (including LPAC staff) found disobeying these stipulations will be subjected to a temporary or indefinite suspension."

One may observe the type of support LPAC provides to neighborhood youth by taking into account all the young visitors that stop in or simply want to "hang out" there. Susan Rivera-León, Rivera's daughter and former director of community-based programs at LPAC, remarks that "Everyone is allowed to roam around here. We don't turn anyone away."[51] Waiting to conduct an interview with an LPAC staff member, a young African American adolescent walks in the door and throws himself down on one of the couches in the waiting area. Wearing black high-top sneakers and a black knit hat, it is evident that this adolescent "knows the street." After taking his coat off, he enters the multipurpose room alone. He has brought only a backpack and a bag lunch, and as he drinks milk from a small carton, he reads the *New York Post*. At LPAC all by himself, the adolescent "comes and goes."

Two days later, the same youth is back at LPAC, sitting in the same spot in front of the auditorium doors. Carrying a rolled newspaper in his back pocket, he fidgets in his seat, doing nothing. One of the basketball coaches comes out from the gym and hugs him. "Hey, Jay!" he exclaims —it is the same Jay from the PRAISE conference. As Jay quietly reads his newspaper on the couch, an LPAC staff member asks him to help carry boxes back to the administrative offices. Jay enthusiastically offers his services. Reyes notes that LPAC is a "nurturing community" for many youth in the South Bronx like Jay who have nowhere to go. Reyes claims that he "has seen individuals' lives transformed"[52] through relationships formed at this organization.

In responding to adverse ethnic, racial, and socioeconomic situations such as those outlined above, it is "ultimately the church that ends up with the broken pieces." Previously on staff with his brother, Reverend Luciano Padilla, at Bay Ridge Christian Center (Bay Ridge) in Brooklyn, one of the oldest Latino Pentecostal churches in New York City, Danny Padilla identifies himself with the Pentecostal tradition. Padilla discusses the situation in which the urban church historically has found itself. Struggling with its unique position in the inner city, he has "seen the church lift itself up" through social action and the generous donation of tithes from the congregation. Like the urban church, LPAC channels monies from the congregation tithes collected at its Sunday services, called "Sanctuary."

This enables the organization to engage in the important social task of providing youth both an access to the cultural arts and an alternative to life on the streets. Striving to create a "safe culture" where "people are not diminished or marginalized," the younger they are, the more LPAC desires to protect their safety.[53] Through LPAC's engagement with the hip-hop culture, the organization's hope is to break down divisions among Latino subgroups as well as quell historical tensions between Latinos and non-Latinos, so that urban youth can focus instead on their own holistic development as children of God.[54]

The Indigenous Religious Community

According to Rivera, membership in the urban church provides a response to the dislocation that so many inner-city youth, particularly those of racial or ethnic minorities, experience in the United States. These young people are subject to the "multiple marginalities" of the inner city, aggravated by extreme poverty and inadequate educational opportunities. Rather than isolate them further, membership in the urban church provides youth with a "re-inscription of locality through the creation of tightly-knit community, and a strong sense of individual identity." In "re-asserting territory," the urban church, or indigenous religious community, functions much like the gang, reaffirming the "self, family (as an extended community), and place." Unlike gangs, however, membership in the urban church, especially that of the Pentecostal denomination, entails the experience of conversion as a "radical transformation . . . of being born again in Jesus Christ." Further, the notion of family as an extended community is rearticulated and accompanied by "a new, cleansed self." As David Martin suggests, Christian denominations, like Pentecostalism and evangelical Protestantism, serve "to implant new disciplines . . . and reverse the indifferent and injurious hierarchies of the outside world."[55]

The indigenous religious community, according to Rivera, develops the process of "re-socialization" to rebuild the "damaged psyche of the Latino youth" who is "crippled by sinful structures" in three main ways. First, the community introduces new role models, namely, the pastor, elders, and the entire leadership structure. Second, the community presents new status symbols who are "articulate, intelligent Latinos." Third, this indigenous community provides new folk heroes, "the people of faith." All of this, claims Rivera, takes place in "historical reality." LPAC's own house of worship, entitled "Sanctuary," whose services are led by Rivera every Sunday from 10 A.M. to noon in the organization's gymnasium, is one example of an indigenous religious community. Another example is the recent creation of LPAC's hip-hop church, called the "Holy Hood," which offers services for urban youth every Friday. Both the Sanctuary and Holy Hood constitute places of worship for African Americans and Latinos against a "culture of ethnic tension." In that these ethnic groups share not only "a common history of oppression" but also a common identity in Christ, Rivera claims that it is only appropriate these groups worship together. In so doing, both services display the marks of the urban church in their manifestation of a "community of affirmation."[56]

Loyal to the neighborhood the organization serves, LPAC provides a number of start-up churches with space in its urban ministry complex for a small fee until they are able to afford their own space. Wounded Healer Fellowship (WHF) is one of these churches. On the temperate afternoon of February 3, 2002, WHF held its Ninth Anniversary Service and Ministry of the Word in a moderately crowded LPAC gymnasium. With nearly two hundred people in attendance, the racial composition of the crowd was mostly Latino and African American, with some white representation. The preacher that day, Reverend Dan Livingston, was a visitor from the South who spoke to the congregation in English.

"God's not saying I don't care how much you have, but give me what you have," proclaims Livingston. "If you come and give God what you have, you'll see the blessings come." Speaking directly to the poverty that exists in this inner city of Highbridge, he adds that it is difficult to have faith "when your wallet is empty and your mailbox is full of bills." Some in the congregation begin clapping and shouting "Alleluia, Alleluia." Livingston remarks that genuine faith is at stake. He refers to his own suffering for two years when false allegations were made against him. He was locked out of his church. All the other pastors in the neighborhood shunned him, except for an African American preacher who would stop by Livingston's house every day. Livingston remarked that as a result of the preacher's visits, the preacher was disowned. In response to his unfortunate situation, the preacher said, "God sent me to your house." Livingston learned from this experience that "not only does God send us somebody, but God keeps his promises," eventually delivering Livingston from his suffering.

Pastor Bert approached the microphone, saying, "God is into restoration and saving people's lives. A bruised reed he will not step on." He continued, "If God has sparked something into your life, it's because he wants to cause a fire." "If for some reason you have not said 'yes' to Jesus, now's the time." Pastor Bert then proclaimed, Jesus Christ is saying, "yo, guess what? I want to have a relationship with you." A man from the congregation raised his hand, signaling his desire to enter into a relationship with Jesus. As Elder Nat rushed over to pray over him, Pastor Bert announced, "I ask in the name of Jesus, heal him, sanctify him, deliver him. I consider it done. Alleluia."

Perhaps most significant about the WHF service was Pastor Bert's admission that "I am so thankful I am messed up, because I can receive all the messes around." WHF's own name emphasizes its ability to navigate in a difficult environment where personal woundedness has unleashed a whole set of social ills. A red banner hanging from the stage best depicts the fellowship's approach to ministry. In the center of the banner are two hands holding a smattering of buildings in New York City, portraying the inner-city's domain and how the faith congregation comes to this domain with open hands.[57]

Nonviolent Social Action

As an indigenous religious community, LPAC strongly emphasizes the formation of partnerships with other community actors to deliver urban Latino youth from the domain of violent captivity of the inner city. Unlike his Pentecostal counterparts, however, Rivera has fashioned these partnerships in a nontraditional way. Reverend Alfonso Wyatt, vice president for Fund for the City, contends that LPAC is organizationally "very different from the mainstream of [Rivera's] mainstream"[58] Pentecostal faith tradition. Rivera's nontraditional style is displayed in how the organization maintains long-standing alliances with those from without the Christian faith tradition—area Buddhists and Quakers, for example—to advance nonviolent methods in the South Bronx. In fact, there is "very little to compare [LPAC from] within its own [religious] tradition," says Reverend Rafael Reyes, superintendent for the Spanish Eastern District of the Church of God, one of the largest Pentecostal denominations in the United States. According to R. Reyes, the organization more easily might be compared to a secular "multiservice organization" in the Bronx or to the defunct Acción Cívica of the 1950s and 1960s.[59]

Through the creation of the Bronx Peace Village/Dojo, Rivera has united forces with Zen Buddhists and Quakers to bring his brand of "spirituality for combat" to New York City. A partnership among LPAC, the Zen Peacemaker Order, and Simeht Ltd. (a Quaker-led organization), Bronx Peace Village/Dojo serves as a "center for meditation, study, and preparation for nonviolent actionists."[60] Through the recruitment of more than forty leaders from religious and community organizations, the center aims to develop what are referred to as "peace warriors" to prevent violent eruptions on the streets. The central objective of the Bronx Peace Village/Dojo is "to connect with those who come, teach them how to reopen their hearts to hope, then train them, body, mind, and spirit, to breathe anew."[61] Seminars utilize methods taken from Aikido, Aiki, Tai-chi chuan, and the Alternatives to Violence Program (AVP)—the latter a verbal practice originating from the Quaker movement in the mid-1970s[62] —to "present non-violence methods, both verbal and physical."[63]

As president of Simeht Ltd., Bill Leicht has a long history of involvement in street work in the South Bronx. A practicing Quaker, Leicht was interested in the advancement of nonviolent social action in New York's poor inner cities. In the 1970s, he helped negotiate gang peace in the neighborhood in collaboration with the Ghetto Brothers, a youth gang, and United Bronx Parents (UBP), a parent-activist group serving the South Bronx for more than thirty years. During the mid-1980s, Leicht began the study of Aikido, putting his interest in nonviolent action into practice. Synthesizing Aikido and the Aiki practice resulted in the formation of the phonetic translation of Aiki, "I-Key Workshops," as a new approach to conflict resolution. I-Key Workshops today serve as the core of Simeht Ltd.'s conflict resolution business and are a core program in many New York City public schools.[64]

The Aiki practice was demonstrated in the Resolving Conflict Creatively Program's (RCCP) "Martial Arts and Conflict Resolution" session led by Leicht on Saturday, April 21, 2002, at the High School for Physical Sciences in New York City. This practice arose from Aikido, the Japanese martial arts form. Like Aikido, the objective of the Aiki practice is to "uncover within conflict the harmony between people and in our world." Moreover, Aiki and Aikido both rely on the body as the teaching instructor and are nonverbal techniques. In contrast to Aikido, the Aiki practice is not a martial art but a way of being that emphasizes the importance of three distinct but related concepts: irimi, relaxation, and turning. Irimi involves learning how to move into or approach a situation, relaxation refers to breathing with the whole body, and turning suggests the ability to change a relationship.[65]

The objective of the RCCP session in April 2002 was to "explore how conflict is physical" in that it "always makes itself manifest in the body."[66] Mostly teachers and graduate students attended the Saturday workshop. Situated in a second-floor classroom with decorative drawings plastering the walls and seated on generic school chairs—too small for most participants—Leicht and Milton Roman, another facilitator, positioned the group in a circle. Also in attendance were two African American high school students, one of whom was a student at Thurgood Marshall Academy High School in Manhattan. This student, named Kariem, remarked that his reason for attending the workshop was to look "for a new way of life and a new way to stay out of trouble." The other student hoped to "learn how to deal on the street." He noted that "trying to solve problems, [often] turns into violence and using weapons."[67]

One of the first activities, entitled "Concentric Circle," required participants to role-play with another person the relationship of boss/employee or teacher/student. Individuals were asked at times not to look at the other person, not to comment, or not to be at the same vantage point (one standing, the other sitting) in an effort to come to terms with interpersonal relationships. All participants remarked that it was extremely difficult to carry out their role-playing task without certain communication essentials like sight, speech, or an agreed upon comfort zone. Subsequently, individuals participated in a "Personal Space" task that involved standing on the opposite side of the room from another person with distance between each person. While one person stood motionless on his or her side of the room, the other person was asked to walk slowly, with sustained eye contact, toward the other side. The motionless person was then asked to put his or her hand out when he or she felt the distance to be too uncomfortable. All believed this task pointed to their inherent physical fear and insecurity. Kariem remarked, "I can't always look at people in the eyes on the street," as that signals a certain vulnerability.[68]

Leicht was the key figure involved in arranging the first meeting between Ramos, a.k.a. "Green Eyes," from the Zulu Nation gang, and Rivera. Through this interaction, coupled with a growing knowledge of Leicht's involvement in gang prevention activities, Rivera asked Leicht to "bring the Aiki practice and AVP to LPAC." Leicht responded to Rivera's request by training Bordoni and Victor Rodríguez, LPAC Aikido sensei, in the techniques of these nonviolent practices. In welcoming Aiki and Aikido to LPAC, Rivera acknowledged the degree of confluence between these Zen practices and the Pentecostal mission. With Leicht's guidance, Rivera understood it was easier to reach people first at the physical level than at the spiritual level. This is especially the case for gang members in the inner city, who tend to have "more comfort with physicality." While not manifesting "stiffness in their bodies," inner-city youth tend to exhibit their physical oppression in muscular tension and tense breathing patterns. Aikido and the Aiki practice aim to regulate this physical oppression through nonverbal techniques like those performed during the April workshop.[69]

The Pentecostal Worldview

The Pentecostal "spirituality" promoted by LPAC is closely attuned to the physicality inherent in the Aiki practice and Aikido. According to Leicht, there is a "cultural overlap" between the physicality of Pentecostalism and the Zen practices of Aiki and Aikido. The word "spirit" comes from the Latin root "spir," meaning "to breathe." Other derivatives of "spir" include "respiration" and "inspiration." For Zen Buddhists, "proper breathing is the way to peace." Pentecostalism, on the other hand, affirms the physicality of the body through the visible display of the "workings of the spirit"—speaking in tongues, laying on of hands, and being slain in the spirit.[70]

Pentecostalism is a grass-roots movement within evangelical Christianity. Such a movement places great emphasis on the "gifts of the Holy Spirit," namely speaking in tongues, prophecy, words of knowledge, divine healing, and the performance of other "signs and wonders," as documented in the Acts of the Apostles, chapters 12–16. As an "experiential, oral, and lived tradition," Pentecostalism differs from other Protestant denominations in that it "breaks away" from *sola scriptura* (only scripture) to include the realm of *pneuma*, or spirit.[71] This movement traces its origins to the 1906 Azusa Street Revival in Los Angeles. The involvement of Puerto Ricans in the movement first began on the island of Puerto Rico, with the preaching of Juan Lugo in 1916. Once in New York City, many Puerto Rican immigrants joined the Pentecostal movement during the surge of migration in the 1920s. The Pentecostal movement has been a central force in the lives of the Puerto Rican community in New York City for more than eighty years. In fact, of the fifty-five Latino Protestant Congregations in New York City in 1937, twenty-five were Pentecostal.[72]

David Martin notes that Pentecostalism shares an affinity with the "informal, spontaneous, flexible, and infinitely varied"[73] nature of Puerto Rican culture. Like Puerto Rican culture, Pentecostalism is an informal faith tradition. This informality is displayed in how Pentecostal worship is free from the constraints of language. In traditional Pentecostal services, "if you could not speak English, you could speak in tongues." However, many churches today offer services in Spanish. This is significant in that "Latinos/ as . . . empower themselves by retaining their language," thus "strengthening their faith." One of the primary reasons Puerto Ricans—and Latinos, generally speaking—entered the Pentecostal movement was because they had been ministered to by church members in the Spanish language.[74] Rivera understands that worship in the Spanish language serves to protect "cultural and linguistic identity" among Latinos. As a second-generation Puerto Rican living in New York City, Rivera relates that it was in the urban church where he first learned the Spanish language.[75]

Social-science researchers typically have characterized the Pentecostal movement as "otherworldly," explaining the lack of social and political engagement by its members.[76] As the paragraphs above attest, however, the

Pentecostal worldview is not confined to otherworldly activities such as speaking in tongues, prophecy, and divine healing. In providing a "communal response to an array of social issues"[77] in the South Bronx, LPAC demonstrates how this worldview is, in fact, more expansive. Rivera realizes his job is not only "to save sinners," but "to do something about the problems in the neighborhood."[78] As an indigenous religious community, LPAC provides urban youth with a response to the dislocation that often plagues life in the inner city. This response is accomplished through the in-house provision of religious services and martial arts classes, as well as an endorsement of nonviolent social action by community partners. Instead of viewing warfare as something external, LPAC leadership— along with its community partners—helps urban youth understand that the greatest battle is one of the spirit. The Pentecostal worldview of the organization serves to aid LPAC's ministry of personal outreach, because "what is above all most evident is the capacity of Pentecostalism simultaneously to conform and transform. It finds out the . . . shape of the local society and participates in the life of the people."[79]

Dimensions of Personal Development

On January 30, 2002, Rivera opened up the morning Job Readiness Workshop in the LPAC multipurpose room offering coffee and orange juice. We are "excited you came," he begins. "Our role as a faith-based organization is to support you." He refers to the story taken from John 8:1–11 in which the scribes and Pharisees bring a woman accused of adultery before Jesus with the intent to stone her. After writing an image in the sand, Jesus proclaims to them, "Let anyone among you who is without sin be the first to throw a stone at her." With that, all the accusers flee the scene. Jesus, turning to the woman asks, "Woman, where are they? Has no one condemned you?" The woman replies, "No one, Sir." He says, "Neither do I condemn thee. Go your way, and from now on do not sin again." Sitting at long cafeteria tables, the nine women present shake their heads. As people of color, we are "not here to accuse, but to help, support, and open doors for you," states Rivera. He refers to the welfare system that both "oppresses and dehumanizes." The "system is such an ugly system that robs us of our dignity." We become "discouraged and depressed at the type of treatment." Rivera emphasizes that LPAC's intention is not to oppress but to "build up." This is because the organization is "motivated by love." LPAC's goal is to lift up "accusations and open up doors to break the cycle of welfare." We "want our people to make it."[80]

Joanne Petty runs LPAC's bimonthly Job Readiness Workshop entitled "Breaking Cycles." Prior to Rivera's greeting, one may observe moderators Petty and Alba Cardona asking participants "Do you need your GED? Do you need computer skills? Do you need job skills?" There are ten people present—nine women and one man. Of the total number, six are African American and a few are black Latinas. "Betsy," as her nametag reads, a black Latina, switches back and forth between English and Spanish. It is obvious Betsy is tense. She exclaims, "I don't want to work for anyone. I want to work for myself!" She turns to Cardona, "*el papel dice que Uds. ayuden que la mujer trabaja.*" In addition to receiving child support, Betsy notes that "*el papa me lleva $1,500 pesos mensual.*"[81] But, with two children, that is not enough money. Betsy states with firmness, "look, I need a job, or else I don't know what to do!"

Petty takes the Breaking Cycles participants through a workbook entitled "Making Career Decisions." She asks the women present to list their values, interests, personal traits, and skills. Petty instructs the women that, even if they do not have a GED, they probably have other skills. For instance, she remarks that getting kids ready for school "is a skill," and a very valuable one at that. Or "maybe you can braid or perm hair. That is a special talent." While the women fill out their goals, LPAC staff member Elizabeth Reyes speaks to them. Reyes' testimony is powerful. She is a single parent who was on welfare for four years. She encourages the women that it is "very easy to get on with your life." Through daily prayer, "God has shown me a lot of miracles." Petty interjects, you "don't have to stay in the situation that you're in." "There is always help if you ask," remarks Reyes, for there is a "whole world of resources and information . . . if you believe there is hope."[82]

LPAC received funding for its welfare-to-work program from the South Bronx Overall Economic Development Corporation (SOBRO), which in turn received monies from New York's Human Resources Administration (HRA). SOBRO managed a borough-wide project with four FBOs in the South Bronx, one of which was LPAC, through its Faith-Based Initiatives Unit. Acting as a "conduit to facilitate joint ventures between churches in the Bronx" and New York City and state government, SOBRO offers technical assistance to religious organizations "in the design, development, and implementation of their community development projects."[83] While LPAC's Job Readiness Program continues to provide career advisement

and résumé preparation to neighborhood clients, the organization no longer works with welfare-to-work recipients, due to SOBRO's decision to
discontinue its funding to the organization.[84]

The influence of Rivera's elaboration of the "Five Dimensions of Personal Development" is present in the Breaking Cycles workshop. As mentioned in chapter three, the five dimensions of personal development are:
spiritual, emotional, mental, physical, and social. Whereas the first four
dimensions relate to the first of Jesus' commandments, "You shall love
the Lord your God with all your heart, and with all your soul, and with
all your mind, and with all your strength," the last dimension, the social,
refers to Jesus' second commandment, "You shall love your neighbor as
yourself" (Mark 12:30–31). The objective of the bimonthly Job Readiness
Workshop, according to Petty, is for participants to address the various
dimensions of personal development so they can "get started to begin a
new life."[85] Acknowledging that the path to personal development is a
step-by-step process, Rivera recognizes that one may make more progress
in one dimension than the others. In viewing LPAC programs as a single
"vision," leadership and staff encourage neighborhood clients to discover
"what makes a holistic person" through the integration of the five dimensions of personal development in all the organization's program areas.[86]

Treating the "Colonized Mind"

Susan Rivera-León argues that the Latino community is "in need of a
very holistic perception and spiritual awakening—[from an] emotional,
physical, and psychological [perspective]."[87] In an attempt to address the
emotional dimension of personal development, LPAC provides pastoral
counseling to its neighborhood constituents from the South Bronx. "The
task with our people is so big," exclaims Dr. Roberto Rivera, former director of LPAC's Pastoral Counseling Program.[88] "Dr. Roberto," as he is
called, originally hails from Puerto Rico. The main obstacle facing Puerto
Ricans living on the mainland, according to Dr. Roberto, is the need to
overcome "our colonized mind[s]."[89]

There are two types of colonization for Puerto Ricans living in the
United States. The first kind is both physical and political and involves
an acknowledgment of the reality that "we are not free as a nation." Although Puerto Rico has a democratically elected government that is an
example to the rest of Latin America, it remains politically dependent on
the United States. This dependence, however, is not the most pernicious

type of colonization. The worst kind of colonization is both intellectual and spiritual; it "is what is in our veins and bones," Dr. Roberto claims. It is an acceptance of the belief "that we are a secondary type of people" who, because of the lack of success in attaining economic and political power, have "not been able to be free and support ourselves."[90]

Puerto Ricans, and other Latin Americans for that matter, come "with a submissive mind" to the United States. This makes itself manifest in interpersonal relationships. Two client couples that Dr. Roberto recently counseled stated that their main problem was "matters of submission and control." Congregational life is not immune to such disorders, admits Dr. Roberto. In fact, many argue that when Christianity came to Puerto Rico, it "helped colonize [the people] even more." Dr. Roberto notes that it is "easy for pastors to become powerful images because of the submissive attitudes of the people." Expressing congregational life in terms of domination and submission, however, sets the stage for a "false faith" and denies that church members actually have the ability "to put into practice the capacities that they have."[91]

As pastor of First Spanish Baptist Church, Dr. Roberto chose to embrace missionary work in the *barrios* (neighborhoods) of New York City. He reflects on a situation in which someone approached him and asked, "Why are you, a well-educated man, coming to work in the barrio?" Dr. Roberto answered him, "*Para qué diablos el Señor me mandó a este ministerio?*"[92] In other words, he found his work in the barrio to be the "most logical thing"—a direct response to God's calling him to the ministry. "It is a devilish barrio where they need help. That is why I am here." Moreover, "I owe it to this people," Dr. Roberto added. After losing his father when he was eight years old, he lived through the difficult reality of his mother raising five children on her own. All the while, however, she instilled in her children the belief that "we were going to be different, because we would get an education." As a Baptist pastor, Dr. Roberto challenged youth in his congregation to obtain as much education as possible. In his first five years of pastoral duties, only one or two youth members graduated from college. After fifteen years, approximately 95 percent graduated from college.[93]

Dr. Roberto considers Viktor Frankl, Jewish psychiatrist, Holocaust survivor, and inventor of Logotherapy, one of his mentors in the field of pastoral counseling. In his work *Man's Search for Meaning*, Frankl reflects on how the prisoners in Auschwitz "suffered from an inferiority complex." He writes that "we all had once been or had fancied ourselves to be 'somebody.' Now we were treated like complete nonentities." Imprisoned by multiple relationships of dependency, Latinos in the United States suffer from a similar inferiority complex, claims Dr. Roberto. Finding solace in the "intensification of [one's] inner life," Frankl found, "helped the prisoner find a refuge from the emptiness, desolation, and spiritual poverty of his existence." In the end, Frankl asserted that "everything can be taken from a man but one thing" remains: "to choose one's attitude in any given set of circumstances, to choose one's way."[94]

Frankl himself made a series of "choices" prior to and during his internment at the Nazi camps. He made a decision to remain with his typhus patients when faced with the opportunity to break free from the Auschwitz camp. However, his imprisonment in the camps was the result of a "choice." In the preface to his work, Frankl relates that an immigration visa to the United States awaited him at the American Consulate in Vienna right before the United States entered World War II. In reflecting on where his real responsibility lay—with his research on logotherapy or with his parents—he chose the latter, after viewing a fragment of one of the Ten Commandments on his parents' table salvaged from a burned-down synagogue in Vienna. This fragment stood for "Honor thy father and mother that thy days may be long upon the land." It was at that moment Frankl decided to let his visa lapse and to "stay with [his] father and . . . mother upon the land."[95]

Frankl's claim that "life is a mission and you have to choose" is a very significant concept in the field of pastoral counseling, remarks Dr. Roberto. One of the most basic elements of counseling is to "transmit a sense of hope to the client"[96] that, regardless of the adverse situations in which one finds oneself, he or she still retains, as Frankl suggests, "inner freedom and personal value."[97] In Dr. Roberto's case, the "client" could be neighborhood residents from the Bronx, LPAC leadership and staff, or Reverend Rivera himself. Dr. Roberto rejects simple responses to life, like "don't worry about it," as this conveys a false sense of hope, thereby denying the reality of the problematic situation at hand. Instead, he opts to address the problem head-on by what he calls "mapping the problem." Once his clients are able to look at the problem in a more realistic sense, they then are able to admit that "now we have to fight together." When the client realizes that a situation exists in which really he or she will have to fight, the client then gives more of himself or herself sacrificially in the process. This is when the element of hope appears. It is the attitude that "I am going to work it out and someone is going to work with me."[98]

In 1996 and again in 1999, the New York Community Trust (the Trust) awarded a two-year grant to the Blanton-Peale Institute, in a joint-venture partnership with LPAC, under its Health and People with Special Needs Program. The Trust is a community foundation with $2 billion in assets that awards approximately $140 million a year in grants. Blanton-Peale, on the other hand, is a "multi-faith, non-sectarian educational and service organization"[99] that strives to combine religion with psychological counseling services. This grant was designed to create a joint mental health training program for both clergy and lay church leaders. At the heart of the funding, maintains Irfan Hasan, Trust program officer, was the understanding that "counseling is not always delivered in traditional mental health settings." Pastoral counseling, in other words, was understood as "part of the continuum of care."[100] Former program officer at the Trust and current vice president of JPMorgan Private Bank, Jacqueline Elias noted that this multiyear commitment to Blanton-Peale and LPAC was "unusual for the Trust." In its history as a foundation, the Trust had never partnered before with any other Latino FBO.[101]

The Trust designated grant money to Blanton-Peale and LPAC for staffing and training costs to serve those Pentecostal and storefront churches that lack appropriate "skills and service infrastructure in the mental health field."[102] Due to a prevalent culture of *machismo* (male chauvinism), the Latino community is reluctant to attend psychological counseling sessions, preferring instead to talk to family members or pastors.[103] While there was a general understanding that Latino churches were heavily active in the mental health field, at the same time many realized that one simply "can't pray something away."[104] Latino pastors themselves arrived at a similar conclusion that "some things don't resolve themselves by just having faith." Through exposure to numerous individuals and families over the past twenty years, pastors like Dr. Roberto have contended that while their central responsibility as pastors was to focus on the "faith component," access to counseling services outside the congregation was necessary.[105] This is one of the main reasons LPAC decided to provide these services with trained counseling professionals at its organization.

Latino Religious Culture

Dr. John Hagedorn, a registered psychologist and director of the Pastoral Studies Program at Blanton-Peale, would agree with Frankl that, amid the harsh reality of life, one may find solace in the "intensification of the inner life." More than anywhere else, the Latino community discovers this haven of inner freedom in the congregation. Within the congregation Latinos discover not only their goals, but also "concepts of right and wrong." Hagedorn likens the congregation to "an emotive system." Many Latinos first speak to their pastors, even about psychological issues.[106] "If you see no one else, you see your minister," comments Elias. This innate "sense of trust with things having to do with the church" stems from the positive experience Latinos have with congregational life in their native land as well as upon their arrival to the United States.[107]

Latino congregations and FBOs can be likened to havens of inner freedom wherein Latinos may come to understand their rights and responsibilities, both as individuals and as members of the larger political community. These religious organizations, however, are also vehicles of "identity transmission" to the degree they strive to preserve Latino religious culture.[108] They play a significant role in the preservation of community at the neighborhood level through the provision of material support (employment opportunities as well as help with housing concerns, health-care expenses, and day-care programs) and nonmaterial support (opportunities for prayer, worship, counseling, and conversation) to their respective populations.

The types of material and nonmaterial support an organization like LPAC offers to its neighborhood constituents are intimately linked to how organizational leadership interprets the Christian narrative in its urban context. It is Rivera's elaboration of a theology of captivity that drives LPAC's ministry of personal outreach. In his theology of captivity, Rivera holds that individuals, systems, and structures have all been held captive and need liberation. However, he ultimately claims that liberation always begins at the individual level. In addition to LPAC's Pastoral Counseling program, the monthly Women's Breakfast and weekly Men's Fellowship are two further examples of how LPAC strives to liberate individuals from captivity through the nonmaterial resources of prayer and conversation. These activities are completely funded by Sanctuary tithes, so the "money goes back to the people."[109] They reflect Paulo Freire's dialogical teaching method in fighting *with*, as opposed to *for*, individuals to "regain their humanity"[110] as residents of the inner city.

Reverend Nancy Márquez, an ordained Pentecostal minister and co-ordinator of social services at LPAC, explains that the main drive behind the Women's Breakfast was to establish a "support group." Márquez, often referred to by staff as "Elder Nancy," has found that the central problem uniting all women in the group is one of "relationships." Among the participants in the group are "mothers of the church" as well as other church-going and non-church-going females. The breakfast takes place one Saturday each month from 9:30 A.M. to noon. Additionally, LPAC hosts a three-day retreat every year for the women. Following Jesus' example in the Scriptures, the first hour of the breakfast is dedicated to eating and fellowship. For Jesus Christ himself, the need to alleviate physical hunger always preceded the more important alleviation of spiritual hunger. Subsequently, a short sermon follows, during which time, claims Márquez, "I sic the Word on them." Women then are permitted to comment on the sermon as well as to both "vent" and "pray for needs." Due to the proximity of one of the Women's Breakfast to Valentine's Day 2002, Márquez reported that preaching for the February gathering centered on the love of God and more specifically on "Jesus [as] the best Valentine."[111]

In December 2001, Percy Howard, LPAC counselor and Sanctuary elder, along with Bordoni and Willie Reyes, established the Men's Fellowship to "simplify" the Word of God for interested men over the age of seventeen. The fellowship runs every Monday night from 7–8:30 P.M., and in just a few months attendance has increased from five to sixteen participants. It serves to call men back to accountability in their everyday lives. "As men of God, we need to be accountable to each other. Without accountability, we go haywire," asserts Howard. In the end, the goal is to "help them to help themselves." To achieve this, LPAC staff must do a lot of listening. He notes that "a lot of the time believers have the tendency to give the answer without understanding the problem." While Christian believers are "accountable to Jesus Christ," Howard urges nonbelievers attending the fellowship to be "accountable to someone."[112]

The Bible teaches that "we all fall short of the glory of God," states Howard. Therefore, believers and nonbelievers alike need "more accountability to check where we fall short and correct it." It "takes time to deprogram" someone who has spent most of his or her life in the "natural world." Howard describes the "natural world" as the world of original sin. According to the Bible, man is "born in sin" and "only through the Holy Spirit is [his] sinful nature made dormant." As a result, "whatever we feed (either the natural or spiritual side) will have dominion." There is a true "spiritual war" that every individual undergoes. But, "prayer changes things." According to Howard, it makes a difference if the foundation is in Christ, because "I can do all things through him who strengthens me (Phil. 4:13)."[113]

As the Women's Breakfast and Men's Fellowship attest, one may regard LPAC as a haven of inner freedom in the South Bronx. LPAC staff and leadership would agree with Patricia A. Wilson that community development first starts with the "individual, interior person by touching the heart [and] changing values and beliefs."[114] Understanding such development as involving an inner transformation nicely summarizes the organization's ministry of personal outreach. In that LPAC "consider[s] [itself] to be a catalyst for change," success is measured by "making a difference in an individual's life."[115] However, the process of community development simply does not end with a client's inner transformation. As the following section on leadership suggests, LPAC makes a deliberate effort to link this transformation to an "outer connectedness" to public and private resources so as to engage in rebuilding the distressed neighborhood of the South Bronx.

Leadership in the Bronx

In the middle of interviewing Rivera in his office, there is a knock at the door. It is a young male member of the Sanctuary who comes to ask for his advice. Rivera is officiating the marriage between this young male and his girlfriend in a few days. After being turned down for a marriage license because he did not have proper documentation, the young adult is extremely concerned. Without hesitation, Rivera quickly interrupts the interview to call a local government official at the Bronx Borough Office with whom he has a personal connection. He is unable to get hold of the official but speaks with someone else from the office on the phone—"The kids don't have a driver's license since they don't drive, a passport because they have never traveled outside of the country, or a Social Security card, but have their birth certificate. . . . Why is it so difficult to get a marriage license?" Rivera continues, "If I have Victor Robles call and vouch for them, is that sufficient?" Not getting anywhere with the individual on the other line, he proclaims, "You dehumanize our people."[116]

As the incident above demonstrates, Rivera's leadership style at LPAC is to "drop things that appear urgent and important" administratively to focus on the more serious problems and address the many "crises" at hand.[117] Rivera could be characterized as a charismatic leader, one who privileges the movement of the spirit over the burden of depersonalized administrative matters. In the Latino community, there is an "expectation of charismatic leadership . . . especially on the spiritual level." Rivera is known to possess an incredible heart and is extremely loyal to his friends. However, this "takes away from running the business," claims Richard Rivera, consultant to LPAC, because the "culture of structured leadership [is] not there."[118]

According to Henry Nixon, Education Coordinator at the organization, LPAC leadership and staff have both "pride in their work" and a "passion for what they do." They believe in doing the "best [they] can with what [they] have." And yet, "everyone," including Rivera, is "in the midst of chaos."[119] LPAC can be quite a frenzied place. The organization, in Hagedorn's view, "has a lot of heart, energy, and will, but is not organized."[120] Francisco "Paco" Lugoviña of the Zen Peacemaker Community and president of New Line Inc. does not consider LPAC's disorganization a liability. He describes the organization as nothing more than a "living laboratory of the human condition, with all its ugliness and all its outrageous beauty."[121]

Whereas some describe Rivera as a "charismatic individual" who is "all over the place,"[122] others comment that he is "like a person with a flat tire who learned how to change it without stopping the car." Even given these characterizations, Rivera still is considered to be "crystal clear what his vision is."[123] Part of Rivera's success has been his connection to key political leaders in New York City and around the United States, thus manifesting the ability for an "inside outsider" from the South Bronx to engage in high-level community collaborations. Richard Rivera notes that some have criticized Reverend Rivera's involvement in the community as too political, arguing that he is divided by "competing interests." But most do not find fault with his political astuteness.[124]

Community Collaborations

As an "FBO link" to New York City government, LPAC has been an "example in how to build collaborations." This is new territory for FBOs, notes Rivera-León.[125] In contrast to LPAC, other neighborhood congregations have not had much exposure in working directly with politicians and other governmental offices in the city.[126] Proudly displayed in the reception area of the LPAC complex is a plaque bestowed on Rivera by former Bronx borough president and 2001 New York City mayoral candidate Fernando Ferrer. It is a "presentation of proclamation" and reads:

> Under the guidance of Dr. Ray Rivera, the LPAC has provided a place for our youth to experience the satisfaction of mastering new skills and excitement of healthy competition by providing recreational, cultural, social, and educational activities for the Borough's youth.

It is signed, "I, Fernando Ferrer, President of the Borough of the Bronx, do hereby proclaim Nov. 6, 1999, Latino Pastoral Action Day." Rivera has "sharp political acumen" and "understands the politics of the Bronx." Partnering with key political players like Ferrer of New York City, Rivera has "placed himself in the place of opportunity."[127]

Ferrer has a long history of collaborating with religious leaders in the Bronx. "Freddy has been there, marching with us, whenever we've needed him," asserts Rivera.[128] Led by Congressman Charles Rangel (D-Harlem), "the city's most powerful black politician," Rivera ranked among supporters of the pro-Ferrer movement for his 2001 and 2005 runs for New York City mayor.[129] With the help of Reverend Al Sharpton, Ferrer assembled an African American/Latino coalition for his 2001 campaign. Representing approximately 350,000 members of their congregations, Latino and African American pastoral leaders stood on the steps of City Hall in 2001, just one week after 80 Latino Pentecostal ministers from the Bronx endorsed Ferrer's Democratic contender Mark Green. Along with twenty-seven Latino evangelical leaders, in June 2001 Rivera publicly endorsed Ferrer as his choice for mayor of New York City. "While we are proud that [Ferrer] is a Latino, that's not the reason why we are endorsing him today," remarked Rivera. "We are here because he has transformed the Bronx."[130]

In December 2001, Ferrer established the Borough Chaplaincy Commission after Rivera proposed that the borough president's office "should have clergy to call on in times of crisis."[131] Noting his heavy reliance on "clergy to provide solace and to help keep the peace," especially after the September 11th attacks, Ferrer created an uncompensated position within the city agency on Grand Concourse near Yankee Stadium, appointing Rivera as its chairman.[132] Rivera has been viewed as an asset to the commission due to his ability to "transcend limitations that have kept faith groups in a particular corner." Because the issues are so similar within the urban church, he can "hang out with Lutherans and Pentecostals just as easily." Rivera has built relationships with leading African American pastors and political leaders like Reverend Wyatt T. Walker, pastor of Canaan Baptist Church of Christ in Harlem; Reverend Floyd Flake, pastor of the Allen A.M.E. Church in Jamaica, New York, and former U.S. Representative (D-NY) from 1987–1997; and Reverend Al Sharpton, contender for the U.S. presidency in 2004.[133] Throughout his position as borough president, Ferrer realized the need to "work with churches, because they were doing the job."[134]

As a member of the Bronx Clergy Task Force, LPAC regularly works alongside other ministers, priests, rabbis, imams, and the New York City Police Department in setting up foot patrols and community policing in the neighborhoods of the Bronx. Like Ferrer, New York City Police Commissioner Howard Safir acknowledged the need for congregations to be involved more in the community. "I think the clergy has a very good sense of what the community feels," Safir commented. "We should utilize that." Meeting with the NYPD in April 2000 to "improve trust between minority communities and the NYPD," the task force has had a history of sowing the seeds of peace in the streets of the Bronx, particularly after the fatal police shootings of unarmed minorities Amadou Diallo, Malcolm Ferguson, and Patrick Dorismond.[135]

The task force "was born of a politically charged moment" after four police officers—who fatally shot Diallo, a twenty-two-year-old West African immigrant, on February 4, 1999—were acquitted by an Albany jury one year later on February 25, 2000. Members of the clergy "literally put themselves between police and angry demonstrators" on the streets in protest of the verdict that February 2000 night. Rivera recalls that the demonstrators were shouting to the police that they were "murderers." The clergy, meanwhile, "asked the police to step back and they wouldn't." "Finally," Rivera remarks, "the crowd turned around at our advice." Part of a long tradition of faith-based community organizing, the actions of the Bronx Clergy Task Force reaffirmed, according to Karen Washington of the Northwest Bronx Clergy and Community Coalition, that "when things were going haywire, it was the church you looked to for healing."[136]

As noted above, Rivera firmly believes in the efforts of the indigenous religious community in providing new role models, status symbols, and folk heroes to its urban constituents in New York City. One is reminded here of the central role played by indigenous pastoral leadership during the civil rights movement. During that movement, black pastoral leaders collaborated with other discontented churches and community groups for the express purpose of social change. These leaders left behind a legacy of "organized nontraditional politics"[137] that has served as a blueprint for political engagement by Latino churches and FBOs in the inner city. Moreover, the development of a "revolutionary Christianity"[138] by proponents of the Social Gospel Movement as well as the understanding by the Salvation Army that the inner city was an "important mission field"[139] have also served to shape the kind of pastoral leadership Rivera provides in the South Bronx.

Rivera also has engaged in a host of multilevel collaborations with community actors of diverse faith traditions in the Bronx. For instance, Rivera has partnered with Francisco Lugoviña of the Zen Peacemaker Community to establish the first Peacemaker Village at LPAC (*La Aldea de Paz del Sur del Bronx*) in July 1997, shortly after Lugoviña's ordination as a Zen Peacemaker priest in Yonkers, NY. Founded in 1996 by Roshi Bernie Glassman and his wife sensei Jishu Holmes, the Zen Peacemaking Order is guided by three principles: (1) "plunging into the unknown," (2) "bearing witness to the pain and joy of the world," and (3) "a commitment to heal oneself and the world."[140] The creation of the LPAC Peacemaker Village was a direct response to Rivera's struggle to overcome the "dichotomy between the sacred and the secular and the personal and the structural, while responding both to those who want to save the soul and those who want to change the system."[141]

As a Zen Buddhist working in a Pentecostal setting, Lugoviña says that he has felt "nothing but acceptance"[142] at LPAC because his mission parallels that of the organization, namely, "to work with people whom I call 'wounded healers' and their organizations in the South Bronx" to "build sustainable neighborhoods with a sound, spiritual underpinning."[143] Like Rivera, Lugoviña admits that he is engaged in holistic ministry, albeit of a different spiritual kind. Lugoviña is currently chairman of the board for LPAC's charter elementary school, the Family Life Academy Charter School (FLACS), and continues to have a consultative relationship with the organization as president of New Line Inc. Located in the Bronx, the company advances what is known as the "Leonardo process" —named after Leonardo da Vinci—to help LPAC leadership understand the whole picture of their organization. Through numerous consultations, Lugoviña aids the organization in effecting change around the Four Principles of Holistic Ministry. The objective of New Line is to "bring out the imaginative part of someone to solve a particular problem." In the case of LPAC, this goal is achieved by asking a series of related questions to leadership and staff, such as, "What can we do to prevent violence in the neighborhood?"[144]

Rivera has been able to address the specific challenges of the Bronx through a host of collaborative partnerships with other Christian churches in the neighborhood. Reciprocal in nature, these partnerships involve not only the provision of technical assistance, but also "prayer and accountability." For instance, while LPAC offers neighborhood churches like the multicultural congregation Love Gospel Assembly technical assistance in grant writing, Love Gospel in turn provides LPAC with the "spiritual support in how to build a ministry." We are each other's "mirror image," notes Bishop Ronald Bailey, pastor of Love Gospel, "in the way in which our ministries help to balance each other. This creates a synergistic effect." For the "dynamic that is produced is greater than LPAC or Love Gospel by themselves."[145]

LPAC's strength in being a genuine grass-roots organization in the Bronx translates into the "desire to help other organizations" in need.[146] Neighborhood churches also turn to LPAC for technical assistance to understand the trends in local, state, and national government policy. LPAC is "very well connected politically, not in terms of favoritism, but in terms of what is going on in the political arena." Just as companies must be cognizant of changes in tax law, so also do congregations and FBOs need to be aware of changes in policy as well as of available funding streams for program development and organizational sustainability. Bailey, who admits that Love Gospel does not have the type of connections LPAC has, acknowledges that "we need the service of LPAC."[147]

Divine Purpose of Leadership

"*Hay una razón porque estoy aqui,*" shouts the pastor. A woman from the crowd yells out, "*Sí señor!*" "*Dios les da a iglesia los ministerios,* says the pastor. "*El ministerio es un proyecto divino.*"[148] The visiting pastor, Reverend Jose Satirio Do Santos from Colombia, proceeded to speak about the need for spiritual leadership, "*el líder necesita ser probado por el fuego,*" all the while realizing that "*el fuego quema.*" Do Santos questioned those present—approximately two hundred from the ministerial profession—"*cuántos quieren ser puro*" like "*el oro*" that is "*el único que resiste*" the flame?[149]

Do Santos' plenary session was part of a larger conference on April 4, 2002, for ministerial leaders entitled "*Llamados a Combatir el Terror,*"[150] hosted by Bay Ridge Christian Center in Brooklyn. The area of Brooklyn in which Bay Ridge is located, Southbrook, is home to the third oldest Puerto Rican community in New York City. Reverend Luciano Padilla, brother of Danny Padilla, LPAC's cultural coordinator, has been pastor of Bay Ridge since 1970 and member of LPAC's advisory board. Green ferns and flags from all North, Central, and South American countries decorate the front of Bay Ridge Christian Center, and the U.S. flag sits on the altar. The stage, in front of which Do Santos stands, is prepared for Sunday service with a set of bongos, percussion instruments, and other Latin American instruments. Male and female ushers, dressed in blue suits, white shirts and red ties, escort conference participants to their seats. With colorful banners carrying the passage from Matt. 28:19 in both English and Spanish: "go therefore and make disciples of all nations" and "*por tanto, id y haced discipulos a todas las naciones,*" Do Santos continued his exegesis on leadership in Bay Ridge Christian Center.

The pastor of a church is not simply its employee, remarked Do Santos. This is the view only of those that "*quieren democratizar la iglesia.*" But "*en el dirigir, hay puntos específicos.*"[151] Do Santos referred to the Book of Acts, chapter 18 and its compatibility with his theme for the day, "*El Dirigir.*" While St. Paul was in Corinth, the Lord spoke to him at night in the form of a vision. He said to Paul, "*No tengas miedo, sigue hablando y no calles, pues en esta ciudad me he reservado un pueblo numeroso. Yo estoy contigo y nadie podrá hacerte daño.*" St. Paul then settled in Corinth for a year and a half and "*siguió enseñando*" (Acts 18:9–11).[152] Drawing on this Bible passage, Do Santos proclaims that, as a pastor, "*Sí Ud. no va, nadie va. Si Ud. no dirige, no va a llegar a ningún punto.*" Like St. Paul, a pastor should "*sigue hablando y enseñando.*"[153]

As Do Santos proclaimed during his plenary session, the ministerial profession is a "*proyecto divino,*" or a divine project. As president and CEO of "the most successful Hispanic ministry" in New York City,[154] Rivera would agree that pastoral leadership is a divine project and has a divine purpose. He is quoted as saying, "When you have an unction, you have no choice."[155] The notion that leadership has a divine purpose stems first from Rivera's personal identity being rooted in Christ. As St. Paul proclaims, "You have stripped off the old self with its practices and have clothed yourselves with the new self, which is being renewed in knowledge according to the image of its creator" (Col. 3:9–10). Once transformed into the "new self," the pastor has a responsibility to live out that personal identity in a faith community. In Rivera's case, the divine purpose of leadership does not end at the level of the congregation. As displayed above, Rivera's leadership is also markedly public. He not only reaches out to thousands of neighborhood constituents through LPAC's ministry of personal outreach, but also personally engages in multilevel collaborations with diverse political, community, and religious actors throughout New York City.

While understanding the divine purpose of leadership to possess personal, communal, and public dimensions, Rivera still views "ministry as ministry" and only secondarily sees ministry as a business.[156] Such a view of ministry makes Rivera more attuned to integrating prayer and worship —such as that witnessed at the Sanctuary and Holy Hood—throughout the organization as opposed to strengthening LPAC's organizational capacity. Not only is LPAC "thinly staffed on top," thereby raising serious questions,[157] but the organization also lacks a strong board of directors with broad representation from the South Bronx community.

A central question will be how Rivera can better institutionalize the divine purpose of leadership at LPAC, taking into account the words the Lord proclaimed to St. Paul, as noted above: "Do not be afraid but speak and do not be silent; for I am with you, and no one will lay a hand on you to harm you, for there are many in this city who are my people" (Acts 18:9–10). Among others areas, this process of institutionalization would involve attracting more professional leadership to LPAC, building a more effective customer service delivery model, and engaging in serious discussions concerning succession planning at the organization. The cultivation of a new generation of leadership is especially important as Rivera becomes less involved in the day-to-day activities of the organization and more interested in advancing his model of ministry through preaching, teaching, and lecturing at universities and conferences.[158]

Conclusion

The objective of this chapter was to present the way in which LPAC operates as a ministry of personal outreach in the inner city of the South Bronx through specific attention to the day-to-day life and work of the organization. In contrast to a secular CBO, LPAC strives to deal with the whole person in its ministry.[159] Therefore, its "*misión [es] muy diferente y distinta que otros. Es única.*"[160] As Bailey suggests, "at the heart of the secular program is a set of rules, dictates, and series of steps to be taken," while "at the heart of the FBO is a person." "That person," notes Bailey, "is Jesus Christ and he is represented in each and every person that our person touches."[161] While most social-services agencies are about "bettering and helping," can each one claim that it is "helping the whole person?" asks Carmen Colón, acting director of community programs at LPAC. Many CBOs are "missing that support piece" and only provide service. At the organization, the idea is to provide activities like those offered through the Greater Heights Ministry and to "help people to transform their life" in other areas. This transformational dimension suggests that at the heart of LPAC's ministry of personal outreach lies building a relationship.[162]

Congressman José E. Serrano (D-NY) has characterized LPAC as an "oasis in a 'challenged' neighborhood." He states, "They have their faith. They have their services. But they don't turn you away if you're not of their belief."[163] For some, the term "faith-based" diminishes the type of work in which LPAC is involved for the community. Reyes notes, "I don't know if we as churches see ourselves as 'faith-based' but as a "Christian ministry." Thomas Reardon, director of finance and administration at LPAC, concurs with the use of the term "ministry."[164] "Ministry is a lot of things," he notes. "It is more than a job."[165] Regardless of being called an FBO or a Christian ministry, it is clear that anyone and everyone is welcome at LPAC. Through its ministry of personal outreach, the organization is "a celebration of life," says Colón. It is here that "people are into people."[166]

5

Nueva Esperanza
A Ministry of Institutional Development

[Nueva's mission] is to develop indigenous institutions in a
community that makes our people self-sufficient, powerful, and
confident within a Christian environment. The faith component of
that vision is very powerful. . . . Nueva wants to create and build.
Its frame of mind is fun and creative. It is not about victimization.

—Juan Torres[1]

Nueva Esperanza began in 1987 with a $60,000 one-year grant.
Twenty years later, Nueva is a force to be reckoned with, not only in the
Latino corridor of North Philadelphia, but also throughout the United
States. With $14.5 million in assets and an annual operating budget of
$18 million, Nueva receives 60 percent of its funding from public sources
and 40 percent from private sources. The strength of the organization is
most visible through the advocacy and capacity-building initiatives of its
subsidiary, Esperanza USA. A national network with more than 10,000
community- and faith-based organizations member institutions,[2] Esperanza USA's most recent involvement in advocacy was the May 31, 2007,
conference call it organized with U.S. Commerce Secretary Carlos M.
Gutiérrez on comprehensive immigration reform. Because of its national
name recognition, the organization continually faces pressure to "make
little Nuevas all over the United States," states Reverend Danny Cortés
(D. Cortés), Reverend Luis Cortés' brother and senior vice president of
Nueva. Realizing that it is not good business "to be everywhere," Nueva
has come to terms with keeping Philadelphia the base of operations for its
ministry of institutional development.[3]

Nueva prides itself on being an organization whose chief aim is to build
community assets through the creation of Latino-owned and -operated

institutions in North Philadelphia. As Juan Torres' quote above states, the organization wants to both "create and build." Through Nueva's ministry of institutional development, states Reverend Luis Cortés, executive director of the organization, "*No solo estamos trabajando por la mancomunidad sino también por el bien común.*" He continues, "*Mejorar el vecindario es un trabajo colectivo, no es sólo un centro de empleos, o una escuela superior o un junior college, tenemos ya todos esos y seguimos construyendo instituciones que le sirvan a la comunidad, además de buscar vías para entrelazarlas.*"[4] Torres, a member of Nueva's board, acknowledges that "the faith component" of Nueva's ministry "is very powerful." The most important aspect of this component is the belief that "a person of great faith can overcome great obstacles."[5] It is Cortés' belief in the transformative power of the Christian message that lies at the heart of the organization's emphasis on institution building. Cortés states that "we start with faith and create institutions around which others can build."[6]

This chapter will explore some of Nueva's national initiatives, spearheaded by the Esperanza USA network. However, because the research contained in this study took place prior to the national direction undertaken by the organization, the chapter will devote more attention to Nueva's ministry of institutional development at the community level, i.e., within the Latino neighborhoods of North Philadelphia. Divided into five sections, the objective of this chapter is to examine Nueva's ministry in light of the following thematic areas: (1) playing the political game, (2) a voice for evangelicals, (3) the business of ministry, (4) competition and coalition building, and (5) educating a community.

Playing the Political Game

"For some people, Jesus' admonition to care for the least of these is an admirable moral teaching. For many Hispanic Americans, it's a way of life," commented President George W. Bush at the first National Hispanic Prayer Breakfast on May 16, 2002. Nueva and Alianza de Ministerios Evangélicos Nacionales (AMEN), an interdenominational association of religious and lay evangelical leaders from Canada, the United States, Puerto Rico, and Mexico, jointly hosted the event in Washington, D.C., bringing together a crowd of seven hundred Latino religious leaders, mostly Protestant, from the United States. After commending the works of those leaders advancing the faith-based effort in their own communities, President Bush noted,

"We . . . know that faith is an incredibly important source of goodness in our country. Throughout our history, Americans of faith have always turned to prayer—for wisdom, prayer for resolve, prayers for compassion and strength, prayers for commitment to justice and for a spirit of forgiveness."[7] Among other speakers at this bilingual event were Mel Martínez, a Cuban American and then secretary of the U.S. Department of Housing and Urban Development. "This breakfast is an opportunity to highlight the bond between faith and government that has stood at America's core since America's earliest days," stated Martínez. Former Congressman J. C. Watts (R-OK), Senator Joseph Lieberman (I-CT), and former Senator Rick Santorum (R-PA), all active forces in faith-based legislative efforts, also spoke at the breakfast.

An ordained Baptist minister and executive director of Nueva, Cortés was lead host of the breakfast. Acknowledging that the breakfast was an historical event, he remarked that "never before has a sitting president led a prayer breakfast with and for Latino people."[8] In his opening remarks at the breakfast, President Bush spoke enthusiastically of Cortés. "One of the things that struck me was, he is a—he'll say sergeant, I'll say general—in the army of compassion in Philadelphia,"[9] to which Cortés retorted, "I would be remiss if I didn't take this opportunity to say your soldiers are ready for war, but we need resources."[10]

As its involvement in the National Hispanic Prayer Breakfast demonstrates, Nueva has understood well the importance of working alongside government to effect change in the ravaged inner cities of the United States. Viewing government as an "extension of the people" and not as a "quasi nonprofit,"[11] the organization has cultivated impressive partnerships with and received numerous grants from federal, state, and local agencies. As mentioned above, Nueva receives 60 percent of funding from public sources, compared with 40 percent from private organizations.[12] Harold Dean Trulear, former director of church collaboration initiatives at Public/Private Ventures, contends that partnering with government to improve the material conditions of community life has biblical roots. He relates the story of how Nehemiah rebuilt the walls of Jerusalem with a government grant from King Artaxerxes.[13] After receiving the grant, Nehemiah sought help from those around him. To the priests, magistrates, and noblemen, he proclaimed, "You see the trouble we are in, how Jerusalem lies in ruins with its gates burned. Come let us rebuild the wall of Jerusalem, so that we may no longer suffer disgrace." He explained to those present "that the hand of my God had been gracious upon me, and also the words that the king had spoken to me." They replied in turn, " 'Let us start building!' " and "committed themselves to the common good" (Neh. 2:17–18).

Whereas Nueva's motivation to engage in urban community development stems from its fervent belief—like that of Nehemiah—that "the hand of my God has been gracious upon me," the organization avoids using overtly sectarian language in its public pronouncements. As noted in chapter one, Rhys Williams explains that the knowledge and use of sacred words is limited to specific religious groups. This is why organizations like Nueva favor the nonreligious response, "Let us start building!" to appeal to a wide variety of public and private actors. Williams contends that once religious language becomes public, it can no longer remain sectarian.[14] In Nueva's case, religious language—once public—should no longer be characterized as sectarian or partisan.

A Nonpartisan Strategy

Nueva has played the political game in a nonpartisan fashion, inviting nationally recognized political personalities from the Democratic and Republican parties alike, such as Senator Hillary Clinton (D-NY), Senator Harry Reid (D-NV), Senator John McCain (R-AZ), Senator Ted Kennedy (D-MA), and former Attorney General Alberto Gonzales, as well as international political figures such as the First Lady of Panama, Vivian Fernández de Torrijos, and the Minister of Tourism for Israel, Avraham Hirschson, to speak at the last five Hispanic Prayer Breakfasts in Washington, D.C. Cortés' strategy at Nueva is simple. When asked where his political affiliations lie, he replied, "I'm not red, and I'm not blue. I'm brown." Cortés continues, "This is what I tell politicians: You want an endorsement? Give us a check, and you can take a picture of us accepting it. Because then you've done something for brown."[15] This strategy has proven to be very successful, given the number of local, state, and national figures from both parties to visit the organization's Hunting Park offices to meet with Nueva leadership on a number of issues pertaining to the Latino community.

During the 2000 presidential campaign, Tom Ridge, then governor of Pennsylvania, brought George W. Bush to the organization for a visit. Ridge referred to this meeting during his nomination speech for Bush at the 2000 Republican National Convention. He stated, "I wish you could have been there when we met with Latino leaders at Nueva Esperanza, here in Philadelphia. There were no reporters in the room. And—I suspect

—very few Republicans!"[16] While Cortés has made numerous appearances with prominent Republicans, such as at Santorum's March 2005 press conference on the Senate Republican Poverty Alleviation Agenda,[17] the political alliances Cortés forges do not break down evenly along partisan lines. In addition to being nominated by Governor Ed Rendell (D-PA) to the Pennsylvania Minority Business Development Authority and to Philadelphia's City Workforce Investment Board by Democratic Mayor John Street,[18] Cortés was one of many Protestant ministers present at President Bill Clinton's atonement speech in 1998. Furthermore, he has criticized openly the policies of the Bush administration, from the nomination of Harriet Miers to the Supreme Court in October 2005[19] to the administration's lack of political will in "ending the atrocities" in Darfur.[20]

Although Bush did not receive Cortés' vote in 2000—his vote went to Ralph Nader[21]—Cortés has been the central Latino religious figure in President Bush's Office of Faith-Based and Community Initiatives (OFBCI), unveiled by the administration in February 2001.[22] The Latino FBO leader testified in June 2001 before the Subcommittee on Human Resources and Select Revenue Means of the House Committee Ways and Means in favor of H.R. 7, the Community Solutions Act of 2001.[23] With forty-four sponsors, H.R. 7 was drafted principally by Congressman Watts. This act, passed by the House of Representatives on July 19, 2001, aimed to "increase charitable giving, to create asset-building financial structures for the working poor, and to form new partnerships between the government and community and faith-based organizations in helping the poor."[24] Furthermore, Cortés promoted the Charity Aid, Recovery, and Empowerment Act of 2002, the CARE Act (S. 1924), sponsored by Senators Lieberman and Santorum, by posting a "CARE Action Alert" notice on the Nueva website to encourage clients and other community residents around the country to write letters to their respective senators to vote in favor of its passage. In addition to leveraging public and private funding for nonprofits, this bill sought to provide technical assistance to small community organizations to qualify for federal assistance. Although the bill was passed by the Senate Finance Committee on July 18, 2002, it faced legislative gridlock on the Senate floor and was not enacted.[25]

More recently, Cortés has been a prominent figure in the discussions surrounding comprehensive immigration reform. Testifying on July 5, 2006, before the Senate Judiciary Committee at a field hearing in Philadelphia, Cortés remarked that "Immigration is the No. 1 issue of concern in our communities. For us, immigration is about family values, about work and living productive lives as contributing members of our communities."[26] Cortés' testimony was in large part a response to the uncompromising language contained in the Border Protection, Anti-terrorism, and Illegal Immigration Control Act of 2005 (H.R. 4437), sponsored by Congressman James Sensenbrenner (R-WI). In particular, Section 202 of the bill assigns a criminal penalty for anyone who "assists, encourages, directs, or induces a[n] [undocumented] person to reside in or remain in the United States."[27] Cortés stated that such a provision amounted to the criminalization of all Hispanic clergy and non-Hispanic clergy aiding the undocumented. He noted that "all clergy must remain free to provide spiritual counsel and to follow their Old Testament or New Testament commandment to feed, clothe, or visit the stranger."[28]

In his public testimony on comprehensive immigration reform, Cortés spoke of the need for pastors to follow freely their biblical mandates; however, he did not point to specific passages from the text. Rather, the bulk of his testimony was directed to the everyday concern of immigration in the Latino community. Only at an August 2006 forum with Hispanic pastors from New Jersey did Cortés engage in the use of a more overt "religious language." During this forum, he made reference to the Book of Leviticus, where it states, "When an alien resides with you in your land, you shall not oppress the alien. The alien who resides with you shall be to you as the citizen among you" (Lev. 19:34).[29]

Shortly after the passage of H.R. 4437 in the House of Representatives in December 2005, Cortés, along with a delegation of fifty other Hispanic faith leaders from across the United States, traveled to Washington, D.C., in March 2006 to convince the Republican National Committee, the Democratic National Committee, and the White House to move quickly on comprehensive immigration reform legislation.[30] Further, in response to a bipartisan comprehensive immigration bill, the Secure Borders, Economic Opportunity and Immigration Reform Act of 2007 (S. 1348), proposed by Senators Kennedy and John Kyl (R-AZ), Cortés convened a conference call—open to the public—with Secretary of Commerce Gutiérrez on May 31, 2007. The central purpose of this call was to educate the Esperanza USA network about the central provisions of the bill through a question-and-answer session with Gutiérrez. During the call, Gutiérrez noted that "like all compromises," the bill is imperfect; however, he emphasized that what is "required today at this historic moment is the leadership to stand up and say . . . this is what we need to do" to bring 12 million undocumented people "out of the shadows." Cortés ended the call, urging everyone to contact their senators in support of the bill and pledging that Esperanza USA would "help our people through the registration process" once the bill is passed.[31]

As his national political involvement demonstrates, Cortés is a "high profile, credible individual" whose views do not swing visibly in the Democratic or Republican direction. Making his decision at the voting booth public, Cortés supported Nader in 2000 and Bush in 2004 for president. Because he does not consider himself to be a separate entity from Nueva, however, Cortés neither endorses political candidates—as in the case of Reverend Raymond Rivera of LPAC—nor financially contributes to political campaigns. When asked why he voted for Bush in 2004, Cortés responded, "I voted my self-interest. For brown, it means that we'll be able to grow our institutions."[32] Those in government circles do not view such a nonpartisan posture as a liability, but rather as an asset. Nueva has proven itself to be a "force to be reckoned with," states Fritz Bittenbender, former secretary of administration for the Pennsylvania state government. Regardless of where one sits on the political spectrum, "no government, no mayor can go in and ignore Nueva."[33]

The Political Significance of Theological Work

As a Latino FBO committed to a ministry of institutional development, Nueva has understood the drawbacks of a Christian theology stripped of any social and political impulse. Building on the legacy of Latin American liberation theology and the civil rights movement, the organization recognizes the political significance of all theological work. Like liberation theologian Jürgen Moltmann, Nueva shies away from the advancement of a privatized faith, stripped of any larger connection to the urban context in which the organization finds itself. Cortés understands that the Latino community struggles simultaneously with both material and spiritual needs. As Nueva's ministry of institutional development suggests, the resolution of one's spiritual needs always presupposes first the solution to a material condition of extreme want. "*La persona que tiene hambre, tiene hambre y punto,*" asserts Cortés. If a starving individual were to pray to God, the prayer would not be "*Señor, como puedo servir,*" but "*Señor, como puedo sobrevivir!*"[34]

Even the kind of popular religion witnessed at Sunday services in those local Philadelphia churches affiliated with Hispanic Clergy carries not merely a personal message, but one that is communal and public. Cortés

—along with six other pastors from the neighborhood of North Philadelphia—formed Hispanic Clergy in the early 1980s, only a few years before the incorporation of Nueva as a nonprofit organization in 1987. To this day, the objective of Hispanic Clergy remains "taking on work that the local church does not," through involvement in social, political, and economic issues affecting the Latino community, such as HIV/AIDS, marriage education, immigration, and youth violence.[35]

At a Sunday service in September 2002 at the Primera Iglesia Bautista Hispana Church—the original site of Hispanic Clergy—Reverend Richard Gúzman proclaimed he was tired of considering religion as mere form. Religion is not about the form, "but it's about a relationship," he shouted. Primera Iglesia Bautista Hispana—one of only three churches ministering to Latinos and the only Latino Protestant community during the early period of Puerto Rican immigration[36]—is a stone church nestled in a residential street of rowhouses at the corner of York and Hancock streets in North Philadelphia. Across the street, a group of Puerto Rican men are eating lunch and playing cards in what appears to be an unpaved outdoor camp area surrounded by chicken wire and a collection of antiquated vans.

Between musical ensembles with tambourines, castanets, and bongos, Gúzman, wearing a black and white Hawaiian shirt, speaks of the difference between a *"teólogo"* and a *"casador."* A teólogo, *"solamente se fue a educar"* and likes to observe events that occurred in the past. A casador, on the other hand, *"busca por senales."* He sees tiger steps and "has the ability to know how much the tiger weighs and whether the animal is male or female." The casador, however, *"no hace su encampamiento aquí"* among the footprints. Rather, *"sigue las huellas a encontrar al tigre."* And, turning to the congregation, Gúzman exclaims, so must each one of us as a people of faith be a *"casador de la presencia de Dios,"* or a "hunter of God's presence."[37]

Gúzman's distinction between a "theologian" and "hunter" is fitting when discussing the political dimension of Nueva's ministry of institutional development. Viewing the organization as a center of spiritual and social survival along the lines of Orlando Costas, Nueva staff and leadership are ever finding innovative ways to "hunt for God's presence" in the urban context of North Philadelphia. In forming partnerships with a host of public figures at the local, state, and national levels, the organization creates varied opportunities to encounter God's presence in the inner city by "making incarnate" the second greatest commandment handed down by Jesus Christ, i.e., "You shall love your neighbor as yourself" (Mark 12:31).[38]

On Lehigh Avenue, near the corner of Sixth Street—just blocks from the Primera Iglesia Bautista Hispana Church—a rowhouse is draped with a gigantic American flag. The side of the house bears the message "*Sin vergüenza para Cristo,*" or "Without Shame for Christ," in vibrant colors with a large cross in the center. Similarly, Nueva has, without shame, proclaimed itself influenced by the message of Jesus Christ. Taking this message to heart, the organization aims to practice actively what it preaches. As the opening quote to this chapter reads, Nueva's ministry of institutional development entails the creation of "indigenous institutions in a community that makes our people self-sufficient, powerful, and confident within a Christian environment." The organization takes its ministry seriously, as evidenced in the nonpartisan way it plays the political game. From the Latin American liberation theology and civil rights movements, Nueva has received a tactical model on which to base its ministry of institutional development, i.e., a ministry that prizes the political significance of all theological work. Concerned with liberating neighborhood residents from poverty, Nueva's ministry reflects the "activist outward journey" of Costas' Misión Integral movement.[39]

A Voice for Latino Evangelicals

In January 2005, *Time* ranked Cortés as one of the "25 Most Influential Evangelicals" in the United States. Among other evangelical powerhouses, such as Reverends Rick Warren, Charles Colson, and Jay Sekulow, Cortés was the only Latino evangelical pastor to make the list. Commenting in *Time* on the Latino community in the United States, Cortés remarked that "part of integrating is understanding power." "Our people have power," he noted, "but they have never used it."[40] This lack of genuine power is particularly striking in the Latino faith community. In contrast to the black, Jewish, and Muslim communities, where the media typically approach the representative clergyperson, "in the Hispanic community, they always go to Hispanic politicians." As a result, the voice of the Latino faith community is rarely heard, Cortés argues, because "when you're not in the media, you don't exist."[41]

According to the 2007 survey *Changing Faiths: Latinos and the Transformation of American Religion*, co-sponsored by the Pew Forum on

Religion and Public Life and the Pew Hispanic Center, the great majority of Latinos—68 percent—self-identify as Roman Catholics, and 15 percent as evangelical Protestants.[42] The high demand for Protestant pastors in poor urban areas has resulted from the exodus of many Latinos from the Roman Catholic Church, leaving evangelical religious ministries like Hispanic Clergy and FBOs like Nueva to work together with the plethora of churches that mark North Philadelphia's interior. One such church with which Nueva is closely affiliated is Iglesia Sinai, A.D., "Asambleas de Dios" (Assemblies of God), one of two Pentecostal churches established in the neighborhood in the 1950s.[43] A member of Hispanic Clergy, Reverend Magaly Martínez is associate pastor of Iglesia Sinai and sits on the board of directors at Nueva.

Iglesia Sinai is a bright-blue church with a white Holy Spirit perched above. A former movie theater, this storefront church is located on Fifth Street between Cambria and Somerset in the Hunting Park section of the neighborhood. Down the street, a mural portraying a primeval jungle scene much like the Garden of Eden, with the caption, "*Lee la Biblia diaramente,*"[44] is painted on the side of a rowhouse. At the corner of Fourth and Cambria, a grouping of boots and sneakers dangles over electrical wires. Near this intersection, there is a red-brick, four-story abandoned rowhouse, while on the other side of the street sits a fenced-in area full of trash, miscellaneous items, and broken furniture.

It is March 31, 2002, Easter Sunday. Arriving at Iglesia Sinai after 1 P.M., the loud music and revelry from Raymond's Night Club next door is in stark contrast to the solemnity of this Christian holiday. Reverend Sergio Martínez (S. Martínez), husband of Magaly Martínez and pastor of this Assembly of God church, speaks to a congregation of approximately one hundred fifty people while Caribbean music plays lightly in the background. An escort walks through the church to ask if anyone needs an ear device that translates the service into English. S. Martínez, resembling a young Harry Belafonte, served in his earlier days as youth minister with his wife in this very church. Behind S. Martínez is a depiction of Calvary. Three wooden crosses are placed in front against a blue sky with white clouds that look like fluffy cotton balls hovering over brown rolling hills. The middle cross, depicting the cross on which Jesus Christ was crucified, is draped with a purple cloth and a crown of thorns.

S. Martínez's sermon emphasizes the necessity of forming relationships. Of utmost importance is the need to develop a personal relationship with Jesus Christ. S. Martínez emotionally shouts, "*Dános tu poder,*" "*Muévete en nuestro lugar."* He then extends an invitation to anyone who *"quiere una relación personal con Jesucristo."* He invites the congregation, *"Vengan esta tarde y formar este pacto con el Señor."*[45] People behind assent, saying in whispered voices, *"Santo Señor, Santo Señor."*[46] S. Martínez continues, *"Siga pasando. Alleluia."* He turns to the congregation, *"Ud. ha venido con alguna necesidad. Se ha sentido congelado."*[47] Then, he switches to English. "You have been frozen in your walk. Come to the altar and the Lord will unfreeze you." People begin streaming up to the altar, kneeling in front of the crosses of Calvary, with their backs to the congregation. Some are crying. There are nine people in total. Others come up to pray over them. An older Latino man with a gray silk suit tries to slay someone in the spirit, but the woman resists falling over. A song plays in the background, *"Jesús es el Señor."* Upon exiting the church, one notes the posting of Psalm 23 on the church's wall: *"El Señor es mi pastor; nada me faltará. . . . Aunque ande en valle de sombra de muerte, No temeré mal alguno; porque tú estarás conmigo: Tu vara y tu cayado me infundirán aliento"* (Ps. 23:1, 4).[48]

Local churches affiliated with Hispanic Clergy, such as Iglesia Sinai, provide a voice for Latino evangelicals in the inner city of Philadelphia. While emphasizing the need to develop a personal relationship with Christ—as S. Martínez does in his sermon—they also promote what Reverend Rivera calls a "holistic evangelism," an evangelism of the gospel of Jesus Christ that "meets the needs of the body as well as the soul."[49] Given the new wave of Dominican, Colombian, Venezuelan, and Mexican immigration to the neighborhood, Reverend Magaly Martínez understands that local churches are challenged to meet newer needs of the body, ones that transcend the common themes of employment, affordable housing, and education for Puerto Ricans living in North Philadelphia. She comments that Latino evangelical and Pentecostal churches—once Puerto Rican strongholds—"are now touched" by the manifold problems that center on issues of citizenship. Undocumented people approach the pastors, worried about the fact that "I don't have legal status."[50]

The Church as Natural Phenomenon

Latinos, immigrants and nonimmigrants alike are connected to their local congregations, continually turning to them "as their primary place of assistance." In many cases, Cortés asserts, the local congregation is the only Latino-owned and -operated institution in the inner city. "Our people turn to that institution because of their trust in it—trust that has been earned through decades of service."[51] From his experience with local congregants, Reverend Esdras Seda, pastor of Lindley Methodist Church and La Resurreción Congregation, comments that the Latino faith community of North Philadelphia is a "quiet community in a sense"—they are not pushy about their needs. This is problematic, especially considering Cortés' observation that this faith community does not utilize its power well. As a pastor and recent member of Hispanic Clergy, Seda continually finds himself reminding his congregants to stand up for their rights.[52]

The "core of the Latino community is the church," maintains R. Andrew Swinney, president of the Philadelphia Foundation, an organization that has collaborated with Nueva since 1998, awarding the organization funding for general operating expenses, program and service support, and technical assistance. Swinney adds that "Nueva Esperanza's identity as a faith-based organization is merely reflective of the fact that this community looks to the church for support. It is a natural phenomenon."[53] Historically the Latino community has trusted Christian churches, not just Roman Catholic ones.[54] This is reflected in the significant majority of Latino evangelical Protestants (85 percent) who say that religion is very important in their lives, versus 68 percent of Roman Catholics.[55] Nueva's identity as a Christian FBO therefore "makes sense," remarks Judith Bardes, manager of the Allen Hilles Fund, a foundation that awarded the organization three one-year grants for its youth summer camp, Camp Esperanza. Steeped in an evangelical Protestant identity, Nueva obtains the "access to and trust of the people" of North Philadelphia.[56]

Even given the importance of religion to evangelical Protestant Latinos, Cortés intends to keep Nueva's ministry of institutional development separate from the evangelism activities of Hispanic Clergy. Hispanic Clergy stands "outside of Nueva," states Cortés, "because we do mass evangelization" through the vehicle of local Philadelphia churches at places like Temple University. These gatherings are "the work of the local church" and should not be confused with Nueva's mission, i.e., the establishment of Hispanic-owned and -operated institutions that lead to the familial, economic, and spiritual development of our communities."[57] While Nueva employees feel comfortable expressing their particular faith persuasion, Cortés makes it clear to leadership and staff that "if they proselytize at Nueva, they will be fired."[58]

Although Nueva cannot proselytize by law, as an organization it responded spiritually to the tragic events of September 11, 2001. D. Cortés welcomed interested staff members to pray together during the terrorist attacks. The next day, Nueva held a religious service in which everyone was invited to participate. Tamara Díaz, administrative assistant to Senior Vice President D. Cortés, recounts that this service made employees feel confident that it "was OK to pray."[59] "This is who Nueva is," remarks Evelyn Pérez, Nueva office manager. People of faith feel very comfortable working at Nueva. Anita Ruiz, director of project development and implementation and assistant general counsel, declares that "Nueva is the first place I could work somewhere that I feel I can be who I am."[60]

Cortés is a Baptist minister who is not "afraid to share faith." He receives no salary from the American Baptist Churches USA (ABCUSA), but its national leadership recognizes his work for the community as "under the auspices of the church." As a person of faith, Cortés admits that he has a distinct "epistemological understanding of the world." He comments that, "Until I become an agnostic—if that day ever comes—I have an epistemological understanding that includes the role of God and life." In terms of the management of Nueva, he is "careful not to impose my epistemological understanding on others, but I would hope that they would see it in my actions."[61]

Evangelicalism and Its Public Side

As a minister affiliated with ABCUSA, Cortés belongs to a Christian faith tradition that historically tends toward theological and political conservatism. American Baptists typically "affirm the classic creeds of orthodox Christianity,"[62] such as the belief that the Bible is the "divinely inspired Word of God" and supreme authority, as well as the belief that eternity is "granted in grace to all who trust Jesus Christ as Savior and Lord."[63] Since the establishment of Nueva in 1987, Cortés admits that he "is not as radical as [he] used to be." But, he notes that "as you institutionalize, you de-radicalize."[64] Community leaders such as Roberto Santiago, executive director of the Council of Spanish Speaking Organizations Inc. (Concilio), the oldest Latino community organization in the Commonwealth of Pennsylvania, call Nueva's core group of Hispanic clergy an "ultra-conservative sector."[65] Roger Zepernick, executive director of Centro Pedro Claver (CPC), a CBO that serves the low-income neighborhood of Eastern North Philadelphia, remarks that "Cortés started conservative with radical clergy. Cortés hasn't changed, but the clergy have increasingly become more conservative." Many community leaders are displeased with the "conservative religious identity that the community has taken on," largely attributable to both Hispanic Clergy's and Nueva's involvement.[66]

Considering the local church as the "fundamental unit of mission" in congregational life,[67] American Baptists place strong emphasis on "individual religious freedom and local church autonomy."[68] Some community actors, however, perceive Nueva's independent streak as an obstacle to community building. Zepernick, a Lutheran minister, contends that the organization has not partnered well with nonevangelical Christian churches in the neighborhood, namely, mainline Protestant and Roman Catholic churches. "Some church groups have trouble dealing with them," he notes.[69] Public figures like Carlos Matos, office manager for Senator Tina Tartaglione and 19th Ward Leader, has seen only what they "do for themselves" versus "what they do for the community." The many Pentecostal and evangelical churches that constitute the impoverished neighborhood, according to Matos, do not empower Latinos. Rather, he finds that "each church is a clique."[70] Angel Ortiz, councilman at-large for the city of Philadelphia, fails to see Nueva as an FBO at all. Instead, Ortiz views the organization "less in terms of projecting a faith" and more as a "tool of economic development."[71]

While Nueva and Hispanic Clergy play key leadership roles in addressing the plight of the Latino poor living in urban North Philadelphia, community organizations and public figures also continue to be powerful and significant forces of neighborhood community building. The trouble with these diverse strands of leadership—as indicated in the passages above— is that they often do not integrate their missions to serve needy residents. Leadership is the main challenge facing the Latino community in North Philadelphia today, argues Maria Quiñones-Sánchez, former regional director for the Puerto Rico Federal Affairs Administration. According to Quiñones-Sánchez, leadership that both knows "how to do business" and can work together peacefully is missing from the neighborhood.[72]

To Nueva's credit, the organization has engaged in many ecumenical partnerships at the local, national, and international levels, thereby displaying the public face of evangelical Protestantism. These partnerships reflect the "social spirituality"[73] of the specific call of American Baptists as a "mission people" to "seek justice for all persons" through involvement in "educational, social, and health ministries."[74] Through these ecumenical collaborations, Cortés has institutionalized the message of Costas' Misión

Integral movement, placing direct emphasis on Costas' call "to take seriously the conflictive world . . . involving its culture, institutions, and structures."[75]

At the local level, Nueva participated in a *"Caminata por la paz,"* or "Walk for Peace," in North Philadelphia in September 1997. Co-sponsored by the Office for Human Relations of the Philadelphia Archdiocese and the Philadelphia Commission on Human Relations, the public rally brought together Catholics and Protestants calling for the end of violence in the Latino neighborhoods of Philadelphia. To a crowd of more than 1,500 in Hunting Park, Cardinal Anthony J. Bevilacqua announced that "the theme that has brought us together here: 'Paz, I can do that!' really says it all."[76] Cortés, representing Hispanic Clergy, spoke at the event, noting that "this is the first time we have consciously planned it and worked together to create something. It brought the whole community together." Also present at the rally were local politicians Angel Ortiz and Deputy Mayor Manuel Ortiz.[77]

More recently, the organization has engaged in a number of educational, social, and health initiatives on behalf of the Latino community at both the national and international levels. In November 2006, Cortés participated in the Second Global Summit on HIV/AIDS at Saddleback Church in Lake Forest, California, where Reverend Rick Warren, best-selling author of *The Purpose-Driven Life* (2003) is pastor. In a public statement, Cortés stated that "it is crucial that we involve the church in education and prevention efforts on HIV/AIDS both in this country and abroad, where more than 40 million people currently live with HIV." One month later, Cortés received the Red Ribbon Leadership Award for Communications from the National HIV/AIDS Partnership for Esperanza USA's innovative multimedia campaign, entitled *Tu eres la respuesta*, or "You are the Answer," to educate the Latino church about HIV/AIDS.[78] A central part of this campaign was the production of a song entitled *"Hay una respuesta"* by internationally recognized Latino musical artists José Luis Rodríguez, a.k.a. "El Puma," Ricardo Montaner, Marcos Witt, and María del Sol.[79]

In addition to ranking among other national evangelical leaders in the Evangelicals for Darfur campaign, Cortés has forged ties between the U.S. Latino community and Israel and between Israel and the evangelical Protestant faith community in the United States. In June 1995, Cortés and two other ministers associated with Hispanic Clergy, Dr. Neftali Ortiz and Reverend Sergio Martínez, visited Israel for a week to observe the progressive community development projects taking place in the country. Accompanied by Rabbi David Wortman and Eviatar Manor, Israel's consul general in Philadelphia, the objective was to gain insight on how to implement such projects in the Latino community of North Philadelphia.[80] Ten years later, under the auspices of Esperanza USA, Cortés led a delegation of Latino leaders to Jerusalem from March 30–April 5, 2005, so as to foster dialogue between the U.S. Latino church and the people of Israel. Cortés viewed the association between the two groups as appropriate, especially given that "as Protestant Christians, we believe that Israel is the Holy Land, that the Jewish People are the Chosen People." He added, "Our Lord our Savior is Jewish. It is important that there be peace, and that the people of Israel be supported."[81]

In May 2005, Cortés and a group of evangelical leaders, including Reverend Ted Haggard and Reverend Jay Sekulow—also included in *Time*'s list of the "25 Most Influential Evangelicals"—traveled to Israel at the invitation of Ariel Sharon, Israel's prime minister. After a series of meetings with Israel's Ministry of Tourism, the Israeli government donated thirty-five acres of land near the Sea of Galilee to this Christian delegation "in a move to foster tourism" by U.S. evangelical Protestants in the country. Haggard noted that, during the course of their visit, former Israeli Prime Minister Benjamin Netanyahu characterized evangelicals as "the best friends Israel has."[82]

These kinds of local, national, and international initiatives are examples of how Cortés desires the Latino evangelical church to adopt a more public face, through empowering the faith community to put into practice the kind of "social spirituality" of which ABCUSA speaks. Although Latino Protestant churches have not reached the level of national political involvement of African American churches, the efforts of Hispanic Clergy have done much to "raise issues of substance that inform the [local] community."[83] Ben Ramos, former Pennsylvania state representative in the 180th District (D-Philadelphia), views Hispanic Clergy as a "new generation of clergy" that must "assume the role as protectors and servants" of the Latino community.[84] Recognizing the impact of Hispanic Clergy in Philadelphia, D. Cortés finds that there is still a pressing need to create a "national voice for Latino evangelicals," a kind of Hispanic Clergy at the national level.[85] The creation of such an organization would serve to embolden Latino evangelical Protestant leadership nationally speaking, in hopes of reversing the media's general trend of treating these pastoral leaders with disregard or even indifference. Such an undertaking would, as Dr. King stated, help the church to "recapture its prophetic zeal,"[86] enabling the Latino faith community a seat at the national political table.

The Business of Ministry

Nueva "know[s] how to play . . . well" its faith identity, notes Maritza Robert, bureau director of community and student services for the Department of Education for the State of Pennsylvania. While accentuating its evangelical Protestant identity in community presentations, the organization tends to downplay being an FBO in grant applications, emphasizing instead its intended outcomes.[87] Always looking at the bottom line, the organization desires to be evaluated first and foremost as a CBO, with tangible measures of its impact on neighborhood revitalization. Thus, Nueva can be characterized best as having a "business approach to ministry."[88] In that all ministries have a "bottom-line reality," D. Cortés does not deem Nueva's approach to ministry inappropriate. It is the duty of all ministries, he states, to be "good stewards of God's resources." In each ministry, regardless of the public theology that informs it, "every budget has to be balanced."[89]

Nueva leadership understands that even if a qualitative difference exists between the mission of an FBO and a CBO, each type of organization is treated equally in the measurement of its project outcomes. "Inasmuch as [both organizations] are providing social services," comments Bittenbender, the perspective of federal and state grant makers is to "treat [all organizations] the same." All funders, whether public or private, ask two central questions: (1) Is the organization in question providing a service? and (2) How effective is such a service? These questions, or "contractual obligations," are identical for both the faith-based and secular provider.[90]

Effectiveness and efficiency are at the heart of Nueva's ministry of institutional development. "Growing up Puerto Rican in a black section of Harlem, [Cortés] developed what might be called a case of institutional envy"[91] with his African American counterparts. After noticing the rich institutional life of black community and religious groups in New York City, Cortés pledged to create Latino-owned and -operated institutions that would compete with their peers. His decision to base Nueva's ministry on the creation of institutional assets in the Latino community of Philadelphia stemmed from his desire to institutionalize the message of the Misión Integral movement, thereby highlighting the Christian's "activist outward journey." Through its development of institutions in poor, urban Latino neighborhoods, Nueva leadership agrees with Brown that human rights are, in fact, "social rights" and that these rights call for the eradication of "structural causes of injustice."[92]

Nueva "sees itself as creating a community within a community." By "creat[ing] an oasis" in the neighborhood through its ministry of institutional development, the organization strives to show Latinos that "this is the way"[93] to urban community empowerment. The word "empowerment" does not have an exact translation in Spanish. Although many have used the invented term "*empoderar*," the closest official word in the Spanish language is "*autorizar*."[94] In an interview with the Philadelphia Spanish-language newspaper, *Al Día*, Cortés described empowerment as "*tú capacidad para hacer possible lo que tú deseas*," or "the ability to implement your will."[95] Building community assets is an exercise of implementing one's will, teaching urban constituents to "be self-sufficient."[96]

Nowhere is this call for self-sufficiency more evident than in the oft-cited Confucian proverb, "Give a man a fish and he will eat for a day. Teach a man to fish and he will eat for a lifetime," which is repeated at Nueva like a mantra. Almost every Nueva staff member alluded to this phrase during interview sessions. Others even included additional lines to characterize fully Nueva's ministry. Tanya Byrd, program manager of job training at the organization, remarked, ". . . teach a man to fish responsibly, he will feed his generations to come." As program manager in the area of work enforcement, she notes that it is not enough to "just give a job, but to show how to get a job" because "children mock what parents do."[97] Anita Ruiz, on the other hand, retorted, ". . . teach a man to own the pond, so he can hire whomever he wants to fish!"[98]

Adorning the front waiting area at Nueva is a plaque entitled "Pride," from which these selected lines come:

Human rights rest on human dignity
Pride is like a heart, it is essential to being
No man is free who is not a master of himself
No bird soars too high if he soars with his own wings
Where there is no vision, our people perish
                                                        —Anonymous

As the plaque suggests, pride involves being self-sufficient, i.e., being a master of oneself. By teaching a man to fish responsibly or even own the pond, Nueva views pride not merely as an individual phenomenon but as a communal and even institutional enterprise. Through its ministry, the organization seeks to advance a kind of Latino pride, as noted in use of the phrase "our people." According to Edwin Aponte, this phrase often is used by "members of the Hispanic Protestant community as a primary reference to other Protestant Christian (*evangélico*) Hispanics."[99] Nueva, however, does not imply the use of this term in its ministry. Speaking more broadly, "our people" suggests a responsibility to and sharing of a common identity with the Latino community. This term is similar to James Cone's notion of a "Latino truth," which arises from the particular experience of an oppressed culture.

Practicing Cultural Competency

From the development of the Second Street Laundromat (*La Lavanderia del Pueblo*) to the building of local housing units and the establishment of the Career Link Center, Nueva's central objective has been to create institutional assets that are culturally appropriate for the Latino community. According to Jeremiah White, chairman of Monarch Consulting Group, Nueva "never loses sight of where the people are. It is rooted in the perceptions of the people."[100] Before Nueva's construction of the laundromat at Second and Huntingdon streets, community residents were asked to participate in a 1988 poll in which they were questioned about the priorities of development projects in the neighborhood. The results of the poll found the neighborhood laundromat to be of utmost importance, as 60 percent of these residents were single, head of household, and using laundromats nearly fifteen blocks away.[101] Although Nueva recently decided to sell the Second Street Laundromat, Cortés described its development as a first-rate example of institution building in the corridor of North Philadelphia. He remarked, "*Nuestro propósito es el de seguir creando proyectos económicos de esta indole donde la comunidad sea dueña de los mismos, y las ganancias se reinviertan en otros proyectos dentro de nuestro comunidad.*"[102]

As displayed in its construction of the Second Street Laundromat, Nueva understands the "Latino truth" of North Philadelphia. According to Leslie Benoliel, executive director of Philadelphia Development Partners (PDP), Nueva "may not be representative of all Latinos." However, she argues that the organization is "aware of Latinos' needs." In that PDP relies on community-serving organizations like Nueva "to give access to their constituency" through aiding the delivery of PDP programs to the Latino neighborhood, Benoliel's comment holds a great deal of weight. Providing technical assistance and grants to community-serving organizations in low-income areas, PDP identifies key Nueva staff and community residents who both understand Latino culture and can speak on behalf of the community at large.[103]

White comments that underlying Nueva's ministry of institutional development is the promotion of a kind of "cultural competency." An outgrowth of the business management concept "core competency," cultural competency involves more than simply an awareness of cultural diversity among social-service recipients. Core competency refers to "collective learning in the organization, especially how to coordinate diverse production skills and integrate multiple streams of technology."[104] Cultural competency, on the other hand, extends this notion of collective learning, by emphasizing not only the "respect for and understanding of" the "histories, traditions, beliefs, and value systems" of diverse cultural groups, but also whether the "specific practices, standards, policies, and attitudes" of social-service providers are actually culturally appropriate, culturally accessible, and culturally acceptable.[105]

Like the neighborhood laundromat, Nueva has engaged in culturally competent practices in the area of housing development. In conjunction with the Institute for Latino Studies (ILS) at the University of Notre Dame, Esperanza USA published a report in June 2005 on the state of Latino housing, entitled *A Roof Over Our Heads*. The study began with documentation of the dramatic growth in Latino "owner-occupied households" between 1990 and 2003, accounting for one-fifth of the total growth in the U.S. homeownership segment. However, this statistic was accompanied by less encouraging data concerning the percentage of homeowners among U.S. Latinos. Whereas approximately 76 percent of non-Hispanic whites report owning their homes in 2003, only 47 percent of Latinos identify themselves as homeowners. Additionally, because a large number of Latinos are urban dwellers, the percentage of income spent on housing by this group, 26 percent, is greater than their non-Hispanic-white counterparts, 19 percent.[106]

More than a decade before the publication of the June 2005 report, Nueva began constructing property for homeownership after noting the poor housing stock of North Philadelphia. In a move to provide "culturally appropriate and culturally responsive"[107] housing development, in 1992 the organization started construction on Villa Esperanza I, a fourteen-unit, $1.6 million project, located at Mascher Street in South Kensington. Made of tan stucco and surrounded by a black metal fence, the housing units of Villa Esperanza I resemble the Spanish Colonial Revival–style architecture of Puerto Rico, with terra cotta–tiled roofs on each unit. Nueva's second and third rounds of homes, Villa Esperanza II and Villa Esperanza III, were constructed in 1997 and 2000, respectively. In response to community residents' desires, this housing stock also reflects a Spanish colonial theme. Admitting that cultural context plays an important part even in the area of housing development, Cortés stated that Nueva is "in close touch with residents before we build anything. It is their neighborhood."[108]

Bilingual assistance for ethnic minorities is an additional feature of a culturally competent social-service program.[109] One such Nueva program providing bilingual assistance for Latinos has been the Betances Job Training Program, which Nueva established in 1996. One of the first welfare-to-work job-training programs in the state of Pennsylvania, the name Betances refers to the Puerto Rican separatist and Creole elite Dr. Ramón Emeterio Betances, a political émigré forced to flee the island to escape harsh Spanish rule after leading an armed revolt against the Spanish forces in 1868.[110] Boasting a 60 percent job placement rate in 2002,[111] Betances is now one of three programs in Nueva's Work Enforcement Unit. Another recent program included in the unit is the Career Link Center. A partnership between Nueva and the Philadelphia Workforce Investment Board, the center assisted 580 clients—in Spanish and English—from its opening in April 2005 to November of that same year. Of those clients, approximately 74 percent were Latino and 26 percent African American.[112]

Cultural competency is considered by some researchers to be a "soft science" in that it lacks an "evidence-based scientific approach for application and utility" in social-service programs. Given Nueva's institutional approach to ministry, however, the inclusion of such a concept is fitting. The organization's business of ministry insists on taking a serious look at bottom-line realities. At the same time, through its attention to the "histories, traditions, beliefs, . . . value systems" and language of the Latino community, Nueva displays the degree to which it puts itself "on the same level" as its clients. Nueva strives to be "*par en par*" ("to know what is going on") in the community. In so doing, the organization is "connected to the community enough to know what is going on to make changes

according to their needs."[113] Through the delivery of its culturally responsive services, argues Byrd of Nueva, the organization allows others "to see
that we are 'the softer side.' There is no set of little eyes and big eyes."[114]

Faith-Based Entrepreneurship

Hanging on the wall in Byrd's office is a copy of *The Prayer of Jabez*. It
reads, "Jabez called on the God of Israel, saying, 'Oh that you would bless
me and enlarge my border, and your hand might be with me, and that you
would keep me from hurt and harm!' And God granted what he asked" (1
Chron. 4:10). Treated in the *New York Times* best-selling book *The Prayer
of Jabez* (2000) by Dr. Bruce Wilkinson, the name "Jabez" means "sorrow
maker." Byrd's visible display of the prayer reveals the degree to which she
feels comfortable showcasing her Christian faith as a program leader at
Nueva. Moreover, it demonstrates her regard for the prayer's contents, especially the firm belief that God would "bless me and enlarge my border."
These last words certainly are consistent with Nueva's business approach
to ministry.

Byrd's posting of this prayer reflects an additional feature of culturally
competent practices in the Latino community, i.e., attention to the religious commitments informing that population. In many ways, the recent
interest the field of public management has taken in fashioning a social-
service system that is culturally appropriate, culturally accessible, and culturally acceptable is an outgrowth of earlier research on political culture.
(Mention has been made in chapter one of the insights contained in such
research, particularly how "beliefs, expressive symbols, and values" shape
the context of political action.)[115] Public management scholars interested
in culturally competent service delivery would extend these insights, understanding that these "beliefs," "symbols," and "values" might be religious
in nature. Religious commitments serve as a reference point, or a cultural
context, for how Latinos approach their lives and work. Taking these commitments seriously, Cortés has promoted faith-based entrepreneurship at
Nueva, putting into practice Jabez's call to "enlarge" the borders of the
Latino community.

Prominent community leaders like Helen Cunningham, executive director of the Samuel S. Fels Fund, have characterized the organization as
a "full-service savior" to its impoverished neighborhood.[116] Nueva's faith-
based status is a "tremendous benefit" in its ministry of institutional development, because Latino churches increasingly are "playing a major role

in the community"[117] of North Philadelphia. Due to Cortés' desire to increase Latino church capacity in the area of community development at the national level, Nueva leadership created the Hispanic Capacity Project (HCP), with funding of $7.2 million from the Compassion Capital Fund. Through training and technical assistance, the chief objective of HCP has been to expand Nueva's model of entrepreneurship to other Latino secular and religious nonprofits in the cities of Seattle, Los Angeles, Tucson, Orlando, Miami, New York City, and Boston.[118] Recognizing that "a small Hispanic group is not going to get the funding to meet the local need unless they partner with a larger organization," Cortés acknowledged the importance that Nueva act as an intermediary between these nonprofits. Mariana Popescu, one of HCP's evaluators, commented that the Spanish language and Latino culture the organization shared with its grantees proved especially helpful in Nueva's role as intermediary.[119]

Nueva considers itself entrepreneurial to the degree that its leadership represents the Latino constituency the organization serves. In this way, the organization can also be characterized as culturally competent in that "cultural diversity in the community is reflected in board membership"[120] at Nueva. Cortés boasts that he only has "neighborhood-based" people on his board "who know the reality" of North Philadelphia or who at one time were residents of the neighborhood, like Juan Torres, senior manager at SEPTA, and his cousin Judy Torres-Lynch, vice president of U.S. benefits at Glaxo Smith Kline.[121] Before a January 2002 board of directors meeting at Nueva headquarters, a traditional Puerto Rican–style dinner was served: pork chops, chicken, and breaded fish with rice and beans and salad. It was clear this gathering was a friendly and familiar environment. That night, five members of the organization's executive team were in attendance to present up-to-date information on their respective departments. Most of the board of directors there appeared to be of Puerto Rican descent, with the exception of Dr. Roberto Araujo, a Brazilian podiatrist.[122]

Torres-Lynch observes that all board members are committed to the fate of the Latino community. Of the nine members, only Torres-Lynch and Torres are business professionals. Three original members of Hispanic Clergy currently sit on the board, Reverend Raúl le Duc, Reverend Bonnie Camarda, and Reverend Magaly Martínez. Considerable representation from clergy on the board makes for "good infrastructure," asserts Torres.[123] While there is a high representation of Protestant pastors on the board, Cortés admits "all people on the board of directors have their own faith."[124] Torres and Torres-Lynch, for instance, are Roman Catholics. As business professionals, however, their board presence brings with it a secular point of view, focusing on the "political, social, and economic aspirations of our people to be an equal player in society."[125]

Essentially, Cortés considers Nueva to be a "staff-led company" along the lines of a Nasdaq corporation.[126] Like the culturally competent board he created, Cortés desires Nueva staff to reflect the "ethnic, religious, and linguistic composition of the community"[127] they serve. There is a good deal of staff loyalty at Nueva due to the organization's genuine belief in investing in human capital. Ongoing mandatory training is a critical part of building human capital at the organization. Furthermore, Nueva "empowers its staff to look at their internal maximum potential" by referring employees to participate in workshops and seminars that foster professional development. According to Evelyn Pérez, head of human resources, the organization has helped its staff complete college, invest in 401(k) programs, and even purchase a newly constructed Nueva home.[128]

Viewing its ministry as a business, Nueva is a model of faith-based entrepreneurship. According to local religious leader Reverend Seda, "the leadership at Nueva keeps moving. If they close the door here, they go around to see the side door. If the side door is not available, they find a way through the window. They have to be creative."[129] Similarly, Benoliel of PDP finds Nueva's entrepreneurial brand of leadership reflected best in how the organization "has been able to change with market needs and navigate in a changing environment while staying true to its mission."[130] Nueva is both progressive in that it "doesn't mind accepting challenges" and aggressive in "seeking out maximum opportunities for its programs."[131]

Much of the organization's aggressiveness is due to the entrepreneurial leadership of Cortés. It is clear that Cortés is a "one-man show" and "the force" behind the organization.[132] Although Cortés asserts that Nueva board members must have a "loyalty to the mission [of Nueva] and not to Luis Cortés," he has admitted that Nueva's "mission and Luis Cortés are sometimes one."[133] Many, however, find Cortés' leadership to be organizationally short-sighted, especially with regard to succession planning. In Torres' view, Cortés needs to foster an environment at Nueva under which new leadership can develop among his staff and on the board. If he ultimately desires Nueva to be a Latino-owned and -operated organization that stands the test of time, "Luis Cortés has to, in a sense, replicate himself."[134]

Competition and Coalition Building

Abandoned rowhouses, one with the inscription "Jesus Love-U" on its side, line the portion of Roosevelt Boulevard at Wyoming Avenue. At this busy intersection sits Iglesia Sion Assembly of God, a stone church, graced at its front with pink rose bushes while at the side of the road lie dozens of shredded rubber tires. On this June 2002 day, a full Latin band played on the stage while many in the congregation waved flags of both gold and red lamé. Nearly two hundred people sang along with the band to the words, "*El Señor está en este lugar . . . Para salvar, para librar . . . Para ganar, para librar mi alma.*"[135] An hour after singing spiritual songs, Reverend Le Duc, pastor of Iglesia Sion and Nueva board member, announced that the congregation would listen to the "word" from Hermana Mirta, a visiting preacher from Argentina. Switching between English and Spanish, Mirta prepared her commentary from a passage taken from the Second Book of Kings concerning a woman from Shunem who decided to visit the holy prophet Elisha after her only son died. The passage reads: "*Llegó al monte Carmelo, donde el hombre de Dios. Eliseo la vio de lejos y dijo a su muchacho: 'Ahí viene nuestra sunamita.' Así que corre a su encuentro y pregúntale: ¿Tú estás bien? ¿Tu marido está bien? ¿El niño está bien? Ella respondió: 'Bien'*" (2 Kings 4:25–26).[136] After telling Elisha about her son, he laid his hands on the dead child and "the flesh of the child became warm" (2 Kings 4:34).

Mirta preached on the amazing faith of the Shunemmite woman. Even after the death of her son, this woman was able to say, "It is all right." In speaking of her journey to the prophet Elisha, Mirta remarked that the woman "knew what to do because she had a spiritual vision. When God speaks, things start happening." Addressing the urban context of North Philadelphia, she commented that "*la gente ha resignado enfrente de tantas imposibilidades*" in the neighborhood. Even though, "*a veces . . . las puertas no se abran,*" stated Mirta, "the Lord has the last word, *la última palabra.*" In the middle of her sermon, she asked the congregation, "How is everything with you?" In unison, the congregation bellowed, "*Bien.*"[137]

In surveying the work that approximately three hundred community-based organizations perform in North Philadelphia, one could assume that saying "it is all right" concerning the urban condition becomes a simple task. This is not exactly the case, however. Given the sheer number of providers in the area, these organizations still "haven't been able to figure out how to work together." Perhaps Nueva's tendency to work alone is due to what Quiñones-Sánchez describes as the "life cycle of working in the community." She notes that organizations like Nueva have "been burned."[138] Regardless of the organization's status as an "independent operator," Le Duc remarks that Nueva has "been looked up to as a model" in the community. "All Hispanic leadership in the city comes" to Nueva, he states, to inquire about its successful ministry of institutional development. The paragraphs below will examine whether Nueva is in fact "the benchmark"[139] for other community organizations as Torres suggests[140] or whether the organization is understood more appropriately as a competitive corporation, building up its enterprise in the neighborhood without consultation with other community actors.

El Bochinche

To assess properly Nueva's actions in the Latino neighborhoods of North Philadelphia, one first needs to consider its urban context. Philadelphia is—as Araujo explains—"a city of groups."[141] Susan Hedden, Nueva's former director of development, echoes this view. Throughout her twenty years working in the nonprofit world, Hedden has found the city to be a "really political town." "It can be a minefield," she emphasizes.[142] Juan Torres refers to "*el bochinche*," a slang word used in Puerto Rico to describe the kind of institutional competition rife in Philadelphia. This word suggests all the various forms of "organizational jealousies and bickering"[143] that take place among a range of political, social, economic, and religious actors within a particular community or neighborhood.

For Nueva, however, a dose of healthy competition lies at the heart of all successful community economic development. Since the case of institutional envy he contracted in Harlem, Cortés has learned that "when you compete, you change society."[144] Understanding clearly that "those who do not own do not play," Nueva has aimed to "create institutions that compete with its peers." According to D. Cortés, institution building has long-term benefits. Not only do institutions "speak to permanence," but they also help build community assets that make, in turn, an "ongoing and lasting impact" on the neighborhood in question.[145]

Cortés has had direct experience with building community assets in Philadelphia. He was one of the founders of the United Bank of Philadelphia in 1992, the first African American commercial bank operating in the city, with deposits of $5 million. Through engagement in competitive market research, Cortés discovered that The Gallery, the largest shopping mall in downtown Philadelphia, experienced multiracial sales during the work week and registered the majority of its total sales—between 70 percent to 80 percent—by African Americans on the weekends. Ideally situated between the Pennsylvania Convention Center and Independence Hall, The Gallery is also the home to Philadelphia's second largest transit hub, where SEPTA trains from all regional rail lines make their stops. In response to these findings, Cortés suggested that United Bank open a branch two blocks from The Gallery and conduct its business even on Saturdays. Two months later, Mellon Bank opened on Saturdays for banking services. First Union Bank later extended its bank week to Saturday. Cortés sees all of this as an example of "how a $5 million bank changed billion-dollar banks."[146]

Additionally, Nueva was the first community development corporation (CDC) in North Philadelphia to develop new homes. In 2002, all CDCs in North Philadelphia were under contract to Nueva in some development capacity. These organizations understood the need to "partner with a CDC with a strong reputation" like Nueva, comments Maritza Ortiz-Santiago, housing director at Nueva. Organizations like Hunting Park CDC and Norris Square Civic Association commissioned Nueva for assistance in their housing development projects, from rehabilitation to new construction. Contracts such as these amounted to a kind of joint-venture partnership under which Nueva performed the actual development work and the other CDCs received the needed publicity. Publicity is crucial for these organizations, according to Ortiz-Santiago, as lending institutions are not likely to give loans to CDCs without a development track record.[147]

Nueva's firm belief in the net benefit of healthy competition is not shared equally by its community peers. According to Alfredo Calderón, executive director of Aspira in Philadelphia, the organization tends to "grab all the funding available" in the areas of housing, job placement and training, and for its charter school, Nueva Esperanza Academy (NEA). In its capitalistic style and without consulting Aspira, Nueva applied for a federal grant that Aspira had received for years, thereby "jeopardiz[ing] [Aspira] for its own greed." Such a move was not appreciated, states Calderón, especially because Aspira helped Nueva leverage resources when Aspira was under the leadership of Quiñones-Sánchez. In addition to helping Nueva obtain the building that currently houses NEA, Aspira had written support letters on behalf of Nueva for grant applications.[148] José Rivera, owner of La Fortaleza wellness centers, would not find these incidents to be uncharacteristic of an organization directed by Cortés. In stating, "*Lo que significa que el dinero que le entra a su institución va para su bolsillo, además, no paga impuestos*,"[149] Rivera regards Cortés as a distinct kind of capitalist, one who—as the head of a Latino FBO—has the privilege of not having to pay taxes.

Like Rivera, Councilman Ortiz argues that Nueva reflects more of a capitalist corporate structure as opposed to a church structure. Ortiz laments the "lack of interagency cooperation" that groups like Nueva have perpetuated in Philadelphia. The organization "jumped the gun before a Latino position emerged," he states. Nueva "has not joined with other organizations to bring about change or programmatic ideas. It is more or less self-insulated." Ortiz admits that city government has helped Nueva launch many community projects over the past years, specifically the Plaza Esperanza commercial district on Fifth Street from Rising Sun to Rockland, where a Rite Aid pharmacy now operates. Nueva, however, has opted for self-insulation over collaboration with other community organizations, attempting, first and foremost, to "be the inside person within the political spectrum."[150]

Claiming to be "political orphans of the city,"[151] Cortés argues that "Nueva doesn't get our fair share," at least not from the city of Philadelphia. Pointing to a grouping of pictures in his office—former U.S. Presidents Jimmy Carter, George H. W. Bush, and Bill Clinton and current President George W. Bush, former Senator Rick Santorum (R-PA) and former Governor Tom Ridge (R-PA)—Cortés clearly understands that the success of his organization revolves around "harnessing political leverage."[152] In addition to Councilman Ortiz, however, state political actors such as Maritza Robert of the Pennsylvania Department of Education, have also voiced their disappointment over the lack of collaboration between Nueva and other Latino community organizations. Robert claims that, instead of conceiving Nueva as a coalition builder, the organization is characterized best as a "*rancho parte*." or a "separate group."[153]

Creating Strategic Partnerships

Since 1962, Concilio, the oldest Latino organization in Pennsylvania, has sponsored the Puerto Rican Festival, with the objective of promoting unity among Latino residents and community groups in Philadelphia. The theme of Concilio's 2002 festival was "Latinos in Philadelphia—A Kaleidoscope of Cultures." This festival featured cultural arts, interdenominational religious services, picnics, job fairs, and a parade.[154] Set on the Ben Franklin Parkway, many young attendees placed their nation's flags on cars, strollers, and even backpacks in solidarity for the event. Amid children blowing whistles and a throng of vendors selling Puerto Rican salsa CDs, straw hats, and shirts with the inscription *"Boricuas con clase,"*[155] numerous floats passed by a crowd of approximately 10,000 people seated on stands around Logan Square. Floats were sponsored by Latinos in the Delaware Valley, Goya, Café Bustelo, the Society of Hispanic Engineers from Drexel University, and the Ursinus College Latino Organization, among others.[156]

As indicated by the theme of the festival, there is a need for Latino community organizations in North Philadelphia "to become more strategic"[157] by taking into account not only the kaleidoscope of cultures in their community, but also the diverse institutional cultures of the organizations themselves. According to Anita Ruiz of Nueva, one is able to divide community organization leaders into "token" and nontoken" Latinos. "Internally" at Nueva "we know who the tokens are versus the real thing," she claims. While it is a general rule that the Latino community "works on a base," there is much infighting. This infighting has lessened some due to the growing national interest in mobilizing the Latino vote. Community organizations now believe that power can be achieved by forming strategic partnerships with other groups as opposed to standing alone.[158]

In a move to build strategic partners among these North Philadelphia-based organizations, the Philadelphia regional office of the Puerto Rico Federal Affairs Administration sponsored a two-day outing in Hartford, Connecticut, to observe the city's state-run public education system, considered a model of successful reform in the United States. Hartford was the first school district in the United States to hand over the management of its educational system to a private, for-profit company. From 1994 until the termination of its contract by the Hartford school board in 1996, Education Alternatives Inc. assumed the role of managing the operations of the district's thirty-two schools.[159] Along with fifteen other community organization representatives, Cortés and Torres from Nueva met with government representatives and the superintendent of schools and also listened to unions and teachers from the Hartford school district tell of their experiences with the school reform process.[160]

Saturated in the history of takeover, we were "flabbergasted at their success," remarks Torres. Intended as an outing to encourage coalition building among these North Philadelphia groups, Nueva representatives viewed such an experience differently. Torres believed that the Hartford trip was "important to dispel negativity around a school takeover and solidify Nueva's position" as a leader in North Philadelphia's educational sector,[161] especially during a much contested debate over the direction of school privatization in Philadelphia. Torres considered the outing a way for Nueva to exert its competitive advantage in the realm of education. Other Philadelphia community groups, however, may not have had the same perspective, viewing Torres' statement as yet another instance of Nueva acting as a "*rancho parte*," or "separate group."

Educating a Community

Nueva's foray into the educational sector of North Philadelphia, however, was not an independent venture. In 1995, CEIBA—a coalition of Latino community-based organizations in Eastern North Philadelphia among whose founding partners is Nueva—initiated a survey of approximately two hundred North Philadelphia residents and businesses, asking respondents about current needs in the community. The research found that "education is an important factor in increasing the quality of life for residents. It is intertwined with employment and economic status." Further, CEIBA reported that while there are many educational programs in the neighborhood geared to elementary and middle school students, "the high school student is included almost as an afterthought."[162]

Two years later, the Cortés brothers applied to the Pennsylvania State Government for grant money to establish a public charter high school primarily for Latino students from the community, "with an emphasis on technology, arts literacy, and Spanish-language arts."[163] The response to this application was a large capital budget grant of $3 million from the Pennsylvania State Government to help Nueva buy and rehabilitate the 6.1-acre industrial complex that now houses Nueva Esperanza Academy Charter High School. Nueva's advocate during this process was Maritza Robert, then the director of the Latino Commission for the State of Pennsylvania. Located at 301 N. Hunting Park Avenue in North Philadelphia, NEA opened its doors in September 2000 with 190 freshmen.

Nueva also sought the assistance of the National Council of La Raza (NCLR) in an effort to ensure that NEA would become a "model academic program" in the community. With NCLR's help, Nueva organized a series of focus groups of high school students, parents, teachers and counselors in mid-April 1999 with specific questions about "the essential characteristics of a successful new high school." Among other responses, recommendations included the need for (1) bilingual/bicultural faculty, (2) computer training, (3) increased attention to the condition of facilities and heightened security at school, and (4) student and family support services. While not officially bilingual, NEA does provide a "bilingual program" to comply with federal guidelines "for educating language minority students."[164]

Nueva's decision to become a provider of educational services was based on strong evidence that the "public school has always let [Latino] kids down in North Philadelphia."[165] According to Angela González, former NEA principal, in 2002 the average NEA student read at the fifth-grade level, while many sixteen- and seventeen-year-olds had entered NEA without even knowing how to read. In response to this dire situation, NEA offered a Developmental English class for third-grade-level and below proficiency. González recognizes that the same children taking this class "were honors students in public school. They are not special education kids, but kids who were neglected."[166]

According to a 2000 report from the U.S. Department of Education, even those who do graduate from high school continue to operate at a critical disadvantage if they come from low-income neighborhoods such as North Philadelphia. Not only are these high school graduates less likely to enroll in a four-year college, but they also lack the skills necessary to succeed in business.[167] Therefore, in the same year that NEA opened its doors to the community as a public charter high school, Nueva officially launched the Nueva Esperanza Center for Higher Education (NECHE), a two-year junior college in partnership with Eastern University. After being accredited by the Middle States Association's Commission on Higher Education in 2005, NECHE officially changed its name to Esperanza College and became a branch of Eastern University, a Christian university of the arts and sciences located in St. Davids, Pennsylvania.

At Nueva's inception, its "two linchpins" were housing and development. As an outgrowth of its ministry of institutional development, Nueva moved into the education realm. In some respects, the movement to get involved in education for the community of North Philadelphia was an "unexpected" one.[168] It began with the question Cortés posed to Nueva's board of directors: "If we don't do it, who will do it for our kids?"[169] Juan Torres asserts that the board always had the same answer: "Nueva has to do it. We owe it to our kids. We owe it to our people."[170] Given the reality of failing educational institutions in the neighborhood, Nueva quickly realized that "educating a community"[171] would be a core feature of its ministry.

Desperate to Save Kids

NEA sits in a renovated industrial-like building, sharing space with a Doors Unlimited Showroom. Across the street from the school is a beverage outlet fenced in with wire, advertising a variety of soft drinks like Franks, RC, and Diet Rite as well as Twin Mountain Natural Spring Water. Upon entering the building, a notice, "*Prohibido El Paso*" (No Trespassing), and a sign stating that "*todo visitante al entrar favor de firmar su nombre en el escritorio de seguridad*" (all visitors must sign in and out at the security desk) greet the visitor. Inside the building, brightly colored artwork adorns the center hallway, announcing, "Welcome to NEA." Next to this is a sign, "Submit your love poems to From the Heart by February 8th for the Valentine issue." In the principal's waiting room, a pamphlet entitled "From the Heart" sits on the table. This pamphlet is the December 2001 issue of poetry selections by NEA students. Turning to a poem, "Prayer" by Jamal Bullock, the first few lines state,

> Lord, it's only the struggles and pain I feel
> All I see is evil
> People being killed
> The love I have for you almost got beaten down
> But now you're in my heart and I've never known love like this before
> I almost lost hope when you took my brother
> I had to live with Grandmom, no father or mother
> But I still don't understand the visions you give me
> I know and trust they are for the good
> So the family and me can up out of the hood.[172]

Bullock's poem speaks to the harsh reality of daily life for NEA students as residents of North Philadelphia: crime, violence, and feelings of abandonment. And yet, even with these difficult challenges, there is a marked display of hope at the school, reflected in the words of Angela González, former NEA principal, "We care. We will not settle for mediocrity. . . . We are desperate to save kids."[173]

González's office has a large window that looks out to the main hallway. In her "no-nonsense" style, she stops now and then to use her walkie-talkie to report unacceptable behavior taking place outside her office. This time, students are piggybacking each other in the front hallway. As the poem above attests, NEA does have its fair share of problems. González shared with me that just recently, a parent chased after a teacher with a bat over some altercation. Additionally, an NEA student pressed charges against another student for assaulting him. González often escorts students to Cortés' office at Nueva to resolve problems. In fact, on January 24, 2002, two NEA students and their families paid Cortés a visit after a quarrel between the students at school almost erupted into gunfire on the street.[174]

Nueva is NEA's parent entity, owner of the school facility and provider of administrative and business services to the school. The connection between NEA and Nueva goes even deeper—Nueva appoints the board of trustees of the charter school, selecting those who "possess a firm belief in the Academy's mission and a commitment to improving public education for Latino and other students."[175] NEA's mission statement reads:

The Nueva Esperanza Academy Public Charter High School is dedicated to providing a quality education that prepares critically thinking, socially capable, spiritually sensitive, and culturally aware young adults who can use English, Spanish, and technology for success in the 21st Century.[176]

Given the inclusion of the term "spiritually sensitive" in the NEA mission statement, one is apt to assume that the school is faith-based. However, this is not the case. González explains that NEA strives to provide a "spiritually sensitive" education by encouraging students to develop "lifelong character attributes" on a daily basis—for instance, in assigning students an adult mentor upon their acceptance to the school.[177]

In addition to the basic math, science and English-language arts classes, NEA requires that students complete one hundred hours of community service to graduate. Students have chosen religious organizations, hospitals, and other CBOs as their preferred service sites. NEA also provides a fine arts program funded through the Arts Literacy Program of NCLR. While this program encourages appreciation and cultivation of the arts, it is also "standards and literacy based."[178] In González's view, an arts literacy program of this kind "directly affects students' academic success" through the reinforcement of reading, writing, and critical-thinking skills.[179]

In January 2002, González pointed out some of the artwork from the arts literacy class displayed on students' lockers in the hallway. Each student was asked to sculpt and paint his or her self-portrait. Remarking that there are "a lot of anger management issues here" at NEA, González commented that viewing the self-portraits would help in understanding further the background of these select students. For example, in one self-portrait, stars and stripes of the American flag cover the face as two blue Twin Towers protrude from a head with no eyes. A medieval hood in black with red crosses accounts for the face of a second self-portrait that has no eyes, nose, or mouth. A third self-portrait presents the image of a girl with no face. In place of the eyes, nose, and mouth is a flowering red rose. A fourth self-portrait displays a green head with no hair. This figure has eyes and other features, but one cannot decipher them fully. Streaks of dripped paint are poured over the head in red, brown, and yellow. These four self-portraits help the onlooker come to terms with how NEA students tend to view themselves. Students may either lack awareness of their personal identity—as the absence of human faces painted on the self-portraits indicates—or they may make a conscious decision to hide such an identity from others' view for fear of vulnerability.

According to David W. Rossi, NEA's CEO, the school "has experienced success in the face of many obstacles," including those suggested "identity" and "anger management" issues the self-portraits above exhibit. Out of a total of seven hundred school districts in Pennsylvania, NEA ranks fourth highest in percentage of students (96 percent) living below the poverty line. Although only 16 percent of NEA's student body does not speak English as a primary language, the school has the third highest percentage of English as a Second Language learners in Philadelphia. Given these challenges, the school has also made some significant strides. The school has outperformed all district high schools in the Central East Region of Philadelphia in math, reading, writing, student attendance rate, graduation rate, and college acceptance rate. In 2006, 70 percent of the senior class graduated, and 95 percent of those graduating received college acceptances.[180]

NEA strives to provide its Latino student population with the educational tools necessary for personal and professional growth. The school boasts an extremely large Latino constituency—92 percent of the student population is Latino, with African Americans constituting the remaining 8 percent. It is Cortés' desire, through the vehicle of NEA, to "educate [these] kids to go to college and come back and improve the community." Whether at NEA or at Esperanza College, as the section below demonstrates, education serves the purpose of inviting Latino youth, young adults, and adults to take a "vested interest in the community"[181] so that they can include themselves among the Latino leaders of tomorrow.

A Hispanic-Serving Institution

In contrast to NEA, NECHE was created as a faith-based junior college in partnership with Eastern University. In 2000, the mission behind the establishment of NECHE—whose name was officially changed to Esperanza College in 2005—was to "get the community educated." Tamara Díaz, former NECHE coordinator, laments the fact that many Latinos are not "joining higher education." Success, according to Díaz, is to "keep our doors open and bring in more opportunities for people to complete higher education." She argues that if Latinos join together in solidarity to help increase educational opportunities in the neighborhood, "we won't have most of our problems, because the community will be motivated and confident."[182]

As a faith-based junior college, students would take the following pledge upon entering NECHE:

Señor, yo creo en el estudio,
Haz que sea una aventura bella y constructiva
que me lleve amar más.
Quiero ser libre,
Haz que crea más en la disciplina interior que exterior.
Quiero ser sincero,
Haz que solo exprese palabras que procedan de mi convencimiento
y mi voz impida a otros a apoyarse en mi silencio
para legitimar sus pretensions y comportamiento agresivos.

. . . Dame el gozo de tener amigos,
Señor, yo creo en el estudio,
Haz que el forje en mis ideas grandes.
Que de mis ideales y experiencias positivas reciban vida,
La familia y la sociedad,
Ellas no solo creen en ti sino que también en mi como lo haces tú.[183]

Now a branch campus of Eastern University, Esperanza College continues to be a faith-based institution, as demonstrated by the "daily devotionals" posted on the college's website. Like NECHE, however, Esperanza College "students do not see it as faith-based." Díaz contends that most of the students do not attend the college "because it is a community of faith, but because of the opportunities" such an institution provides them. Because most of the students are not religious, claims Díaz, they view Esperanza College first and foremost as a place where they can accomplish their professional vocations.[184]

At present, Esperanza College has 120 students in its two-year junior college program, offering concentrations in business administration, communications, and early child education. Students at the college tend to be "nontraditional"—many have not attended school for more than twenty years. Although "90 percent of our students had Spanish as a first language at home," notes Jack Weaver, academic dean of Esperanza College, "now, many are speaking English." To accommodate this changing environment, the college provides different language "tracks" for its students: Language Transition Track A, for native Spanish speakers; Language Development Track B, for Spanish/English and bilingual speakers; and Language Development Track C, for English speakers with little or no exposure to Spanish.[185] With an education from Esperanza College, it is assumed that students will graduate with enough knowledge and English proficiency to enter a bachelor's degree program.

When NECHE was established in 2000, it was the first college dedicated to serve the Latino population in the United States. Now, as Esperanza College, the institution remains "the only program of its kind in the country" and the only Hispanic-Serving Institution (HSI) in the state of Pennsylvania, thanks to a $2.4 million Title V grant awarded by the U.S. Department of Education to "enhance its capacity to serve the Latino community of North Philadelphia." To qualify as an HSI, 50 percent of the student population must be Latino. The monies from the Title V grant—awarded over five years—will be used to expand classroom space, build a new library, and enhance additional concentrations, such as health and human services.[186] The establishment of Esperanza College does not subsume Cortés' entire vision of providing higher education for Latinos. Sometime in the near future, he maintains, there needs to be an equivalent of a Yale or Harvard University for the Latino community in the United States. Cortés claims that his grandiose vision flows directly from

Nueva's core mission of building Latino-owned and -operated institutions that compete with their peers.

Previously a program officer at the Pew Charitable Trusts, D. Cortés admitted that, at first, he believed Nueva's mission to be "short-sighted," and that "creating institutions was not enough." However, over time, he has come to realize that an institution is a broader concept—it "can be a school or family." Educational institutions like NEA and Esperanza College hold prime importance in the stability of the community, asserts D. Cortés.[187] Like other institutions, however, educational institutions are not immune to the pressures of securing funding. In securing the Title V grant for Esperanza College, Nueva has had to be "aware of the reality of funding" for educational institutions as well as ready "to position [itself] appropriately to maximize the opportunity"[188] of new funding streams. Viewing its ministry as a business, Nueva has been entrepreneurial in developing educational institutions that do not merely compete with but outperform their peers.

Conclusion

Nueva brings a highly innovative perspective to its ministry of institutional development, whether in its community development initiatives in the Latino neighborhoods of North Philadelphia or through its advocacy of issues of political significance for all Latinos. In addition to being "top notch" in the way it deals with politicians, Nueva has "good management," is "run up-front," and has "been pretty honorable" as a community-serving organization in North Philadelphia, observes Roger Zepernick of Centro Pedro Claver.[189] Even leaders of those community groups like Concilio that historically have had a "love/hate relationship" with Nueva consider the organization to have "done everything right with the community."[190]

As an FBO, Nueva garners trust from the neighborhood due to its affiliation with those numerous small to medium-sized congregations associated with Hispanic Clergy. In his June 2001 testimony before the Subcommittee on Human Resources and Select Revenue Measures of the House Committee Ways and Means, Cortés commented that "our people turn to [the congregation] because of their trust in it—trust that has been earned through decades of service."[191] Don Jose Stovall, executive director of the Philadelphia County Assistance Office, comments that Nueva "plays an invaluable role" in the Latino community. The organization's very presence, according to Stovall, invokes a "trust . . . that government won't be able to get." The organization "knows best, because they are in the community."[192] Even with this trust, Nueva views institutional development as a long-term journey, inseparable from the financial resources needed to take steps toward its realization.

To this day, Nueva's mission remains the "commitment to the creation of Hispanic-owned and operating institutions that serve the economic and spiritual well-being of the community."[193] The organization realizes the need to "establish institutions so that they are rock solid and people can get what they need."[194] The organization's championing of ministry as institutional development is "not just fluff stuff." Rather, institution building is considered a "vehicle to change the mind-set" of the community.[195] Cortés believes there are two ways to change society. The first is the "Bill Gates way," namely, to use "financial power to change culture." The second is the "old-fashioned way"—"creat[ing] institutions that instill values and ideals, and that continue to foster themselves." The latter way, which lies at the heart of Nueva's ministry, is "the opposite of what society tells you," states Cortés.[196]

6

The Resurrection Project

A Ministry of Community Empowerment

> We wanted to achieve two things at the same time: to promote
> the tangible and intangible assets of the community. By focusing
> on the tangible assets (geographic location, churches, stores, and
> homes), we showed people what was positive about our neighbor-
> hood. Then, by promoting the intangible assets (culture, language,
> faith, life, and spirit), we began building a healthy community.
> —Raúl Raymundo[1]

At the Resurrection Project, building a healthy community involves a combination of tangible and intangible assets. For this reason,
this organization has been called "a prophetic voice in the midst of oppression."[2] According to Raúl Raymundo, executive director of TRP, having a name associated with "new life" drives home the holistic way in
which the organization views a healthy community. Raymundo considers
this kind of community one that includes

> good housing, solid family relationships, strong economic growth, job
> and educational opportunities, and positive attitudes. These things sur-
> face when we work to build the Kingdom of God on earth. Jesus' resur-
> rection is all about new life, and as a primarily Catholic community, we
> believe in his life and message.[3]

TRP's twelve-parish membership base in Pilsen and Little Village—
along with its auxiliary membership of Holy Cross/Immaculate Heart of
Mary (IHM) Parish in Back of the Yards—provides the organization with
the opportunity to remain intimately connected to the Mexican Catholic

community. This connection is significant in a number of ways. According to Salvador Cervantes, community organizer at TRP, "The [Mexican] community supports churches more than government. The church will always be a church." On the other hand, "a politician might come and disappear" due to the ongoing electoral cycle in the political arena. Because of the faith of Latinos, "the church will always speak for the people."[4]

Considered "one of the premier community development corporations in Chicago"[5] and the "most proactive group in Pilsen,"[6] TRP was established in 1990 with an initial investment of $30,000 from its then six member parishes. In addition to an operating budget of $2.8 million as of early 2007, the organization owned $15 million in assets and leveraged an additional $140 million in community reinvestment assets. To date, TRP equally receives one-third of its funding from three sources: (1) government contracts, (2) foundations, corporations, individuals, and TRP member parish dues, and (3) earned income of the organization. While member dues account for a small percentage of organizational funding, Raymundo claims that parish contributions—ranging from $2,000–$6,000 per year—are significant for the kind of statement they make about the parishes' commitment to TRP's mission.[7]

Although TRP is a "nationally significant organization,"[8] unlike LPAC and Nueva, the organization has chosen "not to engage in a national effort," except through its involvement in national coalitions. Remaining committed to its regional community initiatives, "keeping it local" nicely summarizes TRP's community strategy.[9] Simply put, the organization is "one of the institutions that anchors neighborhood work" in Chicago.[10] As one nonprofit leader comments, "I can't put a quantifiable number around [their success], but if a group was coming to Chicago to tour a successful community development organization, TRP would be No. 1 or 2 on my list."[11]

This chapter will explore TRP's ministry of community empowerment in light of five themes: (1) faith-based community organizing, (2) the Patroness of Mexico, (3) the human side of community development, (4) holding leadership accountable, and (5) building a healthy community. These themes will be examined from the vantage point of TRP's new liberationist perspective—the communal praxis of liberation—and additional concepts in religious identity politics.

Faith-Based Community Organizing

On Mother's Day 2001, a group of fourteen young and elderly women from the Little Village neighborhood began a hunger strike that lasted nineteen days. Consuming only liquids, the objective of these *huelgistas* (strikers) was to "prod the Board of Education" in Chicago to build a high school on the vacant lot at Thirty-first and Kostner—the site of a former cooking oil factory. Only three years earlier, the Chicago School Board announced its intention to construct three schools in 2000, two of which were magnet schools built in upper-income neighborhoods on Chicago's North Side. The *huelgistas* were dissatisfied with the city's educational initiatives, arguing that in constructing the magnet schools, Chicago was "practicing discrimination" by neglecting areas in need like the predominantly Latino neighborhood of Little Village. In this neighborhood, the only high school, David G. Farragut High School, accommodated 2,626 students out of a total population of 4,046 students of high school age. In 1998, the city of Chicago—indicating an interest in building a high school in the Little Village area—purchased a plot of land at Thirty-first and Kostner for $5 million. However, plans for construction came to a standstill.[12] This vacant lot became the site for the famous hunger strike.

The hunger strike was regarded as a triumph for the Latino community in Chicago. On August 21, 2001, Chicago Mayor Richard Daley approved construction of the new Little Village High School at Thirty-first and Kostner. With construction costs estimated at $61 million, the new high school was scheduled to open in 2005 with an enrollment of 1,400 students. Considered the *"abuelita"* (grandmother) of the *huelgistas*, 75-year-old Manuelita García discussed the hardships endured by those involved in the hunger strike. She remarked that the strike "was hard, but we survived because the main food we had was our community. They supported us and now, it's all worth it."[13]

At the time of the strike, García was not only a Little Village resident, but also a member of Epiphany Parish. One of twelve parishes affiliated with TRP, Epiphany Parish celebrated the one-year anniversary of the hunger strike victory on Mother's Day 2002 at the site of the future high school. Noticias Chicago television interviewed García, who spoke of the celebration as a way to *"despertar a la gente y a la comunidad."*[14] On this rainy and chilly spring day, Father Peter McQuinn, pastor of Epiphany, celebrated mass under a blue and yellow tent. With his faithful Irish Setter, *"Tano"* (a derivative of the word *"Samitarino"*—"the Good Samaritan"

—Tano was given this name by McQuinn after some parishioners found the dog lying wounded in the middle of the street), at his side and a golden framed picture of Our Lady of Guadalupe placed on the altar, McQuinn preached on the inseparability of Christ's mission from the mission of his people. *"Jesucristo"* says *"mi misión es tu misión." "La misión de Jesus tiene iglesia, parrocos, y Uds."* He added that, *"la lucha no terminó el año pasado."* Rather, as residents of Little Village, there is now the *"segunda nivel de lucha—necesitamos organizar y construir una escuela."* The *"escuela y campo son parte de la misión: formar buenos adultos."* But, in this effort, remarked McQuinn, *"trabajamos como familia"* because *"juntos nada es imposible."*[15] At the conclusion of the celebration, a round of applause went to the seven *huelgistas* in attendance for their perseverance, after which time the *huelgistas* began shouting *"sí, se puede, sí, se puede."*[16]

Opened for business in September 2005, Little Village High School is considered a one-of-a-kind enterprise with four separate schools under one roof: the Multicultural Arts School, the Infinity High School, the Greater Lawndale/Little Village School for Social Justice (School for Social Justice), and the World Language High School. Whereas the Multicultural Arts School gears its education to students interested in the cultural arts, Infinity High School is a community-based school that encourages students to reflect on their community's strengths and challenges. The last two schools prepare students for post-secondary education. The School for Social Justice accomplishes such a task by teaching students to be "reflective about real-world issues." The World Language High School, on the other hand, provides students with an intensive language program and a practical "career-preparatory program." Each of these schools has a capacity of 350 students, thereby accommodating 1,400 students from the neighborhood.[17]

Of the fourteen *huelgistas* participating in the hunger strike, five were members of Epiphany Parish. Epiphany's involvement in the strike manifests how this parish—as a member of TRP—promotes the organization's ministry of community empowerment. In effect, Epiphany parishioners exhibited Raymundo's understanding of "building a healthy community," acknowledging the community's "tangible assets"—the erection of a much-needed high school—along with its "intangible assets" of faith and culture. García's abovementioned quote, "We survived because the main food we had was our community," is further testimony to the central role that community empowerment played in the strike and in its ultimate victory. In McQuinn's view, the hunger strike victory displayed not simply the important "role of the church in community affairs," but reinforced the point that, in the Latino community, "all is integrated, faith, society, and politics."[18]

A Builder of Leaders

Consisting of neighborhood churches like Epiphany, TRP fosters a ministry of community empowerment through direct collaboration with these churches in the area of leadership development. Thus, at the same time the organization actively engages in building homes and rental properties, TRP is also "a builder of leaders."[19] As documented in chapter three, the movement to establish TRP began in 1990 with the formation of approximately sixty CBCs in select Catholic parishes throughout Pilsen. Priests in each parish identified lay leaders, or "coordinators," to represent that particular parish community's interests. Lay leaders and other interested parishioners then met with priests to reflect on Scripture, and in doing so, began to discuss ways to effect change in the neighborhood. Unlike the authoritarian style of leadership witnessed in many Latin American nations, the CBC leadership model reflected a more democratic and collegial approach. In fact, many of the CBC coordinators were not well educated, and some were even illiterate. Because Latino Catholics became more active parishioners through their involvement in CBCs, this leadership model was helpful in staving off aggressive proselytizing efforts by local groups of evangelical and Pentecostal Christians. Like the efforts of their non-Catholic counterparts, door-to-door evangelization by Latino Catholics was central to the mission of the CBCs.[20]

Although the twelve member parishes are epicenters for TRP's organizing efforts in the community—especially in the area of leadership development—TRP "leaves evangelization to the churches."[21] Still, TRP's characterization as a Latino FBO driven by a strong Catholic identity makes sense. According to David Pesqueira, senior program officer at the McCormick Tribune Foundation, Latino Catholics continue to "listen to their shepherds."[22] The Catholic Church is "the most relevant institution for this community in Chicago," remarks Father Ezequiel Sánchez, director of Hispanic evangelization for the Archdiocese of Chicago and pastor of Holy Trinity Parish, for it has engaged in works of charity in the neighborhood, like feeding the hungry, clothing the naked, and opening new schools.[23] Other Chicago community leaders like Trinita Logue, president of the Illinois Facility Fund, contend that the Catholic Church's relevance stems from its sheer power. She maintains that "in this city, if you are Catholic, you can see the mayor. Priests can get anything done."[24]

The churches affiliated with TRP—by providing social services and outlets for community organizing around salient political issues—"add credibility and give a sense of connectedness that other groups don't have."[25] According to Father Don Nevins, pastor of St. Francis of Assisi church, Mexican people "tend to believe when churches are involved." This is because, in their native land, the "church has been there for them."[26] These churches have provided meeting space to host TRP community events, and local church pastors have encouraged parishioners to assume leadership positions in the community on important issues.

From the perspective of the churches, an affiliation with TRP brings its own benefits. TRP was "one of the first Latino organizations" in Chicago working "for systemic change," argues Elena Segura, head of the Catholic Campaign for Human Development (CCHD) and director of Catholic Relief Services for the Archdiocese of Chicago. She remarks that the organization has been very successful in its mission of "empowering the Latino community of Pilsen, Little Village, and Back of the Yards and providing opportunities for leadership development."[27] McQuinn recalls TRP representatives paying a visit to Epiphany, saying, "You tell us what you need and want to do" in your parish. The grass-roots style of TRP differed considerably from the organizing efforts of United Neighborhood Organization (UNO). Heavily involved in community organizing with many Chicago churches during the 1960s and 1970s, at present UNO is nothing more than "a political arm of Mayor Daley," admits McQuinn.[28]

Because many Latinos experience marginality as recent immigrants to the United States, the church often becomes their haven. As an organization dedicated to a ministry of community empowerment, TRP has demonstrated that a link exists between faith-based community organizing and leadership development, especially in the area of immigration reform. This link is present because the "faith-based organizing structure provides local leaders with the tools they need in order to influence city priorities and reshape their own neighborhoods." (The specific tools or "primary motivations"[29] driving TRP's organizing efforts will be examined in more detail in the next section, "Acting on Faith and Values.")

Prior to the September 11, 2001, attacks, community organizations like TRP advocated for a new amnesty program—similar to the Immigration Reform and Control Act signed into law by President Ronald Reagan in

1986—for Latino immigrants. Given the heightened security environment in the United States after these attacks, calls for amnesty from such organizations have subsided. TRP is still concerned with creating a legal path for undocumented immigrants—who make up 37 percent of the population in Pilsen—and has engaged in a "larger political strategy" with the Illinois Immigrant Rights Coalition on the issue of comprehensive immigration reform. TRP's faith-based community organizing efforts on behalf of immigration reform have taken place at the level of advocacy and mobilization. Because local parish leadership has placed this issue at the top of its agenda, TRP affiliated churches were "instrumental" in mobilizing people to participate in the May 1, 2006, marches throughout Chicago as well as in organizing ecumenical religious services for march participants.[30]

TRP's faith-based community organizing transcends the Latino/non-Latino divide. Since 1992, the organization began building a relationship with the Lawndale Christian Development Corporation (LCDC), an African American FBO, over issues of community safety and quality child care. Led by Richard Townsell, LCDC is characterized as a "community-based church" serving Chicago's North Lawndale area, an area that closely borders the largely Mexican neighborhood of Little Village. Townsell admits that TRP is "one of the only [community] groups" he trusts. He emphasizes that, as African Americans, we "need to organize an event" with the Latino community "that TRP needs to be committed to." This need for multiracial faith-based community organizing is particularly important given the history of distrust between Latinos and African Americans in the United States. In political terms, states Townsell, "African Americans and Latinos [are] fight[ing] over who will be the No. 1 minority."[31]

Like African Americans during the civil rights movement, the Latino community is presently urging an honest discussion about the link between faith-based community organizing and Latino leadership development. "We need a Martin Luther King, Jr." states Father Sánchez. Dr. King used "religious imagery to identify with the people and not to manipulate." According to Sánchez, his every speech was a sermon, and through these speeches central theological concepts like salvation and sin were interwoven with questions of political struggle. César Chávez, founder of the United Farm Workers, serves as one example of a Latino faith-based leader grounded in the Catholic tradition. Sánchez claims that Chávez's role as a labor organizer for farm workers was a direct reflection of how he "lived the social teaching of the Church." In addition to employing expressions of popular religiosity—like the banner of Our Lady of

Guadalupe—to promote his cause for the fair treatment of farm workers, Chávez was a "daily communicant, but no one mentions this."[32]

Acting on Faith and Values

In *The Moral Vision of César Chávez* (2003), Frederick John Dalton argues that Chávez was essentially the first person of Mexican heritage to receive "widespread public recognition in the United States." He writes that "more than a labor leader, or the leader of Mexican-Americans," however, Chávez "was regarded by many as a moral leader, as a national prophet of justice." Like Father Sánchez, Dalton holds that Chávez's exercise of moral leadership in the farm-worker struggle was influenced strongly by his Roman Catholic faith. The religious outlook he employed is best described as the "Christian praxis of César Chávez," an outlook rooted in the commitment to and liberation of the poor.[33]

In like manner, the "communal praxis of liberation" characterizes best TRP's approach to a ministry of community empowerment. At the heart of this approach is the acknowledgment of Jacques Maritain's famous distinction between "being with" the people and "acting for" the people.[34] Faith-based community organizing at TRP privileges "being with" the people, through the kind of "critical and liberating dialogue" of which Freire speaks. Through a dialogic relationship fashioned between leadership and the people of a particular community—manifested in the formation of CBCs in Pilsen—the people thereby become "masters of their thinking" and aware of their "significance as human beings."[35]

At TRP, being with the people implies "challeng[ing] people to act on their faith and values to create healthy communities through education, organizing, and community development."[36] This phrase, taken from TRP's vision statement, places a premium on acting on one's faith and values in the field of community organizing. According to Father Nevins, TRP has been careful not to separate community organizing from the Catholic faith and values that inspired it.[37] Similarly, Regina McGraw, executive director of the Wieboldt Foundation—a mid-level funder of TRP's community organizing efforts—regards TRP's Catholic identity as "a vital piece of organizing" and a definite strength for the organization.[38]

It is important to note that the organization was "not simply founded" but "was baptized in a church ceremony at St. Procopius with *padrinos* and *madrinas* [godparents],"[39] one of whom was Chicago mayor Richard M. Daley. Accompanying Daley at the ceremony were other city officials as well as leaders from the banking and construction sectors who were invited to immerse carpentry tools in water, "symbolizing their baptism and their newborn power to give life to the community."[40] This was "one of the most wonderful organizing scenes" ever witnessed, claims Paul Roldan, president of Hispanic Housing Development Corporation (HHDC). According to Roldan, the ceremony concluded with a commitment from Mayor Daley to turn over to TRP vacant lots at no charge "along with sanctifying grace."[41]

TRP's decision to hold the ceremony at St. Procopius demonstrates that there was a "reason why we were doing this, our faith and religion," notes Father Nevins.[42] The organization's identity as an FBO has been a benefit for three main reasons. First, faith is a comfort for most Latinos. "It is a critical piece of who these people are. This is not questioned."[43] Second, faith, and in this case, the Roman Catholic faith, "marries personal faith with a social action component." This means that a member of the community "gets to pray and gets to vote" simultaneously. Third, the Catholic faith has an "organizational structure" in place that lends support to establishing direct lines of leadership.[44]

The establishment of CBCs in Pilsen parishes did much to offset the direct lines of leadership—typically associated with the Catholic Church—by placing more decision-making power in the hands of parishioners. According to Father Charles Dahm, O.P., former pastor of St. Pius V church and founding member of TRP, although there are many Catholic progressives—once missionaries in Latin America—who continue to minister to the Latino community, the number of CBCs has declined in the United States. Subsequent pastors at TRP parishes in Pilsen and Little Village have not voiced strong support for the use of CBCs in pastoral ministry, claims Dahm.[45] As one young pastor observed, CBCs "need a lot of care and feeding."[46] Others maintain that lay leadership training in the parishes should replace CBCs, as the CBCs simply "don't work here." In Father McQuinn's view, the Latin American context for the emergence of CBCs was dramatically different from the situation of the Latino inner city because Latin America was combating terrorism and civil wars.[47]

Because Latinos are a new and growing "dynamic of the Church," the "model of Latino church is evolving," remarks Raymundo.[48] In contrast to preserving the CBC leadership model, TRP decided to unveil a new initiative called Social Ministry Action and Reflection Teams (SMART) at every member parish. The SMART strategy calls for the establishment of a Council of Leaders at every member parish. In addition to being a vehicle for leadership development within the parishes, the Council serves to drive TRP's organizing agenda by recognizing the importance of community organizing as both part of the organization's history and "part of its work moving forward."[49] Desirous of preserving its faith-based community organizing model, the formation of these SMART groups has provided TRP with a way for the organization to continue to act on its faith and values.

The Patroness of Mexico

It is roughly 4 A.M. on a mild Chicago winter day in 2001. Even at this time, on Eighteenth Street in Pilsen, the casual passerby is greeted on the sidewalk by five or six flower-sellers with their assortments of flowers. Upon entering the red-brick Roman Catholic Church of St. Procopius—one of the twelve member parishes of The Resurrection Project—all eyes are transfixed on the large image of the Virgin Mary, located to the right of the altar. It is December 12, the Feast of Our Lady of Guadalupe, perhaps the most significant religious holiday for Mexicans and Mexican Americans. According to official Catholic teaching, the Virgin Mary appeared to Juan Diego, an Aztec peasant, on a hill at Tepeyac in the outskirts of Mexico City in 1531, asking him to petition the local bishop in Tenochtitlán, Fray Juan de Zamárraga, to build a church on the site. The Virgin proclaimed to Juan Diego,

> I very much want and ardently desire that my hermitage be erected in this place. In it I will show and give to all people all my love, my compassion, my help, and my protection, because I am your merciful mother and the mother of all the nations that live on this earth who would love me, who would speak with me, who would search for me, and who would place their confidence in me. There I will hear their laments and remedy and cure all their miseries, misfortunes, and sorrows.[50]

Tepeyac was only miles from Tenochtitlán, the capital of the Aztec empire. When Juan Diego's first visit to the bishop ended in failure, the Virgin Mary asked Juan Diego to cut fresh roses growing on the hillside in the middle of winter, place them in his *tilma* (cloak) and present them to the bishop. Upon opening his *tilma*, the image of the Virgin of Guadalupe miraculously imprinted itself on the cloth. As the thousands of tourists on pilgrimage attest, this *tilma* hangs in the Basilica of Our Lady of Guadalupe in Mexico City.

An abundance of flowers, particularly roses, are placed before the life-size image of Guadalupe at St. Procopius Parish. Parishioners continue to line up the side aisle to place additional bouquets before the Virgin. By 4:30 A.M., the church is completely packed. A group of mariachis—six in number—processes up the center aisle singing "*canciones especiales*" (special songs) in homage to the Virgin Mary. They play for half an hour in front of the image, in a church decorated from front to back with colorful streamers. This tradition in Mexico, known as "*Mañanitas*," involves serenading the Virgin of Guadalupe, the Patroness of Mexico, before sunrise. Singing, "*Madre mía de Guadalupe, dame ya tu bendición, recibe estas mañanitas con un humilde corazón*,"[51] the mariachis pave way for the celebration of the "*Santa Misa*" (Holy Mass) at 5 A.M. By this time, the church is so full that lines of people are streaming out the door. Whole families are in attendance this morning to celebrate their national holiday.

At 5 A.M., mass begins. There are two co-celebrants today, Father Tim Howe, S.J., and Father Charles W. Niehaus, S.J.—pastor and associate astor, respectively, of St. Procopius Church and Jesuit priests—donning stoles with the miraculous image. Sitting on the main altar is a papier-mâché reproduction of the hill where the Virgin Mary first appeared to Juan Diego. Father Howe spreads incense throughout the church, even on the image of Guadalupe at the side altar. The gospel according to Luke speaks of Mary's visitation with Elizabeth, her cousin: "*A los pocos días María emprendió el viaje y se fue de prisa a un pueblo en la región montañosa de Judea. Al llegar, entró en casa de Zacarías y saludó a Elisabet. Tan pronto como Elisabet oyó el saludo de María, la criatura saltó en su vientre. Entonces Elisabet, llena del Espíritu Santo . . .*" (Luke 1:39–41).[52] In the homily, Howe emphasizes how "*La Virgen sale primero para saludar a nosotros*" with the joy that only God can give. The Virgin Mary is a custodian of her beloved son, Jesus, he remarks. In like fashion, he tells the congregation, "*nos vamos a convertirnos en custodios para compartirlo con los demas.*"[53]

Sacred Symbols and Doctrine

The Virgin of Guadalupe is an important image here in Lower West Side Chicago. On Eighteenth and May, just a few blocks from St. Procopius, a mural of Guadalupe graces the side of Taqueria Vegar. Advertising "*lo major en carnitas y chicarron estilo Michoacan: barbacoa menudo y birria, tacos al gusto de su paladar, y licor al gusto y cerveza fría,*"⁵⁴ the mural sits on a vibrant red background amid painted Corona and brandy bottles. The casual manner by which this image permeates Pilsen reminds one of the ordinary, everyday nature of Latino religious culture, as portrayed in Viramontes' novel, *Under the Feet of Jesus*. Instead of a poster of the Virgin placed between rival pictures of Elvis Presley and Marilyn Monroe—as presented in the novel—one finds the image of Guadalupe in the form of a sticker greeting visitors to Pilsen residents' homes or as a bumper sticker placed on neighborhood cars and pickup trucks. Many residents have Guadalupe tattoos that they ask local priests to bless.⁵⁵

Guadalupe is a sacred symbol of faith, hope, and cultural identity for Mexicans everywhere. In Miles Richardson's view,

> nearly all, both conservative anthropologists and radical theologians, concur that the Virgin is one symbol, perhaps the only one, that unites the Mexican people, that brings together the Indian and the white, the poor and the rich, the weak and the powerful into a national identity whose spirituality remains triumphant in the face of threats by the secular giant to the north.⁵⁶

As a revered sacred symbol, the image of Guadalupe provides a way for Mexicans to make sense of their world, whether living in their native land or as immigrants in a foreign land. Father Dahm notes that "being a Mexican is closely intertwined with being a *Guadalupano*, a devotee of the Virgin. She is a national heroine, and, as the founding mother of the nation, casts her religious aura over the country."⁵⁷ For Mexicans, the feast of Guadalupe engages fully the "body and senses." The celebration on December 12 is a "visual feast," as the colorful image displays. Touching the image after offering one's gift, i.e., a bouquet of roses, at the Virgin's feet is an additional act of "adoration and worship."⁵⁸ The feast also manifests a deep appreciation for music, as the lively mariachi band leads the congregation in song. During the celebration of the mass, as the smell of incense fills the church, the congregation shares in the Eucharistic feast, consuming the Body and Blood of Christ.

Considered both an "everyday world and extraordinary"⁵⁹ event, the yearly celebration of the Virgin of Guadalupe is deeply rooted in the sacred doctrine of the Roman Catholic faith. At the heart of this doctrine is the rich sacramental life of the Catholic Church. Accompanying the varied expressions of popular religiosity—pilgrimages, novenas, and Eucharistic processions—is a deep veneration of the Virgin Mary. As evidenced in the *Mañanitas* festivities, the veneration of Guadalupe builds religious identity at the personal level, through acts of individual devotion. However, the belief in sacred doctrine extends beyond what may be perceived as a private exercise of devotion to a communal and public level. Mexicans do not celebrate the Feast of the Virgin of Guadalupe alone; they honor her in solidarity with other Roman Catholics throughout the world in the celebration of the mass. Beyond Catholic believers, this traditional Marian feast increasingly has been celebrated by those outside the Roman Catholic fold, i.e., Latino Protestants. This ecumenical dimension demonstrates the expansiveness of those communal and public orientations implicit in Howe's sermon, that, like the Virgin Mary, we are called "to transform ourselves into custodians in order to share the Lord with others."

As the definition of religious identity politics implies, one must not downplay the religious content that the sacred symbol of Guadalupe provides for Mexican people everywhere. Neither must one disregard the sacred doctrine of Roman Catholicism that serves to lay a foundation for the celebration of this feast in sacramental form, i.e., through the sacrifice of the mass. On the other hand, one must not ignore the fact that the feast also carries with it public implications. Dahm remarks that all homilies on the feast of Guadalupe tend to emphasize two points: (1) "the dignity and value of all Mexican people, primarily the poor and indigenous" and (2) the challenge addressed to contemporary Mexican immigrants to build Guadalupe a "renewed church that will struggle for justice in their new land."[60] In Guadalupe, "Mexicanicity was born," claims Elizondo. He writes, "Guadalupe provides the spark that will allow the people to arise out of the realm of death . . . not just a return to the past but the emergence of a spectacular newness."[61]

Popular Religion and Liberation

The veneration of the Virgin of Guadalupe is one manifestation of what theologians call "popular religion." Elizondo describes popular religion not simply as personal devotion, but as "the ensemble of beliefs, rituals, ceremonies, devotions, and prayers which are commonly practiced by the people at large."[62] The 1987 *National Pastoral Plan for Hispanic Ministry* commented on the familiarity with which Latinos pray to God, even considering God as a "member of the family."[63] Luis Pedraja's book *Jesus Is My Uncle* examines the close, familial relationship the Latino community has with God's son, Jesus Christ, considering him an uncle or even a brother. Latinos and Mexicans, in particular, adopt a similar familial attitude in their relationship with Guadalupe. As Patroness of Mexico, Guadalupe is also honored every year on Mother's Day, because Mexicans regard her as a "second mother," i.e., "their heavenly mother who loves and protects them."[64]

Popular religion reveals the commonly held religious beliefs of a people and, at the same time, defines and shapes a religious identity politics. For decades, the neighborhood of Pilsen has reenacted the *Via Crucis* (Way of the Cross) on Good Friday. Thousands of people flock to the neighborhood to watch the events surrounding Jesus Christ's passion and death. Dahm maintains that this *Via Crucis* reenactment is meaningful for Latinos in that it deepens their spirituality as well as "dramatizes their own sufferings."[65] From his many years serving as pastor of St. Adalbert's in Pilsen, Father Jim Kaczorowski, vicar for priests for the Archdiocese of Chicago, has found that:

> The Mexican community is very spiritual. . . . Their whole lives are built on faith. They identify with Jesus crucified and risen. They see hope, for Christ is a light. They see themselves as living witnesses of the risen Lord, free from poverty, unemployment, and racism.[66]

As the *Via Crucis* procession stops at a local tavern to mourn the deaths caused by excessive drinking and at a nearby corner so that people may reflect on the violence inflicted on the community by gangs, this expression of popular religion is given a communal and public face. Father Sánchez contends that "faith is not different from politics" for the Mexican community.[67] This statement should come as no surprise, especially considering that the development of a religious identity politics in the Latino community views religion and politics not independently, but as continuous entities.

In contrast to some Latin American liberation theologians, new liberationists like Dahm view expressions of popular religion as deeply connected to liberation. Whereas Dahm finds that commemorations of the *Via Crucis* serve to "dramatize" the sufferings of the Latino community, Ada María Isasi-Díaz, *mujerista* scholar, maintains that such events also provide the community with the "strength for struggle."[68] For instance, CBC participants' "critical reflection" on the gospel gave them "strength for the struggle," prompting them to challenge structural injustices in the neighborhood of Pilsen. Gustavo Gutiérrez, acclaimed liberation theologian, acknowledges the sociopolitical value of popular religion in that it mobilizes the people for action.[69] As "highly influential community figures,"[70] Catholic clergy—such as those displayed below—help promote the "liberative potential"[71] of popular religion, by providing a faith context out of which such social and political action can arise.

The *Mañanitas* celebration is preceded in every Latino neighborhood parish by a nine-day novena to Our Lady of Guadalupe that begins on December 3 and ends on December 11. It is 6:30 P.M. on December 7, 2001, at the Immaculate Heart of Mary (IHM) church in Back of the Yards. IHM sits amid pool halls and discotheques on Forty-fifth Street and Ashland Avenue. Tonight it is bursting with worshippers. Amazingly, the average age here is fairly young, approximately twenty-five to thirty years old. At the side altar, a large image of Our Lady of Guadalupe is exposed, behind which is draped a large Mexican flag. On either side of the image are two large bouquets of red, white, and green flowers. The entrance hymn, "*Himno a Nuestra Señora de Guadalupe*," is laced with patriotic themes calling the congregation to attention, "*defendiendo a su patria y a su Dios.*"[72]

Two priests, Father Bruce Wellems, C.M.F., a Claretian priest and pastor of Holy Cross/IHM Parish in Back of the Yards, and Father Alberto Athié, visiting pastor from Istapalapa, Mexico, in the region San Miguel Teotongo, are the co-celebrants of mass tonight. From 1998 until 2001, Holy Cross/IHM Parish was a member institution of TRP. In December 2001, however, Father Wellems' parish formalized a "separation agreement" with the organization. According to Wellems, TRP failed to promote community organizing in Back of the Yards, focusing its attention instead on the expansion of community development in Pilsen and Little Village. Although these institutions continue to be separated, "it is still a marriage," comments Wellems, "so there is still a commitment."[73] Raymundo argues that like TRP, Holy Cross/IHM Parish is creating SMART groups and promoting leadership development and training for the Latino community. Because their missions are relatively similar, Raymundo refers to Holy Cross/IHM Parish as a "quasi" or "auxiliary" member of TRP.[74]

Back of the Yards is a neighborhood most famous for the portrayal of its unsanitary meat-packing plants at the turn of the twentieth century in Upton Sinclair's *The Jungle* (1906). To this day, Back of the Yards has remained a neighborhood of immigrants facing cruel realities. During other nights of the novena, the homily revolves around concerns affecting this community—alcoholism, immigration, affordable housing, domestic violence—but Father Athié cleverly centers his homily tonight on a very serious problem for the neighborhood, namely, *juventud en peligro* (at-risk youth). "*La misión de la iglesia es el apoyo de la juventud en peligro,*" remarks Athié. "*Dios siempre está con los que están en una condición de necesidad. . . . Los jóvenes continuan a perder el sentido de vida. . . . No saben de donde venían ni donde están.*" Athié mentions that Wellems and his ministry team at Holy Cross/IHM Parish are "*interesado en entender a los niños porque no pueden expresar su riqueza creativamente.*" He notes that Our Lady of Guadalupe came to Juan Diego, asking him to go to the bishop and "*muestra a los valores*" to him. Similarly, neighborhood youth must be able to "show their worth" to the larger community, through the creation of "*espacios para niños . . . espacios de dialogo, creatividad, y deporte.*" According to Athié, this is a mission for the whole community.[75]

Athié's homily soon is followed by a lengthy speech from a key individual on Wellems' ministry team, Gonzalo Flores. Flores, twenty-six years old, is a "*joven misionero*" (youth minister) at Holy Cross/IHM Parish who speaks personally about his decision to leave the life of drugs and gangs. Originally from Pilsen, Flores was "*jefe de una pandilla*" in Back of the Yards for five years. "*Le gustaba matar y vender drogas,*" he admits. Flores taught "*cosas de la calle*" to children, helping to destroy his own community. At that time in his life, he did not know that "*la comunidad era llena de fe.*" He was lost—"*no pensaba en Dios, ni en la Virgen de Guadalupe.*" Then, comments Flores, due to God's intervention and with the help of Wellems, "*las puertas de las iglesias se abrieron*" for him. Now Flores does not seek to destroy his community. Instead, he describes societal rupture in Back of the Yards as "*un cáncer, una enfermedad, una ignorancia.*"[76]

This novena celebrated in honor of the Virgin of Guadalupe contradicts the public statement made by the International Week of Catechists in Bogotá, Colombia, in 1968 that popular religion is an obstacle to social transformation. Instead of being subject to "alienation, commercialization, and exploitation," new liberationists such as Dahm, Wellems, and Athié find popular religion to possess a liberative streak, by virtue of its "popular character."[77] As priests, Dahm, Wellems, and Athié show no sign of hesitancy in encouraging their largely Mexican congregations to view participation in the public square as an outgrowth of one's Catholic faith.[78] Linking popular religion with liberation, these new liberationists understand that "saving souls makes little sense apart from transforming the social order."[79]

The Human Side of Community Development

TRP has engaged in community development in an effort to effect social transformation in the neighborhoods of Pilsen and Little Village. According to Raymundo, the organization "operates under a new paradigm in community development." At its inception, TRP "did not set out to build homes, but relationships."[80] In the process of building relationships, however, leadership at the organization realized that there were real issues affecting the Latino community, such as the lack of affordable housing, the need to educate the community about homeownership, and other topics related to financial literacy. Over time, TRP became aware of an additional issue, i.e., the need for dormitory space for college-aged students in the neighborhood. The organization responded by merging physical development, i.e., building affordable homes and rental properties, with a "pro-family" human development. This is rare for community-serving organizations, because it is "so difficult to do," claims Pesqueira of the Mc-Cormick Tribune Foundation. He believes that in viewing community development as a more expansive term, TRP has succeeded in "humaniz[ing] its apparatus."[81]

According to Caroline Goldstein, vice president of community investment for the state of Illinois at Banc One, being faith-based keeps TRP "in a different area of housing development." While other community development corporations (CDCs) enter into more lucrative areas of development—like mixed-income housing—TRP has maintained its focus on providing low- to middle-income housing opportunities for the largely Mexican families of Pilsen and Little Village.[82] Dahm maintains that TRP's success in promoting the human side of community development stems from three factors: (1) "the internal strength of the Mexican family," (2) the confidence this community has in the church, and (3) strong parish commitment in encouraging parishioners to become homeowners.[83] The faith-based connection to community development at TRP was made most apparent, states Raymundo, after the organization unleashed its community development agenda. "For several months," he states, "we had families going to their parish halls and learning how to buy a home. That really created the market."[84]

TRP's emphasis on the low- and middle-income housing market in Pilsen was also a direct response to the wave of gentrification in the neighborhood. Over the years, Pilsen has become an attractive market for rehabilitation and new property development due to its proximity to

Chicago's "Loop." The process of gentrification relies on a heavy influx of capital to the area increasing both land values and rents of residential and commercial space. The end result of this process has led to housing displacement for many of Pilsen's working poor. The tragedy of this situation is that while "Chicago has waved its biggest banner around home-ownership," states Kevin Jackson, director of the Chicago Rehab Network, "some people don't have enough money to own homes." In struggling areas like Pilsen, "the illusion," therefore, "is not about white picket fences, but about lack of housing."[85]

Making Good Neighbors

Victoria Ranta is a tenant in TRP-owned and -managed apartment housing. Ranta is a dignified, older Mexican American woman who has dedicated more than twenty years to community work in Pilsen and ten years to volunteer work with Latino seniors. When asked to comment on her experience as a TRP client, she maintains that "good tenants make good neighbors." This adds a different spin to Robert Frost's oft-cited verse, from his poem *The Mending Wall*, that "good fences make good neighbors." Ranta holds that TRP performs an excellent service in selecting tenants for its many affordable rental units. Furthermore, the organization engages in careful scrutiny of those families seeking to buy a home, imposing a rigorous preapplication process for first-time home-buyers. By seeking out and educating "good neighbors," Ranta claims that the organization has raised the standard of community living in the neighborhood.[86]

Since the construction of its first twenty-four homes in 1991, TRP has transformed nearly 140 vacant lots into "high-quality homes," some for neighborhood families whose total annual income is as low as $20,000.[87] Initially, the organization—then known as the Pilsen Resurrection Development Corporation (PRDC)—was able to purchase vacant lots in Pilsen from the city of Chicago at a price of one dollar each. Furthermore, the organization's housing plans qualified under Mayor Daley's New Homes for Chicago project, a program that awards money to community organizations for renovating vacant lots into affordable homes. In return for receiving a substantial subsidy of $20,000 for each new homeowner, developers in this program are expected to "price the homes affordably for qualified households earning less than 120 percent of the Chicago-area median-income level (no more than $61,555 for a family of four)."[88] Thus,

PRDC was able to sell a $100,000 home to a community buyer for only $80,000. A number of banks, namely, The Northern Trust Company, Citibank, Harris Trust and Savings Bank, and National Republic Bank, agreed to provide thirty-year mortgages at a below-market interest rate of 7⅞ percent and no points for the twenty-four homes. Later on, with more construction, additional banks, such as Comerica, Cole Taylor Banks, and Lake Shore Bank, participated in the financing project.[89] Preceding all the private-sector and government investment, however, was a $250,000 loan to PRDC from the Sisters of Mercy in Chicago.[90]

Raymundo maintains that TRP intends to develop an additional 370 homes and rental units by 2010. By doing so, the organization will have developed more units in the next four years than in the first fifteen years of its history. Raymundo admits that driving the development process is "being intentional about maximizing opportunities" in the neighborhood. Because TRP regards "housing" as equally expansive as "community development," the organization views homeownership workshops—as well as the workshops offered on financial literacy—as central to its work in the housing arena. These educational workshops serve to advance TRP's ministry of community empowerment throughout the organization's four categories of housing: (1) homes for sale, (2) family rental units, (3) senior housing, and (4) student housing.[91]

TRP regards "good neighbors" as those clients who are informed and educated about homeownership and other aspects of financial literacy. The organization hosts a two-part homeownership training session four times a month in Pilsen and once a month in Little Village and Back of the Yards. Each session lasts three hours and is available in both English and Spanish. In contrast to TRP, homeownership workshops provided by agencies such as the Latin United Community Housing Association (LUCHA) and Neighborhood Housing Services of Chicago Inc. run for merely a two-hour session and are generally offered only in English. Still others, like the Spanish Coalition for Housing, charge clients one hundred dollars to attend.[92]

On December 4, 2001, Edgar Hernández, homeownership education specialist for TRP, led part one of the homeownership training session in a large, dimly lit, drafty basement at TRP's "convent site"—future home of the organization's college dormitory initiative, *La Casa*. Most of the thirty-eight participants attended the workshop as a family unit, husband and wife, some with babies in strollers, others rocking infants in their laps. There was a divorced gentleman at the workshop who comically told the group that *"ya tengo una casa, quiero comprarla para mi mujer."*[93] A burst of laughter followed. Single mothers also attended to gather information about homeownership. Lasting 6–9 P.M., the workshop was organized systematically. As Hernández used the flipchart, he made sure participants knew he welcomed interactive dialogue during the session.[94]

According to Hernández, financial literacy and immigration are the two challenges facing the Mexican community in the housing arena today. Community residents "don't trust banks, [so] a lot of people have mattress money," some as much as $20,000.[95] Similarly, Rebecca Lopez, assistant commissioner of housing for Chicago, argues that Mexicans typically "don't go to banks, because they have lost money before" in their native land.[96] TRP has responded to this climate of distrust by providing community residents with courses in financial literacy. Course topics include, among others, "Banking with Confidence," "Budget and Credit Management," and "Credit Banks." While acknowledging that financial illiteracy is an impediment in the housing market, TRP also understands the intimate connection between immigrant status and the possibility of owning a home. As much as undocumented workers would like to save money, "they can't buy a house because they aren't citizens," claims Hernández. These workers can, however, establish credit in other ways, for instance by setting up a checking account.[97]

Latino community residents face additional financial challenges, such as being victimized by predatory lending, which has become more commonplace in the communities of Pilsen, Little Village, and Back of the Yards. Some consider predatory lending an inherently discriminatory practice because it takes advantage of those minorities who have difficulty reading and speaking English. Latinos are particularly vulnerable to this practice, because they often sign documents in English without understanding their content. Along with First Bank of America, TRP has hosted workshops on predatory lending for community residents. The bank considers these workshops as their "faith-based initiative." In partnership with the Archdiocese of Chicago, First Bank of America also visits local parishes to speak on financial counseling and education. The objective of these workshops—delivered in Spanish—is to educate Mexican immigrants on how to protect their money.[98]

According to the U.S. Department of Housing and Urban Development (HUD), there has been growing evidence of this abusive practice of predatory lending in a "segment of the mortgage lending market," particularly in areas with a large concentration of racial and/or ethnic minorities.

Given its discriminatory nature, predatory lending serves to "destabiliz[e] the very communities that are beginning to enjoy the fruits of our nation's economic success."[99] TRP's response has been to expand the traditional definition of housing by offering homeownership sessions and financial literacy classes as a way to build a neighborhood culture that is at once informed, responsible, and self-disciplined.[100]

The "Convent Site"

TRP recognized that "to be a strong presence in Pilsen" in the area of community development, the organization needed to combine an emphasis on "physical development" with one on "people building."[101] This was precisely TRP's intention in renovating the "convent site"—*La Casa*, as it is called—which sits next door to St. Adalbert Parish in Pilsen. *La Casa* was the brainchild of two young adults, Marco Lopez of Back of the Yards and Jaime Esparza of Pilsen. Amid conversations at St. Mary of the Lake Seminary in Mundelein, Illinois, Lopez and Esparza discussed how they could foster an environment for faith-based leadership development among Latino college students in the Pilsen community.[102] That vision conceived by Lopez and Esparza has become a reality, due to a generous grant of $3.4 million from the state of Illinois. Once renovated, the site will serve as a community-based college dormitory, housing seventy-seven students and four resident assistants from the neighborhood.[103]

TRP's decision to rehabilitate this site was based on two factors, one statistical, one anecdotal. First, although 43 percent of residents in the organization's "target neighborhoods," i.e., Pilsen, Little Village, and Back of the Yards, hold a high school degree or GED, only 7 percent hold a bachelor's degree or higher.[104] Second, college students hailing from these neighborhoods tend to live at home during their college years, either because they cannot afford the expense of living on campus or because their families "adhere to traditional values," thereby expecting children—even those of college age—to live with their parents until they are married.[105]

In line with TRP's ministry of community empowerment, the central objective of *La Casa* is to provide a space "where young Latinos(as) can explore their Catholic faith and potential for leadership through reflection, living in community, service and action." According to Alicia J. Rodríguez, community organizer at TRP, this "community-based" dormitory experience aims to integrate five components: (1) leadership and spirituality, (2) collective action, (3) community service, (4) education, and (5) community living. While the leadership and spirituality component en-courages residents to develop leadership skills from a faith-based perspec-tive, the collective action component emphasizes student involvement in special community projects. In addition to requiring each resident to en-gage in ten to fifteen hours of service per month, the community service component invites residents to participate in a mini-internship and men-torship program. The education component demands that all residents be enrolled in a postsecondary educational program. The community living component underlines *La Casa*'s primary mission of living in community and working together in collaboration.[106]

On a sunny day in April 2001, Raúl Hernández, president of TRP's board of directors, drove me to the official site of *La Casa*, 1628 W. Sev-enteenth Street, formerly a convent for Polish sisters. TRP acquired the site and used the downstairs as an annex to its 1818 South Paulina Street site for additional administrative offices. The property sits directly next to St. Adalbert Church, a TRP member parish. Outside the church, a large sign advertises mass in English on Saturdays at 6 P.M. and Sundays at 11:30 A.M.; *Misas en Español* (masses in Spanish) at 10:15 A.M. and 1:15 P.M. on Sundays; and *Msza Po Polsku w niedzeiele o Godz* (masses in Polish) at 9 A.M. on Sundays. The "convent site" is adorned with Polish religious art. Upon walking in the front door, the visitor is greeted with pictures of Di-vine Mercy and Our Lady of Czestochowa—both popular religious devo-tions from Poland—sitting on a small ledge in the front hallway. Upstairs, the Polish sisters' names adorn small golden plaques above the entrance to each room.

Hernández admits that TRP's involvement in education—including the space for college dormitory living—"is my baby." "I know what it's like to go through life without education, so education should be a main pri-ority" at the organization, he states. Rodríguez, however, has a different story for her interest in the *La Casa* initiative. A graduate of Loyola Uni-versity in Chicago, Rodríguez proudly comments that she was the first in her family to earn a college degree. The daughter of parents who work in a candy factory in Des Plaines, Illinois, she says a college degree is quite an accomplishment for a young Latina woman, especially one born and raised in Little Village. Still a resident of Little Village, Rodríguez com-ments that through the creation of *La Casa*, "we want to show that it is possible, that there are students from the neighborhood who are in col-lege and making it."[107]

TRP's involvement in the rehabilitation of the convent site reflects the literature on community building. A recent approach to community development, community building is a holistic term that identifies not only the economic needs of a particular urban community, but also the social and psychological needs. Like Raymundo's definition of a "healthy community" at the start of this chapter, such a literature takes into account the tangible and intangible assets of community life. The desired result of community building, therefore, is not merely the creation of physical development but the establishment of a "sense of accountability and ownership within the community."[108] Central to TRP's ministerial emphasis on community ownership—or community empowerment—in the Latino neighborhoods of Pilsen, Little Village, and Back of the Yards is a religious impulse. Unlike Kathleen Neils Conzen, who states that this religious impulse has been unexplored in the field of urban history,[109] Rodríguez contends that her Roman Catholic faith motivates her to "go the extra mile" for her community "without expecting anything in return."[110]

Amanda Carney, program officer at Local Initiative Support Corporation (LISC), a high-level funder of TRP, commented on the religious impulse driving the community-living space at *La Casa*. She referred to a recent tour of the site that she conducted for an African American community organization so that representatives could get a first-hand look at TRP's plans for college dormitory housing. Carney and the representatives could not fathom how students would be interested in living so close to home, in a place where faith was a "central component." They all murmured that "it must be a Latino thing."[111]

Religion "seems to have gained a new lease on life" in the inner city, states Harvey Cox.[112] TRP could not agree more. Acting on its religious faith and values, TRP has advanced a human side of community development, one that is informed, as Rodriguez states, by "see[ing] Jesus in others and hav[ing] others see Him in myself."[113] This is a "new paradigm" in community development, one that privileges both physical development and people building, states Raymundo. TRP's development of housing units is always accompanied by a consideration of how the organization can better educate and empower the Mexican neighborhood of which it is an integral part. Whether through housing development, homeownership classes, financial literacy programs, or faith-based leadership development at *La Casa*, TRP manifests that community development starts first with building relationships.

Holding Leadership Accountable

Relationship building means many things to a Latino FBO. Such building may involve forming strategic collaborations with powerful institutional actors in the community, or it may entail having face-to-face conversations with neighborhood residents about their needs. At TRP, there is no doubt that building relationships also requires holding leaders accountable. In fact, the phrase "holding leaders accountable" is repeated like a mantra throughout the organization. TRP staff use the word "accountability" in various contexts: (1) holding TRP member churches accountable to their parishioners, (2) holding TRP staff accountable to ongoing leadership development within the organization, and (3) holding external actors accountable to the community. Whereas the first form of accountability has already been discussed in previous sections—especially in regard to the formation of CBCs in TRP member parishes—the second kind of accountability is addressed in the following section. This section will focus on the last form of accountability, holding external actors accountable to those for whom they speak, i.e., the Latino community.[114]

"All politicians are aware of the growing power in the Latino community," states John Donohue, executive director of the Chicago Coalition for the Homeless. However, when it comes to city politics, it is often "Mayor Daley versus the rest of Latino humanity." According to Donohue, Daley has made the middle class his mayoral platform, thereby erecting a "barrier for Latinos trying to make it" in the low-income class.[115] From the perspective of TRP, some degree of political sophistication is required to hold leaders outside the organization accountable to the Latino community. In the past, remarks Rita Cardoso, member of TRP's board, the organization had "tried to keep away from being involved" in politics, to no avail. TRP quickly realized that it "can't forget about politics," though relationships forged with government officials are often unpleasant.[116]

Latino FBOs like TRP should not be regarded merely as social-services agencies, but as "political actors" through the legitimacy these organizations wield with both community leaders and their neighborhood constituencies. TRP begets a kind of "instantaneous camaraderie and trust" in its dealings with a host of government, corporate, and nonprofit institutions for representing its constituency with integrity, maintains Amanda Carney of LISC.[117] Driven by its faith and values, TRP—like LPAC and Nueva—is a mediating institution that helps foster the democratic process by encouraging Latinos to participate actively in public life. While not partisan, Raymundo admits that "TRP is definitely political." Recognizing that "government is not going to answer all challenges in the neighborhood," TRP decided it was necessary to hold government officials accountable for the types of services they provide for the Latino community at large.[118]

Community Policing

One such area in which TRP holds government officials accountable is public safety—an area of great concern for the neighborhood of Pilsen. At 6 P.M. on a December 2001 night, groups of people gather in the basement of Centro Familiar Guadalupano—a community center next door to TRP's headquarters—to attend a 12th District meeting for police beats 1222, 1223, and 1233. Upon entering the room, even the casual observer would view the representation from the Chicago Police Department as impressive: in addition to nine police officers, a detective, a sergeant, and a commander are present. Twenty-five community residents—mostly Latino, but non-Hispanic whites and African Americans as well—attend.

Officer Alex Errum of the Community Policing division for the 12th District opens the meeting with a commemoration of Officer Brian Strouse, a young plainclothes Chicago police officer who was fatally shot in a Pilsen neighborhood alley. Strouse—a member of the Tactical Unit "Tac Team"—was killed early on July 30, 2001, when he responded to gang-related fire. The *Chicago Tribune* reported the following day:

> The slaying in the 1300 block of West 18th Place shook the surrounding neighborhood, where many houses are freckled with bullet holes, residents say they often duck to avoid gunfire, and gangs torment the area with mayhem.[119]

Two gangs, the Ambrose street gang and La Raza, have a history of "nighttime gun battles"[120] in Pilsen. The youth charged with first-degree murder is sixteen-year-old Hector Delgado, known to Ambrose street gang associates as "He-Man." Believing Strouse to be a member of the rival La Raza gang that night, Delgado was "acting as a security guard protecting gang turf."[121] Errum pays tribute to Strouse, emphasizing that he did not just die, but was "murdered in the line of duty."

Commander Ralph Chiczewski then enters the basement room. Immediately, residents called out, "Hey, Commander C!" Others turn to each other and say, "Isn't our Commander a great guy?" Chiczewski presents an award on behalf of the Chicago Police Department to Alvaro Obregon and Salvador Cervantes, TRP community organizers, for their excellence in community service. He mentions that Pilsen has been his "most challenging assignment" to date, even after years spent in narcotics and other high-pressure divisions. In 2001, the 12th District, which includes most of Pilsen, was the leading district in crime reduction for the city of Chicago. In 2001 alone, there was an 18 percent drop in index crimes, homicides, sexual assault, auto theft, and burglary in the district, maintains Chiczewski. With the "help of groups like TRP," he believes that the crime rate for the district will decrease even more steadily in 2002.[122]

Chiczewski exits, allowing Detective Peter La Forta to introduce himself as the Chicago Alternative Policing Strategy (CAPS) coordinator for five Chicago police districts, including the 12th District. According to La Forta, in November 2001 the Detective Division was reorganized into the following subgroups: Violent Crime (homicides and gang crime), Property Crime (robbery and burglary), and Youth (special victims division). This new reorganization is indicative of the chief of detectives' mandate that all Chicago detectives become more involved with the community through the implementation of the CAPS program in every neighborhood.[123]

CAPS is a community-based program that "enables the community to interact with the police department," notes Errum. It is a partnership whereby the "community and police resolve together" issues from a "wide range of concerns"—from garbage pickup to gang activity—affecting Chicago neighborhoods.[124] Chiczewski argues that CAPS has "taken law enforcement to the next level."[125] Implementation of CAPS initially began in five of Chicago's twenty-five districts in 1993. Currently, the CAPS strategy is operational in all twenty-five districts. These "five original prototype districts," however, "continue to serve as a laboratory for testing new ideas and new technology." In addition to holding monthly meetings in each beat (there are 279 police beats in Chicago), with representation from both police and community residents, the CAPS strategy assigns eight to nine officers to each beat, patrolling both on foot and in squad cars. Moreover, CAPS employs technology to target "crime hot spots" and provides sufficient training for police and community residents to combat crime more effectively.[126]

Following the introductions of members of the Chicago Police Department, Obregon of TRP introduces the central theme for the December CAPS meeting in Pilsen—to continue building relationships of accountability between community residents and the police department. He turns to the participants at tonight's meeting, advising them to break into small groups, one accounting for beats 1222 and 1233 and the other accounting for beat 1223. After doing so, he asks residents to reflect on two questions: (1) "What is your role in reducing crimes and creating a healthy community?" and (2) "What is the main concern you bring to this beat meeting?"

Officers Kolasa and Zaber from the Tac Team introduce themselves to residents from beat 1223 as plainclothes officers whose primary areas of responsibility are gang activity and narcotics in the Pilsen neighborhood. Pledging confidentiality, they encourage the small-group participants to come forward with any information they might have about their beat, as does Third Watch Officer Carpenter—who has the 2–10 P.M. shift. Most of the time, claim Kolasa and Zaber, residents are too afraid to report any suspicious and potentially dangerous activity. The participants begin making comments, reporting everything from hangouts of gang members to potential drug-dealing havens. The officers request more specific information from participants, claiming that precise addresses and times of activity will prove useful to them in their quest to combat narcotics and gang involvement in the neighborhood.[127]

TRP has been a proactive force in seeking ways to collaborate with the Chicago Police Department on behalf of the Latino community. Due to past problems in working with the police, the organization built a relationship with Chicago Superintendent of Police Terry G. Hillard. This relationship rested on a desire that both community residents and the police force "hold each other accountable."[128] TRP "wanted a commitment that officers would work with us," states Obregon. As a result, Hillard assigned three commanders to the three Latino communities represented by TRP: (1) Commander Folliard to Back of the Yards, (2) Commander Chiczewski to Little Village, and (3) Commander Prieto to Pilsen. Obregon maintains that of the three commanders, Chiczewski has given "the most personal commitment" to the Latino community, as TRP is his "pet organization."[129] Committed to a ministry of community empowerment, TRP's relationship with the Chicago Police Department rests on the "instantaneous camaraderie and trust" the organization has with its neighborhood constituents.

Cultivating the "One-on-One"

The magnitude of the camaraderie that TRP shares with its constituents was manifested most potently during the Sara Lee Foundation's 1999

Chicago Spirit Award, held May 5, 1999, Mexican Independence Day. Established in 1983, the Chicago Spirit Award, "considered by some the 'Oscar' of Chicago's non-profit community," selects an organization each year that "has improved life for disadvantaged Chicagoans."[130] TRP was the proud 1999 recipient of the $100,000 grant that accompanied the award, designating the grant money to parenting programs for immigrant families through TRP's Esperanza Familiar program. At a reception that day, TRP "not only brought in leaders for the event, but also brought in buses of people from the community" to share in its celebration. "They packed the place," remarks Patricia Garza, manager of corporate contributions for Kraft Foods. Although it was an afternoon event in Chicago, whole families attended together. TRP representatives spoke in Spanish during their acceptance speeches. Garza maintains that TRP's actions that day "drove home the point well [that] this is us."[131]

As demonstrated by the Chicago Spirit Award reception, TRP realizes that relationships are always "people relationships." Building relationships at the client, parish, and community levels, the organization has promoted the cultivation of "one-on-one" meetings. A practice inherited from the organizing tradition of the Industrial Areas Foundation (IAF), the central objective of the one-on-one at TRP is to build networks of trust through ongoing contact with key individuals significant to the organization. Like IAF-affiliated organizations such as PICO, TRP views the one-on-one "as the critical building block of everything they do."[132] Similarly, TRP endorses IAF's foundational belief that all organizing is "relational organizing."[133]

In contrast to earlier accounts of IAF that characterized the network as a top-down, "confrontational protest organization," Mark R. Warren, author of *Dry Bones Rattling*, contends that one must view this network instead as espousing a bottom-up, "nuanced political strategy"[134] that serves to empower local community residents. Pastors affiliated with TRP, however, would not entirely agree with Warren's assessment of IAF. Unlike TRP, Dahm argues that the IAF network does not focus its efforts enough on educating residents "to be empowered individuals." By encouraging people to "act on [their] self-interest," the emphasis of IAF-affiliated groups like COPS and PICO tends to be "all about power" as opposed to genuine "community organizing."[135] Ultimately, Father Howe of St. Procopius asserts that TRP has a more "respectful way" of engaging in community life than the IAF network. Because TRP "stands for values and not for political parties," it pursues a "kinder, gentler way of community organizing."[136]

Central to the cultivation of the one-on-one at TRP is the organization's use of telling stories, a qualitative method employed by the organization to convey to external actors both the needs of the community and its triumphs. To its private and public funders, the story of María Reya has served as a positive example of TRP's success in building relationships with clients. Jesús "Chuy" De León, acting director of supportive housing at TRP, comments that Reya "went through the different divisions of the organization." De León beams with delight when commenting that "her smile is our paycheck."[137] After living for two years in one of TRP's supportive housing units, Reya secured a job as a sales assistant at a Mexican candy shop in Little Village and purchased a home through the organization. In May 2002, only months after attending the previously mentioned December 2001 homeownership workshop, Reya closed on a house with her brother after enrolling in TRP's Individual Development Account (IDA) program in September 2001. The IDA program in Chicago targets those individuals living 80 percent below the median income. Managed by community organizations like TRP, this program establishes savings accounts along the lines of Individual Retirement Accounts (IRAs) for its clients. These accounts, held at local financial institutions, are designated only for large-scale goals, like capitalizing a business, financing an education, or, in Reya's case, purchasing a home.[138]

In effect, the way in which TRP relates these success stories serves to further deepen the one-on-one relationship the organization has with both external actors and clients in two related ways. First, the telling of such stories makes manifest to other external actors in the community the relationships of transparency TRP forms with its clients. Second, these stories demonstrate that TRP accomplishes what it sets out to do, namely, promote a ministry of community empowerment to the Latino neighborhoods of Pilsen, Little Village, and Back of the Yards. While stories like Reya's have served to attract increased financial support to TRP—both at private and public levels—those stories have not always invited positive attention from other CBOs in the neighborhood. Some of these groups tend to view the organization as a "lone ranger" in the community-serving world and regard TRP's "leadership as arrogant."[139]

Evelyn Pérez, community development director for the Midwest branch of the National Council of La Raza (NCLR), suggests that these negative views of TRP may stem from a larger "disconnect among different Latino organizations" in Chicago. Instead of working alongside each other, they "look at each other as competitors."[140] Community organizations tend to form political alliances with select politicians to forward their own interests. Meanwhile, politicians reinforce these alliances, regarding such organizations—faith-based and secular alike—as platforms to advance their own political strategy. Not only has Alderman Ray Frias of the 12th Ward in Chicago commented that priests like Father Wellems "produce votes," but he has also identified FBOs and congregations as "already existing organizations that are cohesive and that we can use to our advantage."[141]

Building relationships one at a time underlies TRP's ministry of community empowerment. Recognizing that relationship building always involves holding leadership accountable, the organization has been able to serve as an effective voice for the community in its many areas of need. One TRP director describes the organization as "a tool, a channel for the community so it can be better after it uses this tool."[142] TRP is committed to developing one-on-one relationships not only with its clients, but also with those government, business, and community actors with which it collaborates. Because "every action is meaningful," states Julie DeGraaf, director of homeownership services at TRP, the organization realizes that there is no time for competition.[143] "Being neighborly is not about individuals or about competition," maintains Raymundo. Rather, "it is about building a kingdom on earth and being our brother's keeper."[144]

Building a Healthy Community

A colonial-style arch on Twenty-sixth Street reads "*Bienvenidos a Little Village*," welcoming visitors to this predominantly Mexican neighborhood. Little Village, or *La Villita*, is known for the Illinois/Michigan Canal. Built in the late 1800s, this canal connecting the Great Lakes to the Mississippi River runs through Little Village's industrial sector. Home to more than 1,200 businesses, the neighborhood consistently registers as the second-highest district in Illinois for sales-tax revenue after Michigan Avenue. Within a few blocks, large banks like Bank One and Citibank sit almost side-by-side along Twenty-sixth Street. Pulaski Street, with its *lavanderias*, *fruterias*,[145] and medley of small shops like Chickie's Beef and Sandwiches, also showcases Chicago's traditional red-and-tan-brick bungalow-style houses. On Central Park West, banners with the words "*Gente con calidad*" (Quality People) and "*Escuela con calidad*" (Quality School) mark the entrance to St. Agnes of Bohemia grade school, which sits next door to the church that bears its name.

"*Para ustedes los creyentes, esta piedra es preciosa; pero para los incred-ulous, 'la piedra que desecharon los constructors ha llegado a ser la pie-dra angular,' y tambien: 'una piedra de tropiezo y una roca que hace caer.' Tropiezan al desobedecer la palabra, para lo cual estaban destinados*" (1 Pedro 2:7–8).[146] These are the words of the second reading proclaimed by the lector at Sunday mass at St. Agnes Church in late April 2002. A young Latino priest, Father Claudio Díaz, Jr., from Brooklyn, New York, celebrates the mass in a Romanesque church with stained-glass windows depicting the mysteries of the rosary. Above the altar and over a rounded arch are words etched in gold letters, "*Adore te devote latens Deitas,*" or "Hidden God, devoutly I adore thee." Father Díaz speaks of the different types of houses constructed during Jesus' time in the country as well as in the city. Those in the city were made of stone, and "*quedan impresión que eran sólidas.*" Our spiritual houses, says Díaz, must also be solid con-structions. Building strong interior houses, "*permite[n] afrontar la vida*" (allows one to face life) with great faith, especially in times of great trial and suffering.[147]

TRP is an enterprise of "faith in action," challenging residents and leaders to live out their faith as a way of building a healthy community.[148] For TRP, building a healthy community is a combination of physical and human development. Advancing a ministry of community empowerment, the organization recognizes the "homeowner [as] critical to a healthy community." "People need a stake in their community," states DeGraaf, and homeownership provides them with that vehicle.[149] As Díaz ends his homily with the words, "*aquí, necesitamos construir nuestras casas. Ahi comieza la construcción,*"[150] one is reminded of the human side of TRP's community development. Although TRP manifests a "much more re-served expression of faith"[151] than its member parish St. Agnes, the orga-nization would consider Díaz's rallying cry of building up God's kingdom on earth—tangible and intangible assets included—as vital to creating a healthy community.

"Quality of Life Plan"

Similar to the method employed in Latin American liberation theology and U.S. Latino theology, TRP's approach to building a healthy commu-nity entails fostering sustainable relationships and lifestyles. Coupled with this approach is the organizational emphasis placed on preserving cul-tural identity, "to the extent that identity centers upon Mexican traditions and culture," argues Raymundo.[152] Since TRP's inception in 1990, the organization has been attentive to empowering the Mexican community in the areas of housing, education, and faith-based community organizing. Due to the organization's desire to "anchor Pilsen as the Mexican center of Chicago,"[153] TRP has realized that the twin forces of cultural preservation and economic revitalization are essential to enhancing the quality of life in the neighborhood.

Working cooperatively with other community organizations and local government actors, TRP has sought to preserve the Mexican character of Pilsen against the threat of further gentrification, so that a "wonderful, vibrant Mexican community" can flourish "in the heart of Chicago."[154] For years, Pilsen residents have feared community displacement by developers and institutions of higher learning through the promotion of incentive plans like tax-increment financing (TIF). TIF provides private developers with the opportunity to "stimulate investment in specific areas that have had difficulty attracting investment," such as the low-middle-income neighborhood of Pilsen.[155] One possible solution to this encroachment is offered by John Podmajersky, lifelong community developer in Pilsen. He maintains that "capitalizing on the area's identity as an arts district is the key to community survival."[156] Since its establishment in 1982, the Mexican Fine Arts Center Museum (MFACM) has been a cultural mainstay in the neighborhood. A sister museum to the Museo Templo Mayor in Mexico City, the MFACM is the largest Mexican and Latino arts institution in the United States and the first such institution to be accredited by the American Association of Museums. As executive director of the MFACM, Carlos Tortolero believes that central to the museum's mission is not only bringing Mexican culture to the larger community, but also having "Mexicans . . . tell our story from our point of view."[157]

On July 22, 2001, the MFACM and the University of Illinois at Chicago (UIC) sponsored a free performance by the Chicago Symphony Orchestra (CSO) entitled "*Plazas de México*" for the residents of Pilsen and Little Village. Held at Harrison Park on Nineteenth Street and Damen Avenue in Pilsen, the 6:30 P.M. performance drew pieces largely from the Argentine tango composer, Astor Piazzolla, and other representatives of classical Latin American music. CSO conductor Daniel Barenboim, a native-born Argentine, played the piano that evening. In addition to the performance, several arts, music, and family activities were scheduled for the day from 11 A.M. to 6 P.M. TRP manned an information booth at the performance all day to participate in this community-wide event.[158]

The CSO performance in 2001 set in motion a larger outreach strategy to the Mexican communities of Pilsen and Little Village. Lee Koonze, director of community relations for CSO, commented that "*nuestra esperanza es que los residents de Pilsen y La Villita sientan que la Sínfonica de Chicago es su orquestra . . . y que esta orquestra es un reflejo de la comunidad y que es accessible a todos.*"[159] In addition to holding after-school classes for community children at the MFACM as part of the *Armonía* program, CSO has collaborated recently with TRP in the *Caminos a la Música* partnership. According to the orchestra's website, through *Caminos a la Música*, CSO and Civic Orchestra of Chicago musicians have agreed to perform concerts in Pilsen and Little Village for the Mexican's community's religious festivals, such as *Día de la Virgen de Guadalupe*, *Via Crucis*, and others. Furthermore, this partnership allows TRP constituents to attend concerts at CSO's Orchestra Hall at a reduced rate. The intention of these concerts and reduced ticket rates, according to the CSO website, is for the orchestra and "classical music to become a part of the fabric of the community."[160]

TRP's motivation as the lead agency in the New Communities Program was similar to that of CSO: to make the celebration of Mexican arts and culture a central part of the fabric of neighborhood life in Pilsen. Spearheaded by LISC, this program assembled a Pilsen Planning Committee (PPC) of 18 prominent actors in the neighborhood, including principals of Catholic and public schools as well as government officials, clergy, and community activists, to engage openly about Pilsen's future. The outcome of PPC's monthly meetings—held November 2005 to August 2006—was the development of a "Quality of Life Plan," unveiled by LISC in early February 2007. This plan delineates a five-part strategy for the preservation and enhancement of Pilsen's Mexican-oriented community by (1) creating more affordable housing, (2) making Pilsen a safer and healthier area to raise families, (3) promoting paths to higher education for residents of all ages, (4) expanding economic development efforts in the neighborhood, and (5) improving the image of Pilsen as center of Mexican arts and culture in metropolitan Chicago.[161]

Under the "Quality of Life Plan," the fifth strategy (i.e., improving Pilsen's image), sets forth a series of suggestions to enhance the value of the neighborhood's cultural and historic assets. Along with expanding the Eighteenth Street business district, such a strategy outlines the need for a "beautification plan" to attract visitors to the neighborhood. Restoring Pilsen's mural art on Sixteenth Street as well as developing Mexican-style gathering places—*El Paseo* and *El Zócalo*—are also featured prominently under this strategy. Whereas *El Paseo* would be redeveloped to create a "pedestrian link" on Sangamon Street between UIC to the north and Cermak Road to the south, the *El Zócalo* site at Eighteenth and Paulina streets—the plaza that sits directly in front of TRP headquarters—would serve as a Mexican-style town square for both local businesses selling their wares and a range of community activities.

To date, TRP has hosted a variety of outdoor events at this site, including *Tardes en El Zócalo*, or "Evenings in the Town Square"—a weekend of cultural programs in late summer—as well as movies, dance ensembles, and information fairs. Capitalizing on the strong sense of Mexican culture in *El Zócalo*, in December 2002 Carlos Santana filmed a video there. Understanding the Christian narrative as "something *lived* and not just *held*,"[162] TRP uses the site every year for *Día de los Muertos* celebrations, a Mexican religious festival honoring the memories of deceased friends and family members. Furthermore, over the last few years, the 33-foot statue of *La Virgen del Nuevo Milenio* has paid a weeklong visit to the site. With thousands of people flooding the site to pray in front of the Virgin Mary and attend outdoor masses by TRP member priests, *El Zócalo* manifests the degree to which it is already "more than a town square." Rather, it is a place "where commerce, faith, politics, and art come together."[163]

At the end of the "Quality of Life Plan," a proclamation issued by Alderman Daniel Solís (25th Ward) expresses his desire to work collaboratively with the PPC to develop a common vision for the neighborhood of Pilsen through the New Communities Program. Beyond lending support to the committee, Solís also agrees to commit the "necessary resources including municipal, financial, and human" to help implement the plan.[164] Recognizing that "many times in the past" members of the committee—including himself—"have worked separately" or as competitors, he views the "Quality of Life Plan" as an important step forward. Solís finds the plan to have provided committee members with "a rare occasion" to work together to build a healthy community.[165]

Leadership and Reinvention

Serving as a committee member in the New Communities Program alongside a host of community activists and public officials like Solís, Raymundo realizes that urban community development is not solely the work of government or community-serving organizations. As one such community organization, TRP was established not to replace government services, "but to enhance local government and the quality of its services." It is Raymundo's belief that organizations like TRP build on government programs, fine-tuning them to meet the needs of the Mexican community.[166] As an FBO, TRP endeavors to meet these needs by acting on the organization's faith and values. Agreeing with Leonardo Boff that Christianity is a "social practice,"[167] TRP does not evangelize. Evangelization is reserved for the member parishes, which are essentially "built-in constituencies" and a good base of community support for the organization.[168]

A complex organization with multimillion-dollar development projects, TRP strives to hold itself accountable through the constant reevaluation of its organizational structure. Under Raymundo's leadership the organization continually engages in a restructuring process, reinventing itself every four to five years. He notes that TRP has launched four periods of reinvention in its organizational lifetime: (1) in 1994, when ICO and PRDC merged to become TRP; (2) between 1996 and 1997, when the organization expanded from a six-parish membership base to fourteen, by including churches in Little Village and Back of the Yards; (3) in 2001, when TRP initiated a strategic planning process that reorganized its services into four main categories: (a) organizing and leadership development, (b) homeownership services, (c) asset management, and (d) economic development;[169] and (4) in 2005, in anticipation of the organization's twentieth anniversary in 2010. The vision underlying TRP's latest strategic plan is for the organization to become a "paragon of community impact through leadership, innovation, and results."[170]

Of all the areas in which TRP is involved, Raymundo claims that leadership development is of utmost importance within the organization. There is "no question that TRP recruits some of the smartest, most highly motivated individuals seen in nonprofits in the city," says Doug Kenshol, director of resource development at TRP. Individuals like Juan Salgado, executive director of the Institute for Latino Progess; Juanita Irizarry Martínez, executive director of Latinos United; and Sylvia Puente, director of the Center for Metropolitan Chicago Initiatives of the Institute for Latino Studies at the University of Notre Dame, all worked at TRP in some leadership capacity in the past. Due to competitive salaries and a scarcity of sophisticated professionals in the nonprofit world, TRP has experienced difficulty with staff retention. In less than one year, for example, there have been three resource development directors. It has "been a struggle not to have consistency," comments Allison Nanni, resource development associate at TRP.[171]

An example of the organization's long-standing commitment to internal leadership development is the weekly staff meetings, held Wednesday afternoons at 1 P.M. The organization's staff meeting in early December 2001 commenced with the sharing of traditional Mexican foods consisting of bulging plastic bags of tamales, both natural-colored and fluorescent pink, from a local neighborhood store. Peeling the corn husks away from the tamale hiding inside, TRP staff listened to presentations on marketing and property management. These meetings are not conducted in a hierarchical, top-down way. Concerned with developing leadership skills in TRP employees—particularly good organizational and public-speaking skills—Raymundo makes sure that all staff members take turns in running the meetings. Susan Lloyd, director at the John D. and Catherine T. MacArthur Foundation in Chicago, attributes these staff-led meetings to Raymundo's ability to delegate leadership at TRP. Although Raymundo is the most visible presence at TRP, he is known to step back and let others within the organization have the spotlight.[172]

And yet, Mexican American institutions like TRP "are still young and are wrapped around who the director is," comments Tortolero.[173] From the perspective of many public and private organizations, Raymundo is considered the "golden boy"[174] for his vision, intelligence, integrity, and ability to work with anyone—community residents, public officials, private corporations, and staff. In the foundation world, he is considered one of a few "thought leaders" concerned with urban community development at the regional level. Because of his prominent status at TRP and in the community at large, many have expressed concern about succession planning after Raymundo leaves the organization. As a "brilliant manager," Raymundo's "transition will be felt," says Lloyd.[175]

In Raymundo's view, leadership development also encompasses the realm of board governance at the organization. At TRP's inception, all pastors from the twelve member parishes sat on the board of directors. It is appropriate that pastors have served as board members, claims Pesqueira of the McCormick Tribune Foundation. Pastors obtain much valuable information from their parishioners about the state of urban community life, and "this is a benefit to the mission of the organization." At the same time, Pesqueria maintains, TRP should keep clergy members on its board—especially if their presence ensures a stronger relationship with the churches—and board membership also should include more representation of Mexican Americans from the community.[176]

In TRP's latest "reinvention," Raymundo has put into place a new governing structure, taking into account—whether consciously or not—Pesqueira's suggestions. The organization has expanded its board of directors to 17 members. Of those 17 board members, ten spaces are reserved for clergy and laity from TRP's member parishes, while the remaining seven spaces are "elected" positions reserved for prominent leaders from the community. Based on this governing structure, there is "at least a three-majority rule from (TRP) member institutions," claims Raymundo.[177] This new structure is rooted in the reality of TRP as a "complex organization," identified by its high-level community-development projects. However, the driving concern for every TRP board member remains the same, that is, to advocate effectively for the interests of the organization and to build a healthy community in the neighborhoods in which TRP serves.

Conclusion

The preceding sections have examined how TRP advances a ministry of community empowerment in the largely Mexican neighborhoods of Pilsen, Little Village, and Back of the Yards. An organization with its roots in faith-based community organizing, TRP has managed to keep such organizing at the heart of its mission, as evidenced by its national, state, and local initiatives on political advocacy issues ranging from comprehensive immigration reform to the formation of SMART groups in member parishes. This is unlike most CBOs, claims Father Dahm, where the increasing demands of economic development triumph over the more intangible needs of community organizing and leadership development.[178] Believing strongly that community residents "can be their own advocates for positive change,"[179] as one TRP staff member put it, "we have to be organizers as much as we are developers and educators."[180]

Being "driven by [religious] values" is in and of itself "an added value" to TRP, claims Lloyd of the MacArthur Foundation.[181] Due to its mission of working with neighborhood parishes, TRP is "held accountable by its member churches."[182] In staying tied to its member parishes, the organization is "less likely to lose [its] community connection."[183] Some public officials view TRP's close alliance with its neighborhood parishes as a great utility. As assistant commissioner of DOH, Lopez contends that "lenders like to know outreach." The kind of outreach that TRP's member parishes provide is significant, she claims, because these parishes "easily are around three thousand members each."[184] Other nonprofit leaders simply point out how TRP, as a group of "hard-core Catholics," is an organization that "integrates faith in [its] decision-making."[185]

At TRP, relationships are always "people relationships,"[186] which has accounted for its success in creating opportunities for its community constituents. With many of the organization's staff residing in the Pilsen, Little Village, and Back of the Yards neighborhoods, the organization views itself not merely as the voice of the community, but, more importantly, as a genuine extension of the community it serves. While the organization does not manifest "a flag-waving kind of faith"[187] in its ministry of community empowerment, as an FBO, TRP's "motives should be purer and more for the people," comments Elena Segura, director of Catholic relief services for the Archdiocese of Chicago.[188] Recognizing that being an FBO means building community, TRP would agree with Father Ezequiel Sánchez that "nothing has the ability to invoke"—or empower—"the community like faith."[189]

7

Speaking the Language of
Religious Identity Politics

[Latino FBOs are] demystifying the language of what faith-based
is. [Being an FBO is] not limited to evangelization. These organizations have shown that they are doing critical work, [typically] not
recognized. The faith-based language is out there and this helps to
name the level of work [accomplished by such organizations].
                                        —Alexie Torres Fleming[1]

During my 1994 study-abroad program in Concepción, Chile,
I lived with a host family, Luisa and Genaro Salgado. Because the Sal-
gados were retired, they were able to spend long periods of time with me
at every meal, teaching me Chilean phrases and correcting my *castellano*
(Spanish). One day while I was in the apartment, the telephone rang.
"*Hola*" (hello), I said to the other person on the line, "*¿de parte de quien?*"
(who is calling?). The man responded, "*Pedro de Valdivia.*" Based on my
studies, I remembered that Pedro de Valdivia was the *conquistador* (conqueror) of Chile. In fact, I had just seen his statue in the central plaza of
Santiago, Chile, only days before. I retorted, "*Ud. es un mentiroso. Pedro de
Valdivia es un estatuo en la plaza*"[2] and quickly hung up the phone. A few
minutes later, the telephone rang again. This time Genaro answered it. After a brief conversation with the caller, he put down the phone, laughing
hysterically. He said to me that the person on the other line was "Pedro"
—his mechanic—from the nearby town of Valdivia, Chile, calling back
again. When someone calls a household in Chile, stated Genaro, one must
announce oneself properly, stating one's name and place of residence.
In this case, the Chilean mechanic happened to have the same name as
Chile's famous conqueror.

Speaking a different language involves many different components. At the earliest stages, one must first memorize vocabulary words in the other language, repeating them over and over to oneself. Then, one studies grammar to learn how to construct sentences in a proper manner. The end goal of sentence construction is the ability to carry on a two-way conversation—stumbling at times initially but then speaking with ease. Beyond grammar, there is a host of idioms or "local expressions" to be learned. Grammatical study and familiarity with local expressions is followed by a keen attention to acquiring the particular "accent" of the language in question. Acquiring this accent is the crown jewel of the language business. It is often said that when one is "fluent" in another language, that person speaks like a "native."

In many ways, speaking the language of religious identity politics is not dissimilar to learning any other language. There is a set of vocabulary words and a proper way to express the religious values, beliefs, and culture of the Christian believer, enabling both the speaker (i.e., researcher) and the believer to have a worthwhile conversation. Furthermore, speaking this language of religious identity politics also requires the possession of a kind of "accent"—or, an indicator that the researcher converses fluently in the language. In an attempt to consider religion only for its instrumental worth, many social-science researchers have misunderstood that religion is not simply a "means" to something else but intrinsically valuable in its own right. In so doing, these researchers have improperly articulated how the religious values, beliefs, and culture of the Christian believer may actually possess meaning apart from the larger social and political order. Researchers often think they know better than their study population, just as I assumed I knew who "Pedro de Valdivia" was, abruptly ending a phone call.

Faith, Hope, and Love

One of the main goals of this book has been to reserve a place for religious identity politics in the conceptual vocabulary of political science. The epigraph to this chapter reveals that the "faith-based language is out there." The goal of the researcher, therefore, is to come to terms with this language, presenting it in the most accurate way to the Christian believer, Christian congregation, or FBO under study. In their research of faith-based social ministries, Unruh and Sider have demonstrated that there are "multiple layers of spiritual meaning" in social ministry, ranging from scriptural authority to personal calling.[3] The Latino FBOs presented in this study—LPAC, Nueva, and TRP—exhibit these layers of spiritual meaning through the public theologies driving their respective Christian ministries. Apart from the distinct kind of social and political action in which each FBO engages, however, all FBO leadership believes in the power of the Christian narrative to shape human action. Central to Christian religious culture is the desire to "become a certain kind of person."[4]

This desire to clothe oneself with the "new self" (Col. 3:9) is manifested in the "dialogic character" of the Christian virtues of faith, hope, and love. The Christian believer deems such virtues as divine gifts infused into the human person. Instead of being characterized as values subject to social construction, these virtues result from an "interpersonal relationship" with God. Displayed throughout biblical tradition, God initiates and the human person—in being "attentive, open, and receptive"—responds.[5] Faith, hope, and love are considered "interconnected" virtues. One might characterize such a "vital interaction" as "reaching in hope, knowing in faith, and accepting in love."[6] Despite the inextricable link that exists among faith, hope, and love, St. Paul claims that of the Christian virtues, "the greatest of these is love" (1 Cor. 13:13). Other liberation theologians like Jürgen Moltmann, however, maintain that the human person is first and foremost a "creature of hope." Moltmann cites a poem from Charles Péguy —French poet, essayist, and philosopher and mentor to Jacques Maritain —to make his case that hope lies at the center of the other two virtues:

Hope leads everything.
For faith only sees what *is*.
But hope sees what *will be*.
Charity only loves what *is*.
But hope loves what will be—
In time and for all eternity.[7]

The Christian is "claimed by hope," asserts Jean Bethke Elshtain.[8] God's liberating power in scriptural tradition—from Exodus to the death and resurrection of Jesus Christ—has shown God to be the "God of hope" and Jesus Christ to be the "Messiah of hope."[9] As exhibited in the poem, the virtue of hope directs one's present attention to the promise of a better future. Steeped in biblical stories of deliverance, the Christian believer also realizes that hope cannot be severed from one's spiritual roots in the past.[10]

In addition to being "faith-based" and charitable organizations, Latino FBOs are institutions of hope. Providing opportunities for urban dwellers to rise above their adverse conditions, Latino FBOs are "enabling institutions"[11] that facilitate real spiritual and structural change in the inner city. Given that the inner city is a place of continuous socioeconomic struggle, FBO leadership and staff affirm with St. Paul that "suffering produces endurance, and endurance produces character, and character produces hope, and hope does not disappoint" (Rom. 5:1–5). As new liberationists, Rivera, Cortés, and Dahm contend that the Christian virtue of hope is not only personal, but also has communal and public orientations. Poignantly displayed in their respective public theologies (Rivera's theology of captivity, Cortés' institutionalization of Misión Integral, and Dahm's communal praxis of liberation), these new liberationists teach their community constituents to "live in hope" by transforming the "wounded" urban culture of which they are a part.[12] With the prophet Jeremiah, these leaders desire to bring the inner city "recovery and healing" as well as an "abundance of prosperity and security" (Jer. 33:6).

The significance of living in hope—and "collective hope"—is not limited to the discipline of theology or the ministerial profession. While much headway has been made in the field of psychology on this topic, recent scholarship has been performed on the relevance of hope in political philosophy and the social sciences, exhibited in the 2004 special edition of the *Annals of the American Academy of Political and Social Science*, "Hope, Power, and Governance." In this edition, Valerie Braithwaite contends that hope implies "goal-oriented thinking." Such thinking involves (1) the clear articulation of goals, (2) the identification of paths needed to achieve those goals, and (3) a sense of agency. Thus, hope can be considered a "human resource for change."[13] According to Victoria McGeer, hope is most pronounced in situations of "limited agency," i.e., when a person faces his or her own limitations as an agent of change. Described as a "social phenomenon," hope necessitates the "scaffolding of others" for one's needs and desires to be fulfilled. In the case of inner-city life, congregations and FBOs often provide this "scaffolding" to the extent that such institutions hold out the promise for living in collective hope, i.e., a hope reserved for the entire community.[14]

Politicians long have recognized the value of employing the "rhetoric of hope" in their public addresses. From Bill Clinton's parting words at the 1992 Democratic National Convention—"I still believe in a place called Hope"—to the recent reiteration of this exact phrase by 2008 presidential contender Governor Mike Huckabee (R-AK), the use of such a rhetoric is alive and well among public officials. Depending on the audience, political leaders infuse this rhetoric with secular or religiously inspired language. In secular contexts, political leaders typically link the language of hope to a policy agenda that serves as the means to bring about the desired public hope. At religious gatherings—such as the annual National Hispanic Prayer Breakfast—political leaders may choose to "tie hope to a religious metaphysic" to highlight the role that supernatural agency plays in the delivery of that desired hope.[15] At the 2007 breakfast, Senator Hillary Clinton proclaimed that "those of us who are motivated by our faith must find ways also to provide hope."[16] In linking hope to a policy agenda or to religious beliefs, politicians exhibit the extent to which hope is "facilitated by institutions."[17]

Religious Identity Politics across the Disciplines

Institutions are the "cultural regulators of life's journey," asserts Braithwaite. Grounded in Latino religious culture, LPAC, Nueva, and TRP are institutions of hope in the inner city that "do the extraordinary" for their urban constituents.[18] These organizations provide their communities with a worldview that privileges economic development, social betterment, and political change.[19] Although such organizations share a common belief in the Christian narrative, their forms of Christian ministry are different from one another. These varieties of Christian ministry—personal outreach, institutional development, and community empowerment—stem from the articulation of a distinct religious identity politics at each organization. As exhibited in the case studies of LPAC, Nueva, and TRP, it is impossible to understand the instrumental worth of these organizations without first taking into account the unique theological commitments that drive such social and political involvement.

Politics is not a starting point of the development of a religious identity politics in the Latino community. Such an identity politics "is not a political realization, though it has political consequences."[20] Advocating a "holistic sociology of the black church," Harold Dean Trulear invites social scientists to engage more fully in a study of the "ideational structures," or the beliefs and values, that ground such an institution. He notes that too much attention has been placed on the role of "social structures," or the institutional constraints that have shaped the emergence of the black church. Social science has erred, comments Trulear, in fixing its scholarly attention on researching the instrumental worth of minority congregations, or *what they do*, at the expense of studying the intrinsic value of such congregations, or *what they are*—i.e., the "faith" in faith-based. It is black religious ideation and not social structures, according to Trulear, "that is essential to understanding and even harnessing the power of the black church." Such religious belief "is the source of its power."[21]

Latino religious institutions—congregations and FBOs alike—are indeed "political," but so too are they "spiritual." Any understanding of the political and social involvement of LPAC, Nueva, and TRP must be traced back to the religious values, beliefs, and culture of the organizations' respective public theologies. To Latino Christians, religion matters not simply because it produces social capital, but because it is a source of personal, communal, and public truth. And the believer considers such truth not as contingent, but as universal, "absolute, and unchallengeable."[22] The fact that there is a universal truth accessible to the believer does not illustrate that there is only "one" kind of religious identity politics. As the Latino FBOs under study attest, there can be many expressions of religious identity politics—even considering the fact that these organizations derive their values, beliefs, and culture from the same Christian tradition and are located in similar urban contexts in the United States.

As evidenced in the Christian ministries of LPAC, Nueva, and TRP, "in the public life of this country, religious convictions spill over into people's aspirations for political action."[23] Nevertheless, religious identity politics does not place its emphasis solely on the same types of values, beliefs, and culture as those of the political order. The spheres of religion and politics both acknowledge the need to cultivate relationships within the political community at large. However, religious identity politics transcends the objectives of the political sphere by recognizing that such cultivation always has a supernatural source. As a new approach in the field of political science, religious identity politics may "contribute to the development of new intellectual spaces"[24] in other academic disciplines. The paragraphs that follow provide suggestions as to how speaking the language of religious identity politics can take place in the fields of political science, religious studies, sociology, and public administration—to name a few.

Political Science

In viewing Latino religious culture as "more than the attitudes people hold to politicians and political institutions,"[25] this study has challenged the traditional boundaries of political science. Most political scientists would agree with Verba et al. that religion is a welcome presence in public life because it is a "democratic arena of activity," especially for those "resource-poor" citizens who lack access to "political resources."[26] In other words, religion helps develop "democratic skills that facilitate democratic participation."[27] In contrast to being a "means" to something else in public life, this study maintains that religion cannot be reduced to simply a political, economic, or social variable.[28] As a politically significant reality, religion influences public culture in six main ways: sacred symbols, sacred doctrine, dynamic presence, divine purpose, public language, and social action. Political scientists might consider how religious actors use public language to explain their world. Stephen Hart has referred to this language as "transcendent talk." He claims that this kind of language is a "rich and complex one," which cannot be described simply as "politics with a religious veneer."[29] Although religious leaders tend to make their language democratically available, such language still abounds with religious truths and imagery. A study of religiously inspired language is politically important, therefore, to the extent that religion provides both "an articulated vision of how the world should be" and a cultural template for "understanding the world, oneself, and [one's] relations."[30] Without fully understanding the religious truths pronounced by a particular group of believers, it is extremely difficult to decipher that group's social and political vision.

The field of political science cannot rely on its own limited language to understand the unique way in which Latino FBOs—and religious believers, generally speaking—operate as political actors in the community. In *Stories of Peoplehood* (2003), Rogers M. Smith contributes to the subfield of identity politics through his presentation of the concept of "peoplehood" as a kind of collective identity in public life. According to Smith, peoplehood is a secular orientation that offers a "sense of belonging [or] a sense of place in the world." Concerned with how political identities "come to exist and become institutionalized," Smith dedicates a central portion of his book to discussing the role that "ethically constitutive stories" play in preserving the values, beliefs, and culture of identity groups or "particular political peoples." Because he likens peoplehood to a Darwinian concept that builds on "more secular accounts of humanity," there is missing a discussion as to how political identities are generated for people of faith. Concurring with David Laitin that "construction and choice . . . is now the standard story line about identities,"[31] Smith's work fails to come to terms with those religious believers who deem identity as something "discovered" through interaction with sacred writings or an interpersonal relationship with God.

Religious identity politics can build on research in political science to provide a more accurate reading of religion from the perspective of the believer. Local communities, faith communities included, are "specific sources of identities"[32] that act as "significant sources of political cues" for members.[33] In that religious identity—like its cultural and political counterparts—"tells us who we are, how we should behave, and how we should act toward those who are not part of us,"[34] such an identity (or "identities," as this study has displayed) exerts an important influence on political behavior. Rather than study religious identity from a secular point of view, the field of political science must "get inside" religion, so to speak, and learn religion's own language in an effort to understand more fully its impact on the life of politics. One way of "getting inside religion" is to conduct more qualitative research or political ethnographies on the interplay between religion and politics.

Religious Studies

Recognizing the important contributions made to promote "cultural affirmation" and "self-identity" in Latino theological scholarship, Benjamín Valentín makes the case that such scholarship needs to fix its attention on how the celebration of local cultures is tied to "community-based political empowerment." According to Valentín, Latino religion has remained narrowly focused on questions of religious identity and culture to the detriment of examining its "broader sociopolitical significance" in the larger community. This one-sided approach neglects Latino religion's public side, he notes, by relegating religion to the private sphere of individual or ethnic community life. Instead of ridding such religion of its emphasis on cultural identity, Valentín desires to unite Latino cultural identity with a "concept of the public," thereby "mapping" out a public theology. His reasons for fashioning a public theology are twofold: (1) to enable Latino theology the opportunity to engage in a "comprehensive project for social justice" and (2) to allow Latino theology to gain a "public voice" in the larger U.S. society.[35]

Gastón Espinosa, Virgilio Elizondo, and Jesse Miranda maintain that Latino religion has played a markedly public role in "political, civic, and social action" in the United States for decades. Whether inspiring United Farm Worker pilgrimages or creating "an ecumenical spirit of cooperation between Catholics and Protestants" in the Sanctuary Movement (a grassroots movement in protest of U.S. immigration policy), Latino religion was at the center of the twentieth-century fight for social justice.[36] Recent findings from the 2007 *Changing Faiths: Latino Religion and the Transformation of American Religion* report, co-sponsored by the Pew Forum on Religion and Public Life and the Pew Hispanic Center, have reinforced the extent to which Latino religion will continue to make an impact on American public life, broadly speaking. First, Latino Protestants and Catholics are practicing a "distinctive form of Christianity," characterized by more expressive forms of worship. This charismatic-style worship—described by researchers as the "renewalist movement"—privileges "God's ongoing, day-to-day intervention in human affairs through the person of the Holy Spirit." Second, Latinos are opting to worship in what are referred to as "ethnic churches," thereby exhibiting how such a population not only is creating "its own form of religious practice" but also "its own religious institutions." Finally, Latino religion continues to influence participation in U.S. political life. Consistent with the decades-long involvement of Latinos in a host of social and political initiatives, this population continues to consider religion an important guide to its political thinking. Religion provides a language from which Latinos can articulate their political views.[37]

Speaking the language of religious identity politics in the discipline of religious studies should not prove too difficult a task. After all, Rivera, Cortés, and Dahm—as new liberationists—acknowledge the political significance of all theological work. Through their ministries of personal outreach, institutional development, and community empowerment, these spiritual leaders advance a "public theology," one that takes into account the "comprehensive project for social justice" of which Valentín speaks. Rivera, Cortés, and Dahm, however, are also aware of the need to link their project of liberation to Latino religious culture. Unlike some Latin American liberation theologians, these three leaders do not support discarding popular expressions of Latino religiosity. Whether they are Latino Pentecostal, evangelical Protestant, or Catholic expressions, the stress on popular religion is not only safeguarded, but also regarded as inseparable from liberation. As nationally recognized Latino FBOs, LPAC, Nueva, and TRP have all gained a "public voice" in the larger U.S. society, tackling issues like at-risk youth, comprehensive immigration reform, and homeownership in their local communities. Although a public theology informs the life and work of these FBOs, such a theology is not considered to be the "same theological or political project" at each organization. Nevertheless, each Latino FBO is committed to providing a response—at once theological and public—to the manifold struggles faced by Latinos in the urban context.[38]

Sociology

Since Robert Putnam's groundbreaking work in *Bowling Alone* (2000), sociologists have maintained that congregations—and religious institutions in general—"represent the country's largest form of social connectedness" and "play the largest role in structuring community life."[39] "Religion is a major generator of social capital," claims John A. Coleman, S.J. The contributions "religious social capital" make to democracy are "not limited simply to its more communitarian vision; it also provides civic skills among those who participate in its structures."[40] Although all forms of social capital are alike, religious social capital differentiates itself from its secular counterparts in five main ways: (1) it generates more social capital than "the level of social capital produced through other means," because a great amount of philanthropy and volunteering is religious in nature; (2) it may, in fact, be more durable than other forms of social capital, "because the motivation to remain faithful may well sustain such efforts"; (3) it transcends "simple calculations of self-interest" by seeking to "give 'voice to the voiceless'"; (4) it may offer stronger foundations for group cooperation, promoting "non-material incentives" to foster collective action; and (5) it distributes opportunities to the disadvantaged and to those who otherwise lack political resources.[41]

While there is general agreement that religious institutions produce varied and valuable forms of social capital, many sociologists have pointed out the limitations of social capital theory in fully capturing faith-based social and political action. Mention has been made already of how social capital theory runs the risk of reducing such action to "self-interested entrepreneurial behavior." Furthermore, in its use of the "language of contract," this theory fails to take into account the "covenantal impetus and moral bases,"[42] i.e., the religious values, beliefs, and culture, that underlie such faith-based activity. Lacking the tools needed to explain the content of religious truths held by individuals or a body of believers, social capital theory is limited in documenting religion's broader influence in American public life.[43]

The case studies of LPAC, Nueva, and TRP demonstrate the limitations of employing a social capital framework to examine each organization's religious identity politics. Building on critiques of this framework and its tendency to instrumentalize faith-based social and political activity, this work has maintained that the Latino FBOs in question are not simply political actors, but also "moral communities." Providing a range of services for their urban constituents, these organizations "walk a tightrope" between being motivated by instrumental and moral values.[44] From an instrumental perspective, LPAC, Nueva, and TRP are concerned with the measurable outputs of their program areas, as they are responsive both to their urban clients and to funding streams. From a moral viewpoint, however, is it a religious identity politics that drives the kind of urban community work performed by these Latino FBOs. The production of social capital is not viewed as the main objective of the Christian believer. As Don Browning et al. assert, "Christians do not live the Christian life to produce social capital but it appears that increased social capital is a long-term, secondary consequence of Christian life."[45] In an attempt to understand both the intrinsic value *and* instrumental worth of the religious values, beliefs, and culture for the Latino FBOs under study, this work contributes to recent calls by sociologists to pursue an "expanded sociology of the sacred."[46]

Public Administration

Over the last decade, the field of public administration (or public management) has discussed alternative approaches to help public managers create "public value more properly and effectively than they do now." According to Mark H. Moore, a public manager could involve anyone from elected officials to interest group leaders and private-sector managers. These latter groups can be conceived as public managers, particularly when interest groups "initiate or halt public sector enterprises" and private-sector managers "produce primarily for government."[47] Amid a growing trend of devolution—the "transfer of social responsibilities [from the government] to the private sector"[48]—a whole range of secular and faith-based non-profit organizations could qualify as public managers, to the extent that these organizations often receive government funding to provide much-needed public services. With respect to the Latino FBOs under study, as of the beginning of 2007, each organization receives a substantial portion of its budget from government contracts. TRP receives 30 percent of its $2.8 million budget from these contracts. The levels of government funding, however, are even higher at Nueva and LPAC. While Nueva receives 60 percent of its $18 million budget from such contracts, government funding makes up approximately 90 percent of LPAC's $2.5 million budget.

Borrowing the concept of customer-service delivery from the private sector, public administrators have sought new ways of finding public value. In Moore's view, this concept of customer-service delivery is valuable to the extent that it encourages public managers to make their encounters with clients "more satisfactory."[49] Recent studies in public administration have extended this concern with customer service, calling for the "delivery of culturally appropriate and culturally responsive public services." Similar to the traditional model of customer service, Mitchell F. Rice contends that cultural competency is about "producing better outcomes," through attentiveness to the strengths of "minority cultures, beliefs . . . and value systems." Cultural competency amounts to a new perspective in public administration for its emphasis on the "importance of culture." Rice suggests that those who provide public services to minority populations take an organizational self-assessment to gauge whether the organization advances, among other things, a leadership and governance structure, communications strategy, and service delivery model that is culturally responsive to the population in question.[50]

Building on this recent scholarship in public administration, LPAC, Nueva, and TRP display how—as public managers—they deliver culturally competent services to their largely Latino urban communities. Based on my interviews with government officials, public agencies could be characterized as culturally "pre-competent," possessing only a limited knowledge of such communities. These Latino FBOs, on the other hand, tend not simply to be culturally competent, but, more importantly, culturally proficient,[51] because their leadership and staff often hail from the same urban neighborhoods as their clients. Through the strong emphasis LPAC, Nueva, and TRP place on the language, ethnicity, beliefs, and religious culture of their minority clients, these organizations help to advance the existing body of literature on cultural competency. Having a "nontra-ditional approach" to public administration, these organizations go be-yond "working from the inside" (i.e., gaining knowledge of the behaviors, perspectives, and values of minority cultures).[52] Such Latino FBOs actu-ally are cultural insiders themselves, providing an alternative method of service delivery in the inner city.

Latinos and Faith-Based Leadership

Addressing the crowd of seven hundred at the National Hispanic Prayer Breakfast on June 15, 2007, former Vermont governor Howard Dean spoke of the common values held by the Latino community, namely, "devotion to family, commitment to hard work, an entrepreneurial spirit, and a deep and abiding faith." As chairman of the Democratic National Com-mittee, Dean stressed how the "Democratic Party shares your values." The concern "for the least of these" (Matt. 25:45), he declared, is displayed in the central goals of the Democratic platform: providing universal health care, alleviating global poverty, and preventing HIV/AIDS—the third largest killer in the Latino community. After a series of inspiring musi-cal selections from leading Latino Christian artists—like "*Dios ha sido bueno*" sung by Marcos Witt[53]—and prayers spoken on behalf of mili-tary personnel, the nation, and U.S. political leadership, Senator Hillary Clinton (D-NY) approached the microphone. Clinton spoke of how she has continued to be "enveloped and protected by my faith." Comment-ing on the passage that "faith, by itself, if it has no works, is dead" (James 2:17), she added, "faith without works is dead, but work without faith is too hard."[54]

A three-hour-long celebration, this breakfast dedicated a central part of the morning to the issue of comprehensive immigration reform. From Dean's comment that immigration reform "brought the Democratic Party and the Hispanic community closer together" to President Bush's expres-sion of gratitude to that morning's gathering for "making comprehensive immigration reform your priority," the breakfast clearly displayed the sig-nificance of Latinos as a powerful public voice. Others, like Senator Ted Kennedy (D-MA), spoke of the "moral imperative" of the pending Sen-ate legislation on immigration reform. A recipient of an Esperanza award that day, Eddie Sotelo, a.k.a. "Piolín"—a California radio personality—discussed his recent bus travels throughout the United States, "collecting one million signatures and prayers" in favor of the legislation. Driven by a moral imperative, Sotelo exclaimed to the crowd, *"yo vengo aquí para decir: con Dios todo es posible"* ("I'm here to tell you that everything is possible with God"). Reverend Luis Cortés remarked how Sotelo's actions —delivering the signatures and prayers to the steps of the U.S. Capitol the day before the breakfast—paralleled Moses' "saying to the Pharaoh: Let my people stay."[55]

Over the years, this breakfast has facilitated a "convergence of [Latino] religious leaders"[56] around issues central to the Latino community. Compared with their African American counterparts, Latino churches are relatively "depoliticized" institutions.[57] Gatherings such as the annual prayer breakfast, however, have provided a vehicle for the empowerment of Latino churches and religious leaders over the last six years. This group of Latino faithful is one that is here to stay in the world of U.S. politics, and the impressive lineup of national political figures speaking at this annual event is testimony to that fact. Instead of expecting Latino believers to use neutral language to express how their religious values affect their political views, national figures like Dean and Clinton have infused their own political messages with value-laden and religiously inspired language. The use of such language suggests two things: (1) U.S. politics is "not value free,"[58] and (2) Latino faith-based leaders increasingly are being viewed by U.S. politicians as national spokespersons for their large and burgeoning ethnic communities.

The emphasis placed on faith-based leadership at the breakfast is noteworthy, especially given the "relative absence of national leadership" in the Latino community. In contrast to a Latino population characterized by a "degree of fragmentation," the National Hispanic Prayer Breakfast has been successful in rallying together a faith community from a wide variety of Christian denominations and across the political spectrum in a national setting.[59] As newly emergent political actors on the urban scene, LPAC, Nueva, and TRP provide additional resources for the development of Latino leadership—at the local, state, and national levels. Not only are such Latino FBOs recent players in the field of urban community building, they are also nationally recognized institutions that serve as incubators for political leadership. The kind of leadership these organizations advance is indigenous in nature—all three FBO leaders were born and raised on the inner-city streets of New York City and Chicago. At its core, however, the leadership model of LPAC, Nueva, and TRP is "faith-based," inspired by the age-old truths and values of the biblical tradition.

James MacGregor Burns, a well-acclaimed leadership scholar, acknowledges the power that values have, both for leaders and their constituents. "Leaders embrace values [and] values grip leaders." And, values are "enhanced" if they are attached to a particular cultural system. Burns observes that the stronger the value system, the more empowered the leader becomes, and the more able that leader is to empower his or her followers.[60] Given their fervent belief in the transforming power of the Christian narrative, one might categorize LPAC, Nueva, and TRP as highly value-laden organizations. As a consequence of their strong Christian values, these organizations are also empowering institutions, responding not merely to the material wants of their clients, but also to their spiritual wants. Considering community building as a holistic enterprise, such FBOs put forth a style of faith-based leadership that is at once innovative and liberating.

In political terms, the future remains wide open for the Latino community. At the breakfast, Dean proclaimed to the gathering of Latino faithful that "it is not enough to ask for a seat at the table. We need you on the ticket."[61] While Republicans have continued to court this community, the recent position of a majority of politicians in the Republican camp against immigration reform has dimmed the prospect of many Latinos remaining in that party's fold for long. Whether Democrat- or Republican-leaning, the Latino FBOs under study are providing creative models of leadership amid the harshness of inner-city life. Driven by their vocation to serve, Rivera, Cortés, and Raymundo are faith-based leaders who have shown that a religious identity politics can drive social and political action in the urban context. They take the following words of St. Paul seriously:

> Consider your own call, brothers and sisters. . . . God chose what is weak in the world to shame the strong; God chose what is low and despised in the world, things that are not, to reduce to nothing things that are, so that no one might boast in the presence of God. He is your source of life in Christ Jesus, who became for us wisdom from God, and righteousness and sanctification and redemption, in order that, as it is written, "Let the one who boasts, boast in the Lord." (1 Cor. 1:26–31)

From their establishment approximately fifteen to twenty years ago, LPAC, Nueva, and TRP remain committed to the call to "associate with the lowly" (Rom. 12:16) and powerless in society. Ending the 2007 breakfast, Cortés proclaimed to those gathered that "as a people of faith, I want to remind us that we are the conscience of this country."[62]

Appendix

Sample Questionnaire: Latino Faith-Based Organizations

Program Establishment
1. When did your particular program begin?
2. What were the initial concerns that drove its establishment?
3. Who were the key individuals involved?

Taking Stock
1. How has your program developed over time?
2. What are its strengths and weaknesses?
3. How do you integrate your mission throughout your program?

Setting Direction
1. What have been your program's main goals?
2. How successful have you been in achieving those goals?
3. What defines success for your program?

Community Outreach
1. How involved is your organization in larger community issues (i.e., social, educational, and political issues)?
2. Does your organization address its concerns to government?
3. Has your organization had success in influencing government/public policy?

Organizational Capacity
1. How has your organization formed strategic partnerships?
2. How has your organization leveraged and managed resources?
3. How has your organization built community support?
4. How important is training to your organization?

5. What are the factors influencing the ability to identify and recruit leaders?

Role of Faith

1. How has your identity as a "faith-based organization" influenced the ability to form partnerships and manage resources?
2. Has this identity been a benefit or a challenge?
3. What makes a faith-based organization different from other community-based organizations?

Community Impact

1. What impact has your organization made on larger community issues (i.e., crime, academic performance, and employment)?
2. What influence has your organization had on other community organizations?
3. How does your program cultivate trust in its partnerships and among the people it serves?
4. How does this organization (and your specific program) hope to address the current challenges of the Latino community in your neighborhood?

Notes

NOTES TO THE INTRODUCTION

1. Charles Dickens, *Our Mutual Friend*, ed. and intro. Michael Cotsell (Oxford and New York: Oxford University Press, 1989), 1.

2. Burton Pike, *The Image of the City in Modern Literature* (Princeton, NJ: Princeton University Press, 1981), 58, 69.

3. Michael Cotsell, "Introduction," *Our Mutual Friend*, xi.

4. Mark R. Gornik, *To Live in Peace: Biblical Faith and the Changing Inner City* (Grand Rapids, MI: Eerdmans Publishing, 2002), 32.

5. Ram A. Cnaan et al., *The Invisible Caring Hand* (New York: New York University Press, 2002), 9.

6. See note 5 above.

7. The term "religious identity politics" has been employed by other scholars to discuss the way in which deeply held religious beliefs have political consequences. See Gritt Klinkhammer, "Modern Constructions of Islamic Identity: The Case of Second Generation Muslim Women in Germany," *Marburg Journal of Religion* 8, no. 1 (September 2003), http://web.uni-marburg.de/religionswissenschaft/journal/mjr/klinkhammer.html. However, Klinkhammer's work does not provide a full elaboration of the term (like that provided in chapter one of this study).

8. Kenneth D. Wald et al., "Church Involvement and Political Behavior," in *Rediscovering the Religious Factor in American Politics,* eds. David C. Leege et al. (Armonk, NY: M. E. Sharpe, 1993), 122.

9. Roberto Suro of the Pew Hispanic Center makes a similar point in a telephone conference call regarding the 2007 study, *Changing Faiths: Latinos and the Transformation of American Religion*. He argues that "among Latinos, religion and politics are intertwined. By some measures there's a closer association of religion and politics among Hispanics than among non-Hispanics. You can't understand the roles Latinos play as political actors without also understanding the ways in which they worship." In "Event Transcript," *Changing Faiths: Latinos and the Transformation of American Religion* (25 April 2007), http://pewforum.org/events/index.php?EventID=R140.

10. A recent case study of Nueva prepared for the Annie E. Casey Foundation

assesses the organization's Hispanic Capacity Project. See Edwin I. Hernández et al., *Leadership Matters: The Role of Latino/a Religious Leadership in Social Ministry* (March 2006): 25–32.

11. This term shares much in common with Benjamín Valentín's characterization of public theology as "a form of discourse that couples either the language, symbols, or background concepts of a religious tradition with an overwhelming, integrative, emancipatory, sociopolitical perspective in such a way that it movingly captures the attention and moral conscience of a broad audience and promotes the culture of those modes of love, care, concern, and courage, required both for individual fulfillment and for broad-based social activism." In *Mapping Public Theology: Beyond Culture, Identity, and Difference* (Harrisburg, PA: Trinity Press International, 2002), 87.

12. Several recent works have documented the varieties of Christian ministry in congregations and FBOs, thereby advancing how the social sciences view the practice of religion. These include, among others: John P. Bartkowski and Helen A. Regis, *Charitable Choices: Religion, Race, and Poverty in the Post-Welfare Era* (New York: New York University Press, 2003); Gastón Espinosa, Virgilo Elizondo, and Jesse Miranda, eds., *Latino Religions and Civic Activism in the United States* (Oxford: Oxford University Press, 2005); Lowell W. Livezey, ed., *Public Religion and Urban Transformation: Faith in the City*, intro. R. Stephen Warner (New York: New York University Press, 2000); Steven Rathgeb Smith and Michael R. Sosin, "The Varieties of Faith-Related Agencies," *Public Administration Review* 61, no. 6 (November–December 2001): 651–671; Nancy Tatom Ammerman, *Pillars of Faith: American Congregations and Their Partners* (Berkeley: University of California Press, 2005); and Heidi Rolland Unruh and Ronald J. Sider, *Saving Souls, Serving Society: Understanding the Faith Factor in Church-Based Social Ministry* (Oxford: Oxford University Press, 2005).

13. The Pew Forum on Religion and Public Life and the Pew Hispanic Center, *Changing Faiths: Latinos and the Transformation of American Religion* (Washington, DC: Pew Research Center, 2007), 18, 59, 9.

14. Luis G. Pedraja, *Jesus Is My Uncle: Christology from a Hispanic Perspective* (Nashville, TN: Abingdon Press, 1999), 109.

15. "Facts for Measures: Hispanic Heritage Month," *U.S. Census Bureau*, http://www.census.gov/Press-Release/www/releases/archives/facts_for_features_special_editions/007173.html.

16. Jorge Ramos and Adam J. Segal, "The Latinization of America," *Baltimore Sun*, 28 April 2004, 19A.

17. Suro in "Event Transcript," *Changing Faiths: Latinos and the Transformation of American Religion.*

18. *Changing Faiths: Latinos and the Transformation of American Religion*, 58.

19. The National Hispanic Prayer Breakfast and Conference, Washington, DC, 15 June 2007.

20. Barack Obama, *The Audacity of Hope: Thoughts on Reclaiming the American Dream* (New York: Crown Publishers, 2006), 8, 52.

21. Ann Swidler, *Talk of Love: How Culture Matters* (Chicago: University of Chicago Press, 2001), 86, 87.

22. Valerie Braithwaite, "Preface: Collective Hope," *Annals of the American Academy of Political and Social Science* 592 (March 2004): 7.

23. See John J. DiIulio, Jr., "The Three Faith Factors," *Public Interest* 149 (Fall 2002): 51–54, 58–59.

24. Studies dedicated to "ecological religion" include: Ram A. Cnaan, *The Newer Deal: Social Work and Religion in Partnership* (New York: Columbia University Press, 1999); Ram A. Cnaan, "Keeping Faith in the City: How 401 Urban Religious Congregations Serve Their Neediest Neighbors," *CRRUCS Report 2000–1* (Philadelphia: University of Pennsylvania, 2000–2001). Studies dedicated to "organic religion" include: Byron R. Johnson, "A Better Kind of High: How Religious Commitment Reduces Drug Use Among Poor Urban Teens," *CRRUCS Report 2000–2*; Byron R. Johnson and David B. Larson, "The Faith Factor: Studies Show Religion Is Linked to the Mental and Physical Health of Inmates," *Corrections Today* 60, no. 3 (June 1998); John M. Wallace, Jr., "Is Religion Good for Adolescent Health?: A Study of American High School Seniors," *CRRUCS Report 2002*; W. Bradford Wilcox, "Then Comes Marriage?: Religion, Race, and Marriage in Urban America," *CRRUCS Report 2002*; and W. Bradford Wilcox, "Good Dads: Religion, Civic Engagement, and Paternal Involvement in Low-Income Communities," *CRRUCS Report 2001–4*.

25. For some recent ethnographies on congregations and FBOs, see Bartkowski and Regis, *Charitable Choices*; Mark R. Warren, *Dry Bones Rattling: Community Building to Revitalize American Democracy* (Princeton, NJ: Princeton University Press, 2001). (Note that Warren actually describes his work as a "political ethnography," 10.); and Richard L. Wood, *Faith in Action: Religion, Race, and Democratic Organizing in America* (Chicago: University of Chicago Press, 2002).

26. Bartkowski and Regis, *Charitable Choices*, 10.

27. Unruh and Sider, *Saving Souls, Serving Society*, 241, 242.

28. The works of Robert D. Putnam, *Bowling Alone: The Collapse and Revival of American Democracy* (New York: Simon & Schuster, 2000), and Sidney Verba et al., *Voice and Equality: Civic Voluntarism in American Politics* (Cambridge, MA: Harvard University Press, 1995), tend to view religion as a means to social capital and political mobilization, respectively. One may also note the title of the recent edited volume: *Religion as Social Capital Producing the Social Good*, ed. Corwin Smidt (Waco, TX: Baylor University Press, 2003). (While this volume represents a great achievement in documenting the manifold ways religious behavior contributes to social capital formation, it does not specifically address the distinct kinds of religious behavior that shape such a formation.) In contrast, recent works that have examined the religious culture of faith-based involvement

include, among others: Stephen Hart, *Cultural Dilemmas of Progressive Politics: Styles of Engagement among Grassroots Activists* (Chicago: University of Chicago Press, 2001); Unruh and Sider, *Saving Souls, Serving Society*; and Wood, *Faith in Action.*

29. Bartkowski and Regis, *Charitable Choices*, 170.

30. Rhys Williams, "The Language of God in the City of Man: Religious Discourse and Public Politics in America," in *Religion as Social Capital*, 173.

31. Miguel A. de la Torre and Gastón Espinosa, eds., *Rethinking Latino(a) Religion and Identity* (Cleveland: Pilgrim Press, 2006).

32. Carl Kravetz, "Latino Identity" (paper presented at the Association of Hispanic Advertising Agencies, 21st conference, Miami, FL, 20 September 2006), 5, 7, 10.

33. See Jorge J. E. Gracia, *Hispanic/Latino Identity: A Philosophical Perspective* (Malden, MA: Blackwell Publishing, 1998) and J. L. A. Garcia, "Hispanic/Latino Identity," *First Things* (June 2000): 64.

34. Arlene Dávila, *Latinos, Inc.: The Marketing and Making of a People* (Berkeley: University of California Press, 2001), 16.

35. John A. García, "Political Participation: Resources and Involvement among Latinos in the American Political System," in *Pursuing Power: Latinos and the Political System*, ed. F. Chris García (Notre Dame, IN: University of Notre Dame Press, 1997), 44.

36. Richard F. Fenno, Jr., *Home Style: House Members in Their Districts* (Boston: Little, Brown, 1978).

37. Anthony M. Orum et al., "Introduction: The Nature of the Case Study," in *A Case for the Case Study*, ed. Joe R. Feagin et al. (Chapel Hill: University of North Carolina Press, 1991), 7.

38. The anthropologist who advocated "going native" was Bronislaw Malinowski after conducting ethnographic fieldwork in New Guinea from 1914–1918. Malinowski argued that "to grasp the native's point of view, his relations to life, to realize his vision of the world," anthropologists should "go native." In Bronislaw Malinowski, *Argonauts of the Pacific* (New York: Holt, Rinehart & Winston, 1922), 290.

39. "Chicana" is a colloquial term for "Mexican American." Sandra Cisneros in Harryette Mullen, "'A Silence between Us like a Language': The Untranslatability of Experience in Sandra Cisneros' *Woman Hollering Creek*," *MELUS* 21, no. 2 (Summer 1996): 13.

40. In designing the questionnaire for the study, I was fortunate to have obtained (via the Internet in 2001) a copy of the questionnaire used by Harold Dean Trulear in his study *Faith-Based Institutions and High-Risk Youth* (Philadelphia: Public/Private Ventures, 2000). For more information on this study, see http://www.ppv.org/ppv/publications/assets/24_publication.pdf. Unfortunately, this questionnaire is no longer available on the Internet.

41. Most of the newspaper articles were taken from clippings that LPAC, Nueva, and TRP had saved over the years. While almost all the articles have page numbers (or Internet addresses) listed in their citations, a few (four, in particular) do not. I was unable to locate page numbers for these articles because the newspaper companies in question did not keep archives past a certain number of years. Additionally, these articles were not available on the Internet.

42. James H. Cone, *A Black Theology of Liberation* (Maryknoll, NY: Orbis Books, 1990), 3.

NOTES TO CHAPTER 1

1. Bishop Roderick Cesar, senior pastor, Bethel Gospel Tabernacle, interview by author, Jamaica Queens, NY, 19 December 2002.

2. Peter Wood, "Afterword: Boundaries and Horizons," in *Conversion to Christianity: Historical and Anthropological Perspectives on a Great Transformation*, ed. Robert W. Hefner (Berkeley: University of California Press, 1993), 319.

3. T. M. Luhrmann, *Persuasions of the Witch's Craft: Ritual Magic in Contemporary England* (Cambridge: Harvard University Press, 1989), 314–315.

4. Verba et al., *Voice and Equality*, 309. See also Michael A. Jones-Correa and David L. Leal, "Political Participation: Does Religion Matter?" *Political Research Quarterly* 54, no. 4 (December 2001): 751–770. In this article, Jones-Correa and Leal support Verba et al.'s main argument that "churches . . . play a unique role in building up the civic skills of many of those least likely to participate in politics" (753). However, they disagree with Verba et al.'s findings that Latino Catholics should be "less likely" to be politically active than their Latino Protestant counterparts (757).

5. Putnam, *Bowling Alone*, 66.

6. R. Laurence Moore, *Selling God: American Religion in the Marketplace of Culture* (New York and Oxford: Oxford University Pres, 1994), 6. See also Roger Finke and Rodney Stark, *The Churching of America: 1776–1992: Winners and Losers in Our Religious Economy* (New Brunswick, NJ: Rutgers University Press, 1992); L. R. Iannaccone, "The Consequences of Religious Market Structure," *Rationality and Society* 3 (1991): 156–177; and L. R. Iannaccone, "Why Strict Churches Are Strong," *American Journal of Sociology* 99 (1994): 1180–1211.

7. Melvin D. Williams, *Community in a Black Pentecostal Church: An Anthropological Study* (Pittsburgh: University of Pittsburgh Press, 1974), 184.

8. Clifford Geertz, *The Interpretation of Cultures: Selected Essays* (Boston: Basic Books, 1973), 167.

9. Ann Swidler pays homage to Clifford Geertz's account of culture throughout her work, *Talk of Love: How Culture Matters* (Chicago: University of Chicago Press, 2001), 11–23.

10. Gabriel A. Almond and Sidney Verba, *The Civic Culture: Political Attitudes*

and Democracy in Five Nations (Princeton, NJ: Princeton University Press, 1963), 13, 16–17.

11. John Street, "Political Culture—From Civic Culture to Mass Culture," *British Journal of Political Science* 24, no. 1 (January 1994): 97.

12. Ronald Inglehart, "The Renaissance of Political Culture," *American Political Science Review* 82, no. 4 (December 1988): 1205, 1204.

13. Lowell Ditmer, "Political Culture and Political Symbolism: Toward a Theoretical Synthesis," *World Politics* 29, no. 4 (July 1977): 553.

14. Street, "Political Culture—From Civic Culture to Mass Culture," 102.

15. Sidney Verba, "Comparative Political Culture," in *Political Culture and Political Development*, eds. Lucian Pye and Sidney Verba (Princeton, NJ: Princeton University Press, 1965), 513.

16. Robert C. Tucker, "Culture, Political Culture, and Communist Society," *Political Science Quarterly* 88, no. 2 (June 1973): 182.

17. Carole Pateman, "The Civic Culture: A Philosophic Critique," in *The Civic Culture Revisited*, eds. Gabriel A. Almond and Sidney Verba (Boston: Little, Brown, 1980), 57–102.

18. Sidney Verba, "On Revisiting the Civic Culture: A Personal Postscript," in *The Civic Culture Revisited*, 394–410.

19. Gabriel A. Almond, "The Intellectual History of the Civic Culture Concept," in *The Civic Culture Revisited*, 1–36.

20. Verba, "On Revisiting the Civic Culture," 394–410.

21. Noted sociologists make the argument that religion serves as a foundation for democratic governance. See John A. Coleman, S.J., "Religion and Public Life: Some American Cases," *Religion* 28 (1998): 135–169; Warren, *Dry Bones Rattling*; and Richard L. Wood, "Religious Culture and Political Action," *Sociological Theory* 17, no. 3 (November 1999): 307–332.

22. Anne M. Khademian, *Working with Culture: The Way the Job Gets Done in Public Programs* (Washington, DC: CQ Press, 2002), 6, 3, 4.

23. Street, "Political Culture—From Civic Culture to Mass Culture," 111, 113.

24. Ronald P. Formisano, "The Concept of Political Culture," *Journal of Interdisciplinary History* 31, no. 3 (Winter 2001): 407. Examples of this nontraditional approach to political culture—one that calls into question the notion that culture is characteristic of the political order—include David D. Laitin, *Identity in Formation: The Russian-Speaking Populations in the Near Abroad* (Ithaca, NY: Cornell University Press, 1998); James C. Scott, *Seeing Like a State: How Certain Schemes to Improve the Human Condition Have Failed* (New Haven, CT: Yale University Press, 1998), and *Weapons of the Weak: Everyday Forms of Peasant Resistance* (New Haven, CT: Yale University Press, 1985); and Rogers M. Smith, *Stories of Peoplehood: The Politics and Morals of Political Membership* (Cambridge: Cambridge University Press, 2003).

25. Tucker, "Culture, Political Culture, and Communist Society," 183. Recent

sociological works that employ a cultural approach to politics include: Hart, *Cultural Dilemmas of Progressive Politics*, and Wood, *Faith in Action*.

26. Khademian, *Working with Culture*, 4.

27. Wood, *Faith in Action*, 261.

28. Geertz, *Interpretation of Cultures*, 11.

29. Ward Hunt Goodenough, *Cooperation in Change* (New York: Russell Sage Foundation, 1963), 96, 97, 98.

30. Clifford Geertz, *Available Light: Anthropological Reflections on Philosophical Topics* (Princeton, NJ: Princeton University Press, 2000), 11, 68.

31. Robert Wuthnow, *The Restructuring of American Religion: Society and Faith Since World War II* (Princeton, NJ: Princeton University Press, 1988), 57.

32. Wood, *Faith in Action*, 263.

33. Geertz, Interpretation of Cultures, 110–112.

34. David I. Kertzer, *Ritual, Politics, and Power* (New Haven, CT: Yale University Press, 1988), 4, 5.

35. Geertz, *Intrepretation of Cultures*, 97, 99, 127, 132.

36. Wood, *Faith in Action*, 240.

37. Cnaan et al., *Invisible Caring Hand*, 9.

38. Anita de Luna, "Popular Religion and Spirituality," in *Handbook of Latina/o Theologies*, eds. Edwin David Aponte and Miguel A. de la Torre (St. Louis, MO: Chalice Press, 2006), 113.

39. Kristy Nabhan-Warren, "Mary," in *Handbook of Latina/o Theologies*, 246, 249.

40. Miguel A. de la Torre and Edwin David Aponte, *Introducing Latino/a Theologies* (Maryknoll, NY: Orbis Books, 2001), 123.

41. Juan Francisco Martínez, "Church: A Latino/a Protestant Perspective," in *Handbook of Latina/o Theologies*, 53.

42. Keith Ward, *Religion and Community* (Oxford, UK: Clarendon Press, 2000), 163, 184.

43. Wood, "Afterword: Boundaries and Horizons," 320.

44. Luis G. Pedraja, *Teología: An Introduction to Hispanic Theology* (Nashville, TN: Abingdon Press, 2003), 22, 23.

45. Ward, Religion and Community, 209.

46. Vincent Brummer, "Religious Belief and Personal Identity," *Neue Zeitschrift fur systematische Theologie und Religionsphilosophie* 38, no. 2 (1996): 162.

47. Holly Diane Hayes, "Col. 2:6–19," *Interpretation* 49, no. 3 (July 1995): 285–288.

48. Edward Sapir, *The Psychology of Cultures: A Course of Lectures*, ed. Judith T. Irvine (Berlin and New York: Mouton de Gruyter, 2002), 139.

49. Albert George Coe, *The Psychology of Religion* (Chicago: University of Chicago Press, 1917), 315.

50. My first encounter with the term "mandate" occurred while I was inter-

viewing Reverend Luciano Padilla, senior pastor of the Bay Ridge Christian Center in Brooklyn, New York, on 26 March 2002. During that interview, Padilla maintained that, in contrast to the mission of secular community-based organizations (CBOs), the mission of FBOs emanates from a "biblical and theological commitment." As a Latino pastoral leader, Padilla stated that he had "a biblical and theological mandate to be the light and salt of the earth. This is not an option for Christians." In an interview on 7 May 2002, Father Peter McQuinn, pastor of Epiphany Parish in the Little Village section of Chicago, echoed Padilla's thoughts on the mandate of pastoral leaders. McQuinn commented that "pastors have a mandate, which is the gospel of Jesus Christ. It is a mandate of social justice."

51. Patrick Primeaux and John Stieber, "Profit Maximization: The Ethical Mandate of Business," *Journal of Business Ethics* 13, no. 4 (1994): 288.

52. Margaret Harris, *Organizing God's Work: Challenges for Churches and Synagogues* (New York: St. Martin's Press, 1998), 196.

53. Noam Chomsky, *Language and Thought* (Wakefield, RI: Moyer Bell, 1993), 17.

54. Reverend Dr. Martin Luther King, Jr., "Strength to Love" (1963).

55. Reverend Jim Wallis, lecture, University of Pennsylvania, 23 October 2003.

56. Williams, "The Language of God in the City of Man," 176, 180, 173, 178.

57. Williams, "The Language of God in the City of Man," 173.

58. Helen Rose Ebaugh and Janet Saltzman Chafetz, *Religion and the New Immigrants: Continuities and Adaptations in Immigrant Congregations* (Walnut Creek, CA: Altamira Press, 2000), 409.

59. Kristin Park, "The Religious Construction of Sanctuary Provision in Two Congregations," *Sociological Spectrum* 18 (1998): 394.

60. Ebaugh and Chafetz, *Religion and the New Immigrants*, 18, 428.

61. Swidler, *Talk of Love*, 71–72.

62. Unruh and Sider, *Saving Souls, Serving Society*, 85, 68.

63. Swidler, *Talk of Love*, 82, 86.

64. John P. Kretzmann and John L. McKnight, *Building Communities from the Inside Out: A Path Toward Finding and Mobilizing a Community's Assets* (Chicago: ACTA Publications, 1993), 143, 155. See also Jo Anne Schneider's article on the social capital advanced by Quaker-based social-service organizations: "Trusting That of God in Everyone: Three Examples of Quaker-Based Social Service in Disadvantaged Communities," *Nonprofit and Voluntary Sector Quarterly* 28, no. 3 (September 1999): 269–295.

65. Meredith Ramsay, "Redeeming the City: Exploring the Relationship between Church and Metropolis," *Urban Affairs Review* 33, no. 5 (May 1998): 621–622.

66. Ernesto Cortés, Jr., "Reweaving the Fabric: The Iron Rule and the IAF

Strategy for Power and Politics," in *Interwoven Destinies: Cities and the Nation*, ed. Henry G. Cisneros (New York and London: Norton, 1993), 316.

67. Usha Nair Reichert, "Revitalizing the Inner City: A Holistic Approach," *Review of Black Political Economy* 24, nos. 2–3 (Fall–Winter 1995): 187, 190.

68. Ross Gittell and Avis Vidal, *Community Organizing: Building Social Capital as a Development Strategy* (Thousand Oaks, CA: Sage Publications, 1998), 1, 13, 14.

69. Kretzmann and McKnight, *Building Communities from the Inside Out*, 376.

70. Ramsay, "Redeeming the City," 620.

71. Patricia A. Wilson, "Empowerment: Community Economic Development from the Inside Out," *Urban Studies* 33, nos. 4–5 (1996): 624, 628.

72. Patricia A. Wilson, "Empowerment: Community Economic Development," 627.

73. Goodenough, *Cooperation in Change*, 219.

74. Charles Hatch Sears, *City Man* (New York and London: Harper & Brothers, 1936), 119.

75. Elijah Anderson, *A Place on the Corner* (Chicago: University of Chicago Press, 1976), 1.

76. Suzanne Keller, *The Urban Neighborhood: A Sociological Perspective* (New York: Random House, 1968), 91.

77. Setha M. Low, "The Anthropology of Cities: Imagining and Theorizing the City," *Annual Review of Anthropology* 25 (1996): 399.

78. An earlier urban ethnographic account that fails to consider religion as one of the "kinds of purposive situational involvements which make up an individual's round of life" in the city is Ulf Hannerz's *Exploring the City: Inquiries toward an Urban Anthropology* (New York: Columbia University Press, 1980), 101.

79. Kathleen Neils Conzen, "The Place of Religion in Urban and Community Studies," *Religion and American Culture: A Journal of Interpretation* 6, no. 2 (Summer 1996): 110.

80. James A. Morone, *Hellfire Nation: The Politics of Sin in American History* (New Haven, CT: Yale University Press, 2003), 3.

81. Harvey Cox, *The Secular City: Secularization and Urbanization in Theological Perspective* (New York: Macmillan Company, 1965), 109, 4.

82. Harvey Cox, *Fire from Heaven: The Rise of Pentecostal Spirituality and the Reshaping of Religion in the Twenty-First Century* (Reading, MA: Addison-Wesley, 1995), xv.

83. David A. Badillo, *Latinos and the New Immigrant Church* (Baltimore: Johns Hopkins University Press, 2006), 208.

84. Gerhard Lenski, *The Religious Factor: A Sociological Study of Religion's Impact on Politics, Economics, and Family Life* (Garden City, NJ: Doubleday and Company, 1963), 43, 44.

85. Badillo, *Latinos and the New Immigrant Church*, 180, 181.

86. Ebaugh and Chafetz, *Religion and the New Immigrants*, 455, 386–389.

87. Segundo S. Pantoja, "Religious Diversity and Ethnicity among Latinos," in *New York Glory: Religions in the City*, eds. Tony Carnes and Anna Karpathakis (New York: New York University Press, 2001), 162, 171.

88. Jones-Correa and Leal, "Political Participation: Does Religion Matter?" 763.

89. One specific kind of Latino religious culture, *ajiaco* Christianity, is explored by Miguel de la Torre. *Ajiaco* Christianity aptly characterizes the religious expression manifested by Cuban exiles in Miami. Such a form of Christianity is more than a sacred doctrine; it is a civil religion that places great confidence in the so-called sacred-space of *el exilio* (the exile), thereby meshing Christian faith with Cuban nationalism. See *La Lucha for Cuba: Religion and Politics on the Streets of Miami* (Berkeley: University of California Press, 2003).

90. Helen Rose Ebaugh and Janet Saltzman Chafetz, "Introduction," in *Religion across Borders: Transnational Immigrant Networks*, eds. Helen Rose Ebaugh and Janet Saltzman Chafetz (Walnut Creek, CA: Altamira Press, 2002), 1.

91. David K. Yoo, "Introduction," in *New Spiritual Homes: Religion and Asian Americans*, ed. David K. Yoo (Honolulu: University of Hawaii Press, 1999), 4.

92. There are multiple definitions for the term "assimilation." A recent anthology on immigrant populations in the United States suggests that assimilation "is about finding a sustainable balance between what makes us different and what we have in common" (Tamar Jacoby, "Defining Assimilation for the 21st Century," in *Reinventing the Melting Pot: The New Immigrants and What It Means to Be American*, ed. Tamar Jacoby [New York: Basic Books, 2004]). The challenges and limits of assimilating Mexican culture in the United States are discussed in Victor Davis Hanson, *Mexifornia: A State of Becoming* (San Francisco: Encounter Books, 2003).

93. Yoo, "Introduction," 11.

94. Robert N. Bellah et al., *Habits of the Heart: Individualism and Commitment in American Life*, rev. ed. (Berkeley: University of California Press, 1996), 230, 247.

95. Bridget Kevane, *Latino Literature in America* (Westport, CT: Greenwood Press, 2003), 12.

96. Other Latin American authors of the "new reality" include, among others, Carlos Fuentes, *La nueva novela hipsanoamericana* (1969) and *Cambio de piel* (1967), and Julio Cortazar, *Rayela* (1963). See Eliud Martínez, "Ron Arias' *The Road to Tamazunchale*: A Chicano Novel of the New Reality," *Latin American Literary Review* 10 (1977): 51–63.

97. Rosario Ferre in Rafael Ocasio, "The Infinite Variety of the Puerto Rican Reality: An Interview with Judith Ortiz Cofer," *Callaloo* 17, no. 3 (Summer 1994): 736–737.

98. Martínez, "Ron Arias' *The Road to Tamazunchale*," 52, 59.

99. "Under the Feet of Jesus," *Publishers Weekly* 242, no. 12 (20 March 1995): 42.

100. Lene Johannessen, "The Meaning of Place: Viramontes' *Under the Feet of Jesus*," in *Holding Their Own: Perspectives on the Multi-Ethnic Literatures of the United States*, eds. Dorothea Fischer-Hornung and Heike Raphael-Hernandez (Tubingen, Germany: Stuaffenburg Verlag, 2000), 101–109.

101. Helena Maria Viramontes, *Under the Feet of Jesus* (New York: Dutton, 1995), 87, 110, 121.

102. Kristen Renwick Monroe, "Morality and a Sense of Self: The Importance of Identity and Categorization for Moral Action," *American Journal of Political Science* 45, no. 3 (July 2001): 494.

103. "Under the Feet of Jesus," 42.

104. Jean Bethke Elshtain, "Christian Imperatives and Civil Life," *Modern Schoolman* 78, nos. 2–3 (January/March 2001): 171, 164–165.

105. Christopher P. Gilbert, *The Impact of Churches on Political Behavior: An Empirical Study* (Westport, CT: Greenwood Press, 1993), 3, 2.

106. Kenneth D. Wald et al., "Churches as Political Communities," *American Political Science Review* 82, no. 2 (June 1988), 533.

107. Alexie Torres Fleming, executive director and founder, Youth Ministries for Peace and Justice, telephone interview by author, 11 December 2002.

108. Daleep Mukarji, "Gospel and the Search for Identity and Community," *International Review of Mission* 85, no. 336 (January 1996): 25.

109. José Ortega y Gassett, *Man and People*, trans. Willard R. Trask (New York and London: Norton, 1957), 237. The word "ministry" comes from the Latin *ministerium*, meaning "office" or "service." While remaining true to its etymology as "office" or "service," various kinds of ministry can be said to exist both in religious and political circles. One may refer to the Ministry of Education in Canada or to the campus ministry that a particular college or university offers.

110. Ortega y Gassett, *Man and People*, 235, 238.

111. Victor Rodríguez, Aikido sensei and handyman, LPAC, interview by author, Bronx, NY, 18 December 2002.

112. Mission statement of Nueva Esperanza.

113. Arthur Haywood, senior vice president, Nueva Esperanza, interview by author, Philadelphia, 9 December 2002.

114. Latino community leader, confidential interview by author, Philadelphia, December 2002.

115. "HHS Funds Faith-Based Organization to Build Service-Provider Infrastructure," http://www.alliance1.org/Public_Policy/2002-11-20_whatsnew_HHS-FaithBased.htm.

116. Raúl Raymundo, executive director, TRP, interview by author, Chicago, 23 April 2001.

117. Motto of The Resurrection Project.

118. Father Charles W. Dahm, O.P., pastor, St. Pius V Church, interview by author, Chicago, 27 April 2001.

119. Alvaro Obregon in Antonio Olivo, "Would You Go to Pilsen for '*Zócalo*'? Mexican-Style Plaza Talk of Neighborhood," *Chicago Tribune* (15 November 2005), http://www.luc.edu/curl/escd/discussions/links/Chicago_tribune%2011-15-2005.shtml.

120. "Santana and Crew Visit the Plaza and Film Hit Music Video!" *The Resurrection Project Winter Newsletter* 1, no. 1 (Winter 2002): 4.

121. Street, "Political Culture—From Civic to Mass Culture," 103.

122. Jim Wallis, *The Soul of Politics: A Practical and Prophetic Vision for Change* (New York and Maryknoll, NY: New Press and Orbis Books, 1994), 32.

123. E. Franklin Frazier, *The Negro Church in America* (New York: Schocken Books, 1974), 16.

NOTES TO CHAPTER 2

1. Patricia Garza, manager, corporate contributions, Kraft Foods, telephone interview by author, 24 July 2001.

2. Gittell and Vidal, *Community Organizing: Building Social Capital as a Development Strategy*, 14.

3. Stacey Wilson, "Old Highbridge Remembered in New Book," *Bronx Beat*, 14–21 May 2001, n.p.

4. Erika Kinetz, "Shadows Across the City; Nine Miles Away," *New York Times*, 23 September 2001, sec. 14, 1.

5. "District 16: Highbridge/Morrisania," *Gotham Gazette*, 2001, http://www.gothamgazette.com/Searchlight2001/dist16.html.

6. Adrian Bordoni, former coordinator of LPAC Gang Prevention Unit, interview with author, Bronx, NY, 29 January 2002.

7. "Hispanic or Latino by Type: Bronx County, New York," *U.S. Census Bureau, Census 2000 Summary File,* http://factfinder.census.gov/servlet/QTTable?_bm=y&-geo_id=05000US36005&-qr_name=DEC_2000_SF1_U_QTP9&-ds_name=DEC_2000_SF1_U.

8. César Ayala, "The 5 Boroughs of New York City," *New York City Population,* http://www.lehman.cuny.edu/depts/latinampuertorican/latinoweb/Census2000/NYC/main.htm.

9. "Hispanic or Latino Origin by Specific Origin, *U.S. Census Bureau, 2005 American Community Survey*, http://factfinder.census.gov/servlet/DTTable?_bm=y&-geo_id=16000US3651000&-ds_name=ACS_2005_EST_G00_&-redoLog=false&-mt_name=ACS_2005_EST_G2000_B03001.

10. Hispanic Federation, "Report 3: Profile of the Puerto Rican Community,"

Annual Survey of Hispanic New Yorkers 1999, http://www.hispanicfederation.org/sv99-3.htm.

11. Nicholas Lemann, "The Other Underclass: Puerto Ricans in the U.S.," *Atlantic Monthly* 268, no. 6 (December 1991): 96.

12. Ayala, "New York City," *New York City Population.*

13. Lemann, "The Other Underclass," 96.

14. Frederick A. Davie, Jr., vice president, National Faith-Based Programs, PPV, telephone interview by author, 1 April 2002.

15. Rafael A. Olmeda, "Latino Churches Reach Out," *New York Daily News,* 6 August 1995, Suburban sec., 3.

16. David Vidal, "Abstracts," *New York Times,* 2 August 1976, 46.

17. George Dugan, "Abstracts," *New York Times,* 31 October 1976, 58.

18. Reverend William Sloane Coffin, Jr., et al., "Barbaro and Unity: A Grass-Roots Team," *New York Times,* 26 October 1981, A22.

19. Independent Progressive Politics Network, "Unity Party," http://www.ippn.org/unsorted/ORUP.htm.

20. Olmeda, "Latino Churches Reach Out," 3.

21. Richard Rivera, adjunct professor, New School, and LPAC consultant, interview by author, New York, 29 March 2002.

22. Dr. Bill Webber, professor, New York Theological Seminary, interview by author, New York, 17 April 2002.

23. Edna Acosta Belén, *Adiós, Borinquen querida: The Puerto Rican Diaspora, Its History, and Contributions* (New York: CELAC, 2000), 16.

24. "There is no excuse for domestic violence" and "Services, Benefits, and Respect."

25. "Hunting Park," *NIS Neighborhoods,* http://phillyneighborhoods.org/NeighborhoodPDF/Hunting%20Park.pdf.

26. "Hispanic or Latino by Specific Origin," *U.S. Census Bureau, 2005 American Community Survey,* http://factfinder.census.gov/servlet/DTTable?_bm=y&-geo_id=16000US-4260000&-ds_name=ACS_2005_EST_G00_&-redoLog=false&-mt_name=ACS_2005_EST_G2000_B03001.

27. "General Information about Latinos Living in Philadelphia," *Congreso de Latinos Unidos,* http://www.congreso.net/factsheets.php.

28. "Latino Philadelphia at a Glance," *Historical Society of Pennsylvania,* http://www.hsp.org/files/latinophiladelphiaataglance.pdf.

29. Anthony S. Twyman, "Once Again the Search for 'Una Vida Mejor,'" *Philadelphia Daily News,* 17 April 1995, 21–22.

30. Roger Zepernick, executive director of Centro Pedro Claver, interview by author, Philadelphia, 26 February 2002.

31. Michael D. Schaffer, "Hispanic Ministers Reaching Out," *Philadelphia Inquirer,* 4 March 1990, 2D.

32. Terence Samuel, "Latino Protesters Turn to Prayer," *Philadelphia Inquirer,* 13 August 1990, A4.

33. M. J. McCollum, "Phila. Clergy Opposes Riverboat Gambling," *Philadelphia Tribune,* 24 February 1995, 3A.

34. David O'Reilly, "Dual Rallies to State Case Against and For City's Police," *Philadelphia Inquirer,* 23 July 2001, A1.

35. Reverend Luis Cortés, executive director, Nueva Esperanza, interview by author, Philadelphia, 24 January 2002.

36. See Samuel Escobar, "The Legacy of Orlando Costas," *International Bulletin of Missionary Research* 25, no. 2 (April 2001): 50–56.

37. Reverend Luis Cortés, interview.

38. Edwin David Aponte, "Latino Protestant Identity and Empowerment: Hispanic Religion, Community, Rhetoric, and Action in a Philadelphia Case Study" (Ph.D. diss., Temple University, 1998), 102–104.

39. Fritz Bittenbender, secretary of administration, Pennsylvania State Government, interview by author, Harrisburg, PA, 4 March 2002.

40. Nueva Esperanza mission statement.

41. Reverend Magaly Martínez, president, board of directors, Nueva Esperanza, interview by author, Philadelphia, 28 January 2002.

42. Angel Ortiz, councilman at-large, city of Philadelphia, interview by author, Philadelphia, 11 June 2002.

43. Reverend Danny Cortés, interview, 8 March 2002.

44. Reverend Danny Cortés, interview, 20 February 2007.

45. *Tenochtitlán:* the capital city of the Aztec empire; *La Diechiocho:* Eighteenth Street; *restaurantes:* restaurants; *panaderias:* bakeries; *librerias:* bookstores; *casas de cambio:* check-cashing institutions; *taquerias:* taco restaurants; *fruteria:* grocery store; *carniceria:* butcher's shop.

46. "Hispanic or Latino Origin by Specific Origin," *U.S. Census Bureau, 2005 American Community Survey,* http://factfinder.census.gov/servlet/DTTable?_bm=y&-geo_id=16000US1714000&-ds_name=ACS_2005_EST_G00_&-redoLog=false&-mt_name=ACS_2005_EST_G2000_B03001.

47. "Pilsen (Lower West Side)," *LISC Chicago's New Communities Program,* http://www. newcommunities.org/printAbout.asp?objectID=10.

48. "Little Village (South Lawndale)," *LISC Chicago's New Communities Program,* http://www.newcommunities.org/communities/littlevillage/about.asp?communityID=6, and "Back of the Yards/Garfield Blvd," *NHS Chicago,* http://www.nhschicago.org/downloads/5980BOY%20profile,%20Final.pdf.

49. Charles W. Dahm, O.P., *Parish Ministry in a Hispanic Community* (New York/Mahwah, NJ: Paulist Press, 2004), 10.

50. See http://home.uchicago.edu/~phlustik/chic-czech.html.

51. "So close to Chicago and so far away from heaven," Raúl Hernández, president, board of directors, TRP, interview with author, Chicago, 17 May 2002.

52. Tara Gruzen, "Mexicans Say Tradition at Risk in Housing Fight," *Chicago Tribune*, 19 August 1996, sec. 1, 16.

53. Teresa Puente, "Pilsen Fears Upscale Push May Shove Many Out," *Chicago Tribune*, 4 November 1997, 6.

54. Dan Alexander, residential development manager, TRP interview with author, Chicago 6 December 2001.

55. Raymundo, interview, 23 April 2001, and telephone interview, 28 February 2007.

56. Raymundo, interview, 23 April 2001.

57. Two good treatments of St. Pius V Church in Chicago are Janise Hurtig, "Hispanic Immigrant Churches and the Construction of Ethnicity," *Public Religion and Urban Transformation: Faith in the City*, ed. Lowell W. Livezey (New York: New York University Press, 2000): 29–55, and Hernández et al., *Leadership Matters: The Role of Latino/a Religious Leadership in Social Ministry*, 15–24.

58. Dahm, *Parish Ministry in a Hispanic Community*, 257, 259.

59. Charles W. Dahm, O.P., with Nile Harper, "St. Pius V Roman Catholic Church and the Pilsen Area Resurrection Project," in Nile Harper, ed., *Urban Churches, Vital Signs: Beyond Charity toward Justice* (Grand Rapids, MI: Eerdmans Publishing, 1999), 171–172.

60. Dahm, *Parish Ministry in a Hispanic Community*, 260, 262.

61. Dahm, *Parish Ministry in a Hispanic Community*, 263.

62. Raymundo, interview, 23 April 2001.

63. David Pesqueira, senior program officer, McCormick Tribune Foundation, interview by author, Chicago, 23 July 2001.

64. James Brewer Stewart, *Holy Warriors: The Abolitionists and American Slavery* (New York: Hill and Wang, 1976), 14, 17.

65. Stewart, *Holy Warriors*, 35, 36, 54, 55.

66. Walter Rauschenbusch, *Christianity and the Social Crisis* (New York: Macmillan Company, 1911), 91.

67. Rauschenbusch, *Christianity and the Social Crisis*, 369, 258, 140, 339, 308–309.

68. Diane Winston, *Red-Hot and Righteous: The Urban Religion of the Salvation Army* (Cambridge, MA: Harvard University Press, 1999), 116, 112–123, 124, 125, 251.

69. Paul A. Carter, *The Decline and Revival of the Social Gospel: Social and Political Liberalism in American Protestant Churches, 1920–1940* (Ithaca, NY: Cornell University Press, 1954), 104, 176.

70. Winston, *Red-Hot and Righteous*, 117.

71. Winston, *Red-Hot and Righteous*, 145, 218, 91, 89, 193, 220, 219.

72. Warren, *Dry Bones Rattling*, 43–45.

73. Warren, *Dry Bones Rattling*, 41–44. Alinsky published these books with strong encouragement from his friend, the French Neo-Thomist Jacques Maritain.

See *The Philosopher and the Provocateur: The Correspondence of Jacques Maritain and Saul Alinsky,* ed. and intro. Bernard Doering (Notre Dame, IN: University of Notre Dame Press, 1994).

74. Saul D. Alinsky, *Reveille for Radicals* (New York: Random House, 1969), 15, xiv, xvi, 16.

75. Warren, *Dry Bones Ratting,* 43–45.

76. Jim Rooney, *Organizing the South Bronx,* foreword Nathan Glazer (Albany: State University of New York Press, 1995), 12, 222, 223, 220, 221.

77. Warren, *Dry Bones Rattling,* x, 191, 245.

78. Wood, *Faith in Action,* 293, 297.

79. Gary Delgado, *Organizing the Movement: The Roots and Growth of ACORN* (Philadelphia: Temple University Press, 1986), 7, 3–4.

80. Aldon D. Morris, *The Origins of the Civil Rights Movement: Black Communities Organizing for Change* (New York: Free Press, 1986), 8, 285–286.

81. Forrest E. Harris, *Ministry for Social Crisis: Theology and Praxis in the Black Church Tradition* (Macon, GA: Mercer University Press, 1993), 40.

82. Reverend Dr. Martin Luther King, Jr., "Strength to Love" (1963).

83. Harris, *Ministry for Social Crisis,* 40.

84. Morris, *Origins of the Civil Rights Movement,* 286–287, 288.

85. Enrique T. Trueba, *Latinos Unidos: From Cultural Diversity to the Politics of Solidarity* (Lanham, MD: Rowman & Littlefield, 1999), 18.

86. Grant Farred, "Endgame Identity? Mapping the New Left of Identity Politics," *New Literary History* 31 (2000): 630, 641.

87. Alberto Melucci, "The Symbolic Challenge of Contemporary Movements," *Social Research* 52, no. 4 (Winter 1985): 789.

88. Silvio Torres-Saillant and Ramona Hernández, *The Dominican Americans* (Westport, CT: Greenwood Press, 1998), 96, 109–110, 97, 102, 96, 121.

89. Ernesto Sagas and Sinita E. Molina, "Introduction: Dominican Transnational Migration," in *Dominican Migration: Transnational Perspectives,* eds. Ernesto Sagas and Sinita E. Molina (Gainesville: University Press of Florida, 2004), 17.

90. David Rodríguez, *Latino National Political Coalitions: Struggles and Challenges* (New York: Routledge, 2002), 50–53.

91. Belén, *Adiós, Borinquen querida,* 2, 3.

92. María E. Pérez y González, *Puerto Ricans in the United States* (Westport, CT: Greenwood Press, 2000), 59, 61, 68, 64.

93. Rodríguez, *Latino National Political Coalitions,* 45–48.

94. Frederick John Dalton, *The Moral Vision of César Chávez* (Maryknoll, NY: Orbis Books, 2003), 155, 162.

95. Ana María Díaz-Stevens and Anthony M. Stevens-Arroyo, *Recognizing the Latino Resurgence in U.S. Religion: The Emmaus Paradigm* (Boulder, CO: Westview Press, 1998), 134.

96. Díaz-Stevens and Stevens-Arroyo, *Recognizing the Latino Resurgence in U.S. Religion,* 143.

97. "The Plan of Delano," in *The Words of César Chávez,* eds. Richard J. Jensen and John C. Hammerback (College Station: Texas A&M University Press, 2002), 16.

98. Dahm, *Parish Ministry in a Hispanic Community,* 254.

99. Elizondo, "Mestizaje as a Locus of Theological Reflection," in *Frontiers of Hispanic Theology in the United States,* ed. Allan Figueroa Deck, S.J. (Maryknoll, NY: Orbis Books, 1992), 107, quoted in Dahm, *Parish Ministry in a Hispanic Community,* 255.

100. *Parish Ministry in a Hispanic Community,* 255–256.

101. Alma M. García, *The Mexican Americans* (Westport, CT: Greenwood Press, 2002), 183.

102. Carol J. Greenhouse, *A Moment's Notice: Time Politics across Cultures* (Ithaca, NY: Cornell University Press, 1996), 78, 79.

103. Raymundo, telephone interview, 28 February 2007.

NOTES TO CHAPTER 3

1. Phillip Berryman, interview by author, Philadelphia, 16 June 2004.

2. Reverend Nelson Rivera, professor, Lutheran Theological Seminary, interview by author Philadelphia, 8 June 2004.

3. Corwin E. Smidt, "Theological and Political Orientations of Clergy within American Politics: An Analytic and Historical Overview," in *Pulpit and Politics: Clergy in American Politics at the Advent of the Millennium,* ed. Corwin E. Smidt (Waco, TX: Baylor University Press, 2004), 5–6.

4. Corwin E. Smidt, "Theological and Political Orientations of Clergy," 8.

5. James L. Guth et al., *The Bully Pulpit: The Politics of Protestant Clergy* (Lawrence: University Press of Kansas, 1997), 14.

6. Orlando E. Costas, *Christ outside the Gate: Mission beyond Christendom* (Maryknoll, NY: Orbis Books, 1982), 126.

7. Ivan Petrella, "Liberation Theology and Democracy: Toward a New Historical Project," *Journal of Hispanic/Latino Theology* 7:4 (2000): 56, 59.

8. Reverend Danny Cortés, interview, 20 February 2007.

9. Petrella, "Liberation Theology and Democracy," 61.

10. Valentín, *Mapping Public Theology,* 44, 45, 67, 80, 87.

11. Michael Leo Owens, "The Political Potential of Black Church-Based Community Development Organizations" (paper presented at annual meeting of Association for Research on Nonprofit Organizations and Voluntary Action, Arlington, VA, November 1999), 7, 19, 24.

12. Kraig Beyerlein and Mark Chaves, "The Political Activities of Religious Congregations in the United States," *Journal for the Scientific Study of Religion* 42,

no. 2 (2003): 236. Frederick C. Harris also remarks on the "different impacts of different religious forms," Frederick C. Harris, "Something Within: Religion as a Mobilizer of African-American Political Activism," *Journal of Politics* 56, no. 1 (February 1994): 48.

13. Kenneth D. Wald, *Religion and Politics in the United States*, 4th ed. (Lanham, MD: Rowman & Littlefield, 2003), 308–309, 310.

14. Beyerlein and Chaves, "Political Activities of Religious Congregations in the United States," 242.

15. Nancy Tatom Ammerman, *Pillars of Faith: American Congregations and Their Partners* (Berkeley: University of California Press, 2005), 57, 24, 26–34.

16. Gastón Espinosa, "Latino Clergy and Churches in Faith-Based Political and Social Action in the United States," in *Latino Religions and Civic Activism in the United States*, 295–298.

17. Unruh and Sider, *Saving Souls, Serving Society*, 20, 110–111, 135–146.

18. Wald, *Religion and Politics in the United States*, 181, 185, 187, 188.

19. Geertz, *Interpretation of Cultures*, 125.

20. Reverend Danny Cortés, interview, 8 March 2002.

21. Reverend Raymond Rivera, telephone interview, 22 February 2007.

22. Reverend Luis Cortés, interview.

23. Reverend Danny Cortés, interview, 20 February 2007.

24. TRP staff meeting, Chicago, 18 July 2001.

25. Wood, *Faith in Action*, 164.

26. Raymundo, telephone interview, 28 February 2007.

27. Wood, *Faith in Action*, 186.

28. Raymond Firth, "Spiritual Aroma: Religion and Politics," *American Anthropologist* 83, no. 3 (September 1981): 583.

29. Reverend Dr. Martin Luther King, Jr., "Where Do We Go from Here: Chaos or Community?" (1967).

30. James H. Cone, *God of the Oppressed* (New York: Seabury Press, 1975), xi.

31. Christian Smith: *The Emergence of Liberation Theology: Radical Religion and Social Movement Theory* (Chicago: University of Chicago Press, 1991), 28.

32. *Third General Conference of Latin American Bishops: Puebla: Envangelization at Present and in the Future of Latin America* (Washington, DC: National Conference of Catholic Bishops, 1979), 178.

33. Leonardo Boff and Clodovis Boff, *Introducing Liberation Theology*, trans. Paul Burns (Maryknoll, NY: Orbis Books, 1987), 3–4.

34. Douglas Sturm, "Praxis and Promise: On the Ethics of Political Theology," *Ethics* 92, no. 4 (July 1982): 741.

35. Gustavo Gutiérrez, "Freedom and Salvation: A Political Problem," in *Liberation and Change*, eds. Gustavo Gutiérrez and Richard Shaull (Atlanta: John Knox Press, 1977), 76.

36. Ernesto Cardenal, "Revolution and Peace: The Nicaraguan Road," *Journal of Peace Research* 18 (1982): 202–203, 206, quoted in John R. Pottenger, *The Political Theory of Liberation Theology: Toward a Reconvergence of Social Values and Social Science* (Albany: State University of New York Press, 1989), 157. Cardenal, as a radical liberationist, contrasts sharply with Gutiérrez. Cardenal was deeply involved in politics, serving as minister of culture in the early 1980s under the leftist government that ruled Nicaragua after the Sandinista National Liberation Front (FSLN) toppled the dictatorship of Anastasio Somoza in 1979. Due to his political involvement with the FSLN, the Vatican suspended Cardenal from the priesthood for a time. See Diego Cevallos, "Religion-Latam: Progressive Theologians Differ on Pope," *IPS-Inter Press Service* (16 October 2003), http://ipsnews.net/news.asp?idnews=20654.

37. David Tombs, *Latin American Liberation Theology* (Boston: Brill Academic Publishers, 2002), 295.

38. Gutiérrez, "Freedom and Salvation," 82.

39. Gutiérrez, "Freedom and Salvation," 86, 57.

40. Sturm, "Praxis and Promise," 739.

41. Jürgen Moltmann, *Theology of Hope: On the Ground and the Implications of a Christian Eschatology*, trans. James W. Leitch (New York and Evanston: Harper & Row, 1967), 329, author's emphasis, quoted in Sturm, "Praxis and Promise," 739–740.

42. Smith, *Emergence of Liberation Theology*, 26.

43. Reverend Nelson Rivera claims that Brazilian theologian Ivone Gebara is the main representative of liberation theology today in Latin America (author's interview with Reverend Nelson Rivera, 8 June 2002). See Ivone Gebara and Maria Clara Bingemer, *Mary, Mother of God, Mother of the Poor*, trans. Phillip Berryman (Tunbridge Wells, UK: Burns & Oates, 1989).

44. Reverend Nelson Rivera, interview.

45. Paul E. Sigmund, *Liberation Theology at the Crossroads: Democracy or Revolution?* (New York and Oxford: Oxford University Press, 1990), 28.

46. Tombs, *Latin American Liberation Theology*, 197.

47. See C. Peter Wagner, *Latin American Theory, Radical or Evangelical?* (Grand Rapids, MI: Eerdmans Publishing, 1970), and J. Andrew Kirk, *Liberation Theology: An Evangelical View from the Third World* (Atlanta: John Knox Press, 1979), in Sigmund, *Liberation Theology at the Crossroads*, 137–138.

48. "Christian Social Responsibility," in *Making Christ Known: Historic Mission Documents from the Lausanne Movement, 1974–1989*, ed. John Stott (Grand Rapids, MI: Eerdmans Publishing, 1997), 25–26.

49. Costas, *Christ outside the Gate*, 13.

50. Orlando E. Costas, *The Integrity of Mission: The Inner Life and Outreach of the Church* (San Francisco: Harper & Row, 1979), 25.

51. Costas, *Christ outside the Gate*, 13–14, 127, 129–130, 131.

52. Smith, *Emergence of Liberation Theology*, 74.

53. Costas, *Christ outside the Gate*, xiv.

54. Lidia Hunter, "Religion-Latam: 'Liberation Theology' Is Not Dead, Author Says," *IPS-Inter Press Service* (10 June 2003), n.p. Other authors like Edward A. Lynch contest this view. Lynch argues that Catholic leaders who were initially opposed to Latin American liberation theology, like Pope John Paul II, have "reclaimed ideas and positions" of the movement. The new position views liberation as a universal concept of the need for all to receive not only material, but also "spiritual sustenance," Edward A. Lynch, "The Retreat of Liberation Theology," *Homiletic and Pastoral Review* (February 1994): 12–21.

55. Some references for these versions of liberation theology are: African American: James H. Cone, ed., *A Black Theology of Liberation* (Maryknoll, NY: Orbis Books, 1990), James H. Cone, *God of the Oppressed* (Maryknoll, NY: Orbis Books, 1997), Diana L. Hayes, *And Still We Rise: An Introduction to Black Liberation Theology* (New York: Paulist Press, 1996), and Robert McAfee Brown, *Spirituality and Liberation: Overcoming the Great Fallacy* (Louisville, KY: Westminster/John Knox Press, 1988); Asian American: Peter C. Phan and Jung Young Lee, eds., *Journeys at the Margin: Toward an Autobiographical Theology in American-Asian Perspective* (Collegeville, MN: Liturgical Press, 1999); Feminist: Elisabeth Schussler Fiorenza, ed., *The Power of Naming: A Concilium Reader in Feminist Liberation Theology* (Maryknoll, NY: Orbis Books, 1997), and Elina Vuola, *Limits of Liberation: Feminist Theology and the Ethics of Poverty and Reproduction* (London and New York: Sheffield Academic Press, 2002); Liberation Theology and Sexuality: Marcella Althaus-Reid, *Liberation Theology and Sexuality* (Aldershot, UK, and Burlington, VT: Ashgate, 2006), and Richard Cleaver, *Know My Name: A Gay Liberation Theology* (Louisville, KY: Westminster/John Knox Press, 1995). Latino liberation theology will be discussed in more depth later in the section of this chapter entitled "Foundations of U.S. Latino Theology."

56. Reverend Raymond Rivera, interview, 14 May 2001.

57. Reverend Bill Howard, senior pastor, Bethany Baptist Church, telephone interview by author, 23 April 2002.

58. Reverend Raymond Rivera, interview, 7 February 2002.

59. Costas, *Integrity of Mission*, 25.

60. Escobar, "The Legacy of Orlando Costas," 53.

61. Reverend Raymond Rivera, interview, 14 May 2001.

62. Reverend Raymond Rivera, telephone interview, 22 February 2007.

63. Reverend Raymond Rivera, interview, 14 May 2001.

64. Reverend Raymond Rivera, telephone interview, 22 February 2007.

65. *The Autobiography of Malcolm X* (New York: Random House Publishing Group, 1964), 254.

66. Paulo Freire, *Pedagogy of the Oppressed*, trans. Myra Bergman Ramos (London: Continuum International Publishing Group, 2000), 48, 49.

67. Webber, interview.

68. Reverend Raymond Rivera, telephone interview, 22 February 2007.

69. Reverend Luis Cortés, interview.

70. "Reverend Lucius Walker, Jr. Biographical Information," *IFCO*, http:// www.ifconews.org/revbio.html.

71. Reverend Danny Cortés, interview, 20 February 2007.

72. Robert McAfee Brown, *Spirituality and Liberation: Overcoming the Great Fallacy* (Philadelphia: Westminster Press, 1988), 116, 117.

73. Robert McAfee Brown, *Makers of Contemporary Theology: Gustavo Gutiérrez* (Atlanta: John Knox Press, 1980), 52.

74. Brown, *Spirituality and Liberation*, 119.

75. Robert McAfee Brown, *Theology in a New Key: Responding to Liberation Themes* (Philadelphia: Westminster Press, 1978), 60, 65.

76. Cone, *God of the Oppressed*, 15, 17.

77. CELEP: Latin American Center for Pastoral Studies; IPLA: Latin American Pastoral Institute.

78. Escobar, "The Legacy of Orlando Costas," 52, 53.

79. Aponte, "Latino Protestant Identity," 195–196.

80. Costas, *Integrity of Mission*, ix.

81. Reverend Danny Cortés, interview, 20 February 2007.

82. Father Dahm, interview, 29 April 2002.

83. Dahm and Harper, "St. Pius V Roman Catholic Church," 170.

84. John Donohue, executive director, Chicago Coalition for the Homeless, interview by author, Chicago, 6 May 2002.

85. Dahm and Harper, "St. Pius V Roman Catholic Church," 175.

86. Freire, *Pedagogy of the Oppressed*, 124, 65, 87, 88.

87. Father Don Nevins, pastor, St. Francis of Assisi church, interview by author, Chicago, 11 December 2001.

88. Dahm and Harper, "St. Pius V Roman Catholic Church," 174.

89. Donohue, interview.

90. Daniel H. Levine, "Popular Groups, Popular Culture, and Popular Religion," *Comparative Studies in Society and History* 32, no. 4 (October 1990): 723, 750.

91. Brown, *Makers of Contemporary Theology*, 30, 43.

92. Gutiérrez, "Freedom and Salvation," 75.

93. Leonardo Boff, *When Theology Listens to the Poor*, trans. Robert R. Barr (San Francisco: Harper & Row, 1988), 83.

94. Gutiérrez, "Freedom and Salvation," 72.

95. Jacques Maritain, *Integral Humanism: Temporal and Spiritual Problems of a New Christendom*, trans. Joseph W. Evans (Notre Dame, IN: University of Notre Dame Press, 1973), 42, 94, 270–271.

96. Raymundo, telephone interview, 28 February 2007.

97. Maria Pilar Aquino, "Theological Method in U.S. Latino/a Theology: Toward an Intercultural Theology for the Third Millenium," in *From the Heart of Our People: Latino/a Explorations in Catholic Systematic Theology*, eds. Orlando O. Espín and Miguel H. Díaz (Maryknoll, NY: Orbis Books, 1999), 20–21, 23.

98. Milagros Peña in Ruy G. Suárez Rivero, "U.S. Latino/a Theology," in *From the Heart of Our People*, 239.

99. For a thorough treatment of leading figures in U.S. Latino theology, see Eduardo C. Fernández, *La Cosecha: Harvesting Contemporary United States Hispanic Theology (1972–1998)* (Collegeville, MN: Liturgical Press, 2000), 38–90.

100. Gilbert R. Cadena, "The Social Location of Liberation Theology: From Latin America to the United States," in *Hispanic/Latino Theology: Challenge and Promise*, eds. Ada María Isasi-Díaz and Fernando F. Segovia (Minneapolis: Fortress Press, 1996), 173.

101. Raymond Rivera, "The Political and Social Ramifications of Indigenous Pentecostalism," in *Prophets Denied Honor: An Anthology of the Hispano Church of the United States*, ed. Antonio M. Stevens-Arroyo (Maryknoll, NY: Orbis Books, 1980), 339.

102. Virgilio Elizondo, *Galilean Journey: The Mexican American Promise* (Maryknoll, NY: Orbis Books, 1983), 18, quoted in Fernández, *La Cosecha*, 39.

103. Virgilio Elizondo, "*Mestizaje* as a Locus of Theological Reflection," in *Mestizo Christianity: Theology from the Latino Perspective*, ed. Arturo J. Banuelas (Maryknoll, NY: Orbis Books, 1995), 19, 20.

104. Ada María Isasi-Díaz, *En la lucha/In the Struggle: A Hispanic Women's Liberation Theology* (Minneapolis: Fortress Press, 1993), 5, 45–48.

105. C. Gilbert Romero, *Hispanic Devotional Piety: Tracing the Biblical Roots* (Maryknoll, NY: Orbis Books, 1991), 19, 21, 117.

106. Juan Luis Segundo, *The Liberation of Theology* (Maryknoll, NY: Orbis Books, 1976), 186, quoted in Michael R. Candelaria, *Popular Religion and Liberation: The Dilemma of Liberation Theology* (Albany: State University of New York Press, 1990), 73.

107. Candelaria, *Popular Religion and Liberation*, xiii.

108. Orientaciones y conclusions de la Semana Internacional del Catequesis; Conclusiones de la commission 6, n. 3, quoted in Candelaria, *Popular Religion and Liberation*, 5.

109. Miguel A. de la Torre and Edwin David Aponte, *Introducing Latino/a Theologies* (Maryknoll, NY: Orbis Books, 2001), 120, 62.

110. Orlando Espín, "Tradition and Popular Religion: An Understanding of the *Sensus Fidelium*," in *Frontiers of Hispanic Theology*, ed. Allan Figueroa Deck (Maryknoll, NY: Orbis Books, 1992), 70, quoted in Roberto S. Goizueta, "U.S. Hispanic Popular Catholicism as Theopoetics" in *Hispanic/Latino Theology: Challenge and Promise*, eds. Ada María Isasi-Díaz and Fernando F. Segovia (Minneapolis: Fortress Press, 1996), 272.

111. Goizueta, "U.S. Hispanic Popular Catholicism," 272, 276, 279.

112. Aquino, "Theological Method in U.S. Latino/a Theology," 28, 32.

113. Pedraja, *Jesus Is My Uncle*, 123, 37, 15.

114. Harold J. Recinos, "The Barrio as the Locus of a New Church," in *Hispanic/Latino Theology*, 183, 184, 185, 189.

115. *Changing Faiths: Latinos and Transformation of American Religion*, 9.

116. Gastón Espinosa in Sara B. Miller, "Planting New Churches, Latinos Alter Religious Landscape," *Christian Science Monitor* (6 February 2004), 2.

117. Miller, "Planting New Churches," 2.

118. Justo L. González, "Hispanics in the New Reformation" in *Mestizo Christianity*, 255.

119. Harreyette Mullen, "'A Silence between Us like a Language': The Untranslatability of Experience in Sandra Cisneros' *Woman Hollering Creek*," *MELUS* 21, no. 2 (Summer 1996): 12.

120. "Cada Día," in Judith Ortiz Cofer, *Terms of Survival* (Houston: Arte Publico Press, 1995), 31. *Padre* (Father) . . . *danos el pan de cada día* (give us this day our daily bread), *Madre* (Mother), . . . *ruega por nosotros* (pray for us), *Hijo Santo, de ojos azules y corazon sangrante y grande* (Son of God, with blue eyes and large bleeding heart).

121. Ana María Díaz-Stevens, "In the Image and Likeness of God: Literature as Theological Reflection," in *Hispanic/Latino Theology*, 91. A further study of religious themes in Latino literature is Elena Olazagast-Segovia, "Judith Ortiz Cofer's Silent Dancing: The Self-Portrait of the Artist as a Young, Bicultural Girl," in *Hispanic/Latino Theology*, 45–62.

122. Roberto S. Goizueta, *Caminemos con Jesús: Toward a Hispanic/Latino Theology of Accompaniment* (Maryknoll, NY: Orbis Books, 1995), 50, 66.

123. Rivera, "The Political and Social Ramifications of Indigenous Pentecostalism," 340.

NOTES TO CHAPTER 4

1. Reverend Raymond Rivera, interview, 7 February 2002.

2. Reverend Rivera, in Joe Feuerherd, "Unanswered questions abound as faith-based plan advances," *National Catholic Reporter*, 21 March 2003, http://findarticles.com/p/articles/mi_m1141/is_20_39/ ai_ 99554451.

3. Reverend Raymond Rivera, telephone interview, 22 February 2007.

4. Feuerherd, "Unanswered questions abound."

5. Susana Rivera-León, Director of Community-Based Programs, LPAC, interview by author, Bronx, NY, 28 January 2002.

6. Reverend Rivera, telephone interview, 22 February 2007.

7. Rivera-León, interview.

8. Tripp Mickle, "Rivera's 'Holistic' Ministry Attracts National Attention,"

Columbia Journalist (5 September 2005), http://www.columbiajournalist.org/rw1_
freedman/2005/article.asp?subj=business&course=rw1_freedman&id=552.

9. Reverend Rivera, telephone interview, 22 February 2007.

10. LPAC's 1st Annual PRAISE Conference, Bronx, NY, 3 April 2002.

11. PRAISE Conference.

12. PRAISE Conference.

13. Universal Zulu Nation, "The Beliefs of the Universal Zulu Nation," http://
www.zulunation.com/beliefs.html.

14. Universal Zulu Nation, "Prophecies," http://www.zulunation.com/proph-
ecies.html.

15. PRAISE Conference.

16. Bordoni, interview.

17. "u.b.n." stands for United Blood Nation. In New York City, the United
Blood Nation accounts for these Blood sets: Nine Trey Gangsta Bloods (NTG),
Miller Gangsta Bloods (MGB), Young Bloods, Valentine Bloods (VB), Mad Dog
Bloods (MDB), One Eight Trey Bloods (183), Mad Stone Bloods (MSB), Gangsta
Killer Bloods (GKB), Five Nine Brims (5-9 Brims), Sex Money Murder Bloods,
and Blood Stone Villains (BSV). From Florida Gang Investigators Association,
"Bloods: A NYC Department of Correction Intelligence Brief," http://www.fgia.
com/cbnycbrief.htm.

18. "Bloods: A NYC Department of Correction Intelligence Brief."

19. "Almighty Latin King and Queen Nation," http://www.gripe4rkids.org/
LKhis.html.

20. Both the poem and prayer were taken from 1st Annual PRAISE Conference pamphlet.

21. "Almighty Latin King and Queen Nation," http://www.gripe4rkids.org/
LKhis.html.

22. PRAISE Conference.

23. Elbert Garcia, "A King's Logic: Interview with Hector Torres," *LATNN.
com*, http://www. latnn.com/grafico/interview/articles/kingsintvw.htm.

24. "Chapter 2: The Magnitude of Youth Violence," *Youth Violence: A Report of
the Surgeon General* (2000), http://www.mentalhealth.org/youthviolence/surgeon
general/SG_Site/chapter2/sec12.asp.

25. Bordoni, interview.

26. John M. Hagedorn, "Globalization, Gangs, and Collaborative Research,"
in *The Eurogang Paradox: Street Gangs and Youth Groups in the U.S. and Europe*,
eds. M. W. Klein et al. (Dordrecht and Boston: Kluwer Academic Publishers,
2001), 41–58, and "The Contribution to Knowledge" (Gangs in the Global City
Conference, Chicago, 16–17 May 2002), http://www.uic.edu/kbc/KennethClark/
glconfcall.htm.

27. Reverend Willie Reyes, Street/Gang Workers, LPAC, interview by author,
Bronx, NY, 29 January 2002.

28. Reverend Willie Reyes, interview.

29. Reverend Raymond Rivera, interview, 14 May 2001.

30. "Providing Recreation, Arts, Inner Healing, Service, and Education for Our Youth" brochure, LPAC.

31. Bordoni, interview.

32. PRAISE Conference.

33. Reverend Rivera, telephone interview, 22 February 2007.

34. PRAISE Conference.

35. Costas, *Integrity of Mission*, 25.

36. PRAISE Conference.

37. Bordoni, interview.

38. William Damon, "Character Education in Schools: Good, Bad, or None of the Above," *Stanford University School of Education* (Spring 2005), http://ed.stanford.edu/suse/faculty/displayFacultyNews.php?tablename=notify1&id=308.

39. Juan Flores, *From Bomba to Hip-Hop: Puerto Rican Culture and Latino Identity* (New York: Columbia University Press, 2000), 138.

40. Julie Delgado, "Capoeira and Breakdancing: At the Roots of Resistance," *Planet Capoeira On-Line Magazine*, http://www.capoeira.com/planetcapoeira/articles/breakdance.htm.

41. Jesse Worker, "Hip Hop," *Urban Folklore*, 3 December 2001, http://www.indiana.edu/~urbanflk/hip_hop/worker2.html.

42. KRS-One, "A Hip-Hop Commentary: When Hip-Hop Was Illegal," *Hip Hop News*, 1999, http://www.daveyd.com/fnvkrsonecom.html.

43. Reverend Danny Padilla, cultural coordinator, LPAC, interview by author, Bronx, NY, 7 February 2002.

44. Reverend Danny Padilla, interview.

45. Reverend Danny Padilla, interview.

46. Reverend Willie Reyes, PRAISE Conference.

47. "William Rodríguez: 1994 Man of the Year," *Black Belt Magazine*, 1994, http://w3.Blackbeltmag.com/halloffame/html/189.html.

48. Reverend Danny Padilla, interview.

49. Reverend Willie Reyes, interview.

50. *The Autobiography of Malcolm X*, 254.

51. Rivera-León, interview.

52. Reverend Willie Reyes, interview.

53. Francisco Lugoviña, president, New Line Inc., interview by author, New York, 20 March 2002.

54. Reverend Danny Padilla, interview.

55. Manuel A. Vásquez, "Saving Souls Transnationally: Pentecostalism and Gangs in El Salvador and the United States," working paper, The Project on Lived Theology, University of Virginia, Charlottesville, VA, http://www.livedtheology.org.

56. Reverend Raymond Rivera, interview, 7 February 2002.

57. "Wounded Healer Fellowship" (9th Anniversary Service and Credentialing Ceremony, Bronx, NY, 3 February 2002).

58. Reverend Alfonso Wyatt, vice president, Fund for the City, interview by author, New York City, 25 March 2002.

59. Reverend Rafael Reyes, superintendent, Spanish Eastern District, interview by author, Old Tappan, NJ, 19 March 2002.

60. "Project," *Simeht Ltd. Project Collaborations,* http://home.earthlink.net/~whiteleicht/articles/Proc-olab.html.

61. *Peace Dojo Project,* http://urbanvisionsinc.org/Articles/esPeacDo.html.

62. Eleanor Seager, "Come to an Alternatives to Violence October Workshop," http://www.peaceactionme.org/sepalternatives.html.

63. Charles Colten, "Aikido-Based Programs for Youth with Special Needs," *Aiki Extensions Newsletter,* http://www.aiki-extensions.org/newsletters/doc/aen1.doc.

64. Bill Leicht, president, Simeht Ltd., interview by author, New York, 18 April 2002.

65. Leicht, interview.

66. Bill Leicht, "Martial Arts and Conflict Resolution Session," Resolving Conflict Creatively Program (RCCP), High School for the Physical Sciences, New York, 21 April 2002.

67. "Martial Arts and Conflict Resolution."

68. "Martial Arts and Conflict Resolution."

69. Leicht, interview.

70. Leicht, interview.

71. Arlene M. Sánchez-Walsh, "Pentecostals," in *Handbook of Latina/o Theologies,* 199, 200.

72. Samuel Cruz, "A Rereading of Latino/a Pentecostalism," in *New Horizons in Hispanic/Latino/a Theology,* ed. Benjamín Valentín (Cleveland: Pilgrim Press, 2003), 206, 207.

73. David Martin, *Tongues of Fire: The Explosion of Protestantism in Latin America* (Cambridge, MA: Basil Blackwell, 1990), 133, quoted in Cruz, "A Rereading of Latino/a Pentecostalism," 213.

74. Sánchez-Walsh, "Pentecostals," 201.

75. Reverend Raymond Rivera, telephone interview, 22 February 2007.

76. John C. Green, "Assemblies of God," in *Pulpit and Politics,* 184.

77. Cruz, "A Rereading of Latino/a Pentecostalism," 184.

78. Webber, interview.

79. Martin, *Tongues of Fire,* 133, quoted in Cruz, "A Rereading of Latino/a Pentecostalism," 214.

80. LPAC Job Readiness Workshop, Bronx, NY, 30 January 2002.

81. "The sheet says that you help a woman find work." In addition to receiving child support, "the father [of my child] gives me $1,500/month."

82. LPAC Job Readiness Workshop.

83. "SOBRO Faith-Based Initiatives Unit," *South Bronx Overall Economic Development Corporation,* http://www.sobro.org/content_new/g1.html.

84. Reverend Raymond Rivera, telephone interview, 22 February 2007.

85. LPAC Job Readiness Workshop.

86. Reverend Raymond Rivera, telephone interview, 22 February 2007.

87. Rivera-León, interview.

88. Reverend Rivera noted in a recent interview that LPAC's Pastoral Counseling Program is not as "fortified" as it has been. It has continued to struggle with funding. At present, there is one person in charge of "spiritual care," namely, Reverend Alfred Correa, MDiv, MSW. Reverend Rivera, telephone interview, 22 February 2007.

89. Dr. Roberto Rivera, former director of Pastoral Counseling Program, LPAC, interview by author, Bronx, NY, 19 April 2002.

90. Dr. Roberto Rivera, interview.

91. Dr. Roberto Rivera, interview.

92. Dr. Roberto answered him, "because the Lord called me to this ministry."

93. Dr. Roberto Rivera, interview.

94. Viktor E. Frankl, *Man's Search for Meaning,* trans. Ilse Lasch (Boston: Beacon Press, 2006), 62, 39, 66.

95. Frankl, *Man's Search for Meaning,* 58, xvi.

96. Dr. Roberto Rivera, interview.

97. Frankl, *Man's Search for Meaning,* 50.

98. Dr. Roberto Rivera, interview.

99. "The Blanton-Peale Institute," *Blanton-Peale Institute,* http://www.blanton peale.org.

100. Irfan Hasan, program officer—Health and People with Special Needs, New York Community Trust, interview by author, New York City, 19 March 2002.

101. Jacqueline Elias, vice president, JPMorgan Private Bank—JPMorgan Chase Bank, interview by author, New York City, 16 April 2002.

102. Elias, interview.

103. Dr. Roberto Rivera, interview.

104. Elias, interview.

105. Dr. Roberto Rivera, interview.

106. Dr. John Hagedorn, dean of students and director of Pastoral Care Studies Program, Blanton-Peale Graduate Institute, interview by author, New York City, 20 March 2002.

107. Elias, interview.

108. Badillo, *Latinos and the New Immigrant Church,* 208.

109. Reverend Nancy Márquez, coordinator of social services, LPAC, interview by author, Bronx, NY, 8 February 2002.

110. Freire, *Pedagogy of the Oppressed,* 48.

111. Márquez, interview.

112. Percy Howard, counselor and elder–Sanctuary, LPAC, interview by author, Bronx, NY, 3 February 2002.

113. Percy Howard, interview.

114. Wilson, "Empowerment: Community Economic Development from the Inside Out," 627.

115. Rivera-León, interview, emphasis added.

116. Reverend Raymond Rivera, interview, 7 February 2002.

117. Lugoviña, interview.

118. Richard Rivera, LPAC consultant and adjunct professor, New School, interview by author, New York City, 29 March 2002.

119. Henry Nixon, education coordinator, LPAC, interview by author, Bronx, NY, 7 February 2002.

120. Dr. Hagedorn, interview.

121. Lugoviña, interview.

122. Elias, interview.

123. Hector Montes, vice president, New Line Inc., interview by author, New York City, 20 March 2002, and Reverend Danny Cortés, interview, 8 March 2002.

124. Richard Rivera, interview.

125. Rivera-León, interview.

126. Thomas Reardon, director of finance and administration, LPAC, interview by author, Bronx, NY, 28 January 2002.

127. Richard Rivera, interview.

128. Mirta Ojito, "Talking the Talk, Sometimes in Spanish," *New York Times*, 19 June 2001, late edition–final, B3.

129. John Toscano, "Coalition for Ferrer: Too Little, Too Late?" *Western Queens Gazette*, 15 August 2001, http://www.qgazette.com/News/2001/0815/Political_Page/001.html.

130. Mirta Ojito, "Latino Pastors Endorse Ferrer for Mayor," *New York Times*, 26 June 2001, late edition–final, B3.

131. "Borough Chaplains' Created," *Bronx Times*, 31 December 2001, http://www.bxtimes.com/News/2001/1213/Boroughwide-News/015.html.

132. "Borough Chaplains' Created."

133. Wyatt, interview.

134. Reverend Rafael Reyes, interview.

135. José Martínez, "Clergy Invited to Attend NYPD Roll Calls," *New York Daily News*, 30 March 2000, 5.

136. Jill Priluck, "Cops and Collars: Clergy Keeping the Peace in the Bronx Want a Reward: The Return of Community Policing," *City Limits Monthly* (June 2000), http://www.citylimits.org/content/articles/articleView.cfm?articlenumber=333.

137. Harris, *Ministry for Social Crisis*, 40.

138. Rauschenbush, *Christianity and the Social Crisis*, 91.

139. Winston, *Red-Hot and Righteous,* 145.

140. Christopher Queen, "Buddhism, Activism, and Unknowing: A Day with Bernie Glassman," *Tikkun* 13, no. 1 (January–February 1998): 64.

141. Francisco Genkoji Lugoviña, "Meeting in the Darkness," *Peacemaker Community,* http://www.peacemakercommunity.org/English/hub/Community/Articles andTalks/Paco/Mtg_in_Darkness.htm.

142. Lugoviña, interview.

143. Lugoviña, "Meeting in the Darkness."

144. Montes, interview.

145. Bailey, interview.

146. Reverend Danny Cortés, interview, 8 March 2002.

147. Bailey, interview.

148. "There is a reason why I am here," shouted the pastor. A woman yelled out, "yes, sir!" "God gives the church ministers. The ministry is a divine project."

149. Reverend Jose Satirio Do Santos ("Llamados a Combatir el Terror," Brooklyn, NY, 4 April 2002). "The leader needs to be tested by fire," all the while realizing that the "fire burns." Do Santos questioned, "who wants to be made pure" like "gold" that is "the only thing that resists" the flame?

150. "Called to Combat Terrorism."

151. This is the view only of those who "want to democratize the church." But, "in leadership, there are specific points."

152. "One night the Lord said to Paul in a vision, 'Do not be afraid but speak and do not be silent; for I am with you, and no one will lay a hand on you to harm you, for there are many in this city who are my people.'" St. Paul then settled in Corinth for a year and a half, "teaching the word of God among them."

153. "Llamados a Combatir el Terror." As a pastor, "if you do not go, nobody will. If you do not lead, you will never arrive at any point." Like St. Paul, a pastor should "continue speaking and teaching."

154. Reverend Luciano Padilla, senior pastor, Bay Ridge Christian Center, interview by author, Brooklyn, NY, 26 March 2002.

155. Reverend Pedro Windsor, administrator, Deputy Chief Education Office, Chicago Public Schools, interview by author, Chicago, 13 May 2002.

156. Reverend Danny Cortés, interview, 8 March 2002.

157. Elias, interview.

158. Reverend Raymond Rivera, telephone interview, 22 February 2007.

159. Rivera-León, interview.

160. Its "mission is very different from [other CBOs]. It is unique." Reverend José La Boy, community and church liaison, LPAC, interview by author, Bronx, NY, 8 February 2002.

161. Bailey, interview.

162. Carmen Colón, acting director of community programs, LPAC, interview by author, Bronx, NY, 29 January 2002.

163. Mickle, "Rivera's 'Holistic' Ministry Attracts National Attention."

164. Reverend Willie Reyes, interview.

165. Reardon, interview.

166. Colón, interview.

NOTES TO CHAPTER 5

1. Juan Torres, senior manager, SEPTA, and Nueva board member, interview by author, Philadelphia, 23 January 2002.

2. Arelis Reynoso, "Cortés: La Ley HR 4437 tiene 'veneno,'" *El Sol*, del 29 de marzo al 5 de abril de 2006, 9.

3. Reverend Danny Cortés, interview, 20 February 2007.

4. Through Nueva's ministry of institutional development, states Cortés, "we are not only working for the community but also for the common good." He continues, "improving the neighborhood is a collective work; it is not only an employment center, or a high school, or a junior college, we already have those and we continue building institutions that serve the community, in addition to finding ways for them to work together." From René Rincón, "Empleos para hispanos," *El Sol*, del 16 al 23 de noviembre del 2005, 9.

5. Reverend Luis Cortés, Jr., interview.

6. Reverend Luis Cortés, Jr., in "Creating Hope through Schools, Jobs, and Homes: Nueva Esperanza," *Philanthropy* 20, no. 6 (November/December 2006): 24.

7. "Remarks by the President at the National Hispanic Prayer Breakfast," *PR Newswire*, 16 May 2002, 1.

8. "National Hispanic Prayer Breakfast," *Worldwide Church of God* (2002), http://www.wcg.org/wn/02july/national_hispanic_prayer_breakfast.htm.

9. "Remarks by the President at the National Hispanic Prayer Breakfast."

10. Adelle Banks, "Bush Meets Hispanic Religious Leaders," *Baptist Standard*, 27 May 2002, http://www.baptiststandard.com/2002/5_27/pages/hispanic.html.

11. Harold Dean Trulear, Civitas Lecture Series, Washington, DC, 1 August 2002.

12. Reverend Danny Cortés, interview, 20 February 2007.

13. Trulear, Civitas Lecture Series.

14. Williams, "The Language of God in the City of Man," 73.

15. Jason DeParle, "Hispanic Group Thrives on Faith and Federal Aid," *New York Times*, 3 May 2005, A1.

16. Governor Tom Ridge, "Bush Nomination Speech," Republican National Convention, Philadelphia, 3 August 2000.

17. "Santorum Rolls Out Senate Republican Poverty Alleviation Agenda:

Santorum Joined by Two Pennsylvania Leaders in Fighting Poverty," *United States Senator Rick Santorum Press Office*, 2 March 2005.

18. "The Reverend Luis Cortés, Jr.," *21st Century Speakers Inc.*, http://www.speakersaccess.com/speaker.php?id=562.

19. Mike Dorning and William Neikirk, "Right and Left Unsure What to Make of Miers," *Chicago Tribune*, 4 October 2005, http://www.chicagotribune.com/news/nationworld/chi-0510040186oct04,1,3559589.story?coll=chi-news-hed.

20. "Without you, Mr. President, Darfur doesn't have a prayer," *Evangelicals for Darfur*, http://go.sojo.net/campaign/evangelicalsfordarfur.

21. DeParle, "Hispanic Group Thrives on Faith and Federal Aid," A22.

22. See note 21 above.

23. "Statement of Reverend Luis Cortés, Jr., president, Nueva Esperanza, Inc.," Testimony Before the Subcommittee on Human Resources and Subcommittee on Select Revenue Measures of the House Committee on Ways and Means: Hearing on H.R. 7, the "Community Solutions Act of 2001," 14 June 2001.

24. "Statement of the Hon. J. C. Watts, Jr., a Representative in Congress from the State of Oklahoma," Testimony Before the Subcommittee on Human Resources and Subcommittee on Select Revenue Measures of the House Committee on Ways and Means: Hearing on H.R. 7, the "Community Solutions Act of 2001," 14 June 2001.

25. "Statement of Senator Joe Lieberman on the Introduction of the Charity Aid, Recovery, and Empowerment (CARE) Act," *United States Senator Joseph Lieberman Press Office*, 7 February 2002.

26. "Testimony of Reverend Luis Cortés, Jr., president and CEO, Esperanza USA," before the United States Senate Committee on the Judiciary: Comprehensive Immigration Reform: Examining the Need for a Guest Worker Program, Field Hearing, Philadelphia, 5 July 2006, http://judiciary.senate.gov/print_testimony.cfm?id= 1983&wit_id=5500.

27. Border Protection, Antiterrorism, and Illegal Immigration Control Act of 2005, 109th Congress, H.R. 4437 (16 December 2005).

28. "Testimony of Reverend Luis Cortés, Jr.," 5 July 2006.

29. "Traten (al inmigrante) como a uno propio," *Impacto Latin Newspaper*, del 24 al 30 de agosto de 2006, 10.

30. Krista Poplau, "Esperanza USA to Discuss Immigration Reform with DNC, RNC, and White House," *U.S. Newswire*, http://releases.usnewswire.com/printing.asp?id=6275.

31. Reverend Luis Cortés, Jr., and U.S. Commerce Secretary Carlos M. Gutiérrez, Esperanza USA conference call on the Secure Borders, Economic Opportunity and Immigration Reform Act of 2007 (S. 1348), 31 May 2007.

32. DeParle, "Hispanic Group Thrives on Faith and Federal Aid," A22.

33. Bittenbender, interview.

34. "Dice Director de Clero Hispano, 'Tenemos Que Regresar a Nuestros Valores,'" *Al Día*, 1 de mayo de 1993, 3. "The person that is hungry, is hungry, period," asserts Cortés. If a starving individual were to pray to God, the prayer would not be "Lord how can I serve, but Lord, how can I survive!"

35. Reverend Danny Cortés, interview, 20 February 2007.

36. Reverend Luis Cortés, Jr., in Aponte, "Latino Protestant Identity," 70, 72.

37. Sunday service, Primera Iglesia Bautista Hispana, Philadelphia, 8 September 2002. Gúzman speaks of the difference between a "theologian" and a "hunter." A "theologian only educated himself." A hunter, on the other hand, "looks for signs." But the hunter "doesn't pitch his tent here," among the footprints. He "follows the footprints to find the tiger." So must each one of us as a people of faith be a "hunter of God's presence."

38. Reverend Danny Cortés, interview, 20 February 2007.

39. Costas, *Integrity of Mission*, ix.

40. David Van Biema et al., "Evangelicals in America," *Time*, 30 January 2005, http:///www.time.com/time/magazine/article/0.9171,1022583-4,00.html.

41. Reverend Luis Cortés, Jr., in Amy L. Sherman, "Good News from the Hispanic Church: The Community Serving Activities of Hispanic Protestant Churches," *Christianity Today*, July/August 2004, http:///www.christianitytoday.com/bc/2004/004/9.18.html.

42. *Changing Faiths: Latinos and the Transformation of American Religion*, 11.

43. Aponte, "Latino Protestant Identity," 73–74.

44. "Read the Bible every day."

45. Martínez emotionally shouts "give us your power," "come into in our place." He then extends an invitation to anyone who "wants a personal relationship with Jesus Christ." He invites the congregation, "come this afternoon and make a pact with the Lord."

46. "Holy Lord, Holy Lord."

47. Martínez continues, "keep coming up to the front. Alleluia." He turns to the congregation, "You have come here with some need. You have felt frozen."

48. "The Lord is my shepherd; I shall not want. . . . Even though I walk through the darkest valley / I fear no evil; for you are with me; your rod and your staff—comfort me."

49. Sherman, "Good News from the Hispanic Church."

50. Reverend Magaly Martínez, interview.

51. "Statement of Reverend Luis Cortés, Jr.," 14 June 2001.

52. Reverend Esdras Seda, pastor, Lindley Methodist Church and La Resurreción Congregation, interview by author, Philadelphia, 5 June 2002.

53. R. Andrew Swinney, president, Philadelphia Foundation, interview by author, Philadelphia, 23 May 2002.

54. Reverend Magaly Martínez, interview.

55. *Changing Faiths: Latinos and the Transformation of American Religion*, 18.

56. Judith Bardes, manager, Allen Hilles Fund, interview by author, Plymouth Meeting, PA, 28 May 2002.

57. Mission statement of Nueva Esperanza, emphasis added.

58. Reverend Luis Cortés, Jr., interview.

59. Tamara Díaz, coordinator for Nueva Esperanza Center for Higher Education, interview with author, Philadelphia, 11 January 2002.

60. Anita Ruiz, director of project development and implementation and assistant general counsel, Nueva, interview by author, Philadelphia, 16 January 2002.

61. Reverend Luis Cortés, Jr., interview.

62. Sherrie Steiner and Donald Gray, "American Baptist Convention," in *Pulpit and Politics*, 19, 25.

63. "American Baptist Identity Statement," http://www.abc-usa.org/identity/idstate.html.

64. Reverend Luis Cortés, Jr., interview.

65. Roberto Santiago, executive director, Concilio, interview by author, Philadelphia, 26 February 2002.

66. Zepernick, interview.

67. "10 Facts You Should Know about American Baptists," Office of Communication/General Ministries, American Baptist Churches USA, 3, http://www.tabcom.org/downloads/10facts.pdf.

68. Steiner and Gray, "American Baptist Convention," 19.

69. Zepernick, interview.

70. Carlos Matos, office manager, Senator Tina Tartaglione and 19th Ward Leader, interview with author, Philadelphia, 6 March 2002.

71. Councilman Ortiz, interview.

72. María Quiñones-Sánchez, former regional director, Puerto Rico Federal Affairs Administration, interview by author, Philadelphia, 25 February 2002.

73. Eldín Villafañe, "An Evangelical Call to a Social Spirituality," in *Mestizo Christianity*, 210.

74. "American Baptist Identity Statement."

75. Escobar, "The Legacy of Orlando Costas," 220.

76. "Peace Rally in Philadelphia," *National Catholic Reporter* 33, no. 44, 17 October 1997, n.p.

77. David O'Reilly, "Walk Crosses Denominations: Catholics and Evangelicals Turned Out for Peace in the Hispanic Community," *Philadelphia Inquirer*, 29 September 1997, B1.

78. "Esperanza USA President Rev. Luis Cortés Joins Rick Warren's Global Summit on AIDS," *Press Release, Esperanza USA*, 29 November 2006.

79. Tara Kathryn Flores, "Entrevista Exclusiva con Luis Cortés," *Nuestra Tarea*, septiembre/octubre de 2005, 9.

80. "Latinos de Fili a Israel," *Al Día*, 1–8 de junio de 1995, 5.

81. Michael Elkin, "A Project of Faith Travels Well, Linking Latino Community to Israelis," *The Jewish Exponent*, 16 June 2005, n.p.

82. "Israeli Government Donates Sea of Galilee Land to Christian Leaders," *Charisma News*, 6 July 2005, http://www.evangelicalnews.org/indiv_pr.php?action=display&pr_id=3703.

83. Reverend Danny Cortés, interview, 20 February 2007.

84. Ben Ramos, consultant, Selecto Consultants, interview by author, Philadelphia, 1 March 2002.

85. Reverend Danny Cortés, interview, 20 February 2007.

86. Dr. King, "Strength to Love."

87. Maritza Robert, bureau director, Community and Student Services, Pennsylvania Department of Education, telephone interview by author, 10 June 2002.

88. Reverend Danny Cortés, interview, 15 January 2002.

89. Reverend Danny Cortés, interview, 20 February 2007.

90. Bittenbender, interview.

91. DeParle, "Hispanic Group Thrives on Faith and Federal Aid," A22.

92. Cone, *Theology in a New Key*, 60, and *Spirituality and Liberation*, 119.

93. Torres, interview.

94. "empower" and "authorize."

95. "Poder o no Poder," *Al Día*, 31 de marzo a 14 de abril de 1994, 1. An adequate definition of this term is "your capacity to make possible that which you desire . . . that is empowerment."

96. Tanya Byrd, program manager, job training, Nueva, interview by author, Philadelphia, 15 January 2002.

97. Byrd, interview.

98. Ruiz, interview.

99. Aponte, "Latino Protestant Identity," 186.

100. Jeremiah White, Chairman, Monarch Consulting Group, interview by author, Philadelphia, 7 June 2002.

101. Udayan Gupta, "Community-Loan Funds Bridge Inner-City Capital Gap," *Wall Street Journal*, 13 January 1993, B2.

102. Efraín Roche, "Nueva Esperanza inauguará Lavandería del Pueblo," *Community Focus*, 29 October 1992, 1. He remarked, "Our purpose is to continue creating economic projects of this kind where the community is the owner and the earnings are reinvested in other projects within our community."

103. Leslie Benoliel, executive director, Philadelphia Development Partners, interview by author, Philadelphia, 1 March 2002.

104. C. K. Prahalad and Gary Hamel, "The Core Competence of the Corporation," *Harvard Business Review* 8, no. 3 (May–June 1990): 79–93.

105. Mitchell F. Rice, "Promoting Cultural Competency in Public Administration and Public Service Delivery: Utilizing Self-assessment Tools and Performance Measures," *Journal of Public Affairs Education* 13, no. 1 (Winter 2007): 42, 50.

106. Eileen Díaz McConnell and Timothy Ready, *The Roof Over Our Heads: Hispanic Housing in the United States* (Philadelphia: Esperanza USA, June 2005), 5, 6, 11.

107. Rice, "Promoting Cultural Competency," 41.

108. Reverend Luis Cortés, Jr., in "Nueva Esperanza: Bringing New Hope to Philadelphians," *Resources*, Fall 1997, 3–4.

109. Rice, "Promoting Cultural Competency in Public Administration," 44–45.

110. Belén, *Adiós, Borinquen querida*, 13, 15.

111. "Nueva Esperanza: Bringing New Hope to Philadelphians," 4.

112. "Empleos para hispanos," *El Sol*, del 16 al 23 de noviembre del 2005, 8.

113. Tamara Díaz, interview.

114. Byrd, interview.

115. Verba, "Comparative Political Culture," 513.

116. Helen Cunningham, executive director, Samuel S. Fels Fund, telephone interview by author, 21 May 2002.

117. Ramos, interview.

118. "Creating Hope through Schools, Jobs, and Homes: Nueva Esperanza," *Philanthropy* 20, no. 6 (November/December 2006): 25.

119. Claire Hughes, "Nueva Esperanza Targets Help to Hispanic Faith-Based Groups," *Roundtable on Religion and Social Welfare Policy* (13 June 2006), http://www.religionandsocialpolicy.org/homepage/article_print.cfm?id=4415.

120. Rice, "Promoting Cultural Competency," 47, 49.

121. Reverend Luis Cortés, Jr., interview.

122. Board of directors meeting, Nueva Esperanza, Philadelphia, 10 January 2002.

123. Torres, interview.

124. Reverend Luis Cortés, Jr., interview.

125. Torres, interview.

126. Reverend Luis Cortés, Jr., interview.

127. Rice, "Promoting Cultural Competency," 49.

128. Evelyn Pérez, office management, HR, Finances, Nueva, interview with author, Philadelphia, 11 January 2002.

129. Reverend Seda, interview.

130. Benoliel, interview.

131. Don Jose Stovall, executive director, Philadelphia County Assistance Office, interview by author, Philadelphia, 8 March 2001.

132. Judy Torres-Lynch, vice president, U.S. benefits, Glaxo Smith Kline and Nueva Board member, interview by author, Philadelphia, 23 January 2002.

133. Reverend Luis Cortés, Jr., interview.
134. Torres, interview.
135. "The Lord is in this place . . . to save, to free . . . to win, to free my soul."
136. "So she set out, and came to the man of God at Mount Carmel. When the man of God saw her coming, he said to Gehazi his servant, 'Look, there is the Shunammite woman; run at once to meet her, and say to her, Are you all right? Is your husband all right? Is the child all right? She answered, "It is all right."
137. Sunday service, Iglesia Sion, Philadelphia, 2 June 2002. "People have resigned themselves in the face of so many impossibilities" in their very own lives and neighborhoods. But although "sometimes . . . the doors do not open," the Lord has the last word.
138. Quiñones-Sánchez, interview.
139. Reverend Raúl le Duc, pastor of Iglesia Sion and Nueva board member, interview with author, Philadelphia, 8 March 2002.
140. Torres, interview.
141. Dr. Roberto Araujo, Nueva board member, interview with author, Philadelphia, 25 January 2002.
142. Susan Hedden, director of development, Nueva, interview by author, Philadelphia, 16 January 2002.
143. Torres, interview.
144. Reverend Luis Cortés, Jr., interview.
145. Reverend Danny Cortés, interview, 20 February 2007.
146. Reverend Luis Cortés, Jr., interview.
147. Maritza Ortiz-Santiago, housing director, Nueva, interview by author, Philadelphia, 11 January 2002.
148. Alfredo Calderón, executive director, Aspira, interview by author, Philadelphia, 5 March 2002.
149. "Pelea sobre el terreno," *Al Día*, junio 3–9 de 2001, 2–3. In stating, "this means that the money that enters his institution goes directly to his pocket, in addition he does not pay taxes," Rivera characterized Cortés as a distinct kind of capitalist, one who—as the head of a Latino FBO—has the privilege of not having to pay taxes.
150. Councilman Ortiz, interview.
151. Larry Copland, Lea Sitton, and Larry Fish, "Poor Vie for Slice of Federal Aid Pie," *Philadelphia Inquirer*, 28 March 1994, A12.
152. Ruiz, interview.
153. Robert, interview.
154. "Welcome to the Puerto Rican Festival 2002," *Concilio*, http://elconcilio.net/Festival/Intro PRF 2000.htm.
155. "Puerto Ricans with class."
156. Puerto Rican Parade, Philadelphia, 29 September 2002.

157. Quiñones-Sánchez, interview.
158. Ruiz, interview.
159. Jacques Steinberg, "Private Groups Get 42 Schools in Philadelphia," *New York Times,* 18 April 2002, A22.
160. Quiñones-Sánchez, interview.
161. Torres, interview.
162. Reverend Luis Cortés, Jr., et al., "Section I: School Design," *Nueva Esperanza Academy Charter School: A Public Charter High School* (Charter School Application Presented to the School District of Philadelphia), Philadelphia, 10 November 1999, 3.
163. NEA Brochure.
164. Cortés et al., "Section I: School Design," 3–4, 13–14.
165. Torres-Lynch, interview.
166. Angela González, former Nueva Esperanza Academy Charter High School principal, Philadelphia, interview by author, 15 January 2002.
167. U.S. Department of Education in Rochelle Nicols Solomon, *Data Presentation: Gear Up Partnership Meeting,* Philadelphia, 27 February 2001, 18.
168. Reverend Danny Cortés, interview, 15 January 2002.
169. Torres-Lynch, interview.
170. Torres, interview.
171. Reverend Raúl le Duc, Pastor—Iglesia Sion and Nueva Board member, interview with author, Philadelphia, 8 March 2002.
172. "From the Heart," Nueva Esperanza Academy Charter School (December 2001).
173. González, interview, 15 January 2002.
174. Reverend Luis Cortés, Jr., interview.
175. Reverend Danny Cortés et al., "Section III: Governance/Management," *Nueva Esperanza Academy Charter School*, 38.
176. Nueva Esperanza Academy's mission statement, emphasis added.
177. González, written interview, 19 December 2002.
178. González, interview, 15 January 2002.
179. González, written interview, 19 December 2002.
180. David W. Rossi, CEO, Nueva Esperanza Academy Charter High School, written interview by author, 20 February 2007.
181. González, interview, 15 January 2002.
182. Tamara Díaz, interview.
183. "Lord, I believe in study, / Make it a beautiful and constructive adventure / that leads me to love more. / I want to be free, / Make me believe in interior discipline more than in exterior discipline." "I want to be sincere, / Make me only express words that proceed from my conviction / and my voice impede others who might use my silence / to legitimize their pretensions and aggressive

behavior." ". . . Give me the joy of having friends, / Lord, I believe in study, / Make it forge my great ideas." "That from my ideals and positive experiences, / family and society receive life, / So that not only they believe in you but also in me as you made me."

184. Tamara Díaz, interview.

185. Sandra Gardner, "Unique Esperanza Targets Hispanics," *Hispanic Outlook*, 3 July 2006, 30–32.

186. Gardner, "Unique Esperanza Targets Hispanics," 32.

187. Reverend Danny Cortés, interview, 15 January 2002.

188. Reverend Luis Cortés, Jr., interview.

189. Zepernick, interview.

190. Santiago, interview.

191. "Statement of Reverend Luis Cortés, Jr.," 14 June 2001.

192. Stovall, interview.

193. Nueva mission statement, emphasis added.

194. Hedden, interview.

195. Ruiz, interview.

196. Reverend Luis Cortés, Jr., interview.

NOTES TO CHAPTER 6

1. Raymundo, in *Parish Ministry in a Hispanic Church*, 278.

2. Donohue, interview.

3. Raymundo, in *Parish Ministry in a Hispanic Church*, 263.

4. Salvador Cervantes, community organizer, TRP, interview by author, Chicago, 27 April 2001.

5. Caroline Goldstein, vice president, community investment (State of Illinois), Banc One, interview by author, Chicago, 26 July 2001.

6. Mark McDaniel, program officer, Polk Brothers Foundation, interview by author, Chicago, 27 July 2001.

7. Raymundo, telephone interview, 28 February 2007.

8. Susan Lloyd, director, building community capacity, MacArthur Foundation, interview by author, Chicago, 11 December 2001.

9. Raymundo, telephone interview, 28 February 2007.

10. Lloyd, interview.

11. McDaniel, interview.

12. Kari Lydersen, "Hunger Stikers Prod Chicago for New School," *Washington Post*, 28 May 2001, A2.

13. Fran Spielman, "New High Schools Will Accent Thinking Small," *Chicago Sun-Times*, 26 June 2002, special ed., 9.

14. Noticias Chicago television interviewed Garcia, who spoke of the celebration as "a way to wake up the people and the community."

15. "Jesus Christ" says "my mission is your mission." "The mission of Jesus has a church, parishes, and you." He added that "the struggle did not end last year." There is now the "second level of struggle—we need to organize and build a school." The "school and grounds are part of the mission to form good adults." But in this effort, "we have to work as a family" because "nothing is impossible if we work together."

16. "yes we can, yes we can."

17. "Mayor Daley Dedicates New Little Village High School: Community-Driven, Small-Schools Campus Opened in September," *Public Building Commission of Chicago,* 11 October 2005, http://www.pbcchicago.com/subhtml/press/pr_little_village.asp.

18. Father Peter McQuinn, pastor, Epiphany Parish, interview by author, Chicago, 7 May 2002.

19. Peter Skerry, "Citizenship Begins at Home: A New Approach to the Civic Integration of Immigrants," *The Responsive Community* (Winter 2003/4): 30.

20. Dahm, *Parish Ministry in a Hispanic Community,* 97, 98, 100, 105.

21. Pesqueira, interview.

22. Pesqueira, interview.

23. Father Ezequiel Sánchez, pastor, Holy Trinity Parish, interview by author, Chicago, 14 May 2002.

24. Trinita Logue, president, Illinois Facility Fund, interview by author, Chicago, 17 December 2001.

25. Julie DeGraaf, director of homeownership services, TRP, interview by author, Chicago, 2 May 2002.

26. Father Nevins, interview.

27. Elena Segura, program director, Office for Peace and Justice, Archdiocese of Chicago, interview by author, Chicago, 18 December 2001.

28. Father McQuinn, interview.

29. Wood, *Faith in Action,* 71.

30. Raymundo, telephone interview, 28 February 2007.

31. Richard Townsell, executive director, Lawndale Christian Development Center, interview by author, Chicago, 19 December 2001.

32. Sánchez, interview.

33. Dalton, *The Moral Vision of César Chávez,* 2, 3.

34. Father Alberto Athié, resident pastor, Holy Cross/IHM Parish, interview by author, Chicago, 30 April 2002.

35. Freire, *Pedagogy of the Oppressed,* 124, 88.

36. TRP vision statement, *The Resurrection Project,* http://www.resurrectionproject.org/.

37. Father Nevins, interview.

38. Regina McGraw, executive director, Wieboldt Foundation, interview by author, Chicago, 24 July 2001.

39. Susana Vásquez, "TRP: Baptized to Transform Pilsen," *PRAGmatics* (Fall 1988): 17.

40. Dahm, *Parish Ministry in a Hispanic Community*, 199.

41. Paul Roldan, president, Hispanic Housing Development Corporation, interview by author, Chicago, 20 December 2001.

42. Father Nevins, interview.

43. McGraw, interview.

44. McGraw, interview.

45. Father Dahm, interview, 29 April 2002.

46. Father Tim Howe, S.J., pastor, St. Procopius, interview by author, Chicago, 14 May 2002.

47. Father McQuinn, interview.

48. Raymundo, interview, 23 April 2001.

49. Raymundo, telephone interview, 28 February 2007.

50. This is an excerpt from the *Nican Mopohua*, a text that gathered the events of 1531, written by a Nahuatl scholar in the Nahuatl language for his people, Virgil Elizondo, *Guadalupe: Mother of the New Creation* (Maryknoll, NY: Orbis Books, 1997), 8, v. 23–25.

51. "My Mother of Guadalupe, give me your blessing, receive these mañanitas with a humble heart."

52. "In those days Mary set out and went with haste to a Judean town in the hill country, where she entered the house of Zechariah and greeted Elizabeth. When Elizabeth heard Mary's greeting, the child leaped in her womb. And Elizabeth was filled with the Holy Spirit."

53. Mañanitas celebration, St. Procopius Church, Chicago, 12 December 2001. Howe emphasizes that "the Virgin first goes out to greet others" with the joy that only God can give. In like fashion, Howe tells the congregation, "we transform ourselves into custodians in order to share the Lord with others."

54. "offering the best in meats and pork in the Michoacan style: barbecued often, tacos made to your liking, liquor of your choosing, and cold beer."

55. Father McQuinn, interview.

56. Miles Richardson, *Being-in-Christ and Putting Death in Its Place: An Anthropologist's Account of Christian Performance in Spanish America and the American South* (Baton Rouge: Louisiana State University Press, 2003), 244.

57. Dahm, *Parish Ministry in a Hispanic Community*, 162–163.

58. Richardson, *Being-in-Christ*, 221, 222.

59. Richardson, *Being-in-Christ*, 239.

60. Dahm, *Parish Ministry in a Hispanic Community*, 166.

61. Virgilio P. Elizondo, "Popular Religion as Support of Identity," in *Mestizo Worship*, 27.

62. Elizondo, "Popular Religion as Support of Identity," 24.

63. The 1987 National Pastoral Plan for Hispanic Ministry, in *Parish Ministry in a Hispanic Community*, 157.

64. Dahm, *Parish Ministry in a Hispanic Community*, 163.

65. Dahm, *Parish Ministry in a Hispanic Community*, 173.

66. Father Jim Kaczorowski, TRP board of directors, interview by author, Chicago, 4 May 2001.

67. Father Sánchez, interview.

68. Isasi-Díaz, *En la lucha/In the Struggle*, 48.

69. Candelaria, *Popular Religion and Liberation*, 8.

70. Ted G. Jelen, "Roman Catholic Priests," in *Pulpit and Politics*, 235.

71. Romero, *Hispanic Devotional Piety*, 117.

72. "Hymn to Our Lady of Guadalupe"; "defending one's country and one's God."

73. Father Bruce Wellems, C.M.F., pastor, Holy Cross/IHM Parish, interview by author, Chicago, 30 April 2002.

74. Raymundo, telephone interview, 28 February 2007.

75. "The mission of the church is to support at-risk youth." "God is always with those who are in a condition of need. . . . Young people are continuing to lose the meaning of life . . . they do not know where they are coming from or where they going." Holy Cross/IHM Parish is "interested in understanding why youth are not able to express themselves in a creative fashion." He notes that Our Lady of Guadalupe came to Juan Diego, asking Juan Diego to go to the bishop and "demonstrate his worth" to him. In like manner, neighborhood youth must be able to "demonstrate their worth," through the creation of "spaces for youth . . . spaces of dialogue, creativity, and athletics."

76. Our Lady of Guadalupe Novena, Immaculate Heart of Mary Parish, Chicago, 7 December 2001. Flores was "head of a gang" in Back of the Yards. The gang "liked to kill and sell drugs," he admits. Flores taught "the life of the street" to the children, helping to destroy his own community. He did not know that "the community was full of faith." He was lost—"he did not believe in God or in the Virgin of Guadalupe." Then, comments Flores, due to God's intervention and with the help of Father Wellems, "the church opened its doors" for him. Instead he describes societal rupture as "a cancer, a sickness, and ignorance."

77. Candelaria, *Popular Religion and Liberation*, 5, 8.

78. Ted G. Jelen, "Roman Catholic Priests," 242.

79. Richardson, *Being-in-Christ*, 113.

80. Raymundo, interview, 23 April 2001.

81. Pesqueira, interview.

82. Goldstein, interview.

83. Dahm, *Parish Ministry in a Hispanic Community*, 266–267.

84. Raymundo, in *Parish Ministry in a Hispanic Community*, 266.

85. Kevin Jackson, director, Chicago Rehab Network, interview by author, Chicago, 18 December 2001.

86. Victoria Ranta, TRP focus group, Chicago, 30 July 2001.

87. "Affordable Housing: Ownership," *The Resurrection Project*, http://www.resurrectionproject.org/Housing.

88. "Mayor to Transfer City-Owned Property to Pilsen Resurrection Development," *Lawndale News*, 22 September 1994, 16.

89. César Guerrero, "New Homes for Chicago: Pilsen Families Win Lottery for New Homes," *Nueva Vida* 53, no. 38, 19 September 1991, 1.

90. Raymundo, interview, 23 April 2001.

91. Raymundo, interview, 28 February 2007.

92. Edgar Hernández, homeownership education specialist, TRP, interview by author, Chicago, 10 May 2002.

93. "I already have a house, I want to buy one for my [ex-]wife."

94. TRP Homeownership Workshop, Part I, Chicago, 4 December 2001.

95. Edgar Hernández, interview.

96. Rebecca Lopez, assistant commissioner of housing, Department of Housing, interview by author, Chicago, 17 December 2001.

97. Edgar Hernández, interview.

98. Pamela S. Voss, "How to Reach Mexican-American Immigrants That Are Unbanked and Convert to Mainline Banking" (ABA National Community Development Conference, Baltimore, MD, 18 March 2002).

99. "Predatory Lending," *Homes and Communities: U.S. Department of Housing and Urban Development*, http://www.hud.gov/offices/hsg/sfh/pred/predlend.cfm.

100. Skerry, "Citizenship Begins at Home," 31.

101. McGraw, interview.

102. Alicia J. Rodríguez, community organizer, TRP, interview by author, Chicago, 6 December 2001.

103. "La Casa," *Housing: The Resurrection Project*, http://www.resurrectionproject.org/Housing.

104. "Education," *The Resurrection Project*, http://www.resurrectionproject.org/Education.

105. Oscar Avila, "For Latino Students, a Place to Call Home," *Chicago Tribune*, 20 January 2004, 2C.

106. Alicia J. Rodríguez, interview.

107. Rodríguez in Avila, "For Latino Students, a Place to Call Home," 2C.

108. Reichert, "Revitalizing the Inner City," 190.

109. Conzen, "The Place of Religion in Urban and Community Studies," 110.

110. Alicia J. Rodriguez, interview.

111. Amanda Carney, program officer, LISC, interview by author, Chicago, 23 July 2001.

112. Cox, *Fire from Heaven*, xv.

113. Alicia J. Rodríguez, interview.

114. For additional analysis on the concept of "holding leadership account-able," from the point of view of PICO—an IAF-affiliated organization—as well as a consideration of the difference between "internal accountability" and "external accountability," see Wood, *Faith in Action*, 44.

115. Donohue, interview.

116. Rita Cardoso, vice president, TRP Board of Directors, interview by author, Chicago, 2 May 2001.

117. Carney, interview.

118. Raymundo, interview, 6 December 2001.

119. E. A. Torreiro and Diana Strzalka, "Cops Charge Teen in Officer's Death," *Chicago Tribune*, 1 July 2001, C1.

120. Mickey Ciokajlo and John Chase, "Suspect in Officer's Killing Dropped Family for Gang," *Chicago Tribune*, 2 July 2001, N1.

121. Ciokajlo and Chase, "Suspect in Officer's Killing Dropped Family for Gang."

122. Commander Ralph Chiczewski, City of Chicago Department of Police, 12th District, interview by author, Chicago, 15 May 2002.

123. 12th District Police Beat Meeting, Centro Familiar Guadalupano, Chicago, 5 December 2001.

124. Officer Alex Errum, Community Policing, City of Chicago, Department of Police, 12th District, interview by author, 15 May 2002.

125. Chiczewski, interview.

126. "What Is CAPS?" City of Chicago, Department of Police, http://www.ci.chi.il.us/CommunityPolicing/AboutCAPS/HowCAPSWorks/WhatIsCAPS.html.

127. 12th District police beat meeting.

128. Cervantes, interview, 19 July 2001.

129. Alvaro Obregon, community organizer, TRP, interview by author, Chicago, 9 May 2002.

130. "Sara Lee Doubles Its Spirit Award," *StreetWise*, 11 May 1999, 17.

131. Garza, interview.

132. Wood, *Faith in Action*, 35.

133. Warren, *Dry Bones Rattling*, 51.

134. Warren, *Dry Bones Rattling*, 163.

135. Father Dahm, interview, 29 April 2002.

136. Father Howe, interview.

137. Jesús De León, acting program manager of supportive housing, TRP, interview by author, Chicago, 10 May 2002.

138. Raúl Hernández, interview.

139. Allison Nanni, resource development associate, TRP, interview by author, Chicago, 9 May 2002.

140. Evelyn Romero, community development director (Midwest), National Council of La Raza, interview by author, Chicago, 18 December 2001.

141. Alderman Ray Frias, 12th Ward, City of Chicago, interview by author, Chicago, 6 May 2002.

142. Guacolda Reyes, director, asset management division, TRP, interview by author, Chicago, 15 May 2002.

143. DeGraaf, interview.

144. Raymundo, interview, 23 April 2001.

145. "Laundromats" and "fruit shops."

146. "To you then who believe, he is precious; but for those who do not believe, 'the stone that the builders rejected has become the corner,' and 'a stone that makes them stumble, and a rock that makes them fall.' They stumble because they disobey the word, as they were destined to do."

147. Sunday mass, St. Agnes of Bohemia Church, Chicago, 28 April 2002. Those in the city were made of stone and "gave the impression that they were solid." In building strong interior houses, "this allows one to face life" with great faith.

148. Pesqueira, interview.

149. DeGraaf, interview.

150. Sunday mass, St. Agnes of Bohemia Church: "Here, we need to build our homes. The construction begins here."

151. Nanni, interview.

152. Raymundo, telephone interview, 28 February 2007.

153. Doug Kenshol, director of operations, TRP, interview by author, Chicago, 9 May 2002.

154. Kenshol, interview.

155. Puente, "Pilsen Fears Upscale Push May Shove Many Out," 6.

156. Patricia Richardson, "Under Construction: Building Boon: Pilsen Attracting Redevelopment, Higher Prices," *Crain's Chicago Business,* 3 June 2002, 13.

157. Nancy Moffett, "Museum Boosts Pilsen, Director Says," *Chicago Sun-Times,* 22 April 2001, 18.

158. TRP staff meeting, Chicago, 11 July 2001.

159. Lee Koonze, in *Exito!* 19 de Julio de 2001, 39. Lee Koonze commented that "our hope is that the residents of Pilsen and Little Village feel that the CSO is their orchestra and that this orchestra is a reflection of the community and that it is accessible to all."

160. "CSO Community Partnership Programs," *Chicago Symphony Orchestra —Education and Community,* http://www.cso.org/main.taf?p=10,1,1.

161. "Pilsen: A Center of Mexican Life," *Quality of Life Plan* (Chicago: LISC/Chicago's New Communities Program, November 2006): 5–6.

162. Street, "Political Culture—From Civic Culture to Mass Culture," 103.

163. Antonio Olivo, "Would You Go to Pilsen for 'Zócalo'?: Mexican-Style

Plaza Talk for Neighborhood," *Chicago Tribune*, 15 November 2005, http://www.luc.edu/curl/escd/discussions/links/Chicago_tribune%2011-15-2005.shtml.

164. "Pilsen: A Center of Mexican Life," 21.

165. Alderman Solís in "New Communities Program," *The Resurrection Project*, http://www.resurrectionproject.org/New-Communities-Program.

166. Raymundo, interview, 6 December 2001.

167. Boff, *When Theology Listens to the Poor*, 83.

168. Florencia Ramírez, former director, resource development, TRP, interview by author, Chicago, 19 July 2001.

169. Raymundo, interview, 23 April 2001.

170. "Strategic Plan: 2006–2010," *The Resurrection Project*.

171. Nanni, interview.

172. Lloyd, interview.

173. Carlos Tortolero, executive director, Mexican Fine Arts Museum, interview by author, Chicago, 19 December 2001.

174. Romero, interview.

175. Lloyd, interview.

176. Pesqueira, interview.

177. Raymundo, telephone interview, 28 February 2007.

178. Father Dahm, interview, 29 April 2002.

179. "Community Organizing," *The Resurrection Project*, http://www.resurrectionproject.org/Community-Organizing.

180. DeGraaf, interview.

181. Lloyd, interview.

182. Estela Balderas, grants manager, TRP, interview by author, Chicago, 3 December 2001.

183. Carney, interview.

184. Lopez, interview.

185. Pesqueira, interview.

186. Tortolero, interview.

187. Sunny Fischer, executive director, Driehaus Foundation, interview by author, Chicago, 10 December 2001.

188. Segura, interview.

189. Father Sánchez, interview.

NOTES TO CHAPTER 7

1. Alexie Torres Fleming, executive director and founder, Youth Ministries for Peace and Justice, telephone interview by author, 11 December 2002.

2. "You are a liar. Pedro de Valdivia is a statue in the plaza."

3. Unruh and Sider, *Saving Souls, Serving Society*, 68, 69–72.

4. Swidler, *Talk of Love*, 73.

5. Bernard Häring, C.Ss.R., *Hope Is the Remedy* (Garden City, NY: Doubleday, 1972), 35, 31.

6. Otto Hentz, S.J., *The Hope of the Christian* (Collegeville, MN: Liturgical Press, 1997), 8.

7. Charles Péguy, *Mystère: Le Porche de Mystére de la Deuxiéme Vertu* (1911), in *Oeuvres Poétiques Complétes* (Paris: Editions Gallimand, 1957), 539–540, quoted in Jürgen Moltmann, *The Experiment Hope*, ed. and trans. M. Douglas Meeks (Philadelphia: Fortress Press, 1975), 189.

8. Elshtain, "Christian Imperatives and Civil Life," 163.

9. Moltmann, *The Experiment Hope*, 46, 53.

10. John Macquarrie, *Christian Hope* (New York: Seabury Press, 1998), 28.

11. Valerie Braithwaite, "Preface: Collective Hope," 7.

12. Elshtain, "Christian Imperatives and Civil Life," 165, 171.

13. Valerie Braithwaite, "The Hope Process and Social Inclusion," *Annals of the American Academy of Political and Social Science* 592 (March 2004): 130.

14. Victoria McGeer, "The Art of Good Hope," *Annals of the American Academy of Political and Social Science* 592 (March 2004): 103, 104, 105, 108, 125.

15. Peter Drahos, "Trading in Public Hope," *Annals of the American Academy of Political and Social Science* 592 (March 2004): 19, 33.

16. National Hispanic Prayer Breakfast.

17. Drahos, "Trading in Public Hope," 31.

18. Braithwaite, "Preface: Collective Hope," 7.

19. Sasha Courville and Nicola Piper, "Harnessing Hope through NGO Activism," *Annals of the American Academy of Political and Social Science* 592 (March 2004): 81.

20. Emmanuel McCall, "Black Liberation Theology: A Politics of Freedom," *Review and Expositor* 73, no. 3 (Summer 1976): 333.

21. Harold Dean Trulear, "A Critique of Functionalism: Toward a More Holistic Sociology of Afro-American Religion," *Journal of Religious Thought* 42 (Spring/Summer 1985): 38–40, 48–49.

22. Firth, "Spiritual Aroma," 583, 584.

23. Jacob Neusner and William Scott Green, "Why Study About Religion? The Contribution of the Study of Religion to American Public Life," in *The Power of Religious Publics: Staking Claims in American Society*, eds. William H. Swatos, Jr., and James K. Wellman, Jr. (Westport, CT: Praeger, 1999), 71, 74.

24. Birgit Meyer and Annelies Moors, "Introduction," in *Religion, Media and the Public Sphere*, ed. Birgit Meyer and Annelies Moors (Bloomington: Indiana University Press, 2006), 19.

25. Street, "Political Culture—From Civic Culture to Mass Culture," 113.

26. Verba et al., *Voice and Equality*, 317, 320.

27. Wood, "Religious Culture and Political Action," 308.

28. Street, "Political Culture—From Civic Culture to Mass Culture," 113.

29. Hart, *Cultural Dilemmas of Progressive Politics*, 18, 79.

30. Williams, "The Language of God in the City of Man," 182.

31. Rogers M. Smith, *Stories of Peoplehood: The Politics and Morals of Political Membership* (Cambridge: Cambridge University Press, 2003), 101, 12,14, 8–9, 166, 37.

32. Manuel Castells, *The Information Age: Economy, Society, and Culture, Volume II: The Power of Identity*, 2d ed. (Malden, MA: Blackwell Publishing, 2004), 68.

33. Christopher P. Gilbert, *The Impact of Churches on Political Behavior: An Empirical Study* (Westport, CT: Greenwood Press, 1993), 171.

34. Kenneth D. Wald et al., "Making Sense of Religion in Political Life" (paper presented to the 2003 Annual Meeting of the American Political Science Association, Philadelphia, 28–31 August 2003), 7.

35. Valentín, *Mapping Public Theology*, 67, 68, 70, 72, 73.

36. Gastón Espinosa et al., "Introduction: U.S. Latino Religions and Faith-Based Political, Civic, and Social Action," in *Latino Religions and Civic Activism in the United States*, 5, 11.

37. *Changing Faiths: Latinos and the Transformation of American Religion*, 3, 29, 49, 58.

38. Valentín, *Mapping Public Theology*, 85.

39. Warren, *Dry Bones Rattling*, 20, 21, 22.

40. John A. Coleman, S.J., "Religious Social Capital: Its Nature, Social Location, and Limits," in *Religion as Social Capital*, 33, 35.

41. Corwin Smidt, "Religion, Social Capital, and Democratic Life: Concluding Thoughts," in *Religion as Social Capital*, 217–218.

42. Bartkowski and Regis, *Charitable Choices*, 19, 170.

43. Smidt, "Religion, Social Capital, and Democratic Life," 219–221.

44. Wood, *Faith in Action*, 186, 193.

45. Don Browning et al., *From Culture Wars to Common Ground: Religion and the Family Debate* (Louisville, KY: Westminster/John Knox Press, 1997), 268, quoted in Coleman, "Religious Social Capital: Its Nature, Social Location, and Limits," 45.

46. N. J. Demerath, "Diagnosing the Reverend Dr. Dumpty 'After the Fall,'" in "Progress and Cumulation in the Sociology of Religion: A Symposium," *Journal for the Scientific Study of Religion* 42, no. 1 (2003): 3.

47. Mark H. Moore, *Creating Public Value: Strategic Management in Government* (Cambridge, MA: Harvard University Press, 1995), 21, 3.

48. Unruh and Sider, *Saving Souls, Serving Society*, 10.

49. Moore, *Creating Public Value*, 36.

50. Rice, "Promoting Cultural Competency," 41, 42, 43, 49.

51. Rice provides a range of possibilities on the "negative-positive continuum" of working in "cross-cultural situations," taken from the work of T. Cross

et al., *Toward a Culturally Competent System of Care*, vol. 1 (Washington, DC: Georgetown University Child Development Center, 1989). The six possibilities are: (1) cultural destructiveness; (2) cultural incapacity; (3) cultural blindness; (4) cultural pre-competence; (5) cultural competency; and (6) cultural proficiency, quoted in Mitchell, "Promoting Cultural Competency," 42.

52. Rice, "Promoting Cultural Competency," 51, 50.

53. "God has been good."

54. National Hispanic Prayer Breakfast.

55. National Hispanic Prayer Breakfast.

56. Pantoja, "Religious Diversity and Ethnicity among Latinos," 168.

57. Hernández et al., *Leadership Matters: The Role of Latino/a Religious Leadership in Social Ministry*, 7.

58. Obama, *Audacity of Hope*, 64.

59. Karen M. Kaufmann, "Cracks in the Rainbow: Group Commonality as a Basis for Latino and African-American Political Coalitions," *Political Research Quarterly* 56, no. 2 (June 2003): 207.

60. James MacGregor Burns, *Transforming Leadership: A New Pursuit of Happiness* (New York: Atlantic Monthly Press, 2003), 211, 206, 183.

61. National Hispanic Prayer Breakfast.

62. National Hispanic Prayer Breakfast.

Index

About the Author

Catherine E. Wilson is Assistant Professor in the Department of Political Science and in the Center for Liberal Education at Villanova University, where she also serves as the Nonprofit Coordinator in the Master of Public Administration Program. She is a Non-Resident Senior Fellow in the Program for Research on Religion and Urban Civil Society at the University of Pennsylvania.